Comparative Aspects of Scottish and Irish
Economic and Social History 1600-1900

Comparative Aspects of Scottish and Irish Economic and Social History 1600-1900

Edited by
L.M.Cullen & T.C.Smout

JOHN DONALD PUBLISHERS LTD
EDINBURGH

© John Donald Publishers Ltd.

ISBN   0   85976   017   0

Printed in Great Britain by Bell and Bain Ltd.,
Glasgow

Preface

THE idea for a seminar to compare aspects of Scottish and Irish economic and social development 1600-1900 occurred to the editors at a meeting at Trinity College, Dublin, in 1973. Even on the most superficial examination it was clear that both countries have been profoundly affected by a similar geography, by a Celtic heritage, and by a history of close political and economic links with England. Both countries within the period have exchanged populations in the Scottish movement to Ulster in the seventeenth century and the equally significant movement of Irishmen to Scotland in the nineteenth. In both countries the cattle trade was a leading commercial sector in the seventeenth century and the linen trade was the main manufacture of the eighteenth; both countries attempted a cotton industry, which was much more successful in Scotland in the nineteenth century; both countries are famous for whisky (or for whiskey); both countries had important growth in their foreign trade before the American War of Independence, but Scotland was granted direct access to the colonies and Ireland denied it; both countries were affected by the improving landlords of the eighteenth century and the Highlands like Ireland were obsessed by the movement for tenants' rights in the nineteenth. In both countries economic development was threatened by recurrent imbalances between food supply and population growth; most of Scotland escaped the trap but Ireland, in 1846, failed to do so. Were these topics that Scottish and Irish historians could fruitfully examine together?

Thanks to the generous support of the Social Sciences Research Council it proved possible to hold an exploratory seminar with about 40 participants in Dublin in September 1976. All the topics mentioned above were examined in the papers printed here though we were unable (through an unavoidable cancellation) to obtain a study of tenant rights in the nineteenth-century Highlands. However, as a bonus we secured Ian Robertson's paper on the problems exported when Scottish and Irish tenants became settlers together in Prince Edward Island, Canada. Only Chapter 1 was not presented at the seminar; it represents our reflections on the course of Scottish and Irish history formed after reading the papers and attending to the subsequent discussion within the seminar.

In addition to funds from the SSRC, we wish to acknowledge financial help from the U.S. Government via the American Cultural Attaché to the Republic of Ireland and from the Department of Modern History at Trinity

College, Dublin. Many of the participants were also assisted by their own universities, and Dr. Robertson by the Canada Council. None of the grant-giving bodies have any responsibility for the opinions expressed in this book. The burden of organising the meeting itself was primarily borne by David Dickson of Trinity College, Dublin, to whom we owe special thanks.

We hope the book (as it has now become) will be read both by specialists and by a wider audience. Several of the papers represent summaries of recent research on key topics, and as such should interest anyone with a general interest in the course of Scottish or Irish history.

L.M. Cullen
T.C. Smout

Dublin and Edinburgh

Contents

PART I

INTRODUCTION

1. Economic Growth in Scotland and Ireland

L.M.Cullen and T.C.Smout

THE three centuries from 1600 to 1900 provide an apt framework in which to study the comparative economic development of Scotland and Ireland. (1) The regal union of 1603 between Scotland and England coincided with the final and effective conquest of Ireland: for both nations the seventeenth century became an age of peace and order, broken though it was by the long campaigns of 1641-52 and the shorter ones of 1689-91. In 1707 Scotland entered into parliamentary union with England and Wales; her population was then perhaps scarcely more than a third of that of Ireland. In 1801 Ireland followed suit, and joined England, Wales and Scotland in the union; as late as 1841 she still had over three times the population of Scotland. Then came the Great Famine of 1846, with catastrophic results to one society but not to the other. By 1901 Scotland and Ireland had virtually the same population, but Scotland had an industrial sector about four times the size and an agriculture about twice as productive. Nothing could better illustrate either the scale of the transformation of the Scottish economy compared to the Irish, or the sustained drive behind it.

Which nation was the more developed to begin with? Plainly in 1600 both were extremely underdeveloped, with large areas of semi-subsistence economy scarcely involved in outside markets. But neither was stagnant. Scotland in the last quarter of the sixteenth century and until at least the end of the first quarter of the seventeenth experienced significant development in several directions — her overseas and overland trades expanded, her fisheries grew, her textile, coal and salt industries all became larger. Especially her towns grew. As late as the 1640s, Edinburgh (with upwards of 20,000 or 30,000 souls) was clearly larger than Dublin, which alone of Irish towns bore comparison with Glasgow, Dundee and Aberdeen. The size of the Scottish urban sector indicates an agriculture, which, while neither sophisticated nor undergoing the same rapid changes as farming in England, was nevertheless productive enough to keep substantial towns fed.

In the second half of the seventeenth century, however, Scottish growth faltered except along the Clyde. She ran into trouble in external markets. Her industries proved uncompetitive. Her agriculture, Dr. Woodward suggests, proved incapable of expanding cattle production sufficiently to take advantage of the opportunity left in the English market by the prohibition on the sale of Irish beasts imposed in 1667, raised in 1679 and reimposed in 1681. Even the prosperity and enterprise of Glasgow, stimulated perhaps by the vigour and trade of nearby Ulster, was unable to compensate. The century ended in a serious famine and the fiasco of the Darien venture.

Ireland, on the other hand, appeared to do remarkably well, though the performance varied in its timing from one region to another, with Munster to the fore in some of the early decades and East Ulster in the closing decades. Population growth was apparently vigorous due both to a high rate of natural increase among the Irish and to a large though intermittent immigration of Scots moving to greener and emptier pastures. This had been taking place since early in the century and became a flood in Ulster in the 1690s when crops failed in Scotland. It represented a substantial transfer of capital as well as labour from one economy to the other. After the Restoration, products of Irish farming were so competitive on the market elsewhere in Britain that both the English and the Scottish Parliaments passed protective legislation against sundry items, though the Scots were glad enough to get Irish victual in the famine. The Irish woollen industry attracted similar attention in Westminster's Woollen Act of 1699. Meanwhile Dublin had increased astonishingly: with perhaps 60,000 inhabitants at the end of the century she was then about twice the size of Edinburgh, and other towns – especially Cork – had also grown significantly. Even as adventurers in the Caribbean and North American plantations it was often the Irish rather than the Scots who made the most mark.

Rough calculations of the value of exports in the two countries are suggestive. Total Irish exports in the period 1698-1700 were valued at £888,000: with a population believed to be a little under three million, this gives a per capita value of about 6s. Scottish exports to England in the same period were valued at £114,000, and it is unlikely that the total value of trade to other markets matched them; assuming a final figure of £200,000 and a population of about one million, the value of exports per head would be only 4s. Both figures are of course very low, surely indicating the large size of the subsistence sectors in Scotland and Ireland. England itself and the market-oriented colonies in North America, for example, enjoyed per capita exports of several times this magnitude. But the evidence from exports joins other indications that Ireland seemed to hold more promise of a bright economic future than Scotland at the opening of the eighteenth century.

Between the Anglo-Scottish Union of 1707 and the British-Irish Union of 1801 the fortunes of the two countries plainly crossed again. When? Even thoughtful contemporaries were of two minds. As late as 1785 John Knox could write his *View of the British Empire* as though it was self-evident that Ireland was at least as developed as Scotland, though that must have been about the last possible date at which such an attitude would have seemed plausible. Nine years earlier Adam Smith had stated categorically that 'in Ireland the inferior ranks of people are still poorer than in Scotland'. (2) If migration from one part of the British Isles to another is an accurate indicator of relative income levels, it is significant that no-one seems to have moved in either direction between the two countries in the first half of the eighteenth century: Alexander Webster could only find two Catholics in Lanarkshire in his enumeration of 1755. Thereafter a trickle of Irish immigrant workers began, first becoming notable in the 1780s, and forming sizeable communities in towns in the West of Scotland by the early 1790s.

It is not easy to make calculations from the trade figures, but they may nevertheless contain a clue as to when the change occurred. There are no Scottish figures before 1755, and thereafter they are only directly informative about trade (at constant c.1755 prices) between Scotland and foreign (i.e. non-English) ports. In that year Scottish domestic exports to foreign ports were worth £285,000. What were exports to England worth? If 60 per cent of the linen made was sold in England this item would be worth £207,000; if 40,000 cattle were driven south at £1.10s each, their value would be £60,000. Adding these items together a conservative estimate of the value of Scottish domestic exports of £552,000 is reached: with a population of 1.25 million, exports would be worth about 9s a head — a clear increase on the start of the century. The value of total Irish exports in 1755 was £1,820,000; with a population of 3.2 million they were worth 11s a head — also clear growth since 1700. (3) Given the very crude nature of the calculations, Scotland and Ireland look about equal.

How did things go from there? Scottish domestic exports to foreign ports doubled between 1755 and c.1780 (at constant prices) and had doubled again by 1800. Total Irish exports grew by about two-thirds between 1755 and 1770 and after stagnating in the 1770s increased by a further 80 per cent to a peak of £5.4 million in 1791/2. The pace of growth was however irregular, and a contraction in the 1790s contrasted with an unprecedented upsurge and broadened base in Scottish exports. This would support the suggestion that the significant difference in the course of the two economies arose only towards the end of the eighteenth century. Scottish exports to foreign ports were worth £1,343,000 in the years 1797-9: adding £250,000 for the value of cattle and £231,000 for linen, and guessing that by then the sales of cotton in England must have exceeded the sales of linen, one reaches a rough guess of £2,070,000 for a population of 1.6 million — or exports worth at least £1.6s. (4) Total Irish exports were worth £4,351,000: if population had reached 5.0 million (as seems likely enough), exports would be worth about 17s a head. This probably understates, and perhaps substantially understates, the value of Scottish trade to England: if it does, the divergence between the two economies must have been even more marked.

Table I   Estimated approximate *per capita* values of domestic exports (in shillings):

	Irish	Scottish
1698-1700	6	4
1755	11	9
1797-99	17	26+?+

(*N.B.*   This Table should be read in conjunction with notes 3 and 4)

So both economies appear to have been rather successful for most of the century, but Scotland appears to have drawn rapidly ahead of Ireland at the end of the century. Why? Several of the papers in this collection bear on that problem.

Devine makes a strong plea for considering the direct trade between Scotland and the colonies as a major factor in Scottish growth before c.1780, not merely in the Glasgow enclave but in Lowland Scotland as a whole. This, of course, would have been impossible without the Act of Union and Scotland's inclusion within the navigation acts. Re-exports (mainly of tobacco) were certainly a valuable item in the Scottish balance of trade, exceeding the value of Scottish domestic exports to foreign ports until 1777 (though they presumably would seldom have exceeded Scottish domestic exports to England and foreign ports combined). Ireland, excluded from the privilege of direct colonial trade, had virtually no re-exports to compare with this Scottish bonus.

On the other hand, Ireland certainly had large port towns. Dublin, which handled over half the import and export trade of Ireland in the second half of the eighteenth century, had a population not much below 200,000 by 1800, which made her one of the top ten towns of Europe and the second town of the British Isles by an enormous margin. Of course, Dublin had other advantages than those conferred on her by trade. She was an active administrative capital, invigorated from the 1690s by the regularity with which the Irish parliament met: this brought the business of the gentry to the consumer goods industries and the service sector. Edinburgh, which had lost her parliament but not her function as a legal and ecclesiastical capital and which also had a gentry season, was nevertheless much smaller: she still had only 67,000 inhabitants at the end of the century despite building her famous New Town. Cork and Glasgow make another instructive comparison. Cork, the capital of the Atlantic provisioning trade, was substantially larger than Glasgow, the capital of the Atlantic tobacco trade, until about 1780: then Glasgow accelerated as industry increased, and by the end of the century contained about 77,000 people compared to some 60,000 in Cork. (5) The provisioning trade with its demand for butchering and barrelling facilities probably had more direct linkages than importing and re-exporting tobacco, apart from the perhaps vital ones in banking, though as Devine shows, the Glasgow merchants were deeply involved in many other activities as well.

In fact both countries gained something from the colonial trades, and one reason for the buoyancy of their commerce down to c.1780 was American demand (though we would hazard the guess that straight English demand was more important to both countries as it certainly was to Ireland). On the other hand, even if one accepts that Scotland gained more than Ireland, there was not, as Devine emphasises, any sign that the tobacco merchants played any critical direct role in supplying capital or enterprise to Scottish or even to Glaswegian industrialisation after 1780. It is therefore difficult to argue that Scotland's privileged position under the navigation acts was a critical factor in her acceleration past Ireland at the end of the century.

Yet that is not quite the whole story. Scotland, with permission to trade directly to the colonies, developed a network of mercantile contacts in the New World which was often reflected in the successful return of her adventurers to Scottish commercial life and landownership. They were confident men with wide horizons who added appreciably to the vigour and spirit of their native land. Ireland's seventeenth or early eighteenth-century adventurers on the other hand drew comparatively few recruits in the rest of eighteenth century from families not already involved overseas, and as Jacob Price observed at the seminar, they were much less likely to return; they tended, for one reason or another, to stay abroad as successful merchants or landowners when they had made their pile or even to settle in London.

What about the industrial side? The linen industry, the staple manufacture and largest domestic export of both countries for most of the century, is considered here by Gribbon and Durie. There are time-series for both countries, though they do not measure the same thing: the Scottish figures relate to total production brought to the market (i.e. net of unstamped linen made for private sales), the Irish only to exports. Nevertheless, placed side by side, while both again show substantial growth over the period, they do not at all suggest that the secret of Scotland's success lay in superior competition in linen. Scottish market output, on trend, came to equal a diminishing proportion of Irish domestic exports of linen, especially in the 1770s (when there were many bitter complaints in the West of Scotland of inability to meet Irish competition in the finer linens), and much more strikingly in the 1790s (when Scotland was beginning to decide that her comparative advantage in textiles lay elsewhere). Growth in linen was no doubt an important factor in the development of both countries, but not in the better performance of one compared to the other.

Table II   Millions of yards of linen cloth, annual averages (6)

	A	B	
	Manufactured for sale in Scotland	Exported from Ireland	A as % of B
1730-9	4.53	5.26	86
1740-9	5.69	7.49	76
1750-9	9.04	12.71	71
1760-9	12.41	16.10	77
1770-9	12.83	20.32	63
1780-9	17.47	25.01	70
1790-99	20.89	40.73	51

Colonial trade, incidentally, was relatively less important to the Irish linen industry than to the Scottish, which exported to the colonies either from her own ports or through England some 25-30 per cent of her manufacture.

The cotton industry, discussed here by Dickson and Butt, perhaps brings us nearer to the crux of the matter of comparative development. Both Ireland and Scotland were toying with the use of cotton wool, mainly in mixed fabrics, in the third quarter of the eighteenth century. Perhaps in Ireland the industry even got off to a better start when first it began to accelerate: raw material imports to Irish ports were well above those to Scottish ports before the late 1780s. But the lead was short-lived, as Table III demonstrates:

Table III   Annual Imports of cotton wool (six-year periods), million lbs. (7)

	A	B	
	To Ireland	To Scotland	A as % of B
1781-86	0.62	0.43	144
1787-92	1.49	2.27	66
1793-98	1.15	2.05	56
1799-1804	1.55	7.19	22
1805-10	3.41	9.05	38
1811-16	3.00	8.08	37
1817-22	3.31	12.00	28

If raw material inputs are a guide, this seems to show how even on the eve of the Union of Ireland and Great Britain in 1801 the Irish cotton industry was lagging while the Scottish one began a classic take-off. After the Union, interestingly, the Irish made some headway in cutting back the Scottish lead: around 1810 there were about 50 mills in Ireland and about 110 in Scotland. But it could not last: the Irish industry contracted and almost disappeared after 1825, while the Scottish went on growing until mid-century and was still large in 1900.

If our exposition so far has been along the correct lines, both countries did about equally well in the 'proto-industrialisation' period down to c.1780, so had equal chances to accumulate capital, skilled labour and entrepreneurial experience in the textile sector. The industry was still dispersed in Scotland and England alike in the eighteenth century, and access to coal fuel for steam motive power was not an important factor until the nineteenth century. Perhaps at first the Irish kept mainly to linens, increasingly to fine linens moreover, because they were still making a good enough return from them in the 1790s, while Scottish manufacturers left the older textile in the west of Scotland because they were finding they could not compete, and they started cotton factories instead. The Scots made a fine cotton which they could sell in a buoyant home market and export extensively to England and Europe. The Irish made a coarse cotton (with lower value added) which they could only sell on rather a weak home market. Lastly, with the coming of self-acting mules and the big powerloom weaving sheds after 1825 there were strong centralising forces drawing the industry to the coalfields: cotton declined in the east and south of Scotland as well as in Ireland at this point.

Next, there is the difficult problem of the role of agriculture in eighteenth-century growth. In the complete absence of statistical data it will be a long time before scholars in either country can agree on what really happened, who made it happen, and when. Crawford and Campbell in their papers on the eighteenth century tend to play down the role of the landowners in determining the outcome of events. Crawford shows that 'Ulster tenant right' was the consequence of the economic balance of power between the tenant and the landlord becoming tilted in favour of the tenant by the historic difficulties of settling the north, rather than the consequence of specially enlightened attitudes by landlords there. Certainly in eighteenth-century Scotland tenants enjoyed no such privilege as those in Ulster, and Scottish landlords were dictators in comparison. Campbell maintains, however, that the landowner in Scotland played a much more unimportant role than historians have sometimes allowed. Perhaps, but in countries where owner-occupiers are so scarce the general inclination of the landlord to accelerate or to withstand change (to manage land actively or passively) has considerable significance. Woodward argues that in the previous century the new men in Ireland seemed to have more energy for commercialisation than the old men in Scotland. No one could doubt that in the eighteenth century at least some landlords in both countries were on the side of change: model villages on each side of the water are one abiding testimony to their zeal and optimism. Of course they wanted the rents, but who in eighteenth-century Britain would not have supposed that self-interest and social were the same?

What has still to be determined is the extent to which, in Ireland, land resettlement and the penal laws affected economic development adversely. Woodward's point cannot be disregarded, but it is equally necessary not to underestimate indigenous commercialisation. The continued (and for Ireland unique) contact between the landed classes and commerce in eighteenth-century Co. Galway, the one region where there was continuity in landownership, is a reminder that land resettlement as well as bringing in new entrepreneurial talent can have upset old. The penal laws, by limiting Catholic outlets in landownership and the professions, have often been represented as favourable to Catholic involvement in trade; but in so far as they reduced Catholic profits from land, office or the professions that might have been invested in trade they must often have had quite the reverse effect.

Certainly in Ireland the upheavals of the seventeenth century had the consequence of introducing a new landed class in most of the country, and, outside Ulster and Galway, of creating a cultural gulf between the landlord on the one side and the tenant and the priest on the other that had no close parallel in eighteenth-century Scotland. Adverse tenurial relationships can be exaggerated, and moreover it is necessary to make allowance, as Vaughan argues, for the fact that a more pastoral economy provides less scope for landlord initiative. But, even so, the greater the discontinuity and the deeper the gulf, the larger the obstacle to the successful diffusion of ideas sponsored by agent or landlord. The relative cultural gulf may have been affected by greater adaptability in Scotland than in Ireland, a consequence of the emerging – and sharp – contrast in literacy and schooling. The Scots, less successful as adventurers than the Irish in the seventeenth century, were conspicuously more mobile in the eighteenth century, and drawn from a wider range of society, whereas Irish initiative overseas with some notable exceptions continued to come from almost unchanging family groupings. The land resettlement may account for some of this inflexibility, but the rigidity and the lack of wider involvement must reflect other factors as well. Significantly, the Ulster Scots, whose society reproduced some of the characteristics of Scottish society, furnished the main stream of Irish popular emigration in the eighteenth century.

Many speakers at the seminar wished to emphasise the peculiar belief in 'improvement' which swept the intellectuals of the Scottish Enlightenment in the universities, the ruling Moderate faction in the Church of Scotland and the Scottish landed classes themselves in the decades after 1750. It was compounded of uncritical optimism about the beneficence of economic change and boundless confidence and determination to bring such change about. It was a national search for 'opulence', an energy and a feeling of hope that permeated many aspects of Scottish life. Though there were 'improvers' in both countries, the sense of a country vigorously determined to twist its fate to its advantage is peculiarly Scottish. Of course it could work no miracles without the right market conditions; given the right conditions, it could perhaps generate the psychic energies to overcome all sorts of traditional inertias. Here again the greater cultural unity of Scotland compared to Ireland might be of singular importance.

A crucial question is when in the eighteenth century did agricultural change occur fastest, and in which country more basically? Farming output for the market obviously increased in both countries throughout the century, as rising urban populations and increasing exports of grain (from Scotland only until mid-century and in Ireland after mid-century) and animal products testify. Ireland, however,

B

endured famine in 1728-9, a very serious famine in 1740-1, near-famine in 1744-5 and in 1756-7, and among the labouring population near-famine in 1799-1800. One paper in this collection argues that Scotland had dearths, but that the only eighteenth-century scarcity that led to a marked surge in deaths was in the Highlands in 1782-3. Does this mean that already from the second quarter of the eighteenth century Scotland had a more productive agriculture? The point cannot be determined because there are too many variables. The shortfalls in the harvests in Scotland might have been smaller due to climatic accidents. Charity might have been greater or better organised: it is argued here that there were significant improvements in Scottish charity, but in Ireland although private efforts made their appearance as early as 1740-1 and parish and municipal authorities were involved in famine relief in 1756-7, it is possible that efforts were neither as effective nor as general as those in Scotland.

It is only by the 1780s, however, that one can begin to feel certain that a difference in kind is emerging between Lowland Scottish and Irish agriculture; it took the form of enclosures, modern rotations, turnip husbandry, and, especially in south-east Scotland, the emergence of highly capitalised and large commercial farms. Everywhere in Scotland sub-tenancies were discouraged. The *Statistical Account* of the 1790s shows few Lowland counties unaffected, though in some the transformation was only beginning and would hardly be complete even thirty years later. In Ireland different traditions of tenure and inheritance combined with a much greater density of population and, perhaps, (in many areas) the very success of the small weaver tenant or sub-tenant in the linen industry precluded such basic agrarian reorganisation. Since so much depended not merely on the attitudes of landowners but on the initiative of tenants, the high level of literacy might have been an important bonus to Scotland: an educated peasantry more readily turns its back on immemorial tradition because it finds on the printed page an alternative form of authority, and much of the new farming technology was disseminated in books and articles. There is even the question as to how far the details of the new husbandry were really applicable to the wetter climate of Ireland before the coming of deep field drainage in the middle quarters of the nineteenth century.

Whatever the reason, the fact that agriculture was being transformed in Scotland but not in Ireland at the end of the eighteenth century was a critical difference between the two countries, probably the most critical of all. Scotland at the end of the century was enjoying 'balanced growth' in the agricultural and industrial sectors simultaneously, with all the advantages that implied in the interchange of labour and capital between the two sectors and the buoyancy of demand for each other's products. One obvious gain was in savings capacity: traditional Scottish 'thrift' had a rural base. Ireland, however, was severely handicapped by a lagging agricultural sector with all that implied in low income, low savings, and weak demand for industrial goods. No country has ever been transformed into a modern economy without a successful agricultural revolution preceding or coinciding with industrialisation: Ireland could not be an exception to that rule.

We did not in this collection attempt to obtain a comparison of Scottish and Irish banking in the eighteenth century but that, too, could prove a fruitful field for investigation. Initially, Ireland, despite the absence of either national or chartered banks, was ahead: note issue there may have amounted to £400,000 by the 1720s, but it was still only £55,000 in Scotland as late as 1744. Moreover, Scottish banking was confined to Edinburgh until 1749, when the first provincial bank opened in Glasgow, but in Ireland at mid-century banks either existed or had made an appearance in no less than seven centres apart from Dublin. However, Irish banking lost its impetus in the crisis of the mid-1750s: the note issue at that time, said to be over £1 million, was probably halved and even with some recovery was not exceeded until the early 1790s. In Scotland, however, the second half of the century was a period of marked growth: note issue reached £864,000 by 1772 and £3 million in 1802. On a per capita basis the Scottish circulation in the 1770s was probably between three and six times the Irish. In other words, notes had effectively replaced cash in much Scottish trade by that date, a situation that was not effectively attained in Ireland until the renewed growth of banking during the Napoleonic War inflation.

Two striking contrasts between early Irish and Scottish banking were the absence of extensive partnerships in Irish banking (although they were not precluded by law until the Bank of Ireland Act in 1782) and the low level of capitalisation, a situation more akin to that of the Edinburgh private bankers than to the Scottish chartered banks. Funds were shorter in Ireland; bills, even in the final decade of the eighteenth century, rarely exceeded two months in contrast to as much as four months in Scotland, and interest rates, legal and market, were fractionally higher. The strength of Scottish financial institutions was an important aspect of the ability to mobilise savings for the agricultural and industrial revolutions: in Ireland the main purpose of banks was less to provide credit than to transfer payments by short-dated bills between country and town, or between the island as a whole and London.

After the Irish-British Union of 1801 and throughout the nineteenth century the gulf between the economies of Ireland and Scotland grew wider. Ireland's failure to modernise agriculture led to reliance upon the potato to sustain her rapid increase of population, which had reached 8.2 million in 1841 compared to 2.6 million in Scotland. Then came blight, and the Great Famine; it put 3 million people at risk in Ireland compared to a mere 100,000 in the Western Highlands of Scotland. £10 million of money was pumped into Ireland compared to perhaps £300,000 into the Highlands. Nevertheless the Irish problem was too huge for the British state to over-come. Irish population dropped by 19 per cent, 1841-1851, and continued to fall until it was no more than 4.5 million in 1901 — a tragic demographic collapse unique in nineteenth-century European history. Scotland sidestepped the Malthusian trap, though only by a narrow margin in the Western Highlands, as Flinn shows. In that area there was a four per cent drop in population, 1841-1851: but it was easily swallowed up in a 10 per cent increase in Scottish population as a whole over that decade, and it continued to grow until it, too, reached 4.5 million in 1901. In migration Ireland's loss was Scotland's gain. Table IV shows how very much more important Irish settlers were to the Scottish economy than to that of England and Wales.

In Scotland there were about 200,000 inhabitants of Irish birth in 1901, and today about one Scot in six is a Catholic, almost all the members of this church being the descendants of nineteenth-century immigrants.

Statistics from the end of the period measure something of the industrial gulf between the two countries. In 1897, for example, Ireland had 74,000 workers in textile factories and workshops; 69,000 of these were in the 'flax, hemp, jute' group,

Table IV   Percentage of Population returned as Irish-born at the censuses (8)

	Scotland	England and Wales
1841	4.8	1.8
1851	7.2	2.9
1861	6.7	3.0
1871	6.2	2.5
1881	5.9	2.2
1891	4.9	1.6
1901	4.6	1.3

mostly linen workers. Scotland had 144,000 textile workers, 76,000 in the 'flax, hemp, jute' group (mostly jute), and the rest in strong cotton and woollen industries that had then no parallel in Ireland. However, textiles were relatively less important in Scotland than in Ireland. In the 1907 Census of Industrial Production textile output accounted for only 14 per cent of gross output in Scotland compared to 24 per cent in Ireland. The striking contrast between the two economies was in mining and quarries, and iron, steel, engineering and shipbuilding combined: these provided 41 per cent of gross output and industrial employment in Scotland compared with nine per cent of output and 14 per cent of industrial employment in Ireland.

In absolute terms, the only industrial groups in which output was larger in Ireland than in Scotland were butter production, bacon, grain-milling, brewing, shirtmaking and linen. The Irish produced 230 million yards of linen in 1907, or not far off three times the Scottish total production; on the other hand as linen was the textile with the lowest net output per employee and the highest proportion of females and juveniles the growth of the Irish linen industry may be regarded as the counterpart to the shift of Scottish resources into more remunerative branches of textiles and into carpeting. In the food and drink trades, while the gross output of the sector was larger in Scotland, net output per worker was larger in Ireland, reflecting in particular the high degree of organisation of milling, brewing, bacon and butter.

Whiskey (or whisky) is an intriguing case in point. In the 1907 census of production, value-added was relatively higher in Ireland than in Scotland, and while Irish whiskey output was only half the Scottish, Irish exports probably accounted for 60 per cent of shipments beyond the U.K. although the main market then was in the Antipodes rather than in America as it became since. The great success of Scotch on the foreign market in the twentieth century could not therefore be foreseen from nineteenth-century data. Weir stresses in his paper the incentive for patent distillers to amalgamate, and notes that by 1922 the Distillers Company Ltd. in Edinburgh controlled all but one of the Irish patent distillers. For Ireland, there might have been an important difference between short-term and long-term advantage. After 1922 these Scots-owned plants both in the Free State and in Northern Ireland were regarded as peripheral by the company and readily closed down in the difficult inter-war years. These circumstances offer a clue to the striking change of fortune of the two industries.

Table V below shows how very much more developed the industrial sector was in Scotland than in Ireland at the time of the 1907 census. While Scottish industrial workers were only about a fifth more productive per head than Irish ones, net industrial output in Scotland was nearly four times net output in Ireland. England and Wales are added for further comparison: Scotland was neither less industrialised nor much less productive than the largest partner in the United Kingdom.

Table V   Net Industrial Output, 1907 (9)

	Net output (million £)	Net output per employed indust- rial worker (£)	Net output per inhabitant (£)
England and Wales	603	104	18
Scotland	86	98	18
Ireland	23	78	5

The logic of Table V is that agriculture played a much larger part in the economy of Ireland than of Scotland by the early twentieth century. Indeed, in Ireland in 1911, 51 per cent of the occupied population were engaged in agriculture as against 11 per cent in Scotland, which had a lower farming proportion than any other country in the world except Belgium and England and Wales. In 1908, gross output in Irish agriculture was twice that of Scottish, but the Scots were very much more productive farmers: in per capita terms Scottish gross agricultural output was more than twice the Irish − £109 to £46. (10) As deductions from gross output to arrive at net output and income respectively are fairly modest for agriculture, the figures may be regarded as not greatly out of line with relative per capita incomes in farming in the two countries.

The tertiary sector in Scotland was rather larger than in Ireland (36 per cent of occupied population compared to 29 per cent), but the important contrast was the degree to which her insurance, investment and banking houses had emancipated her trade from the heavy dependence on England that was apparent in the Irish case. In 1907 Ireland shipped a total of £60.5 million exports, but only £2.7 million (four per cent) directly from home ports. (11) We do not know the value of Scottish trade by land and sea to the rest of the United Kingdom, but £48.2 million were shipped directly to foreign parts − eighteen times the value of the Irish figure. Similarly, though Ireland owned foreign investments, they were far less extensive than those of Scotland, which possibly grew from around £60 million in 1870 to over £500 by 1914: (12) at the latter date Ireland's must have been between £100 and £150 million. Such a sum could only have come from a highly self-reliant economy with a strong propensity to save: bank deposits in Ireland were £7 a head in 1890 and £9 in 1900, compared to £23 and £24 in Scotland. (13)

So what was the approximate difference in relative incomes in the two countries? Edgar Crammond's attempt in 1912 to calculate the Gross National Product (G.N.P.) of both countries certainly failed by being an underestimate for Scotland (£36) and for Ireland (£19). (14) One of the authors of this article has recently calculated Irish G.N.P. per head as high as £34 at 1911 prices (i.e. 62 per cent of the figure for the United Kingdom). This would seem to put Ireland in an intermediate position between Belgium and Sweden on the one hand and France and Germany on the other, a superficially impressive figure for a country with 51 per cent of its occupied population in agriculture, and in part accounted for by its unique emigration which exceeded the natural increase of population. (15) The margin between the Irish and the Scottish figure must have been substantial if total net output in the industrial sector in Scotland was four times the Irish, and if total foreign investments were at least three times the Irish: roughly equal tertiary sectors (enjoying equal rates of remuneration, although with the Scots biased towards the more remunerative employments) and an Irish net agricultural output twice that of Scotland would only go a limited way in reducing the disproportion. Scotland stood then near the historic peak of her economic performance relative to that of the other regions and nations of the British Isles. Perhaps we would not be wrong in supposing that Scottish G.N.P. at market prices in 1911 was not more than five per cent below the average for the United Kingdom as a whole, which Feinstein estimates at £55 per head.

A ratio to United Kingdom per capita G.N.P. of 95 per cent for Scotland and 62 per cent for Ireland probably aptly, although somewhat uncertainly, reflects the different levels around 1911. The more reliable estimates for the inter-war years offer some confirmation of relativities. Scottish per capita income, depressed in relation to pre-war, has been estimated in the 1920s at about 92 per cent of that of the United Kingdom; the income of the Irish Free State in 1926 was 67 per cent of that of the United Kingdom. (16) Of course all attempts to calculate national income statistics for component parts of the same kingdom involve heroic assumptions: Scottish economists are unable to agree on a figure for the 1970s, let alone the 1900s. All we can safely say is that our statistical straws in the wind point in the same direction – to the conclusion that Scotland had in contemporary terms by 1900 an outwardly highly successful economy but Ireland was still seriously lagging behind her by a substantial margin. What is not shown, of course, is Scotland's reliance on a few heavy industries, which was to cost her dear after 1920.

What are the main reasons for the divergent fortunes of the two countries in the nineteenth century? The most obvious is certainly one of the most important – Scotland had the raw materials needed in Victorian industry, and Ireland had not. Coal ultimately proved decisive to the location of the cotton industry, as we have seen, but the main dynamic in Scottish industry from the middle decades of the century was provided by the iron trade, a lucky bonus based on the discovery of the blackband ores and their exploitation by the hot blast process: that in turn laid the foundations for the heavy engineering and shipbuilding of Clydeside at the end of the century, though it ultimately had to use imported ores for acid shipbuilding steels. Ireland had no equivalent resource bonanza. Even the rise of Belfast as a shipbuilding centre was in a marginal location to the Clyde: in the best years before 1914 shipping tonnage launched there was barely a third of the Scottish total figure.

Absence of raw materials, though serious, was not, however, necessarily a fatal handicap to a nineteenth-century economy. Why was it Denmark and not Ireland that grew so fast and so triumphantly on butter and bacon exports to the U.K. in the 40 years before the first world war? One must not underestimate the extent of the achievement in Irish farming in the second half of the nineteenth century or overestimate the obstacle of landlordism to growth in the post-famine period, as Vaughan's contribution to these papers shows. It may be that Irish concentration on summer dairying as opposed to all-the-year-round butter production was, on the principle of comparative costs in free trade conditions, a rational economic decision.

If half agricultural output was exported, the Irish farmer cannot be faulted too sweepingly on the grounds of inefficiency or uncompetitiveness. In butter, as Ireland was an established supplier — and at one stage the major supplier of the world market — new competition may, as it has done for industrial countries on many occasions, have presented particular problems: in the case of butter the change in taste was from a traditional heavily salted product to a lightly salted product more palatable to the British urban market.

Nevertheless, the low absolute level of Irish farm incomes and the conspicuous difficulty the dairy industry had meeting foreign competition shows how limited Irish success was compared to that of the Danes by the early twentieth century. The Irish farmer and the exporter cannot escape blame for their tardy recognition of change, or for their reluctance or inability to adjust rapidly enough to new market conditions. There was a failure to realise the benefits of all-the-year-round production for a constant market and a tendency to cling to the old pattern of seasonal product- ion on which the early Irish dominance had been based: and it cost Ireland dear at precisely the time when the Danes were using agricultural exports as a base for one of the fastest rates of economic growth experienced in Europe before the first world war.

In explaining the difference we are surely thrown back again on the importance of earlier history. In Denmark there was basic reform of tenures and agricultural practices from the late eighteenth century; there was rapid population growth there- after, but never even in the hardest decades did it outstrip growth of G.N.P: as in Scotland, great emphasis was laid on literacy and schooling. These were Denmark's solid foundations for the producers' co-operatives and rural credit organisations. In Ireland, the Land Acts of 1870 and subsequently in themselves scarcely affected economic trends, but one cannot therefore dismiss as irrelevant the contrast between ongoing reform in Denmark from the time of the Great Rural Commission in 1784 and the lack of drive behind the governments and social leaders of pre-Famine Ireland in producing new agrarian structures. The achievement in Ireland of mass literacy and universal schooling in the second half of the nineteenth century may also have come too late to produce as flexible and self-reliant a peasantry as the Danes or Low- land Scots. Once Ireland had dropped behind, however much the Irish might imitate the forms of Danish practice (and they had 236 dairy co-operative societies by 1902), it was impossible for them to equal Denmark. (17) On external markets in a free trade world the supplier who loses by a small margin loses nevertheless.

The case of an economy crippled by early agrarian problems and excessive populat- ion growth was not uncommon in nineteenth-century European history. Interesting comparisons could be made with those provinces of Flanders and Silesia where very small farms and a rural linen industry in decay also led to harrowing crises in the 1840s (though the presence of coal and iron ore in the same countries changed their histories thereafter). Norway was another overpopulated potato-eating country, with exceptionally heavy emigration in the second half of the century and like Ireland with a record of economic growth between 1850 and 1900 that was quite good by previous recent standards, but not very good by comparison with her nearest neigh- bours. Finland was equally a Malthusian case, with a famine of comparable mortality to that of Ireland striking two decades later. Perhaps there are even points of contact with parts of south Europe, like Galicia, or Romania, where Michael Davitt was a much-admired author. (18) What all these economies have in common is failure to start an 'agricultural revolution' before the middle of the nineteenth century, and thereafter considerable trouble in trying to close the gap between themselves and the 'successful' economies: and what the successful economies have in common is a good clear start in agricultural change, generally in the eighteenth century itself. Carney makes the point in his paper on pre-famine household size — Ireland's case is only exceptional if compared with England or Scotland. But then it is notorious that the Industrial Revolution in Great Britain was without close parallel elsewhere in the world.

Lastly, what of political factors? For England, Union with Ireland, as with Scotland a century before, was not on economic grounds but for reasons of national security. But if Ireland had kept her parliament she would still have been hard put to do better than nineteenth-century Norway or Finland. It is true that we could not expect early nineteenth-century Westminster to consider the needs of underdeveloped provinces for one moment — the Highlands learnt that as well as Ireland. Possibly an Irish government would have come earlier to decisions about land law and rural credit. On the other hand, however, Union probably made it very easy, for example, for Ireland to finance a generous railway-building programme. Scotland, for her part, found eighteenth-century Union advantageous by opening the colonies to direct trade and by bringing Scottish linen and cattle into the biggest free-trade area in Europe; in the nineteenth century Union was presumably still advantageous to a Scotland industrialising with the same speed as England because of the freedom of opportunity and factor mobility which it conferred. In any case, it worked and gave satisfaction in Scotland; and while it neither worked nor gave satisfaction in Ireland, the attack upon it there was more obviously political and nationalist than economic.

The big factors in the differing development of the two countries, then, seem to us not political but geological (coal and ore), agrarian and, in so far as adaptability is concerned, cultural. In the papers presented here the element of explicit comparison is much more marked in some than in others, but all of them fulfil an essential purpose of clearing the way for deeper study of the history of each country. If we were to suggest an agenda for further comparative research, the period of most critical interest would surely lie roughly between 1780 and 1820, when population growth threatened to swamp economic growth in Ireland but appeared to fuel economic growth in Scotland; and the most fruitful line of investigation would be of the historic nature of farming and the social, cultural and demographic dynamics of the rural community in the two countries in the eighteenth and nineteenth centuries.

NOTES

1. We are indebted to all the members of the seminar, and in addition, to Prof. A.S. Milward, for much information and many stimulating ideas: but we accept full responsibility for the mistakes, quirks and directions of this chapter. We were not trying to represent any consensus within the seminar, but to put our own interpretatioⁱ on the course of events in the light of the papers and the discussions.

2. J. Knox, *View of the British Empire* (London, 1785), pp.99-101; Adam Smith, *Wealth of Nations* (Everyman edn.), II, p.421.

3. The values of Irish trade are at irregularly and inadequately adjusted prices, of Scottish trade at c.1755 prices. Irish exports are substantially undervalued compared to Scottish, and comparisons of officially recorded exports undoubtedly underestimate Ireland's relative weight. For the linen trade with England, see Devine, below, p185; for the cattle trade, see A.J. Youngson, 'Cattle exports and highland clearances', unpublished paper presented at New Orleans seminar on exports and economic growth, December 1975.

4. Values of Irish trade continue to be given in intermittently adjusted valuations, and of Scottish domestic exports to foreign ports at c.1755 prices. The figures for 1797-9 are closer on the two sides than in 1755 (see L.M. Cullen, *Anglo-Irish Trade 1660-1800* (Manchester, 1968), p..220), so that distortion is minimised. Moreover, the value of Scottish cattle sold in England is given at *current* prices (about twice 1755 prices) and of linen similarly at current prices (though here the increase was much less). These qualifications mean that Table I in particular should be used with great caution, but we believe the *trends* which it reveals are valid despite doubts over individual figures. As the official valuations on the two sides concord better for 1797-9 than for 1755, comparison if anything must understate the emerging Scottish superiority.

5. We are obliged to Mr. David Dickson for this information from his own research into the history of Cork.

6. Statistics from Henry Hamilton, *An Economic History of Scotland in the Eighteenth Century* (Oxford, 1963), and C. Gill, *The Rise of the Irish Linen Industry* (Oxford, 1925). Both the Scottish and the Irish figures will tend to give the impression of greater increases in *output* than actually took place: presumably in Scotland, as the power of the market grew, a higher proportion would be brought to be 'stamped for sale'; in Ireland, in 'export-led growth', a higher proportion of output would be exported. It is therefore important this should *not* be read as an output table.

7. Statistics from Henry Hamilton, *op.cit.*; Scottish Record Office, customs ledgers in RH 2/4 and RH 20; Dickson, below, pp.105, 108. Some cotton wool may have been re-exported from Scotland to England or vice versa and cannot be found in the books: certainly a great value of yarn moved in this way.

8. We are obliged to Prof. M.W. Flinn for this table.

9. *Final Report of the First Census of Production*, P.P. Vol. CIX (1912-13), p.iii.

10. *The Agricultural Output of Great Britain 1908*, P.P. Vol.X (1912-13), *The Agricultural Output of Ireland 1908* (HMSO, London, 1912). The latter publication was not included in the parliamentary papers. As deductions are smaller for the less commercialised Irish agricultural industry, net comparisons are more to Ireland's advantage. Moreover, if farm food consumption is valued at retail prices and turf consumption estimated, the net figure is significantly higher: net farm income adjusted for national accounting of £50 per capita as against gross output per capita of £46.

11. Data on exports from annual returns in the Parliamentary Papers, *Annual statements of the trade of the United Kingdom,* and from 1904 *Reports of the trade in imports and exports of Irish ports,* compiled by the Irish Department of Agriculture and Technical Instruction.

12. S.G.E. Lythe and J. Butt, *An Economic History of Scotland, 1100-1939,* (Glasgow and London, 1975), p.236 and sources cited there.

13. For this and other Scottish banking statistics in this paper, see S.G. Checkland, *Scottish Banking: A History, 1695-1973,* (Glasgow and London, 1975).

14. E. Crammond, 'The Economic Position of Scotland and her financial relations with England and Ireland', *Journal of the Royal Statistical Society,* Vol. LXXV (1911-12), pp.157-82; Crammond, 'The Financial difficulties of Home Rule', *Nineteenth Century,* Vol.LXX (1911), pp.601-26.

15. L.M. Cullen, 'Income, Foreign Trade and Economic Development: Ireland

as a Case Study', unpublished paper for New Orleans seminar on exports and economic growth, December 1975. Information supplied by Profs. A.S. Milward and S.B. Saul from their forthcoming second volume of *The Economic Development of Continental Europe* suggests that by 1909 the Scandinavian countries, Belgium, the Netherlands, France and Germany comprised a group of countries with a G.N.P. of approximately $150 per head and that France and Germany had improved their position to about $200 per head by 1919.

16. A.D. Campbell's calculations suggest that Scottish G.N.P. was then a little over 90 per cent of the U.K. figure. By then Scotland was clearly relatively less prosperous than England, and the Southern Irish figures had also been removed from the U.K. total, so they were not present to bias the U.K. figure downwards as they had done in 1911. See A.J. Cairncross (ed.), *The Scottish Economy*, (Cambridge, 1954), pp.46-64. For the 1926 estimate of the national income of the Irish Free State, see T.J. Kiernan, 'The national income of the Irish Free State in 1926', *Economic Journal*, vol.XLIII (March 1933). The 1926 ratio of Irish per capita income to Britain's is also Kiernan's; and is expressed on a different basis to the other ratios, i.e. as a percentage of British income *excluding* Irish. If an estimate for Northern Ireland were available, the all-Ireland per capita figure would be somewhat higher. The ratio for 1926 would be higher — even if re-expressed on a United Kingdom *and* Ireland basis — than the pre-war estimate. The war and post-war inflation had strengthened Ireland's relative economic position (see L.M. Cullen, *An Economic History of Ireland Since 1660* (London, 1972), pp.172-3).

17. Cormac Ó Gráda, 'The beginnings of the Irish Creamery System 1880-1914', forthcoming in the *Economic History Review,* argues that the Irish adaptation of Danish technology was better than is usually allowed.

18. We are obliged to Prof. A.S. Milward for this information.

PART II

POPULATION

2. Famine and Famine-relief in Scotland

T.C.Smout

FAMINE is almost as familiar and important a concept to Scottish historians as to Irish ones. There are few books on the course of Scottish history, however general, that do not refer to the great dearths of 'King William's Ill Years' in the 1690s, (1) or to the serious harvest failures of the eighteenth century, (2) or to the so-called 'potato famines' in the Highlands in the first part of the nineteenth century, particularly in 1846. (3) Very little has been written, however, on the frequency or severity of famines or on efficacy of their relief in Scotland. It is the thesis of this brief paper that they were comparatively frequent and severe between the middle of the sixteenth and the middle of the seventeenth centuries; that they occurred with decreasing frequency between the middle of the seventeenth and the middle of the eighteenth centuries, that *potential* famine situations recurred again with increasing frequency between the middle of the eighteenth century and the middle of the nineteenth, but that loss of life was then effectively limited by relief; thereafter they disappeared. The research reported on here was largely carried out by a team working on Scottish historical demography under Professor Flinn's direction at Edinburgh; it was financed by the SSRC and forms part of the subject matter of a book, *Scottish Population History from the Seventeenth Century to the 1930s*, to be published by Cambridge University Press in due course.

What is a famine? Obviously the word is used in common parlance to denote a gross shortage of food, but for our purposes we shall define as 'famines' only those shortages of food that are also associated in some way with 'mortality crises'. Not all shortages led to a mortality crisis; not all mortality crises were associated with famines, though many were.

But what are 'mortality crises'? In non-quantitative sources crisis years can often be readily identified: certain seasons are perceived at the time to be abnormally fatal over a large area, and arouse contemporary comment (in chronicles, diaries and government sources) about starvation, epidemic or the urgent migration of population out of the affected zone. They create manifest alarm. In quantitative terms definition is difficult because there exist only defective statistics on the registration of deaths before the establishment of the Scottish Registrar-General's office in 1855. The parish registers of burials usually survive in rather short runs, and are often seriously deficient or at least inconsistent in recording certain classes of deaths — especially those of infants, children, vagrants and paupers. Nevertheless, certain years showed up as crises in an index of mortality for Scotland that we created from the early seventeenth century by piecing together runs of the best surviving burial registers. (4) When the index figure for burials ran at 30—50 per cent or more above that of the surrounding quarter of a century, we found that non-quantitative sources were full of comment and alarm. So we identified crises from the index and found we could confirm them from other sources.

Certain points need to be made about this figure, which is much lower than, for instance, those found by French demographers studying the seventeenth century. (5) Firstly, poor registers are likely to become worse in a crisis, either because deaths occur in disproportionately large numbers among a badly recorded group (for instance, pauper vagrants), or because the man responsible for keeping them dies or flees. They are, therefore, likely to understate but never to overstate the true magnitude of the surge in mortality. Secondly, we are talking here of a national mortality index — or at least of one compiled from parishes scattered through the Lowlands from the Moray Firth south to the Border with England (we have no runs of burial registers for the far north before the eighteenth century, and none for the Western Highlands before the coming of civil registration in 1855). Locally it was quite common to experience surges in deaths 30—50 per cent above the 25 year norm without any sense of crisis: in fact the national index is derived from a number of local fluctuations, often of this magnitude, but normally cancelling each other out as a 'good' year in one parish is frequently a 'bad' one in the next. But in a mortality crisis of the kind we are talking about there is a strong tendency for burials in most parishes to move up together: in some parishes the surge in burials may be a hundred per cent above the norm or much more; in others the level may only increase by a few per cent. In other words a *national* crisis consists of extreme suffering in many places but not in all places; it will be a widespread, but scarcely ever a universal, disaster.

On the same kind of criteria we can also talk of *regional* crises affecting many parishes within a region, associated with soaring burial numbers and widespread local comment and alarm but not being a generalised experience for the whole, or for most, of Scotland.

How often did mortality crises of any kind (famines or otherwise) occur in the early part of our period? Our quantitative study did not begin until the seventeenth century, but the work of Professor Lythe on the sixteenth century (using non-quantitative sources alone) enables us to reach back in a more tentative way at least to the 1560s. (6) He identifies apparent crises associated with the high price of grain and which we might therefore regard as famines in 1562-3. 1571-3, 1585-7 and 1594-8: to these he would add non-famine crises associated with plague in 1568-9, 1574, 1584-8 and 1597-9. The two types frequently coincide or overlap, but plague was a disease of the burghs, not of the wider countryside — famine affected town and country alike. In the first half of the seventeenth century we found one extremely serious national mortality crisis associated with famine in 1623, and apparently three local ones (these latter were necessarily identified from non-quantitative sources) — in the Highlands in 1604 and 1650, and in the far north in 1634-6: in addition there were two serious waves of plague, in 1600-09 and in 1644-9, when food prices were low. This suggests up to eight famines (of which three were only regional) in a hundred years.

While there were no mortality crises other than these associated with food

deficiencies or bubonic plague, it should not be assumed that those who died in
the former type of crisis were mainly the primary victims of hunger: the principal
killers were 'fevers' (probably mainly typhus) and 'fluxes' (dysentery). The pattern
of disaster can be illustrated from the events that led up to the catastrophe of
1623. It originated with a bad harvest in 1621, which was followed by high prices
and heavy imports of Baltic grain to the east-coast burghs. The problem of vagrancy
increased in the following winter as the relatively well-to-do, finding themselves
pressed, got rid of such servants and dependants as they could – in the words of
one chronicler, 'everie man was carefull to ease himself of suche persones as he
might spaire, and to live als retiredlie as possiblie he might. Pitiful was the lament-
ation not onlie of vaging beggars, but also of honest persons'. (7) Mortality rose in
some parishes in the twelve months following the harvest of 1621, but not by very
much: it was a second harvest failure in 1622 that did the damage the following
year, as the table below illustrates. (8)

	Burials		
	Dunfermline	Kelso	Dumfries
1621	57	59	91
1622	123	86	87
1623	442	417	408+
1624	99	131	
1625	29	71	
1626	25	42	

Apparently the mortality at Dunfermline in 1623 was equivalent to a quarter
or a fifth of the total population of the town; that at Dumfries to rather under a
fifth; at Burntisland in the same year 329 people were buried, but the burgh
cannot have exceeded much above 1,000 in its total population. Nevertheless it
would be wrong to assume that national mortality was necessarily on this scale; in
times of famine towns attracted the starving because they were market centres to
which food might be imported, and many of those buried were plainly vagrants
or 'outland men'. The Scottish Poor Law of the period was rudimentary and inefficient, although Privy Council made strenuous efforts to restrict vagrancy and
to compel parishes to look after their own destitute poor. One cannot, however,
escape the feeling that nothing effective was done. As Edinburgh Town Council
put it, the legislation had been framed when 'thair wes nather sick greit famyn,
sick great number of pure, nor sa greit a visitation be seikness' (9): it had not
worked in the past and could not be expected to work now in an unforeseen emer-
gency.

The century from 1651-1750 had fewer crises of all kinds. Plague never re-
appeared after the 1640s, partly, no doubt, due to strict quarantine laws for
shipping, and partly because Scotland benefited from the gradual elimination of
the disease from Western Europe. But it also had fewer famines; there was a
distinct mortality crisis associated with shortage of food that affected many areas
in the years 1674-6; there was a regional crisis in the far north in 1693-5; there
was the very famous run of famine years, 'King William's Ill Years', 1695-1700;

prices rose to disconcerting heights at least three times in the first half of the eighteenth century, 1709, 1728, and 1740-1, but after 1700 there was definitely no corresponding national or regional surge of mortality to constitute a crisis. From this one can consider the whole period as probably more benign than the century that preceded it, and the second half of the period as exceptionally trouble free compared to the sixteenth and the seventeenth centuries.

How can one account for this? If it were English history it would be very tempting to seek an explanation in terms of improved food supply following an 'agricultural revolution' of the type Dr. Kerridge has described for Tudor and Stuart England. (10) But in Scotland structural change in agriculture simply did not occur on a sufficient scale. Nevertheless, grain prices did fall during the 1650s and remained generally low over the next hundred years except in the famine periods of the mid-1670s and late 1690s. The standard problem of the countryside was seen to be glut rather than dearth, underconsumption rather than underproduction. The export trade in grain became important, and the policy of the government (whether Scottish before 1707 or British thereafter) changed to encourage the farmer by protective corn laws and export bounties as a way of finding a market for the surplus. (11)

There seem to be only two ways of explaining how this could have come about — by a reduction in the pressure of population on available resources, or by an improvement in the performance of agriculture brought about by natural rather than human agencies. It is difficult to know which to prefer. The plague of 1644-9, though very severe in the burghs (it would not be surprising if 20 per cent of Scottish urban population was killed by it) had little significance in the countryside except possibly in parts of Argyll and southern Perthshire: as the losses in the towns were very quickly made up by an inrush from the countryside it is difficult to argue that low prices from the 1650s are due to demographic losses in the consumer market. The famine of the 1690s, however, affected the countryside badly: furthermore it was accompanied by the emigration of tens of thousands to Ulster. Possibly the total Scottish population by 1701 was 5-15 per cent below what it had been six years earlier, and it may well be that mortality did not increase after the next bad harvest in 1709 because there were marginally fewer people left to feed anyway.

The argument from improved agricultural performance presumably would have to rest on climatic amelioration. Lamb has outlined what are considered to be the broad outlines of changes in the British weather — a period of deterioration in the later middle ages, temporarily arrested in the first half of the sixteenth century, resumed apace in the second half: most of the seventeenth century was a cold epoch, but around 1700 (possibly a little before) a period of improvement set in. (1? Parry, working on changes in the level of cultivation in the Lammermuirs in southeast Scotland, has demonstrated how vital even very small changes in summer climate can be for the cultivation of oats in marginal areas. He believes that subsistence farmers will give up and move away from a marginal area if the risk of two harvests failing in succession is greater than once in twenty-five years, and he can demonstrate that the likelihood of such a double crop failure is doubled for marginal farmers if the mean summer temperature falls by $0.16^{\circ}C$, or 5 per cent.

Applying Lamb's model, he indicates that the intensity of average summer warmth
at about 940 feet altitude fell by 6 per cent in the second half of the sixteenth
century, that it remained at this level for most of the seventeenth century, but
that between about 1680 and 1750 most of the sixteenth-century losses were
made up once more. (13) Much of Scotland is, of course, marginal in some senses —
either lying at a high altitude or exposed to strong winds along the coasts: small
alterations in mean summer temperature could therefore be expected to make
much larger changes to the volume of grain harvested than would be the case in
England, and particularly after 1700 it is tempting to see climatic changes as a
factor in diminishing the frequency of famine.

There is, however, at least one other factor to be considered if one contemplates
the difference in mortality between the crisis of the late 1690s and the crisis of
1740-1: the former was a national disaster the memory of which lasted for generations and in some parts still persists: the latter saw an inconsiderable rise in the
number of deaths despite forebodings of catastrophe in the face of what contemporaries described as the worst harvest for forty years, exacerbated by an industrial
depression and the disruption of the economy by war. Certainly the crisis of 1740-1
was not as prolonged as that of the 1690s when it was the repetition of several bad
harvests that did the damage. The other main difference appears to be in the efficacy
of poor relief. In the 1690s the picture was very mixed and perhaps on average
already a little better than in 1623. Edinburgh, for example, established famine
relief camps in the Greyfriar's churchyard, and the parish of Yester in East Lothian
organised assessment for the relief of paupers so effectively that few or none seem
to have perished. Privy Council was, as in 1623, busy trying to make certain that
parish authorities enforced the existing law and properly maintained their own poor:
but some only feigned obedience and here — as Mrs. Mitchison was able to demonstrate for the parish of Spott (also in East Lothian) — the number of dead could
be very high. (14) One also hears reports in the 1690s of the failure of social
obligation, for example, in Andrew Fletcher's call to public action and private self-
denial in a situation where 'so many thousands of our people ... are this day dying
for want of bread', and Patrick Walker's moral tale of the mean farmer who refused
sustenance to the poor and was fated to starve in turn himself. (15)

In 1740 the atmosphere was quite different. Burgh councils and landed proprietors alike appear to have organised themselves quickly and efficiently to act
both within and without the strict letter of the poor law, especially in buying up
grain to sell at less than the market price. (16) Sir John Clerk described in his
private memoirs how 'we had brought from England and Holland many thousands
of bolls to support [the country people], yet they asserted that all was done for
our own private advantages, not believing it possible that we had bought victual
for them at a 3rd or a 4th dearer than we sold it to them, and yet this methode
of providing for them cost the gentlemen of this shire above 2,000 lib. ster.' (17)

This activity cannot fail to have had a benevolent effect on the levels of
mortality during the dearth. What the improvement in social provision was due
to is hard to say. There are no grounds for supposing that, in the poor decades
after the Union, the charity-giving classes had a higher income (and therefore a
bigger surplus to be generous with) in 1740 compared to 1700. There seems, though,

C

to have been more pressure from rioters in 1740, acting in the way E.P. Thompson has described for England (18) to force the magistrates to regulate the market, by, for instance, forbidding the export of grain or the use of barley in the distilleries. But the improvement must also be seen as part of a long-term effort by kirk sessions and by the landowners in good years as well as bad to cope with the problem of the poor in the parishes; this effort appears to become intensified in the Lothians in the 1720s and to have spread in the following decade to other parts of Scotland. (19) In most ways the crisis of 1740 is more like those of the remainder of the eighteenth century than like those of the previous century — the break between one period and another is only approximate.

Nevertheless, the years from 1751 to 1850 did have their own characteristics. The country for much of the century was still hardly able to feel that its food supply was secure, and, indeed, there was more manifest anxiety on that score than there had been in the first half of the eighteenth century. Grain prices began to rise on trend, and continued to do so until the second decade of the nineteenth century. There were numerous years in which the price leapt suddenly upwards following a deficient harvest; 1756, 1762, 1772, 1782, 1799-1800, 1812 and 1816-8 all caused widespread alarm, and there were various others which gave rise to local anxiety. Thereafter supply seems to have improved and grain price fluctuations (set against a tendency to deflation) were less marked. But the poor were far from safe. In the growing industrial sector there was a marked tendency for cyclical unemployment to remove the subsistence of thousands in an unforeseeable way: it happened first following the Ayr Bank crisis of 1772, and recurred at more or less regular intervals throughout the nineteenth century. Also, in the Highlands, the first half of the nineteenth century saw repeated and ever more serious failures of subsistence in both oat and potato crops culminating in the great potato blight of 1846.

How did mortality crises strike in this environment? Our statistics are only valid for the Lowlands, but here high mortality did not come as one might expect, in years of high grain price. There were no Lowland mortality crises in the eighteenth century at all. There were, however, five (of increasing severity) in the first half of the nineteenth century — in 1808, 1818, 1832, 1837 and 1847-9: the last reached proportions that had not been seen in Scotland since the famines of the seventeenth century.

Various problems arise from all this. Firstly, how did the eighteenth century avoid famine despite increasing pressure on food supply? Secondly, were the nineteenth-century crises in the Lowlands in any sense related to deficient food supply? Thirdly, what happened in the Highland shortages? We know from non-quantitative sources that hundreds died of famine there in 1782: this does appear to have been a regional mortality crisis. (20) But did the more famous potato failure of 1846 precipitate a catastrophe in any way comparable to events in Ireland?

The first problem can be approached in a number of ways. By the 1780s one can talk at least of Lowland Scotland as a country already set on the path of rapid economic growth, with a flourishing textile industry and the beginnings of an agricultural revolution in the south. One consequence was that more money was saved even by the common people against a rainy day: friendly societies in town and country alike grew apace in the last two decades of the century, and in the dearth of 1799-1800 also entered the grain market to buy up grain and distribute it at less than cost price to their members. Another was that landowners and the middle classes did now have a larger surplus to be generous with: and as social tension increased (there were grain riots in the depression of 1772 (21) and extensive radical disturbances in the 1790s) they perhaps also found their generous impulses quickened as never before. Transport was also greatly improved by road, canal and sea — one observer attributed the avoidance of catastrophe in the Western Lowlands in 1782 to the fact that it was now possible to move food into the area in sufficiently large quantities. (22) Lastly, the potato became available as a second crop, an alternative staff of life if oats gave way. Its introduction was accelerated by its manifest usefulness in relieving dearth — for example that of 1756.

If there is one single factor that stands out in the Lowlands, however, it is the greater sophistication in organising relief. The dearth of 1782 was relieved by levying 'voluntary assessments' in the parishes on a very wide scale and by greatly increased expenditure by the kirk sessions. Often local authorities went to considerable lengths to alleviate the situation. In Aberdeenshire, for example, the heritors made an estimate of the local shortfall. They reckoned that normally a given input of seed would yield 100 bolls of oats, of which 25 would be needed for seed again and the remainder would yield 70 bolls of meal; the bad harvest meant that the same input yielded only 18½ bolls of meal. Over the whole county there would be a shortfall of 220,000 bolls, which they proposed to cover as follows: 35,000 bolls would be saved by the poor eating less food, 25,000 would be saved by consuming last year's stocks (the previous harvest had been good), 25,000 would be saved by reaping the harvest as early as possible, and by planting early potatoes, 60,000 would be saved by restrictions on brewing and distilling, converting bear or barley into meal instead — this left 75,000 bolls to be found by imports, which they proposed to help organise and subsidise. (23)

The government also intervened directly for the first time in 1783 to distribute thousands of bolls of peas worth £17,000, purchased for military stores in the American War, to Highland and other remote areas as far north as Orkney and Shetland. (24) The usefulness of this intervention was mixed: where access was easy it appears to have saved lives, but in the remoter corners of the Highlands too little was given, and too late, to prevent heavy mortality. Nevertheless, the involvement of the state in famine relief was a new and important feature, related to a new view of Scotland (especially the Highlands and Islands) as a nursery for the armed services. Indeed, it may not be too much to suggest that all authorities — government, landowners and kirk sessions alike — were coming to regard manpower in a different and more modern way, as an economic resource to be husbanded to fight or to labour rather than as a profitless surplus to be squandered in death.

In the scarcity of 1799-1800 many of the same features are evident again: not only did landowners, kirk-sessions and friendly societies buy up grain and distribute it at less than cost price, but in some places landowners forbade the movement of corn out of the parish until the poor had been satisfied — showing a 'moral economy' in Thompson's sense that in this case evidently did not even

need to be prompted by the crowd. In the burghs use was made for the first time
of the soup kitchen, copied from English example (they were known as 'Rumford
kitchens' or 'public kitchens'): in Edinburgh alone 200,000 meals were distributed
by them between November 1799 and April 1800. (25)

All in all, it is clear that Scotland was not only a very much richer country
than she had been in the dreadful 1690s when the import of even a few score
thousand bolls of grain had evidently been enough to put a severe strain on her
balance of payments; she was also run with unprecedented efficiency in local
government and with sufficient public spirit and generosity to be able to organise
to avoid demographic disaster when the price of food went up.

Our second problem was whether the nineteenth-century recurrence of Lowland 'mortality crises' can fairly be related to food supply and be described as
the rebirth of famine. At first sight it seems unlikely. Of the four crises, only the
last coincided with a sharp increase in the price of food. These are partly (but by
no means exclusively) urban crises and it is customary to think of the urban problem essentially in Chadwickian terms as due to uncontrolled epidemics in a bad
sanitary environment. So, in part, it must have been; but there is reason to think
that hunger played an important part as well. The mortality crises of 1808, 1832,
1837 and 1847-9 correspond with troughs in the trade cycle when tens of thousands
in towns and villages were unemployed: food may not have been unduly expensive,
but if purchasing power disappeared the effect was the same; in 1842, in the trough
of another trade cycle, food remained unusually cheap, and an expert on the
Glasgow bills of mortality believed that this had counteracted the bad effects of
unemployment and kept the death rate low. (26)

There is no doubt, too, that poor law and charity which had worked well in
the country areas and smaller towns was all too often not working at all in the
towns as they grew larger. The campaign for the reform of the Scottish Poor Law
led by W.P. Alison was based on the belief that the high urban mortality was
caused by inadequate relief — that the system which worked in communities
where everyone could know everyone else's need was impossibly casual and inefficient to cope with the anonymity and hopelessness of a great Scottish city
of the 1830s and 1840s. The Poor Law Commission of 1844 heard many reports
of the poor starving in town garrets with nothing in their houses but straw, and
as one minister said: 'I never knew what destitution was, among the poor in the
country. I never saw a case of destitution that I could not relieve before the sun
went down; but here there are thousands of cases that you cannot relieve'. (27)
Urban society had outgrown the institutions which kept hunger-related mortality
within bounds in the eighteenth century. One would not wish to exaggerate this
point, or to deny the obvious importance of the deteriorating public health environment. But there was in some senses a regression towards the seventeenth-century
relationship between the hunger and death in the towns.

Lastly, what of the nineteenth-century Highlands? One must admit at once
that any quantitative study of what happened in the Highlands is ruled out by
the virtual absence of burial registers there — though of course there are for the
nineteenth century the decennial censuses to give statements of absolute levels
of population. The clear evidence of population increasingly pressed up against

the limits of resources is marshalled in another paper in this collection by
Professor Flinn. (28) The great dearth of the later 1840s was preceded by extensive
scarcities in 1817-18, when the government again stepped in to help provide grain,
and in 1836-7 when £50,000 was subscribed to a charitable relief fund organised
from Glasgow by which 'the inhabitants of the Highlands and Islands were, for
the time at least, rescued from the fell grasp of famine'. (29) But there was a
sense in which by the late 1830s everyone was waiting for the next blow, so
great was the dependence on potatoes along the western seaboard and so obvious
the destitution of the population there.

Nevertheless the great blight of 1846, and the appalling harvest conditions
of the rest of the decade, caused a total failure of subsistence on a scale that took
contemporaries by surprise. There is no doubt that scores of thousands of lives
were at risk, and that many enfeebled people reduced to the last extremities of
destitution died of typhoid and typhus. (30) If we had the statistical evidence
it might indeed prove to have been a regional 'famine' in the sense that we defined
it at the start of this paper. But the intercensal decline 1841-51 was only 4 per
cent in the worst affected area, and much of this was plainly due to emigration
rather than to mortality. All well-informed contemporaries (and there was no
shortage of experts of all shades of opinion on Highland destitution in these years)
agreed that mortal catastrophe had been clearly averted, and Sir Edward Pine
Coffin, the principal government official in charge of the relief programme, said
in reply to a specific enquiry about the extent of disease that 'the very remarkable
answer to my question on this point has almost invariably been *so healthy a
season has seldom been known'*. (31) One recent historian has called it 'a human
tragedy on a scale unparalleled in modern Scottish history'. (32) It was certainly
a social and economic tragedy in the sense that the blight utterly destroyed the
crofters' way of life and led to an acceleration of eviction and emigration – but
it was not apparently a demographic tragedy in any way comparable to the Irish
experience, or even to the Highland crisis of 1782 when 'many hundred persons
languished and died through the want of sustenance...they were found dead on
the roads, in caverns and amongst thickets where they had taken shelter'. (33)

The reason for the better outcome in 1846 was very plain, and will perhaps
now seem familiar: famine relief had become well organised. The credit for this
must, on this occasion, go to the British Government and to external charity.
The landowners' record was mixed. Sir Edward Pine Coffin commented acidly
that 'the moral obligation supposed to attach to the landowners cannot be relied
on'. While there were some examples of quixotic generosity such as that of Macleod
of Macleod on Skye, and the Duke of Sutherland who spent £18,000 on relief,
there were probably more of appalling meanness by absentees like Gordon of Cluny,
the owner of Barra, South Uist and Benbecula, whom Sir Edward threatened with
public exposure for leaving the islanders to starve.

The role of the Government was much more effective in Scotland than in
Ireland, partly because they had learnt something from experience the previous
year in Ireland, partly because there were fewer people to relieve. Two depot ships
with food were sent to the west, one to Tobermory and one to Portree. In the
first critical period they provided £24,000 worth of meal sold directly to the

crofters and £12,000 sold to the landlords for distribution to the crofters. At the same time the Free Church (only three years old in 1846) distributed £15,000 of relief from a steam yacht that cruised the worst afflicted islands. Meanwhile a massive charitable relief fund was set up in the Lowlands under a voluntary body called the Central Board of Management of the Fund for the Relief of the Destitute Inhabitants of the Highlands: £250,000 was donated through them in the period 1847-51, most being distributed as pittance wages for public works such as road making. It was not an attractive way of providing for people in great need but if the aim was to keep them alive it appears to have worked. (34)

If there is one conclusion that we can draw from this survey it is that avoidance of catastrophe when the price of food went up depended not merely on the general level of economic sophistication and wealth that Scotland had reached but also, and perhaps to an unexpected degree, on the generosity of those who had it in their power to relieve a famine and on their increasing efficiency in devising social organisations capable of the task. Charity may have been cold but it unseated one of the horsemen of the Apocalypse.

NOTES

1. See, for example, George S. Pryde, *Scotland from 1603 to the Present Day* (London, 1962), pp.67-8; W. Ferguson, *Scotland 1689 to the Present* (Edinburgh, 1968), pp.78-9; T.C. Smout, *A History of the Scottish People 1560-1830* (London, 1969), pp.154-5; J.A. Symon, *Scottish Farming Past and Present* (London, 1959), pp.103-4.

2. Symon, *op.cit.*, p.116; J.E. Handley, *Scottish Farming in the Eighteenth Century* (London, 1953), pp.35-6; J.E. Handley, *The Agricultural Revolution in Scotland* (Glasgow, 1963), pp.71-2.

3. Malcolm Gray, *The Highland Economy 1750-1850* (Edinburgh, 1957), chapter 4; A.J. Youngson, *After the Forty-Five* (Edinburgh, 1973), pp.189-90; Eric Richards, *The Leviathan of Wealth* (London, 1973), chapter 17.

4. Details of the methodology are available on request.

5. E.g. P. Goubert, *Beauvais et le Beauvaisis de 1600 à 1730* (Ecole Pratique des Hautes Etudes – VIe Section), p.52.

6. S.G.E. Lythe, *The Economy of Scotland in its European Setting* (Edinburgh, 1960), pp.17-23.

7. D. Calderwood, *The History of the Kirk of Scotland* (Wodrow Society, 1845), VII, 512-3.

8. The Dumfries burial register ceased to be kept in the last quarter of 1623.

9. *Register of the Privy Council of Scotland,* first ser., XIII, 817.

10. Eric Kerridge, *The Agricultural Revolution* (London, 1967).

11. T.C. Smout and A. Fenton, 'Scottish Agriculture before the Improvers: an Exploration', *Agricultural History Review,* XIII (1965).

12. H.H. Lamb, *The Changing Climate* (London, 1966).

13. M.L. Parry, 'Secular Climatic Change and Marginal Agriculture', *Transactions of the Institute of British Geographers,* publication no.64, March, 1975.

14. Rosalind Mitchison, 'The Making of the Old Scottish Poor Law', *Past and Present* no.63 (May, 1974), pp.76-80.

15. A. Fletcher, *Political Works* (Glasgow, 1749), pp.84ff; P. Walker, 'Some Remarkable Passages in the Life and Death of Mr Daniel Cargill', *Biographia Presbyteriana* (Edinburgh, 1827), II.

16. James McIntyre, '1740 – Dearth and Harvest Failure', Edinburgh University Department of Economic History M.A. dissertation, 1973.

17. *Memoirs of the Life of Sir John Clerk of Penicuik, 1676-1755* (Scottish History Society, 1892), p.159.

18. E.P. Thompson, 'The Moral Economy of the English Crowd in the Eighteenth Century', *Past and Present*, no.50 (Feb. 1971).

19. Information kindly supplied by Mrs R.M. Mitchison from research in progress.

20. John Knox, *A View of the British Empire more especially Scotland* (London, 3rd edition 1785), II, 616-8.

21. S.G.E. Lythe, 'The Tayside meal mobs 1772-3', *Scottish Historical Review,* XLVI (1967).

22. Knox, *op.cit.,* II, 409-10.

23. J. Anderson, *General View of the Agriculture of the County of Aberdeen* (Edinburgh, 1794).

24. James Hunter, *The Making of the Crofting Community* (John Donald Publishers Ltd. Edinburgh, 1976), p.50; Handley, *Agricultural Revolution,* p.72.

25. Graham M. Birnie, 'Tradition and Transition: The Scottish Poor Law, Harvest Failure and the Industrious Poor, 1799-1801', Edinburgh University Department of Economic History M.A. dissertation, 1976.

26. *Report of the Royal Commission on the Poor Law (Scotland),* P.P. 1844, Vol. XX, pp.365-6.

27. *Ibid.,* p.119.

28. See below, pp.47-63.

29. A. Fullarton and C.R. Baird, *Remarks on the Evils at Present Affecting the Highlands and Islands of Scotland* (Glasgow, 1838), p.5

30. Hunter, *op.cit.,* chapter 4 *passim.;* R.N. McMichael, 'The Potato Famine of the 1840s in the Western Highlands and Islands of Scotland', Edinburgh University Department of Economic History M.A. dissertation, 1973.

31. Scottish Record Office, Final Reports of Sir Edward Pine Coffin, p.275, (uncorrected) Treasury Correspondence relating to Highland Destitution, Feb.-Sept. 1847.

32. Hunter, *op.cit.,* p.50.

33. Knox, *op.cit.,* II, 616.

34. Many of the details come from Hunter, *op.cit.,* chapter 4 *passim.*

3. Aspects of Pre-famine Irish Household Size: Composition and Differentials

F. J. Carney

THE contour of pre-famine Irish demographic history is generally well known, if still unexplained. On the basis of revised population estimates for the eighteenth century and the Censuses of Ireland from 1821 to 1841, (1) K.H. Connell concluded, 'that the doubling of population which they show in the sixty years before the Famine reflects at least as great a rate of natural increase.' (2) Connell then forwarded the fertility hypothesis. He argued that the growth of population from 1780 to 1840 was fundamentally due to an earlier age at marriage which produced a double-barrel effect: it allowed women to bear more children over their fecund interval and it decreased the length of time in which one generation succeeded another. (3) An alternative proposal, the mortality hypothesis, has been argued by Michael Drake. He suggested that the diffusion of the potato in the late eighteenth century increased fecundity and led to a 'once and for all drop in the general level of mortality'. (4) These conflicting interpretations have given rise to a stimulating debate in Irish history in which the parties seem to agree on the magnitude of the population growth if not on its causes, components, or effects. (5) Indeed, Thomas Newenham's comment in 1805 remains timely, 'that the progress of the population of Ireland has not as yet been sufficiently illustrated; that much matter connected therewith still remains for investigation'. (6)

One aspect of nineteenth century pre-famine Irish demographic history which has never been investigated is the size and the composition of households. The purpose of this paper is to analyze how the various elements of the household combined to establish the mean household size, to determine whether the households were large, and whether differentials existed in household size. It will not be possible to directly compare Ireland with Scotland (7), or the Irish in Ireland to the Irish in Scotland (8), in the first half of the nineteenth century. This is all the more regrettable since the manuscript censuses of Scotland are, unlike those of Ireland (9) or England and Wales (10), 'fully available for the whole of the nineteenth century and open to public inspection'. (11)

This study explicitly adopts for its present purposes the 'lists of inhabitants' methodology with the definitions and classificatory schema as developed by P. Laslett (12) and E.A. Hammel and Laslett. (13) The unit of analysis and the emphasis of the investigation rests on the household as the coresident domestic group. Most studies of the household employ either ecclesiastical *libri status animarum* estate censuses, hearth tax returns, or as in this analysis, manuscripts of census returns. Data which were assembled initially for altogether different purposes but which now can be utilized to answer some questions concerning the size and the composition of households in the past.

Generally, these lists arrange the names of inhabitants in groups which include not only the family proper but also satellite members associated with the family, for example, servants, lodgers, or boarders. The prime criterion of the household is shared residence. However, aside from shared location, members of the household can also be linked with reference to at least two other criteria: shared activities (a functional criterion) or kinship (a familial criterion). (14)

Answers to questions about the household and the family based on census manuscript data are constrained as to what they can reveal about the family as a web of personal relationships either within a given household or beyond the confines of the house. (15) The entire kin network is not necessarily the residential family or household. If one's interest is not centered on these familial links but instead is focused on the family and the household as the common unit of consumption and production, either of children or of goods, then census manuscripts may provide invaluable information to demographic and economic historians. (16)

In all the studies to date, no comparable quantitative evidence on Ireland has been presented. This paper shall attempt to widen the representativeness of the British Isles through some of the findings from an inquiry into Irish households in 1821. The study presents data on five counties in Ireland: Cavan, Meath, Fermanagh, King's, and Galway. The choice of these counties was necessitated by the exigencies of data survival. They collectively represent the widest possible information on Ireland in the nineteenth century. The data analyzed herein are drawn from a one-in-six random systematic sample of all the surviving manuscripts for 1821. (17) The sampling unit for the study was the census household. The enumerators for the census criss-crossed townlands by parishes throughout Ireland commencing in May, 1821. They assigned a unique number to each house within a given townland. Then they proceeded to determine for each house and its household: the number of stories to the house; the name, age, and occupation of the household head, and, if an occupier of land, the size of the holding; the name, relationship to the household head, age, and, if any, the occupation of each inhabitant residing within the house.

Table 1 details the distribution by county of the 2663 households sampled.

Table 1   *The household sample, Ireland 1821*

County	Sample size (N)
Cavan	857
Meath	528
Fermanagh	271
King's	501
Galway	506
Total	2663

The sample of households in this study is composed solely of what might be termed 'private households'. No hospitals, gaols, poorhouses, police or army barracks, that is, no institutions, were sampled. Several schools were included in the sample but in each of them, only the schoolmaster and, where applicable, his family household were listed. In each school encountered, the pupils would have been enumerated in their households of origin and not in the institution.

Since sample sizes vary from county to county, where appropriate, two averages will be reported: the mean of means and the weighted average. Discussions will rely on the weighted average but preference for the mean of means could be predicated on a desire to represent 'Ireland' equally by each available county, rather than on a basis determined by the fortunes of survival size.

To answer the questions concerning the size and composition of Irish households, the advantage of having comparable data for other areas is obvious. It is relatively easy to measure the mean, median, and modal size of household, but to establish that it is 'large' one needs some measuring standard or index. For Ireland, the 'English standard 100 communities', developed by the Cambridge Group for the History of Population and Social Structure (18), and on occasion some other countries, will provide information to allow a confirmation or a denial that an Irish household was large. It may be objected that the English standard represents too long a time span to compare to Ireland in 1821. This may be true, but detailed information useful for the comparisons to be made here is only available for the full standard or Ealing (Middlesex, England) for 1599. The English standard was constructed specifically to be used as an index against which pre-industrial, rural, European communities could be compared. This consideration largely explains the decision to adopt the lists of inhabitants methodology. Furthermore, the definitions and the categories outlined in that particular system of analysis appear to be entirely congruent with the economic and social setting of Ireland in 1821.

There are a number of possible measures of household size because alternative definitions of the household are a function either of shared residence, shared activities, or blood and marriage ties. The measure which represents all the inhabitants of a single residential structure is denoted the 'household size'. This should be considered the global measure of household size in that it includes all the occupants of a given house. It could include a family, their servants, visitors, lodgers, and boarders, all treated as one unit. When the size of all these units are aggregated and divided by the total number of houses, the 'mean houseful size' results.

Once a departure from measuring the size of the household on the criterion of sharing a single residence is made, complications concerning the criterion of shared activities are encountered. Here any indicators employed will depend critically on what is meant by 'shared activities'. If one simply means sleeping in the same premises or eating at the same table, then all inmates (the more inclusive term for lodgers and boarders) should be included and thus this measure of household size would equal definitionally what has been termed houseful size. Rather than employ a redundant measure, inmates, whether they reside as individuals or as members of a household unto themselves, are subtracted from houseful size leaving 'household size'. (19)

This measure of household size includes the family related by blood or marriage and their servants. Servants shared either domestic or productive activities with the family. The first set of activities could be subsumed under the rubric of 'in-house'

service: tending to the daily requirements of the master, the head of the household, and his family. The second set of activities is denoted 'productive' because
it provides for the possibility of servants who shared non-domestic tasks with
the family. These servants worked in the fields and/or tended cattle or sheep
(occasionally expressly called 'out-door' servants in the census). In the case of
crafts and trades, some servants were apprentices, or yet another possibility, some
were shop-assistants. Servants at this point, much more clearly than inmates,
demonstrably fit the stricter construction of the shared activity criterion and
hence servants are included in, and inmates excluded from, the second measure
of household size. It is through this measure that 'mean household size' is produced.

The last measure which uses the criterion of shared kinship remains to be
established: the size of the family which forms the core of the household. This
measure is simply called 'family size'. It includes the head of the household and
all the inhabitants of the house who are related to him directly by blood or indirectly by marriage.

On the basis of the alternative criteria, three measures of the size of coresident
domestic groups have been developed: (20)

1. houseful size (the total number of inhabitants in each house)
2. household size (all the members of a household related directly or
        indirectly plus their servants)
3. family size (all the members of a household related by blood or by
        marriage).

Another presentation of the definitions, expressed in terms of averages per household, may prove useful:

1. mean household size = mean family size + mean number of servants
2. mean houseful size = mean household size + mean number of inmates.

The statistic most commonly cited in this paper and the studies it draws upon
for comparisons is the mean household size.

Table 2 summarizes the main statistical measures used to discuss household
size for the five counties sampled. Houseful sizes in the 1821 Irish sample ranged
from 1 to 21 inhabitants, with a mean of approximately 5.7 persons. As the
table shows, the range in average houseful size across counties was small, varying
only from 5.45 to 5.86, about 0.4 persons per house, or 7.3 per cent of the
average houseful. The range of Irish household size was also 1 to 21 inhabitants.
However, since inmates are disregarded for purposes of this measure, the size of
the coresident group contracts. Mean household size varied from 5.26 to 5.60,
0.34 persons per house. This represented 6.3 per cent of the mean household
size. The range of family size also contracts relative to the other measures, but
varied from 1 to 16 members. However, the greatest diversity among the measures
of coresiding groups occurs when attention is turned to the mean family size.
It varied from 4.86 to 5.25, or 0.39 persons per house, that is, 7.7 per cent of
the mean family size. In all cases, the sample from Galway, a western county,
exhibited the greatest mean size; Meath, a county in the east, displayed consistently
the lowest household sizes. Galway maintained its preeminence despite a much
lower than average number of servants and a slightly higher than average number
of inmates. On balance, Galway had the smallest average number of servants and

Table 2 *Summary measures* by county*

Measure	Cavan	Meath	Fermanagh	King's	Galway	Weighted mean	Mean of means
Mean houseful size	5.69	5.45	5.82	5.68	5.86	5.68	5.70
Mean household size	5.54	5.26	5.49	5.34	5.60	5.45	5.45
Mean family size	5.13	4.86	4.97	4.94	5.25	5.05	5.03
Mean number of servants	0.40	0.40	0.52	0.40	0.35	0.40	0.41
Mean number of inmates	0.15	0.19	0.33	0.34	0.26	0.23	0.25
N	857	528	271	501	506	2663	–

* In all the summary tables, the appropriate measures may not sum exactly due to rounding.

inmates collectively, 0.61 per house. Thus the explanation for the largest household size is that the largest families were found in that county. Likewise, Meath's lower than average number of servants and inmates combined with the smallest family size explains the lowest mean household size in the counties sampled. The other eastern county, King's, consistently ranks in the fourth position in the table for all measures. The average family household in King's was only slightly larger than Meath's, the average number of servants was identical, but the number of inmates per house in King's was almost twice that of Meath. For the remaining two counties, the relative positions do not change if either mean household size or mean family size is the criterion: Cavan is second and Fermanagh is third. However, Fermanagh changes position in the rank order if the measure of mean houseful is used. The relatively high number of servants per household means that Fermanagh was just slightly smaller on average in mean household size compared to Cavan, but since Fermanagh showed the second greatest incidence of inmates, this pulled the county up into second position, just beneath county Galway in the average size of housefuls.

Across all counties, the striking feature is the consistency of the relative importance of family size in explaining household size. On average, family size always exceeded 90 per cent of household size (the mean is 93 per cent), within an extremely narrow range: from 90.5 for Fermanagh to 93.8 per cent for Galway. The size of Irish households is largely explained by the numbers of people who resided together and were related by blood or marriage. The rank order of average family size in this study determined the rank order of average household size.

Table 3 compares the Irish sample to the English standard 100 communities by means of the summary measures developed.

Table 3   *Summary measures: Ireland, 1821 and English standard*

Measure	Irish sample	English (21) standard	Per cent (22) difference
Mean houseful size	5.68	4.77	19.1
Mean household size	5.45	4.45	22.5
Mean family size	5.05	3.82	32.2
Mean number of servants	0.40	0.63	-36.5
Mean number of inmates	0.23	0.32	*

*   The English standard was unable to classify 'unidentified persons'. They amounted to 0.25 persons per household. For purposes of this table they have been placed with the inmates so as not to cloud the visual comparison of family size and servants, the components of household size. Since they resided in the house they must be members of the 'houseful', but they need not be members of the 'household' — that depends entirely on their identification. See text.

No matter which of the three main measures is employed, Irish households were substantially larger than English ones. Irish households were from 19 to 32 per cent larger. The mean Irish family size represents 93 per cent of the mean household size; in England, the respective proportion is only 86 per cent. Irish households are larger overall despite the fact that English households included

about 37 per cent more servants. This significant differential is more than compensated for by the fact that the mean family sizes differed by slightly more than
32 per cent.

There is however one problem with the comparison. It is biased. The English
standard household contained on average 0.25 'unidentified persons'. (23) Adjustments can be made for these masked souls when comparing mean household and
mean family size through various assumptions. Firstly, if all the unidentified persons
were servants, the difference in mean household size between the Irish sample and
the English standard would decrease from almost 20 per cent to 16 per cent.
Secondly, if they were all family members, the mean family size difference would
decline from 32 to 24 per cent. Thirdly, if the unidentified persons were appor-
tioned to each measurement category according to its existing relative weight, the
percentage difference between Irish and English mean household size would be
25 instead of 32 per cent and the mean family size difference would change from
22.5 to 16 per cent. Even under the more extreme assumptions, one and two,
Irish households were still significantly larger than their English counterparts: for
every four persons in an English household there were five in an Irish household.
Moreover, a comparison of Table 2 and Table 3 reveals that there existed no Irish
mean *family* size smaller than the English mean *houseful* size. The comparison
also shows a much greater diversity in household size between Ireland and England
than between the Irish counties sampled no matter which summary measure is
used.

In terms of statistics of central tendency, any measure of average household
size devised and then compared to the available data on England clearly indicates
that Irish households were larger. Depending on the specific ratio chosen, Irish
households are from 16 to 32 per cent larger on average. However, measures of
central tendency by themselves may hide as much as they reveal. To insure that
means or averages are not obfuscating in this instance, Table 4 compares the
frequency distribution of household sizes and the number of persons in each
household size by several classes.

Table 4 *Distribution of households and persons: Irish sample, 1821 and English
standard (24) by size of coresident group percentages*

Size	Households		Persons	
	Irish sample	English standard	Irish sample	English standard
1	2.7	5.6	0.5	1.2
2 - 3	20.2	30.7	9.6	16.4
4 - 5	31.3	30.5	25.9	28.9
6 - 7	26.3	19.8	31.2	26.8
8 - 9	13.5	8.5	20.7	15.0
10 - 11	4.6	3.0	8.7	6.5
12	1.4	2.0	3.4	5.2
Total	100.0	100.1	100.0	100.0

The Table confirms the general results of larger mean household size and
shows the dispersion of how people clustered themselves. The proportion of

English households larger than Irish households occurred in only three classes: the two smallest and the largest. Viewed from a different perspective, 36.3 per cent of all English households contained from 1 to 3 persons; only 22.9 per cent of Irish households fell into this range. At the other end of the spectrum, 45.8 per cent of all Irish households were formed by 6 or more members, whereas only 33.3 per cent of English households were as big.

The distribution in the number of inhabitants per house similarly shows on average a higher proportion of the English in smaller groups and a higher proportion of Irish people in the larger units. Of all persons in the Irish sample, 64 per cent of them lived in groups of 6 or more. Only 53.5 per cent of the English did so. At the lower end of the scale, 17.6 per cent of the English lived in households of 1, 2, or 3; and only about 10 per cent of the Irish did.

The evidence from the Irish sample for 1821 when compared to the English standard 100 communities indicates that Irish households were larger. Table 5 was constructed to place the Irish sample in a wider setting to help determine if Irish households were large when other areas are used as an index.

Table 5   *Mean household size (MHS) (25) International sample*

Location	Date	MHS	N
Heidenreichstein, Austria	1763	5.63	651
Essex, England	1796	5.48	210
English standard	1811	5.48	432
Belgrade, Serbia	1733-4	5.46	178
Irish sample	1821	5.45	2663
Aros-in-Mull, Scotland	1779	5.25	211
Yokouchi, Japan	1823	5.10	98
Longuenesse, France	1788	5.05	66
English standard	1821	4.62	1007
English standard	1801	4.51	1332
(Full) English standard, 100	1574-1821	4.45	–

It has already been argued that Irish mean household size was significantly larger than the English standard. As the table shows, if the comparison had been between the Irish sample, and the part of the English standard derived only from sources of the same date, Irish mean household size would have appeared slightly smaller, 5.45 to 4.62 persons – a difference of 18 per cent rather than the 22.5 per cent reported in table 3. Comparing the Irish sample to a few samples from other nations reveals that the Irish figure tends to fall into the middle range of mean household size. These particular countries are not a random sample: they were selected on the basis that they used the same definitions and methodology and they fell within a tolerable time span near to 1821.

The conclusion of this section of the paper then is that Irish households in 1821 were significantly larger than English households but that future studies of other European, rural societies will probably indicate that mean Irish household size was not uniquely so in a wider historical context.

The question about differentials in mean household size related to other factors remains. It has already been shown that when geographical differentials are explored there are only modest differences between the areas sampled in Ireland. This is not the case when the age or the occupation of the household head is investigated.

It is important to realize that studies of the family and household based on censuses are photographs cut from a movie and placed in isolation. The concern is with an institution that is essentially dynamic: people marry, children are born, they grow, some leave home, they die. Though not necessarily in that order, changes in households could be expected to trace a cycle of growth and decline from household formation through household dissolution. Table 6 presents the usual summary measures according to the age of the household head grouped into six categories. (See page 41).

No matter what measure of household or family size is used the rank order never varied: the largest households were headed by persons aged 45 to 54 years; second came households headed by 35 to 44 year olds; then 55 to 64; 65 and over; 25 to 34; and lastly, households where the master or mistress was less than 24 years of age. The rise and fall of households over time seems a fairly safe inference to make from this cross-tabulation. The pattern that emerges from the table varies slightly depending on whether mean family size, mean household size, or mean houseful size is the measure of interest. Table 7 arranges the three measures into indices with the respective maximum household size as the base of 100.

Table 7   *Summary measures: indices of household size by age group of household head*

Measure	-24	25-34	35-44	45-54	55-64	65+
Mean houseful size	57	76	98	100	91	85
Mean household size	56	77	99	100	91	86
Mean family size	54	75	96	100	90	82

By differencing the indices across rows, an indication of the rate of increase and decrease of household sizes results. The picture is one of high growth in households headed by persons 20 to 30 years old, the mid-points of the two youngest age groups. This is followed by slightly higher rates of change for households headed by people from 30 to 40 years old. The peak is reached around the time the household head is aged 50 with surprisingly low — in relation to the increases — rates of decrease in household size on the downhill side of the cycle. Increases in the indices for mean household size were influenced by subcycles in the number of servants per household. Households seem to take on servants fairly rapidly over the family formation stage, say from ages around 25 to 40. Presumably the period when most if not all of the children born into the household would be below adult productivity. When the children were young, the family took on servants. But as more of the children approach adulthood, say 15 years of age, servants are quickly sloughed off for about a ten year interval. Then there is a build-up in the number of servants residing, gradually at first, but more rapidly as the household head reaches 60: just over the same period when

Table 6 *Summary measures: by age group of household head*

Measure	-24	25-34	35-44	45-54	55-64	65+
Mean houseful size	3.60	4.80	6.20	6.31	5.74	5.38
Mean household size	3.35	4.65	5.97	6.02	5.49	5.16
Mean family size	3.09	4.25	5.46	5.70	5.13	4.66
Mean number of servants	0.27	0.40	0.51	0.32	0.36	0.49
Mean number of inmates	0.25	0.15	0.24	0.29	0.25	0.22
N	93	565	672	627	469	237

D

his family is contracting. Servants seem then to be a substitute for young children earlier in the family cycle; later, after the peak of family size is attained and passed, servants seem again to be substitutes but this time for the departing children who by now have reached adulthood.

No simple hypothesis is suggested when the age of a household head and the average number of inmates is compared. Since inmates are likely to be a source of supplemental family income, and thus relatively more important to households the lower their income, one expects to find a stronger relationship between inmates and family income than between inmates and the age of the household head.

The final portion of this paper involves the relationship between the size of the household and the occupation of the household head. What one would like to know, all other factors being constant, is whether larger household sizes are associated with higher family incomes. Then it would be useful to establish the direction(s) of the relationship. But unfortunately, the census of 1821 did not seek information on income. It did however attempt to ascertain the occupation of the members of the household.

From the occupational data, a 'socio-economic status' index was constructed which is more properly entitled an 'occupational classification'. Counting the categories of 'no occupation' and each dual occupation, e.g. farmer and weaver, separately, the sample distinguishes seventy-four different occupations. Ireland at the time was predominantly rural and agricultural: 69.4 per cent of all household heads were either farmers (42.3), farmers and laborers (7.2), or laborers (19.9 per cent). A further 2.3 per cent of household heads returned themselves as following a dual occupation which without exception involved some farming. Craftsmen with occupations of undoubted differences in remuneration and skill accounted for another 11.5 per cent. Adding to this the 6.9 per cent of households headed by persons with no occupation, a relatively small number of occupations encompassed slightly more than 90 per cent of all household heads. The occupations of the remaining 10 per cent showed tremendous variety if not great weight of numbers. There are publicans, huxters, members of the clergy, distillers, a horse-gelder, car men, rat catchers, land surveyors, and even that *rara avis,* a capitalist. The problem was to compress these callings into a manageable classificatory scheme which approximates an economic and social grading of occupations. The approach adopted was to establish two gradations and then merge them into one. One gradation was composed of all household heads involved in agriculture. The other category was the residual: people engaged in the professions, trades, crafts, unskilled work and laboring. The grading of agricultural occupations was simplified by the information provided in the census on the size of the holding and the assumption that an acre in any one county, *ceteris paribus,* was about as profitable as an acre in any other county. The agricultural segment was then split into five classes according to the size of the holding expressed in Irish acres (26): the first land class were holdings above 50 acres; second, from above 10 to 50 acres; third, from above 2 acres to 10 acres; fourth, any holding less than or equal to 2 acres; and finally, all agricultural workers without any land. The non-agricultural occupations were likewise subdivided into five classes: first, gentlemen, clergy, surgeons, and attorneys; second, the middle and lower professions (e.g. revenue officer, school teacher, land surveyor, land steward), the higher trades and skilled crafts (innkeeper, spirit dealer, publican, watch maker). The third class was composed of all dual occupations, the remaining trades, and the crafts (masons, carpenters, smiths, victuallers, shoemakers). The fourth group comprised female work (spinning, sempstress, mantua-maker, washer woman) and unskilled labor (gaol keeper, car man, coach driver, rat catcher). The fifth class was reserved for persons without occupations, paupers, beggars, and two unclassified occupations: 'maley' and 'jurner'.

The two classifications, called 'land' for agricultural pursuits and 'group' for non-agricultural occupations, were meshed in such a fashion that an index of 1 on land was assumed to generate an economic or a social status equivalent to an index of 1 on group. Dual occupations were sorted with both indices and assigned ultimately the higher index. Thus a farmer and weaver with 11 acres would be given an index of 2, but a farmer and weaver with 9 acres was assigned to class 3. Patently, the system involved a high degree of 'guestimation'. (27)

Table 8 presents the summary measures for the Irish sample of 1821 according to the above classification.

Table 8 *Summary measures: by occupational index*

Measure	1	2	3	4	5
Mean houseful size	8.92	6.80	5.79	5.00	4.41
Mean household size	8.75	6.60	5.58	4.78	3.89
Mean family size	5.86	5.72	5.25	4.66	3.71
Mean number of servants	2.89	0.87	0.33	0.12	0.18
Mean number of inmates	0.17	0.20	0.21	0.22	0.53
N	64	452	1098	856	193

Scanning down the columns, the highest socio-economic status class is associated with the largest household and family sizes, the greatest average number of servants and the smallest average number of inmates. At the other end of the scale, the lowest occupational groups evidenced the smallest household and family sizes, but a proportion of servants slightly higher than occupations of index 4, partly due to the non-classifiable occupations, but not entirely. By a considerable amount, the lowest occupational group coresided with the highest average number of inmates. The remaining classes take exactly intermediate rank order positions between these extremes according to the index assigned to the occupation of the household head. Thus on the evidence of the data and the index scheme, there does seem to have existed a negative (because higher statuses were assigned lower indices) relationship between occupational index and the household and family size, i.e. lower index number − higher status − is associated with larger sizes; a negative relationship between the occupational class of the household head and the number of servants resident. A positive association is found between the occupational index and the mean number of inmates, reminiscent of an hypothesis advanced earlier.

There are several other differentials which could be investigated to clarify differences in household and family size: rural versus urban residence, the marital status and sex of the household head, the number of residing kin beyond the nuclear family of husband, wife, and own children. These matters will have to wait for a future conference.

This work on Ireland will continue under the guiding assumption that, 'if the family thrives, the nation thrives, and if we can find out how the average family thrives we are in a fair way to knowing the roots of the progress of the economy as a whole.' (28)

In the interim, the results from this investigation should prove of wider interest than simply extending our knowledge of nineteenth-century households and families in the British Isles beyond England. Aside from any spark of curiosity it ignites in the other Celtic parts of these islands, the information on the household in pre-famine Ireland should provide welcome evidence useful for comparative purposes to historians of urban households in the second half of the nineteenth century. From the 1830s and more especially from the end of the 1840s, large numbers of the Irish emigrated to the cities of the United States, Canada, and Great Britain. Studies on urban households in these areas invariably single out ethnicity as an important variable explaining differences in many observed patterns. (29) Up to now they have not been able to draw upon any quantitative evidence dealing with Ireland which indicates even in general terms the historical conditions of the household from which the Irish projected themselves overseas.

NOTES

1. K.H. Connell, *The Population of Ireland 1750-1845* (Oxford, 1950), Chapters I and II.

2. K.H. Connell, 'Land and Population in Ireland, 1780-1845' in D.V. Glass and D.E.C. Eversley, eds. *Population in History* (London, 1965), p.424. At least one commentator, R.C. Geary, believed that 'Connell's upward revisions, though drastic, seem too conservative' and thus that the estimated rate of increase is too liberal. See Geary, 'Review of the Population of Ireland 1750-1845 by K.H. Connell', *Studies*, XXXIX, 156, (1950), 472-473. Also see the discussion by Geary of K.H. Connell's 'Marriage in Ireland after the Famine: The Diffusion of the Match', *Journal of the Statistical and Social Inquiry Society of Ireland*, XIX, (1955-6), 98-100.

3. K.H. Connell, 'Some Unsettled Problems in English and Irish Population History, 1750-1845', *Irish Historical Studies*, VII, 28 (1951).

4. Michael Drake, 'Marriage and Population Growth in Ireland, 1750-1845, *Economic History Review*, 2nd series, XVI, 2 (1963), 312.

5. Some tributaries of the debate stream may be explored in: the 'Bibliography of the Writings of Professor K.H. Connell', *Irish Economic and Social History*, I (1974), 14; Raymond D. Crotty, *Irish Agricultural Production...*, (Cork, 1966), Chapters I and II; Joseph Lee, 'Marriage and Population in Pre-Famine Ireland', *Economic History Review*, 2nd series, XXI, 2 (1968); L.M. Cullen, 'Irish History without the Potato', *Past and Present*, no.40 (1968); G.S.L. Tucker, 'Irish Fertility Ratios before the Famine', *Economic History Review*, 2nd series, XXIII, 2 (1970); for a useful summary, see, Brendan M. Walsh, 'A Perspective on Irish Population Patterns', *Eire-Ireland*, IV, 3 (1969).

6. Thomas Newenham, *A Statistical and Historical Inquiry into the Progress and Magnitude of the Population of Ireland* (London: 1805), p.iv.

7. But see Eric R. Creegan, *Inhabitants of the Argyll Estate, 1779,* (Edinburgh, 1963).

8. For an example of a study of the Irish in Scotland, see, Michael Barke, 'Census Enumeration Books and the Local Historian', *The Local Historian*, X, 5 (1973).

9. In June 1922 the Army of the Provisional Government of Ireland shelled its own Public Record Office, which was, and is, housed in part of the Four Courts in Dublin, in order to extricate Irregulars; for an account see *The Irish Times,* June 29, 1922, p.5.

10. For a full review of the Censuses of Great Britain see, Interdepartmental Committee on Social and Economic Research, *Guides to Official Sources, No.2: Census Reports of Great Britain 1801-1931,* HMSO, (London, 1951). Census manuscript for the British censuses are not available until 100 years have passed from the time of the census.

11. M. Anderson, 'The Study of Family Structure' in E.A. Wrigley, ed., *Nineteenth-century Society...* (Cambridge, 1972), p.414, fn. 30.

12. See Peter Laslett, 'Social Structure from Listings of Inhabitants', in E.A. Wrigley, ed. *An Introduction to English Historical Demography* (London, 1966) and Peter Laslett, 'Introduction: the History of the Family', in Peter Laslett, ed. with the assistance of Richard Wall, *Household and Family in Past Time* (Cambridge, 1972).

13. E.A. Hammel and Peter Laslett, 'Comparing Household Structure Over Time and Between Cultures: A Suggested Scheme for Representation and Classification with a Provision for Handling by Computer', *Comparative Studies in Society and History,* XVI (1974).

14. Laslett, 'Introduction...', *op.cit.,* pp.23-25.

15. See Lutz K. Berkner, 'The Use and Misuse of Census Data for the Historical Analysis of Family Structure', *Journal of Interdisciplinary History,* V, 4 (1975), 724-726. Berkner raises three specific criticisms against Laslett's methodology. The first point about kin networks is granted in the text above. The remaining two points are not applicable to the Irish Census of 1821: first, the Irish census did ask questions about the age of each member of the household. The response rate was 99.87 per cent of the enumerated population. The last criticism concerning the explicitness of the relationship to the household head in the data itself is treated below in note 23.

16. For three types of models which could use the data generated here to test and/or to refine their theories, see A.V. Chayanov, *The Theory of Peasant Economy,* edited by Daniel Thorner et al., (Homewood, 1966); Frank Lorimer, 'The Economics of Family Formation under Different Conditions', *UN World Population Conference, 1965,* III (New York, 1967); and Richard A. Easterlin, 'Relations between Population Pressure and Economic and Demographic Change', International Union for the Scientific Study of Population, *General Conference,* III (London, 1969).

17. Public Record Office, Ireland. Census of 1821, Copies of Returns, county Cavan; Original Returns for counties Meath, Fermanagh, King's, and Galway. PRO, 1A.45.series 3-20.

18. Laslett, ed. *Household and Family..., op.cit.*

19. Inmates living in family groups within the household of the 'main' family are not dealt with in this paper. Although they are included in all 'inmate measures'.

20. To see a range of alternative measures, consult P. Laslett, 'Mean Household Size in England since the Sixteenth Century', in Laslett, ed. (1972), *op.cit.,* Table 4.2, p.133.

21. Laslett, 'Introduction...', *op.cit.,* Table 1.13, p.83.

22. As England is the standard, per cent difference was calculated: (Irish sample, 1821) — (English standard) / (English standard).

23. This might be considered an index of the quality of the English data. Ireland's census acts from 1821 explicitly required an answer to the question about each member's relationship to the household head. (See Census of Ireland, 1821, (Brit. Parl. Papers, 1824 XXII) xiv-xv.) Out of this sample, there were nineteen persons for whom presumptions were made because the appropriate entries were lacking: that amounts to 0.007 persons per household. British censuses did not require that this information be given until the Census of 1841. (See *Guides to Official Sources, No.2, op.cit..*) The Federal censuses of the United States of America had no provision for this information until 1880. (See Barbara Laslett, 'Household Structure on an American Frontier: Los Angeles, California in 1850', *American Journal of Sociology*, LXXXI, 1 (1975), 112.)

24. Laslett, 'Introduction...', *op.cit.*, Table 1.7, p.77. It should be noted that the 'persons' column in Laslett's table only sums to 99.8 per cent. I have added 0.1 per cent to the groups sized 4-5 and 6-7 for the English standard persons per household size.

25. Most of the sample is taken from Laslett, 'Introduction...', *op.cit.*, Table 1.3, p.61. Parts of the English standard 100 communities, for the years, 1801, 1811, and 1821 were calculated from information in Laslett, 'Mean household Size...', *ibid.*, Table 4.1, p.131. The data for Austria is taken from Lutz K. Perkner, 'The Stem Family and the Developmental Cycle of the Peasant Household: An Eighteenth-Century Austrian Example', *American Historical Review*, LXXVII, 2 (1972), 398-418.

26. See Census of Ireland, 1821, *op.cit.*, x, xii, xvi. Also see, P.M. Austin Bourke, 'Notes on Some Agricultural Units of Measurement in Use in Pre-Famine Ireland', *Irish Historical Studies*, XIV, 55 (1965), 236-245.

27. See John Hall and D. Caradog Jones, 'Social Grading of Occupations', *The British Journal of Sociology*, I (1950), 31-55; Lawrence Stone, 'Social Mobility in England, 1500-1700', *Past and Present*, no.33, (1966), 16-55; L.A. Clarkson, *The Pre-Industrial Economy in England 1500-1750*, (London, 1971), Chapter 4, notes to Table 2, pp.90-92; W.A. Armstrong, 'The Use of Information about Occupation', in Wrigley, ed. (1972), *op.cit.*, pp.191-310.

28. J.D. Chambers, *Population, Economy, and Society in Pre-Industrial England* (London, 1972), p.34.

29. For example see Lynn Lees, 'Patterns of Lower-Class Life: Irish Slum Communities in Nineteenth-Century London', in Stephen Thernstram and Richard Sennett, eds., *Nineteenth-Century Cities: Essays in the New Urban History*, (London, 1969), pp.359-385; Michael Anderson, *Family Structure in Nineteenth-Century Lancashire* (London, 1971), Chapter 7; Edward T. Pryor, Jr., 'Rhode Island Family Structure: 1875 and 1960' in Laslett, ed. (1972), *op.cit.*, pp.571-589; Tamara K. Hareven and Maris A. Vinovskis, 'Marital Fertility, Ethnicity, and Occupation in Urban Families: An Analysis of South Boston and the South End in 1880', *Journal of Social History*, VIII (1975), 69-93.

4. Malthus, Emigration and Potatoes in the Scottish North-west, 1770-1870

M.W. Flinn

THE problem that exercised Malthus, and for which the history of the Scottish north-west in the century between about 1770 and 1870 provides an apposite case-study, (1) relates to the relative rates of increase of population and food supplies. In Malthus's view, while most societies tend to be able to increase the food supplies available to them 'in arithmetic proportion' (i.e. like simple interest), their populations tend to grow 'in geometric proportion' (i.e. like compound interest). Given these basic assumptions, there must come a time, sooner or later, when populations reach a ceiling set by their available food supplies whether home-grown, or a combination of home-grown and imported. When this happened, Malthus suggested, population would tend to be held to this ceiling by the 'positive checks' of war, disease or famine — that is, by some augmentation of mortality. To avoid such tragedies, he recommended the gentler wisdom of reduction of fertility — his 'preventive check', by which societies would control their population growth to a rate no greater than that of the growth of their food supplies. This was best achieved by delaying marriages. He was, of course, thinking in a context of societies with uncontrolled fertility, when marriage was commonly followed by the births of children in a regular spacing for the remainder of the wife's natural reproductive period. In such conditions there was a direct correlation between women's ages at first marriage and completed family sizes. Though Malthus's proposition is most easily demonstrated to be wrong in respect of his arithmetic progression of food supplies, it is most likely to be correct in conditions of minimal agricultural resources such as exist in the Scottish north-west. It is true, of course, that societies are rarely completely isolated from their neighbours; but most can supplement the food they provide themselves only by producing something additional and exchanging this for extra food.

The society whose experiences I propose to consider in the light of this Malthusian approach occupied the islands off the west coast of Scotland (the inner and outer Hebrides) and the parishes on the mainland that lie to the north and west of the Highland watershed north of the Great Glen, but excluding Caithness and the northern isles. Almost all these parishes border a stretch of coastline. In terms of the civil parishes employed in the nineteenth-century censuses, this region embraced 38 parishes — 20 in the islands and 18 on the mainland. For simplicity's sake, I am calling this area the 'north-west', though readers will recognise it, I hope, as possessing a certain social and economic homogeneity and distinctiveness. It corresponds, of course, to the area north of the Great Glen designated by Fraser Darling in his *West Highland Survey* of 1955. Table 1 sets out the inter-censal

Table 1 *Growth of population, North-west Scotland, 1755-1861*
(Cols. (a) = percentage increases in intercensal periods; Cols. (b) = annual compounded rate of growth)

Area	1755 - 1801		1801 - 1811		1811 - 1821		1821 - 1831		1831 - 1841		1841 - 1851		1851 - 1861	
	(a)	(b)	(a)	(b)	(a)	(b)	(a)	(b)	(a)	(b)	(a)	(b)	(a)	(b)
Islands														
Outer Hebrides (1)	59.9	1.02	12.8	1.19	20.3	1.85	8.9	0.86	11.1	1.05	1.1	0.11	1.2	0.12
Skye (2)	40.3	0.74	7.7	0.74	22.5	2.03	9.3	0.89	1.4	0.14	-2.4	-0.22	-12.4	-1.32
Mull (3)	61.5	1.04	9.9	0.95	13.1	1.23	-0.7	-0.08	-4.5	-0.46	-16.8	-1.84	-12.4	-1.32
Others (4)	84.0	1.33	3.9	0.38	1.4	0.14	-4.1	-0.42	0.8	0.07	-16.0	-1.74	-20.7	-2.32
Total	56.2	0.97	9.6	0.92	17.5	1.61	6.2	0.60	4.8	0.47	-3.9	-0.40	-6.3	-0.65
Mainland														
Sutherland (5)	11.9	0.24	0.8	0.88	1.0	0.10	18.4	1.69	-1.3	-0.13	-3.0	-0.30	1.2	0.12
Ross (6)	48.3	0.85	23.8	2.13	28.1	2.48	2.2	0.22	2.9	0.28	-4.1	-0.40	0.0	0.00
Inverness (7)	49.8	0.88	-1.6	-0.16	15.2	1.42	1.3	0.13	-3.7	-0.38	-5.2	-0.53	-20.6	-2.30
Argyll (8)	11.1	0.23	1.8	0.18	5.4	0.53	5.2	0.51	-5.8	-0.60	-4.9	-0.51	-15.3	-1.66
Total	29.3	0.56	8.1	0.78	14.9	1.39	5.9	0.57	-0.9	-0.09	-4.1	-0.42	-5.9	-0.61
North-west total (Islands and mainland)	44.4	0.80	9.0	0.87	16.5	1.52	6.1	0.59	2.6	0.26	-4.0	-0.41	-6.1	-0.63

Notes:

1. Parishes of Barvas, Lochs, Stornoway, Uig, Harris, Barra, North Uist, South Uist.
2. Parishes of Bracadale, Duirinish, Kilmuir, Portree, Sleat, Snizort, Strath.
3. Parishes of Kilfinichen, Kilninian, Torosay.
4. Parishes of Tiree and Coll, Small Isles.
5. Parishes of Assynt, Eddrachilles, Farr, Tongue.
6. Parishes of Applecross, Gairloch, Glenshiel, Kintail, Lochalsh, Lochbroom, Lochcarron.
7. Parishes of Glenelg, Kilmallie.
8. Parishes of Ardnamurchan (including Arisaig and Moidart), Morvern.

rates of growth of population (using Webster's 1755 private census and the first
seven censuses of population) of this north-west region, and of its principal component areas. The notes to the table indicate exactly which civil parishes have
been included.

Like all studies within a fairly rigidly theoretical framework, this paper must
involve much over-simplification. It is hoped, however, that what is lost by distortion from this cause and by the failure to take account of some other important
influences on the social and economic evolution of this area will be offset by the
gains of exposing, more clearly than a more comprehensive survey would achieve,
the structure of the principal forces involved in the determination of the course
of north-west Highland history.

There is no reason to suppose that, short of the point at which the checks
envisaged by Malthus began to operate, the population of this area would not show
the same tendencies as populations elsewhere to natural increase. The limited
nature of the physical resources of this area merely set a lower ceiling to the density
of population that could be accommodated than would be set in more favourably
endowed areas. Paucity of sources prevents us from discerning when, in modern
times, Malthus first showed his hand in the Scottish north-west. In the great
European famines of the seventeenth century it is always hard to decide whether
there was a true Malthusian crisis or not. Pre-industrial peasant societies rarely
planned for substantial surplus production in normal and good years, and so, having
few non-food products to trade for imports of foods, were perennially at risk in
the event of serious harvest deficiency. We cannot, therefore, assume that a major
famine, like that of the late 1690s in Scotland, indicated a true Malthusian situation:
the evidence that the ceiling had been reached can only be a population held to
long-run stagnation by its inability to raise additional food year-by-year on the
available land with the going technology and subject, in consequence, to recurring
famines.

Whether or not the famine of the late 1690s was a manifestation of a true
Malthusian situation, it is likely that the cut-back in population that it produced
left the population of the north-west, as of other parts of Scotland, so reduced
that there could be no serious question of a Malthusian situation being reached
for several decades. Soon after the mid-eighteenth century, however, signs began
to appear of pressure of population on resources. There are, unfortunately, no
sources for the statistical assessment of the growth of population in the north-west
before the mid-eighteenth century and accordingly no means of ascertaining just
when or why the great eighteenth-century acceleration in the rate of growth of
population began. Comparison of Webster's parochial figures for 1755 (2) with
those of the first census of 1801 shows that, whatever growth had or had not
taken place before 1755, there was substantial growth over the whole area in the
second half of the eighteenth century, and in some parishes dramatic growth. (3)
The first real indication – since people do not easily forsake their homelands – of
overcrowding was produced shortly after 1770 by the first of what later proved to
be several great waves of emigration. At this time it became a commonplace for
commentators to draw attention to the apparent excess of population. Pennant
commented in 1772 on over-population and under-nourishment on Canna and

Skye, and observed that the people of Rhum 'carry famine in their aspect', (4) while Crevecoeur's 'Andrew the Hebridean' had left Barra for Pennsylvania in the same year with the comment, 'There were too many of us'. (5)

There are, of course, many alternatives open to a society when it first finds itself confronted with a Malthusian situation of this kind. It can turn to Malthus's own alternative of the preventive check and reduce its tendency to natural increase by lowering fertility through delayed marriage. Or, following the law of comparative costs, it might shift the structure of its existing agricultural production in such a way as to produce more of a particular commodity which it can exchange in the market for a greater quantity of other foodstuffs. Or it can seize every opportunity provided by advancing agricultural technology to raise the productivity of its strictly limited acreage of cultivable land. Finally, of course, the pressure can be eased by temporary or permanent out-migration. Migrants not only reduce the immediate Malthusian pressure, they also frequently add to cash resources: temporary out-migrants bring some of their earnings back with them, while longer-term or permanent emigrants send remittances home. Both of these increase the purchasing capacity of the remaining population for imported foodstuffs. All of these alternatives except the first, of course, merely raise the Malthusian ceiling, they do not remove it.

In the second half of the eighteenth century several of these possibilities were, in fact, available to the people of the north-west to help them to accommodate their growing numbers, and were adopted by them. First, there was cattle-raising. The export trade in 'black' cattle, particularly to England, offered a resource that could be exchanged for a greater quantity of traditional grain food than could have been produced on the same area of land. This was primarily because cattle could feed on land too poor to sustain grain crops, and the north-west had no shortage of sub-marginal land. (6) The second possibility was kelping. Kelp was burnt, dried seaweed, one of the three main sources of raw material for the manufacture of alkali. Though its collection and preparation by many of the inhabitants of the western mainland and by almost all those of the Hebrides was begun as early as the 1750s, the discovery by landlords that kelp production could significantly augment estate revenues, a realisation heightened by the inaccessibility of supplies of the alternatives to kelp — potash and barilla — during the French wars, encouraged an immense increase in production from the 1790s. (7) Third was the potato. Cultivated in the Outer Hebrides first in the 1740s, the potato was gradually adopted as a major item in the diet of the inhabitants of the north-west during the later decades of the eighteenth century. The potato, like cattle, could be accommodated on land that would not support grain crops, and it responded in a different way from grain to variations in the weather and so mostly did not fail in years of deficient grain harvest. It could, moreover, support families on much smaller acreages than were required for grain crops. (8)

These important developments permitted, though with varying chronologies, either directly through an increase in food productivity, or indirectly through an increased purchasing power for imported foodstuffs, (9) the accommodation of much of the natural increase of population during the second half of the eighteenth century. Together with out-migration they helped to stave off what must certainly have otherwise been a gathering Malthusian crisis.

The great burst of emigration (10) from the north-west in the years 1772-5 is perhaps the clearest indication of the recognition by the people of that region that they were in danger of outgrowing their own capacity to feed themselves. Malthusian pressure shows itself fitfully rather than regularly: in a Malthusian situation, above-average, or even average, harvests may for a time continue to meet, or almost to meet, the needs of the population; it is in the years of below-average harvests that the reality of the threat is first revealed. 1771 and 1772 were both years of poor harvest in many parts of Scotland, (11) and it may be that harvest deficiency was responsible for the timing of this first great emigration. It was perhaps also the first acute crisis since the opening-up of new possibilities of emigration with the acquisition of French Canada in 1763. Not the least of the consequences of the 1763 peace for the Highlands had been the disbandment of all but one of the ten Highland regiments raised during the war. The demobilisation of possibly 10,000 young adult male Highlanders (12) might in itself have amounted to the equivalent of several years' natural increase of the Highland population and must have led within the next few years to a not inconsiderable short-run rise in marriage and fertility rates. Alternatively, many of the emigrants themselves and some other commentators of that period attributed their decision to leave to sharp increases of rents around 1770. (13) These, in their turn, possibly also reflected the increasing pressure of numbers on limited acreages of usable land, though many contemporaries were satisfied to ascribe the rises to nothing more than the cupidity of landlords.

Though this wave of emigration may not be exactly measured statistically, there is no lack of evidence for it. Already in the winter of 1771-2 the *Caledonian Mercury* had recorded the intentions of groups of people in the Highlands to emigrate. (14) There is evidence of 831 people leaving the County of Ross in 1772 and 1773, 288 leaving Bute and Argyll, and 735 from the Countess of Sutherland's estate alone in the same two years. (15) Two different official sources show respectively 2,773 and 3,607 people leaving Scotland in 1774 and 1775, most of them Highlanders. (16) Boswell, fortuitously journeying with Johnson in the north-west in 1773, spoke, on observing two ships taking emigrants from Skye, of 'the present rage for emigration', (17) a phrase that found echoes elsewhere. (18) By 1773 the scale of the outflow began to concern the government in Edinburgh and London. The cause of these fears was not a humanitarian concern for the welfare of people driven by remorseless economic pressures to quit their native land, but the imagined dangers of contamination by American democratic and republican ideologies, and, more urgently, of the drying-up of the flow of recruits to the Highland regiments. (19)

One result of the government's concern was a remarkably detailed set of passenger lists for emigrant ships leaving Scotland in 1774 and 1775. (20) These returns, invaluable as they are for indicating to us the sex- and age-composition and places of origin of the emigrant parties, almost certainly under-state the numbers leaving. But given that they include some Lowlanders as well as parties from other parts of the Highlands and from the northern islands, it hardly seems likely that even in the peak years 1774 and 1775 emigrants from the north-west would have exceeded 2,000 each year. We might estimate the population of the

north-west in 1770 in round figures at 70,000. Emigration on this scale could, however, temporarily have more than absorbed the probable natural increase: clearly, while the 'rage' lasted, it played a part in keeping Malthus at bay.

But the 'rage' was soon over, cut short by the outbreak of the American war. While we do not find again until the second half of the nineteenth century quantitative evidence concerning emigration from Scotland comparable in detail with that available for the 1770s, shreds of evidence (also mainly from shipping lists) indicate that emigration from the north-west continued as fitfully as the intervals of peace permitted between 1783 and 1815. (21) As Walker expressed it in 1808, 'such an overflowing population must induce many of them to leave the country'. (22) In both American and French wars, however, the drain from emigration was replaced by the call to arms. The peculiar power of the Highland landlords to enforce enlistment by threat of eviction led to a quite astonishingly disproportionate share of the Highlands in the supply of war-time military man-power; (23) and, by removing so many young adult males from their homelands for long periods, necessarily reduced marriage and fertility rates. It is not possible to judge the extent to which the alternation between emigration and military service contributed to easing the pressure of continuing population growth, and it is unfortunate that it is on just the point of absolute levels of population that the parochial accounts in the *Old Statistical Account* (1791-9) are at their weakest: it would be unwise to rely on them in any attempt to estimate growth rates in the decade before the 1801 census. (24) For the first decade of the nineteenth century we are more fortunately placed, however, thanks to the censuses and the recent discovery of answers to a parish-by-parish questionnaire conducted in conjunction with the 1811 census. (25) While these answers indicate a wide range of demographic experience in north-west parishes, they show both emigration and population growth continuing. The variations between parochial experiences reflected the extent to which different parishes and their landlords responded to both pressures and opportunities.

New factors, too, were being brought to bear on the situation. The introduction of vaccination in 1803 sharply reduced, within a very few years, the mortality from smallpox, and therefore tended to accelerate the rate of natural increase. (26) Hunter has shown how the 1803 Passenger Act tended to reduce emigration by pushing the cost beyond the reach of many who otherwise felt that the time had come for them to bow before the pressure to leave. (27) On the other hand, the wars greatly increased temporary absences of adult males on service in the army, the navy and the merchant navy. (28) At the same time, harvests were good and, in the outer islands at least, fishing supplemented the diet. Several parish enumerators in 1811 also commented on the tendency to early marriages induced by the desire to evade militia service. Many of these points are summed up in the parish enumerator's reply from Barra: 'The number of persons in 1801 was 1,925, of which about 300 emigrated to America in 1802, leaving about 1,625, which in 9 years has increased 489. This increase is to be attributed to early marriages and at all times to a plentiful supply of food together with a total absence of epidemic or other deadly distempers.' (29) At the same time, however, and more significant, perhaps, having regard to the longer run, some parish commentators referred (approvingly, in most cases) to the retention and accommodation of the natural increase of population by the sub-division of holdings. The entry in the 1811 questionnaire for Coll spoke of how the proprietor, Colonel MacLean, divided land 'into small lots or crofts for the better accommodating his tenants, and many poor families in the island. In one part of the island where formerly two or three families only resided there are at present twenty-two families accommodated with crofts and a number of acres of moss lands for improvement ... A few of these people some years ago intended to emigrate to North America but instead of crossing the Atlantic and improving wild tracts of land in that country, are now usefully employed in improving their native soil.' (30)

While these varied and occasionally conflicting pressures worked themselves out, an ominous threat appeared in 1799 and 1800 in the shape of terribly deficient harvests. Absence of burial registers for the north-west throughout the period covered by this paper prevents us from tracing the effect of these failures on mortality rates, and their timing — just after the completion of the *Old Statistical Account* and just before the first census — deny us access to much contemporary local comment. They were reminders, however, that though the normal or good harvests of the ensuing years seemed to be reassuring, the inevitable poor harvests of the future could evoke the horrible reality of the positive check.

The actual growth of population between the first two censuses is therefore the net outcome of many interacting forces. Greater under-counting in the first than the second census means that the recorded growth of 9.0 per cent in the north-west area (as defined above) was probably a slight overestimate. (31) The war clearly contributed to the reduction of the rate of natural increase, but the disturbance it created to demographic growth in this decade was sufficiently great to make it impossible to detect the underlying 'real' secular trend.

We may perhaps attempt to summarise the ways in which, between 1770 and 1815, the society of the north-west had contrived to prevent the axe of the positive check from falling. Spasmodic emigration after an initial burst in the early 1770s probably eased the pressure no more than temporarily, though enlistment in the Highland regiments replaced emigration in the war years as a means of keeping the young adult males away from matrimony and parenthood. Probably equally important in enabling the region to accommodate its swelling numbers was the access to supplies of imported food made possible by the exploitation of the resources of seaweed and rough grazing. Some improvements in agrarian organisation and steadily increasing resort to the cultivation of the potato helped to allow some of the natural increase to be retained. In these ways, population could continue to grow at a modest rate without any necessary diminution of customary living standards, though there were naturally considerable variations from parish to parish in the ability to absorb the many changing pressures.

The society of the north-west was not, of course, left by the landlords to find its own destiny. The shifting and sometimes contrary pressures of economic and demographic change were further confused by the exercise of landlords' powers. Scottish landlords interfered with the natural playing-out of the Malthusian drama in a variety of ways. At one time they facilitated population growth by encouraging kelping and fisheries. At other times they exacerbated the situation by removal and re-grouping which had the tendency of diminishing the amount of land available for subsistence. The nature of Highland land tenure gave landlords the power, rare in other parts of Britain, to shift population on a massive scale and accelerate or delay, at least in the short run, the consequences of demographic growth. Until tenurial relations became rigid after the Crofters' Holdings Act of 1886 we would expect the demographic pressures to contribute to the shifting of the balance of economic advantage in favour of the landlords. (32) There are some signs of this happening during the late eighteenth and early nineteenth centuries. Gray has illustrated the rise in rents before 1815 and has also shown vividly the extent to which the landlords were able increasingly to capture the increments of wealth created by kelping. (33)

It is after 1815 that the north-west really entered its most severe Malthusian crisis. With the great reduction in the armed forces after 1815 it comes as no surprise to find that the actual growth rate of population – at 16.5 per cent – was appreciably higher in the second decade of the nineteenth century than in the first. Though quantitative confirmation beyond the evidence of the censuses is hard to come by, there is no shortage of literary evidence of mounting population pressure after 1815. (34) The return of men from their war-time absences must have raised marriage and fertility rates, though neither can be measured satisfactorily in this period. Even before the end of the war, the re-opening of international trade had allowed imports of potash and barilla to drive down the price of kelp. Kelping, which had begun to decline when Wellington's Peninsular Campaign gave British importers access to supplies of Spanish barilla, never recovered, and this source of the region's purchasing power for imports fell away very rapidly. The cattle trade, too, though less severely affected than kelping, was hit by the post-war fall in prices. (35) Continued out-migration eased the pressure, but this could produce no more than a mitigation. Cameron has recently demonstrated a marked switch about this time in the attitudes of landowners to emigration. (36) As late as 1802 the Highland Society of Scotland had been invoking the aid of Telford in the belief that his proposals for public works schemes might provide the livelihoods that would discourage emigration, (37) while the 1803 Passenger Act, as Hunter has shown, was a deliberate attempt to arrest the great burst of emigration sparked off by the Peace of Amiens in the previous year. (38) But barely a dozen years later the evidence pointed very clearly to the mistakenness of a policy aimed at retaining population. Whether or not the attitude of landlords was a significant influence on population movements, the relatively low rates of actual growth of the population of the north-west after 1821 – 6.7 per cent between 1821 and 1831, and 2.6 per cent between 1831 and 1841, rates appreciably lower than likely rates of natural increase at this period – indicate that out-migration remained fairly heavy. But even these low rates involved nearly 10,000 additional mouths to be fed in a region already exploiting its exiguous resources to the limits allowed by the agrarian policies of the landlords.

In such a situation the only remaining expedient available to stall off the immediate Malthusian pressure was more intensive resort to the potato. The thirty years between 1815 and 1845 were, for the Scottish north-west as Cullen has argued they were for Ireland, (39) the age of the potato. The process was nicely illustrated by W.F. Skene, who, as secretary of the Central Board that organised Highland relief after 1846, had access to a great deal of local information. In a single Skye parish he noted that in 1801, when its population stood at 2,555, 1,600 bolls of oats and bere and 5,000 barrels of potatoes were produced: by 1841, by which time the population had risen to 3,625, there were produced 1,618 bolls of grain and 32,000 barrels of potatoes. Potatoes, he said, 'consequently furnished the sole additional production to meet the requirements of the additional population'. (40) But, as Alison pointed out in 1847, 'when we find a population... living chiefly on potatoes, and reduced to absolute destitution, unable to purchase other food when the potato crop fails, we have at once disclosed to us the undeniable fact, that that population is redundant'. (41)

In this period of intensification of pressure, landlords made use of their augmented economic power in various ways. Some sought to raise their incomes from rent by the creation of 'farms', often, but not invariably, sheep farms: this involved shifting tenants from their holdings and increasing population and holdings density in other areas. This power to enforce peasant migration was comparable with early medieval powers of preventing migration. In a similar way, also redolent of medieval rather than modern practice, landlords used their enhanced powers of control in attempts in some instances to regulate their tenants' marriages. 'Early marriages', commented one witness before a Select Committee of 1841, 'have been greatly discountenanced [during the last ten years] by the resident factors, by clergymen, and influential gentlemen'. (42) This was associated with a growing movement on the part of the landlords to discourage or prohibit the sub-division and sub-letting of holdings. Having contributed by clearance to the over-crowding of coastal areas, landlords then aimed to use their power to complete the process by creating the conditions in which the surplus of population had no choice but to emigrate.

For a time the potato served the north-west well enough. Its principal disease at this time was the 'curl', which was spread by a variety of greenfly, and it has been shown that this greenfly rarely moves from a host plant when the wind rises above eight miles an hour, while heavy rainfall will wash plants clear of this parasite. (43) Thus the prevailing climate of the north-west provided a natural protection against the 'curl', though in parts of the North of England its ravages were so severe in the late eighteenth century that it was feared that the cultivation of the potato must be abandoned altogether. Curl was said to be general in England by 1820, 'but ... never did much injury to this part [the Scottish Highlands] of the United Kingdom'. (44)

The warning of ultimate catastrophe first appeared in the shape of 'blight' in 1833, and the potato harvest was very seriously damaged in 1836 and 1837. Widespread starvation was prevented, however, on this occasion by the mounting of a vigorous, charitable famine relief operation. But the writing was on the wall. 'Do you consider the great distress of 1836 and 1837 likely to occur again?' the Rev. N. McLeod, secretary of the Glasgow relief committee was asked in 1841. 'It most probably shall', he replied, 'and we feel in awful terror of its recurring, for the slightest failure of the crop in any one season, even falling short of that

which occurred in 1836 and 1837, must occasion it, where there is no employment.' (45)

The disaster occurred nine years later. (46) There was partial failure in 1845,
when the disease was selective of the areas it attacked, but in 1846 failure was
complete almost throughout Scotland. 'The failure may be taken as absolute',
wrote the Lord Advocate to the Home Secretary on 2 September. 'Little or nothing
will be saved; and the suffering from scarcity and disease will be very severe indeed
in the districts where the population depends mainly on that food'. (47) On 7
September, 176 inhabitants of Lochcarron (Ross), petitioning the government for
assistance, stated that 'from time immemorial the inhabitants of the parish of
Lochcarron depended entirely for subsistence on potatoes, and the produce of
herring fishing... That the potato crop is this season completely and utterly destroyed
by disease in Lochcarron, and ... it is obvious that these persons will be immediately
plunged into a gulph of the deepest destitution.' (48) In the presbytery of Mull
(including neighbouring islands) it was anticipated that 17,000 or 18,000 out of
a population of 22,000 would 'in the course of a few weeks' be in a state of
starvation. (49) By early October 400 of Lismore's (Argyll) 1,400 inhabitants were
on the verge of starvation. The worst destitution, because of the highest potato-
dependence, however, was in the islands of Lewis, Harris, Mull, Eigg, Tiree and
Coll.

In Ireland the iron law of Malthus's positive check asserted itself through death
by disease and starvation. In the Scottish north-west, a combination of government,
landlords and charity came to the rescue and prevented the same from happening. (5
In spite of this massive famine relief operation, however, the area planted with seed
potatoes in 1847 was a mere one-sixth of the usual, and severe food shortage continued in the north-west until 1850. During a five-year period, therefore, a substantial proportion of the population, ranging in some areas up to three-quarters,
subsisted entirely on food or income made available by government, landlord or
charity. Perhaps because the scale of the problem was infinitely less than in Ireland,
or because the configuration of the land made it so much easier to supply food by
water, there seems to have been virtually no starvation. There were reports of some
disease, but they were of common illnesses, and it is not possible to assess whether
the incidence was higher than usual. In response to specific enquiries about the
extent of disease, Coffin, the Commissioner appointed by the government to report
on the crisis, found in 1846 that 'the very remarkable answer to my question on
this point has almost invariably been, *so healthy a season has seldom been known,*
and the appearance of the people bore testimony to the truth of the assertion'.
He went so far as to say that in many cases the people were better fed than they
usually were. (51)

The almost complete absence of burial registers for this region in the pre-civil
registration era makes it impossible to check the accuracy of Coffin's assertion or
to discover whether the continuance of famine conditions during the rest of the
decade began to show in heightened mortality. (52) Had this been the case, however, it is likely that it would not have escaped attention, since the area was kept
under fairly close scrutiny by government and charitable agencies.

Preventing death from starvation, however, carried the corollary of not reducing the population. In fact, it made the problem more urgent: it was clear to everyone that the potato, which had bridged the gap for the last generation, was effectively no longer available. There was no *status quo* to return to. In the face of this new reality, nobody, it seems — government or landowners — could propose any solution other than emigration. So landowners set about organising parties from their over-burdened estates, and the Central Board, in charge of charitable relief, contributed towards the cost of several large parties. The official emigration statistics, unfortun-ately, though they show a substantial increase in the outward movement from Scottish ports in the years 1847-9 in comparison with 1844-6, are too imperfect to provide an accurate indication of the numbers leaving in the late 1840s. (53)

In the immediate famine period, however, emigration was accessible only to those able to afford it, or to the few fortunate enough to get assistance from their landlords or the Central Board. The really needy, particularly the numerous cotters, were for the most part prevented by lack of resources from following even though an acceleration of clearances intensified the pressures on them in some areas. It was only later following the influential report by Sir John McNeill to the new poor law Board of Supervision in Edinburgh in 1851, (54) that wider financial assistance was made available by the Emigration Act of that year and by the newly-formed Highland Emigration Society. These developments, moreover, coin-cided with the discovery of gold in Australia. Though the emigration statistics improve in 1853, measurement from 1851 is still difficult; but it is likely that 100,000 Scots emigrated between 1851 and 1855, though the proportion of those from the north-west among them cannot be estimated. Over the whole 20-year period from 1841 to 1861, the total population of the north-west declined by 9.9 per cent. Since the natural increase of the area is likely to have been not less than 10 per cent per decade, we may not be far from the truth if we estimate that almost one-third of the pre-famine population of the north-west left — mostly, we may be sure, between 1846 and 1854. (55)

If the age- and sex-structure of the emigrant parties had been the same as that of the population they left behind, the story might have ended there. But this was far from being the case. Curiously, we know more about these aspects of the eighteenth-century emigrant groups than we do of the post-famine parties. An analysis of the emigrants listed in the shipping muster rolls of 1774-5 shows a high proportion, as might be expected, in the young adult group — 14.6 per cent in the 15-19 age-group compared with 9.2 per cent in Webster's age-structure table for the whole of Scotland in 1755 and 10.4 per cent in the 1821 census; 28.0 per cent in the 20-29 age-group (compared with 17.0 per cent and 16.4 per cent respectively). Though family parties were common among the emigrants, children were nevertheless disproportionately few — 22.9 per cent aged 0-14 in the shipping lists compared with 33.4 per cent in 1755 and 38.0 per cent in 1821. The sex-ratio in the 1774-5 parties was 178 males to every 100 females (compared with 86 in the five Highland counties of Sutherland, Ross, Inverness, Argyll and Bute in 1801). The sex-ratio of Scottish-born settlers in England and Wales in 1861 was 122 males to 100 females, and when in the late 1870s the official emigration statistics distinguish between the sexes of emigrants from Scotland, there were nearly three males to every one female.

E

These figures do not relate, of course, exactly to the sex- and age-composition of the emigrants from the north-west in the 1840s and '50s, but they support the general view that males, and particularly young adult males, tended to be disproportionately represented, sometimes heavily so, in the emigrant groups of this period. What was more important than the demographic structure of the emigrant parties, however, was the age- and sex-structure of the population left behind. For the purposes of the analysis that follows, I am obliged, having regard to the sources of the data, to use figures relating to whole counties. I shall, therefore, refer to a region I will call the Highland Counties, comprising the registration counties of Sutherland, Ross, Inverness, Argyll and Bute. In 1841, the sex-ratio in this region, at 89.7, was very close to that of Scotland as a whole. In 1851 it had fallen to 86.4, recovering somewhat to 88.7 in 1861. In the latter year, however, in the reproductive age-group 15-49, the sex-ratio was 83.7, and in the 'marrying' age-group 25-29, it was 76.2. Thus, even if all males married, one woman in every four or five was not going to be able to find a mate of approximately her own age. The outcome of this situation was inevitably low marriage rates. In 1861, 41.1 per cent of the women in the Highland Counties aged 25-29 were married compared with 54.0 per cent in the whole of Scotland, and 59.1 per cent in the age-group 30-34, compared with a Scottish percentage of 68.9 per cent. The data do not, unfortunately, permit us to calculate average ages at first marriage regionally at this period, but in 1861 the median age at marriage of females (which, of course, includes re-marriages) was 25.3 in the Highland Counties, compared with a Scottish median of 24.0.

Given low illegitimacy rates, (56) fewer and later marriages in the female population amounted to a social control on fertility. In 1861, before the beginning of the general European fertility decline, and when the crude birth rate in Scotland still stood at 34.8, in the Highland Counties it was 27.0. Moreover, against a constant national rate, the Highland Counties rate showed a decline to 25.7 already by 1871. But the crude birth rate is a deceptive measure, influenced as much by age-structure and marriage patterns as by 'real' fertility levels. A somewhat better measure, though one by no means perfect, is the general fertility rate (the number of live births per 1,000 married and unmarried women aged 15-49). In 1861 a Highland Counties rate of 106.7 compared with a national rate of 131.5. One would expect the low marriage rates of the Highland Counties to account for some of this disparity, and so they do. A marital fertility rate (legitimate live births per 1,000 married women aged 15-49) gives 223.3 for the Highland Counties and 247.1 for Scotland. A difference remains, however, and given what we know of marriage ages, the important and interesting question as to whether Highland births were reduced by low marriage rates or by controlled fertility within marriage remains unanswered.

In the first year of civil registration in Scotland, fortunately in the present context located in 1855 when the new, post-famine demographic structure could be said to have become established in the north-west, very comprehensive registration schedules produced such a wealth of demographic data that it has lain unprocessed ever since in the original books in the Edinburgh office of the Registrar-General for Scotland. In 1872, however, the Registrar-General, also interested in

this problem, made some use of these 1855 data. Of the geographical regions he
selected for analytical purposes his 'insular' region — comprising all the Hebrides,
Orkney and Shetland — comes nearest in economic character to the 'north-west'
of this paper. He showed that, whereas in Scotland as a whole 52.5 per cent of
all births in 1855 to mothers stating their ages (only 1.4 per cent failed to do so)
were to mothers under the age of 30, only 39.1 per cent of births in 'insular'
districts were to mothers in this age-range. Conversely, in Scotland as a whole
only 24.4 per cent of births were to mothers of thirty-five and over, while in
'insular' districts 33.4 per cent of births were to mothers of these ages. The
Registrar-General was of the opinion that 'the difficulty of procuring a livelihood
in the 'insular' districts is so great that marriages are delayed beyond that of the
inhabitants of the other parts of Scotland.' (57)

The 1855 data, however, also permit the calculation on a regional basis of
age-specific fertility. Taking, to minimise the labour, the single county of Ross-
shire as a proxy for the north-west, Table 2 compares the resultant age-specific
rates with those for the whole of Scotland in that year. Apart from the comparatively low rates in the two youngest age-groups which certainly produced a
very small proportion of the total number of births, it seems that, once married,
the women of Ross were no less fertile than the women of other parts of Scotland.
We should not be far wrong in concluding that the low crude birth rates in the
Highland Counties after 1855 were the result mainly of low marriage rates and
late marriages. These, in their turn, were consequences of imbalances in the sex-
and age-structure in the population left behind after the emigration.

Table 2   *Age-specific legitimate fertility rates, Ross-shire and Scotland, 1855*
(legitimate births per 1,000 married women in each age-group)

Age-group	Ross-shire	Scotland
15-19	300.0	511.2
20-24	373.6	427.0
25-29	386.5	366.0
30-34	324.5	302.4
35-39	255.0	242.0
40-44	138.4	113.3
45-49	15.1	18.1

Sources: For Ross-shire: General Register Office, Edinburgh, 1855 Registration
books; Censuses 1851 and 1861. (The populations in each age-group
have been estimated for mid-1855 by calculating the change between
31 March 1851 and 30 June 1855 as 42.4% of the total intercensal
change, 1851-61.) For Scotland: C.J. Lewis and J.N. Lewis, *Natality
and Fecundity* (Edinburgh, 1906.)

The rate of natural increase of population is determined, of course, by the
actual difference between crude birth and death rates, and in the decade 1861-71
the natural increase in the Highland Counties amounted to 8.9 per cent, compared
with an overall Scottish figure of 13.6 per cent. In successive decades the Highland
Counties rate fell as follows (Scottish rates in brackets): 7.8 per cent (14.0 per cent);
8.4 per cent (13.6 per cent); 5.7 per cent (12.4 per cent); 4.4 per cent (12.1 per

cent); 1.2 per cent (9.1 per cent); 1.0 per cent (7.2 per cent); and (for 1931-39)
-0.6 per cent (4.4 per cent). Though declining fertility accounted for much of this
drastic fall of the rate of natural increase, the failure of the crude death rate to
fall more than marginally over the whole period from 1861-1939, in sharp contrast
to the rate for Scotland which fell by nearly 38 per cent over the same period,
must also have played a part. Partly this was due to its low starting level, partly
to the ageing of the population, but partly also to the importation into the Highland
Counties during the 1860s of tuberculosis as a major killing disease. Of course,
emigration from the Highland Counties continued after 1861, and the comparatively
low rates of natural increase were converted in every decade into negative rates of
actual growth.

In these ways emigration and out-migration to other parts of the United Kingdom led — though the outcome was no part of the intentions of the inhabitants —
to the creation of conditions in which the preventive check operated naturally, and
enabled the region to bring under control, in a way that Malthus would have
approved, its own population growth. The nearest approach to the positive check
was the sharp rise in mortality from tuberculosis during the 1860s. This can most
probably be explained in terms of infection caught by the greatly increased numbers
of out-migrants from the north-west in the 1850s who brought infection back with
them when they returned home to die. (58)

In these various ways, in the century following the emergence of Malthusian
pressure, the north-west contrived for the most part to evade the ultimate penalty
of the positive check. At first, war, lack of opportunity and, probably, shortage of
funds, restrained the initial attempt to allow emigration to ease the pressure; but,
so long as the external market permitted it, the area's feeble natural resources of roug
grazing and seaweed were, for a period, developed and the products exchanged for
imports of foodstuffs. For much of the first half-century too, recruitment to the
Highland regiments drew a significant proportion of the young adult males away
from their families with inevitable temporary repercussions on marriage and fertility
rates. Then, when the ending of war brought the men back and caused kelp and
cattle prices to fall, the potato came increasingly to be relied on to accommodate
the increments of population growth. Finally, when the time bought by the potato
ran out, the people turned once again to emigration as the only escape from the
Malthusian pincers. This time the emigration was on a scale not only to relieve the
immediate pressures on food supplies, but also to lead, albeit without conscious
forethought, to the secular — and, in the event, final — solution of the preventive
check. Though under the threat of the positive check for almost a century, the
north-west contrived by one means or other to avoid paying the penalty.

To demonstrate that the north-west escaped, against all the odds, the horror
of Malthus's positive check is not, of course, to suggest that its history in this
period was free from suffering. The responses to Malthusian pressures enumerated
in this paper formed but one of several groups of forces battering Highland society
at this climacteric of its history. Some of the other influences, too, may themselves
have stemmed indirectly from demographic sources. Highland history of the eighteen
and nineteenth centuries has most commonly been written in terms of tenurial relationships and cultural clashes, but to leave the demographic developments out of
the picture is like presenting *Hamlet* without the Prince of Denmark.

NOTES

1. This paper owes much to discussions with Professor T.C. Smout and Mrs Rosalind Mitchison in the course of joint research over several years into Scottish demographic history. Mrs Mitchison has also given me valuable help with the calculations involved in Table 1. I would further like to thank Mrs Ailsa Maxwell, Mrs Judith Gillespie, and Mrs Nancy Hill for much laborious spade-work in the abstraction and presentation of data from the censuses and civil registration returns on which parts of this paper are based. A Malthusian approach to the problems of west Highland history was implicit in Malcolm Gray's *The Highland Economy* of 1957, and much more explicit in A.J. Youngson's *After the Forty-five* of 1973: this attempt to interpret the history of the Scottish north-west even more explicitly in Malthusian terms is offered in the hopes of emphasizing what I believe to be the principal forces underlying the social and economic development of the area.

2. J.G. Kyd, *Scottish Population Statistics,* Scottish History Society, 3rd ser. XLIV (1952).

3. At 44.4 per cent between 1755 and 1801, and taking no account of inaccuracies in both the counts, the growth was appreciably faster than that of Scotland as a whole (28.5 per cent). Tiree and Coll, however, increased over the same period, according to the same sources, by 91.1 per cent, Kilfinichen on Mull by 88.4 per cent, and South Uist by 103.5 per cent.

4. T. Pennant, *A Tour in Scotland and Voyage to the Hebrides,* 3rd edition (Warrington & Chester, 1774), II, 271-2, 305-6, 278.

5. J. Hector St. John Crevecoeur, *Letters from An American Farmer* (London, 1782). See also *Calendar of Home Office Papers, 1773-1775,* nos. 324, 331, 345, 609, 610 and 1091.

6. See M. Gray, *The Highland Economy, 1750-1850* (Edinburgh, 1957), pp.36-7. On occasions, as Telford commented in 1802, the high price of cattle 'furnished the old farmers with a portion of capital which enables them to transport their families beyond the Atlantic'. (*Survey and Report of the Coasts and Central Highlands of Scotland by Thomas Telford, Parliamentary Papers,* 1802-3, IV, p.15.)

7. M. Gray, 'The kelp industry in the Highlands and Islands', *Economic History Review,* 2nd ser. IV (1951), 197-209.

8. We are fairly well informed about the progress of potato cultivation in this area, thanks to the surveys of agriculture and diet in the *Old Statistical Account,* and the relevant volumes of the two series of *General Views of Agriculture.* For a survey of the spread of potato cultivation in Scotland and its place in the diet of people, see Part 5, section 7 of M.W. Flinn (ed.), *Scottish Population History from the Seventeenth Century to the 1930s* (Cambridge, forthcoming).

9. Gray, *Highland Economy,* pp.43-4; and M. Gray, 'Economic welfare and money income in the Highlands, 1750-1850', *Scottish Journal of Political Economy,* II (1955), 49-53. In many instances the kelping population was deliberately concentrated by landlords into subdivided holdings too small for subsistence, so that the earnings from kelping must have been employed to some extent on the purchase of food grown elsewhere. Nonetheless, it is clear that the lion's share of the proceeds of the sale of kelp went, not to the kelpers, but to their landlords, who almost certainly did not employ it to bring food into the area except possibly in rare years of acute harvest failure. (See James R. Hunter, *The Making of the Crofting Community* (Edinburgh, 1976))

10. See Margaret I. Adam, 'The Highland emigration of 1770', *Scottish Historical Review,* XVI (1919). Miss Adam's conclusion that the emigrants of this period were comparatively wealthy is not wholly supported by the evidence of the shipping lists, where comments under the heading 'Reasons for leaving', as well as the correspondence of officials suggest considerable poverty and economic pressure. The title of Miss Adam's article, and, indeed, its content, suggest a somewhat different short-run chronology from that revealed by more recent study.

11. *Caledonian Mercury,* 2 December 1771; 23 March, 3 April and 10 April 1772; R.C. McLeod, ed. *3rd Spalding Club* (Aberdeen, 1939), pp.2, 10; T. Pennant, *A Tour of Scotland and Voyage to the Hebrides* (London, 1790), I, 263, 313; R.J. Adam, *Survey of Assynt,* p.xxix.

12. John Prebble, *Mutiny, Highland Regiments in Revolt, 1743-1804* (London, 1975), pp.93, 97.

13. P.R.O. T.47/12, fos. 117-8; T.1/500, Customs Officer, Inverness to Treasury, 3 January 1774; and see John Walker, *An Economical History of the Hebrides and Highlands of Scotland* (Edinburgh, 1808), II, 406.

14. *Caledonian Mercury,* 26 January 1771; 5 and 12 September 1772.

15. *Calendar of Home Office Papers, 1773-1775,* No.585.

16. *Ibid.,* No. 1091; P.R.O. T.47/12.

17. James Boswell, *Journal of a Tour of the Hebrides* (Everyman edition), pp.129, 141, 192.

18. See, for example, a report by the Wigtown Customs Officer in 1774 in P.R.O. T.1/500; and the minister for Lismore and Appin in the *Old Statistical Account.*

19. *Calendar of Home Office Papers, 1773-1775,* No.1091, 14 August 1775.

20. The extant returns are preserved in P.R.O. T.47/12. Some of them — particularly those from Greenock — are in weekly form as ordered, but others are random, usually relating to the departure of individual emigrant ships.

21. See, for example, the *Old Statistical Account* entries for Ardnamurchan (Argyll) and Bracadale (Skye); P.R.O. H.O.102/13, and C.O.226/23; *Survey and Report ... by Thomas Telford, Parliamentary Papers,* 1802-3, IV, 16. And see also Margaret I. Adam, 'The causes of the Highland emigration of 1783-1803', *Scottish Historical Review,* XVII (1920). Replies to the 1811 census questionnaire indicate that there was a considerable outflow after the Peace of Amiens in 1802: parties of 300 from Barra and 300 from Glenelg are specifically mentioned for that year, while similar parties left Morvern and South Uist at unspecified dates between 1801 and 1811. (B.M. Add. MS. 6897).

22. John Walker, *An Economical History of the Hebrides and Highlands of Scotland* (Edinburgh, 1808), II, 403.

23. John Prebble, *Mutiny,* p.271.

24. Rosalind Mitchison, however , in Part 4, section 4 of Flinn, ed. *Scottish Population History* (forthcoming), using the Princeton model population tables, has estimated rates of natural increase of various regional populations in Scotland from *Old Statistical Account* data.

25. B.M. Add. MS 6897. This document contains returns from about two-thirds of all the parishes in Scotland. Unfortunately there are no returns for the counties of Ross and Sutherland.

26. For the introduction of vaccination into Scotland and an assessment of its demographic impact, see Part 5, section 6 of Flinn, ed. *Scottish Population History* (forthcoming). Vaccination was specifically mentioned in 1811 as a principal explanation of the recent increase of population in Harris, and Sleat (Skye) (B.M. Add. MS 6897).

27. James R. Hunter, *The Making of the Crofting Community* (Edinburgh, 1976), p.25.

28. See, for example, the *Old Statistical Account* entries for South Uist, Sleat (Skye) and Tiree; and 1811 questionnaire entries for Bracadale (Skye) and Glenelg (B.M. Add. MS 6897).

29. B.M. Add. MS 6897.

30. *Ibid.*

31. For a variety of reasons it might not be unreasonable to suppose that under-counting in 1801 was 2-3 per cent greater than in 1811. If this were so, then the actual growth of the north-west between 1801 and 1811 would have been as little as 6-7 per cent.

32. There is a useful discussion of the role of tenurial institutions in the analysis of Malthusian situations in R. Brenner, 'Agrarian class structure and economic development in pre-industrial Europe', *Past and Present,* no.70 (1976).

33. Gray, *Highland Economy,* pp.145-7; and *Economic History Review,* 2nd ser. IV (1951), 200-3.

34. See, for example, *Report of the Select Committee on Emigration from the United Kingdom, Parliamentary Papers,* 1826, IV, q.628; A. Fullarton & C.R. Baird, *Remarks on the Evils at Present affecting the Highlands and Islands of Scotland* (Glasgow, 1838), pp.50-1; *Report on the Applicability of Emigration to Relieve Distress in the Highlands, dated 29 July 1837, Parliamentary Papers,* 1841, XXVII, p.1; and Gray, *Highland Economy,* chap. 4 *passim.*

35. Gray, *Highland Economy,* pp.182, 186; and *Economic History Review,* 2nd ser. IV (1951), 205-9.

36. J. Cameron, 'The changing role of the Highland landlords relative to Scottish emigration during the first half of the 19th century', *Scottish Colloquium Proceedings,* IV-V (1972), 77-87.

37. *Survey and Report ... by Thomas Telford, Parliamentary Papers,* 1802-3, IV; and see *Prize Essays and Transactions of the Highland Society of Scotland,* II (1803), p.vii.

38. James R. Hunter, *The Making of the Crofting Community,* p.25.

39. L.M. Cullen, 'Irish history without the potato', *Past and Present,* no.40 (1968).

40. W.F. Skene, *Celtic Scotland: a History of Ancient Alban* (Edinburgh, 1890), III, 374-5. The parish may be identified as Kilmuir.

41. W.P. Alison, *Observations on the Famine of 1846-7* (Edinburgh, 1847), p.18. See also *Second Report of Select Committee on Emigration, Scotland, Parliamentary Papers,* 1841, VI, qs. 195-6, 848; and Robert Graham's 'Report on distress in the Highlands, 6 May 1837', App. I to *First Report of Select Committee on Emigration, Scotland.*

42. *Second Report of Select Committee on Emigration, Scotland, Parliamentary Papers,* 1841, VI, q. 848. On the Macdonald estate in Skye from 1831 any tenant's son marrying before inheriting land directly from the landlord would be evicted (Hunter, *The Making of the Crofting Community,* p.42).

43. R.N. Salaman, *The History and Social Influence of the Potato* (Cambridge, 1949), pp.179-84.

44. William Aitken, *The Potato rescued from Disease and restored to Pristine Vigour* (Edinburgh & London, 1837), p.17.

45. *First Report of Select Committee on Emigration, Scotland, Parliamentary Papers,* 1841, VI, qs. 805-6.

46. There is no comprehensive modern study in print of the potato famine in Scotland. In spite of its title, M. Gray's article, 'The Highland potato famine of the 1840s', *Economic History Review,* 2nd ser. VII (1955), is almost exclusively concerned with the tenurial, social and agricultural background to the events of the 1840s. The best available accounts are by R.N. Salaman, *History and Social Influence of the Potato,* pp.375-90; and by J.P. Day, *Public Administration in the Highlands and Islands of Scotland* (London, 1918), pp.95-106. R.N. McMichael's unpublished dissertation, 'The Potato Famine of the 1840s in the Western Highlands and Islands of Scotland' (Edinburgh University Department of Economic History M.A. dissertation, 1973), provides an original and valuable account of the famine and its relief. And see James R. Hunter, *The Making of the Crofting Community,* ch. 4.

47. *Correspondence from July 1846 to February 1847 relating to the Measures adopted for the Relief of Distress in Scotland, Parliamentary Papers,* 1847, LIII, p.8.

48. *Ibid.,* p.15.

49. *Ibid.,* p.10.

50. For an account of the relief operation, see T.C. Smout's contribution to this volume.

51. Highland Destitution Papers (temporary reference), Scottish Record Office, fo. 275. Coffin's italics.

52. There is actually a single burial register for the island of Gigha (outwith the north-west as defined in this paper), where the very small annual number of burials makes it unwise to draw conclusions. Here, however, the burials averaged 8.2 per year during the four years 1842-5, and rose in 1847, 1848 and 1850 to 13, 14 and 16 respectively.

53. Official emigration statistics are conveniently brought together in N.M. Carrier and J.R. Jeffrey, *External Migrations* (HMSO, London, 1953).

54. *Report to the Board of Supervision by Sir John McNeill, G.C.B., on the Western Highlands and Islands, Parliamentary Papers,* 1851, XXVI.

55. There was a sharp fall in the numbers of Scots emigrating between 1854 and 1855, and the numbers remained relatively low or fell further up to 1861. If this estimate is even approximately correct, Hunter's estimate of 16,000 leaving the north-west between 1847 and 1856 is almost certainly quite a severe underestimate. (James R. Hunter, *The Making of the Crofting Community*, ch.5, n.38. Hunter's 'north-west' is very closely identical with the north-west of this paper.)

56. For a discussion of regional variations in illegitimacy, see A. Leffingwell, *Illegitimacy and the Influence of the Seasons upon Conduct* (London, 1892). Part 5, section 4 (by T.C. Smout), in Flinn, ed, *Scottish Population History* (forthcoming); and T.C. Smout, 'Aspects of sexual behaviour in nineteenth-century Scotland', in A. Allan MacLaren, ed, *Social Class in Scotland Past and Present* (Edinburgh, 1976).

57. *Report on the Returns of Births, Marriages and Deaths for the Decade 1861-1870* (Registrar-General for Scotland, Edinburgh, 1872).

58. The evidence for this trend is to be found in the *Detailed Annual Reports* of the Registrar-General for Scotland. As late as 1855, the Registrar-General had specifically commented on 'the small comparative mortality from phthisis in the western islands and Argyll' (*Detailed Annual Report,* 1855, p.iii). And see D. Macdonald, 'The cause and prevention of pulmonary consumption in the West Highlands and rural districts of Scotland', *Caledonian Medical Journal,* n.s. VI (1904-6), 247-66, 302-13; and R. McNeill, *On the Public Health of the Insular and Inland Rural Districts of Scotland* (Edinburgh, 1890), pp.5-6.

5. Some Aspects of Nineteenth-century Irish Emigration

Cormac Ó Gráda

'For to live poor I could not endure
like others of my station:
So to Americay I sailed away
And left this Irish nation.'

AS the standard works by O'Brien, Redford, and Forbes Adams have shown, large-scale emigration from Ireland began not with the Great Famine, but several decades earlier. (1) However, many central aspects of the pre-Famine outflow require further examination. Not only do we know too little of the socio-economic and regional backgrounds of pre-Famine emigrants: there are no reliable estimates of even total emigration during the years between Waterloo and the Famine. This earlier emigration is significant in its own right: indeed, Cornewall Lewis felt entitled to argue that it was 'perhaps nearly unparalleled in the history of the world.' (2) But further research would also tell us more about the nature of the pre-Famine economy at large. For instance, did pre-Famine emigration tend to diminish or increase inter-regional income differences within Ireland? Elementary textbook economic theory would suggest the former, but the recent developmental experience of many countries implies the latter for early stages of development. More concrete information on the social class background of emigrants would thus determine whether the pre-Famine economy was 'modern' or 'backward' when compared with less developed countries today. (3)

Then there are external effects. However, not until more is known about the nature of the demand for labour in Britain before 1840, and the spread and volume of Irish emigration there, can one assess the effect on British living standards. Certainly there were fears that continued emigration would reduce the population of the three kingdoms to a common 'potato standard'. 'Is anyone sanguine enough', cried Henry Booth, the Liverpool railway entrepreneur, 'to imagine that the independent character of the British labourer .. can be sustained amidst the debasing competition, resulting from the eternal influx of poverty and degradation of Irish peasantry.' (4) Such forebodings implied that Irish labour supply at the time was infinitely elastic in the long run at the going wage: on more realistic assumptions about supply, though, such fears were exaggerated. (5) Still, the importance of Irish immigration as an ingredient in the famous 'standard-of-living debate' has never been properly considered. Besides, what should one make of Dr. E.H. Hunt's recent claim that pre-Famine immigration tended to increase inter-regional wage

*An earlier version of this paper was given, in Irish, at University College, Galway in May 1976. I am grateful to Gearoid Ó Tuathaigh and Louis M. Cullen for their comments and suggestions.

differentials within Great Britain itself — an interesting idea, but one which is not easy to interpret in terms of economic theory? (6)

Part I of the present chapter draws attention to one previously neglected source on pre-Famine emigration, and assesses its bearing on just a few of the issues raised above. The exodus during and after the Famine is better chronicled and better understood, and its tragic elements are — not surprisingly — still part of oral tradition. But it has been subjected to less theoretical analysis than many other quantitatively less important emigrations. Part II is concerned with an aspect of post-Famine emigration: we discuss there the regional variation in the outflow during the 1850s and 1860s, and question the findings of some recent work on the topic.

I

In Ireland, unlike Great Britain, none of the census enumerators' manuscripts for the 1861-1891 period survives. Only snippets remain for 1821-1851. All that is left, in usable form, for 1841 is the evidence for some townlands in the neighbourhood of Killeshandra in County Cavan, and for a few pockets elsewhere. The Killeshandra sample is small to begin with — 2274 families, a population of 12313 — and hardly representative of the population of the country as a whole. Nevertheless, the data do contain a number of implications regarding pre-Famine emigration. (7)

The relevant information occurs in Table 2 of the enumerators' Form A. It is there almost by accident and, indeed, was not used by the census commissioners in collated form in their published report. The table contained the following heading: 'Return to Members of this Family now alive, and whose home is in this house, but who are absent on this night of Sunday, the 6th June, 1841.' The Killeshandra manuscript reports record over 320 emigrants to America under this heading, and a substantially lower number to Britain and elsewhere. Though the instruction on the form is clearly stated, it is safe to assume that the vast majority of those listed never returned.

It is possible — if only in a rough-and-ready way — to gauge the social backgrounds of these emigrants by examining the occupation of the head of the household, given elsewhere on the same form. We have divided the emigrants into two categories, 'rich' and 'poor' — relative and arbitrary ones, it is readily admitted. In thus dividing the observations, it was assumed that the emigrating relatives of farmers, teachers, coopers, publicans, shopkeepers, and the like were 'rich', while the relatives of labourers, weavers, spinners, and so on, were designated 'poor'. In some ambiguous instances, incidental information on the enumerators' form is sometimes helpful: thus if the family is recorded as having a servant living in, or as employing labour on an occasional basis, it was consigned to the 'rich' category.

Calculations by this crude schema suggest that 183, or 56 per cent of the recorded emigrants, were from a 'rich' background, while this category accounted for only 43 per cent of the entire population of Killeshandra. The difference is highly significant in the statistical sense. (8) The implication is straightforward: in the Killeshandra area at least, the 'rich' were substantially more mobile outward than the 'poor'. This is to be expected for two reasons. First, the cost of getting to America presumably prevented many of the 'poor' from leaving. Secondly, insofar as social status was a relevant consideration for prospective emigrants, the 'rich' man's sons and daughters were more likely to resist a labourer's job at home than a farm labourer's family: 'when they went to America and perhaps did much the same work they felt and also their people at home that they had not lowered their social standing.' (9)

Indeed, what is surprising, in view of the wealth of impressionistic comment in the *Poor Inquiry* evidence and elsewhere, is the number of 'poor' recorded as emigrants. However, too much should not be made of this. The area around Killeshandra, while already in decline by 1841, was relatively prosperous when compared with most of Ireland. Thus according to the entry in Lewis' *Topographical Dictionary*, published only a few years prior to the census, '(the) town .. has a cheerful and thriving appearance. The linen manufacture, which is carried on extensively in the neighbourhood, has contributed greatly to its prosperity, and, upon an average, coarse linens are sold in its market to the amount of £1,500 weekly. The market is on Wednesday and is abundantly supplied with provisions ..' (10) Besides, the *Poor Inquiry* assistant commissioners, though they did not conduct an inquiry in Killeshandra itself, report 'emigration to a considerable extent .. among all classes, but especially servant boys, farmers and weavers,' from the adjoining, and similarly circumstanced, baronies of Upper and Lower Loughtee. Few reports from other areas examined by the commissioners make such claims. It seems safe to assume that had the enumerators' returns for any part of, say, Mayo or Clare survived, they would imply a greater contrast in the proportions of the 'rich' and 'poor', as far as emigration was concerned. (11) The returns thus do not necessarily contradict the earlier and contemporary qualitative accounts.

The Killeshandra emigration data also provide some slight insight into a further problem, that of family succession practices. In this instance the information is even skimpier, but one must be grateful for even small mercies. The existing literature on Irish succession practices, it must be said, is rather thin. However, it is sometimes suggested, by way of generalisation, that the Great Famine destroyed the tradition of partible inheritance and subdivision, while the post-Famine decades saw the evolution of a system of impartible inheritance, associated with late marriage and the 'match'. (12) This seems to us an over-simplified scenario: we believe that impartible inheritance was common, if not the norm, in the farming community before the Famine. We have thus sought some preliminary guidance on the following problem from our data: *which* son succeeded his father on the land? With primogeniture, one might expect the younger sons of a man of some property, faced with the prospect of labouring work at home, to be helped emigrate. Neither of the acknowledged experts on past Irish marriage and family patterns, Conrad Arensberg and Kenneth Connell, discusses the issue in detail. Arensberg is content with stating, of a later period, that 'the farmer has full power over his sons,' a point echoed by Connell. Thus, at least by implication, they seem to be arguing for a random inheritance pattern. (13)

The scant Killeshandra data do not support such a picture, for in 35 of the 45 unambiguous cases, the emigrant is the eldest recorded farmer's son, who left one or more younger brothers behind on the farm. This prompts a hypothesis worth further research elsewhere: male emigration from Irish households was supportive of a system of ultimogeniture. The hypothesis is sociologically appealing. The eldest son may not have relished staying around in a subordinate role, with potential in-law tensions in the event of his being married, so the farm fell by default to others. In America, too, it has been suggested by Easterlin that 'the question of who moved [who left the farm] depended primarily on birth order.' (14) The possibility has been stated recently by Robert Kennedy for Ireland, though without any supporting evidence. (15) But note the following from William Carleton: (16)

Shortly after his marriage his father died and Dennis succeeded him on the farm; for you know that among the peasantry the youngest usually gets the landed property – the elder children being obliged to provide for themselves according to their ability, or otherwise a population would multiply upon a portion of land inadequate to their support.

Carleton was writing of an area within thirty or forty miles of Killeshandra, and in the same decade as the census. Further research should establish how widely the family status hypothesis holds in space and in time.

In passing, we note that the surviving records from Killeshandra also imply that emigration had a levelling effect on the emigrants themselves. Judging from the entries in Form A, the great majority of them, whether 'rich' or 'poor' to begin with, became labourers and house servants in the New World. Male emigrants exceeded females by a ratio of eleven-to-nine in the area, but by definition the data can shed no light on family emigration.

II

I have suggested elsewhere that Irish emigration statistics for the nineteenth century contain some serious inconsistencies and fail to show the true extent of the post-Famine outflow. In particular, it would seem that emigration to Great Britain was far greater than the figures imply. (17) But where did these 'hidden emigrants' come from? Age-cohort analysis of censal data can shed some light on this question. By definition, a particular base-year age-cohort in county or province j can be accounted for in a succeeding period in terms of survivors in j, emigrants, migrants in other counties or provinces, and deaths. Given appropriate assumptions, one could in principle calculate emigration estimates $\hat{E}$ for all Irish counties and all pre-First World War intercensal periods. (18) In this preliminary exercise, however, we focus attention on the periods 1861-71 and 1901-11 only, and derive estimates for the four provinces. Our approach is based on comparing the survivors in 1871 with the original returns of 1861, and the same again for 1901 and 1911, respectively. The reasons for this choice of period will be seen below. All calculations refer to the 5-30 years base-year age-cohort.

We assume zero net internal migration, zero immigration, and a death rate consistent with the 'disappearance' of five per cent of the base-year age-cohort. These assumptions mean substantial computational economies, for they give us

$$\hat{E} = 0.95 \, AC_t^J - AC_{t+1}^J$$

where AC = age-cohort, $\hat{E}$ = estimated emigration, and t = time period. Thus for instance there were 723,662 people in the 5-30 years age-cohort in the province of Leinster in 1861, and 524,123 in the 15-40 years cohort in 1871. It follows that calculated emigration from Leinster in this age-cohort during 1861-71 equalled [.95(723,662) - 524,123], or 163,356.

Besides, in our opinion the assumptions are broadly justifiable for the areas and time periods chosen. Immigration was small in proportion to emigration, perhaps three to five per cent, and can be safely ignored in the present context. While there are no age-specific mortality statistics for the 1860s, the earliest available figures imply a death-rate only slightly higher than that assumed above for the 5-30 years age-cohort:

Deaths per 1,000 per annum in different age-groups: Ireland, 1870-2

Age	Males	Females
5-9	5.4	5.4
10-14	8.2	3.7
15-19	5.4	5.5
20-24	8.1	6.4
25-34	9.0	8.1

Source: B.R. Mitchell and P. Deane, *Abstract of British Historical Statistics* (Cambridge, 1962), p.44.

Coale and Demeny's tables for a 'western population' like nineteenth-century Ireland's, also seem to imply a somewhat higher age-specific death rate than five per cent, but it should be noted that our assumed figure excludes members of the base-year cohort who died outside the country. (19)

Table I   Estimated emigration (5-30 years age-cohort), recorded emigration: the four provinces, 1861-1871 and 1901-11.

Province	1861-71			1901-11		
	$\hat{E}$	E	$E/\hat{E}$	$\hat{E}$	E	$E/\hat{E}$
Leinster	163,356	149,802	0.92	45,060	42,490	0.94
Munster	233,428	307,098	1.32	104,318	112,340	1.08
Connacht	158,520	114,493	0.72	91,017	85,133	0.94
Ulster	242,048	199,718	0.83	110,822	105,982	0.96

Source: For $\hat{E}$, see text. For E, emigration for 1861-70 and 1901-10 calculated from *Census of Ireland for the Year 1871* (Dublin, 1875), pp.434-5, and *Census of Ireland for the Year 1911* (Dublin, 1913), pp.292-3.

In the first place, the results reassuringly confirm our earlier argument about under-recording for Ireland as a whole. This is seen when $\hat{E}$ is adjusted to account for emigration outside the age-cohort. Assuming that four-fifths of all emigration in 1861-71 and ninety per cent of the total in 1901-11 was in the 5-30 years age-cohort, the data imply under-recording of between ten and fifteen per cent at least in the 1860s, though not in the 1900s. (20)

More interestingly, though, the $\hat{E}$'s in Table I also suggest that under-recording was most serious in Connacht in the 1860s: by the 1900s $E/\hat{E}$ varied far less between provinces. We are thus led, in roundabout fashion, to the conclusion that the 'hidden emigrants' of the early post-Famine period came mainly from the west and north-west of the country. Contrary to what the recorded statistics imply, it is possible that the true emigration rate from those areas exceeded the national average. (21) This finding rather conflicts with the dominant interpretation of post-Famine economic change in the west.

In a series of influential papers published in the early 1960s, Dr. S.H. Cousens, in attempting to explain regional variations in the emigration statistics, argued that the west was too poor and backward to adjust in the expected, orthodox manner. (22) Thus the apparent paradox of low recorded emigration is resolved, at least in part, by appeal to a Myrdal-style argument: 'Lack of movement from the west was a result of a reluctance to leave as well as inability to pay the passage to America .. The poverty of western Ireland still restricted emigration between 1861 and 1881, despite population pressure and therefore the need to reduce it. The result was a lack of regional variation in emigration from Ireland at that time.' (23) Cousens' interpretation has been widely endorsed. (24) It is certainly ingenious and persuasive, but leaves a few basic points unresolved. For instance, if inability to pay prevented emigration even in normal times in the west, then why should the outflow — by Cousens' admission, largely unaided — have tended to peak at times of harvest failure, or more general economic depression? And why, if emigration from the west was lightest and most sporadic, did incomes there rise more than in any other province, not simply in the wake of the Famine, but also in the decades preceding the Land War? Cousens has drawn attention to the peaking of emigration at times of crisis. There is evidence that some landlords did in fact aid destitute tenants to leave in bad years, as part of a land clearance policy. But Cousens does not rely on this debating gambit, and such action can hardly explain more than a small part of the peaking. (25) Thirdly, Cousens' interpretation does not explain why emigration from the west should have 'taken-off', as it were, in the 1870s. Surely, if the west was too backward to begin with, increasing population pressure there — in the absence of sharp domestic demographic adjustment (for which no evidence is adduced) — must have made large-scale emigration a more difficult proposition as the years passed. (26)

It is doubtful whether the factors mentioned can be comfortably accounted for within Cousens' framework. But Table I shows, I believe, that the dichotomy between east and west has been exaggerated in the literature. To be sure, it is possible that emigration overseas from the poorer areas was restricted by the lack of funds or credit; however, to the extent that emigration to Britain was important, the problem posed by the data is a *faux problème*. Evidence on the county origins of emigrants to Britain is thus far lacking. Still, given the prevalence of seasonal migration and the resultant emigration flows, it seems not far-fetched to argue that substantial numbers of westerners settled permanently in Great Britain, though unrecorded. That the west remained (and remains) poor in comparison with the rest of the country is self-evident: more interestingly, however, it seems that emigration alleviated, rather than exacerbated, this regional inequality from the Famine period on.

NOTES

1. G. O'Brien, *An Economic History of Ireland from the Union to the Famine* (Dublin, 1921), pp.207-21; A. Redford, *Labour Migration in England 1800-50* (Manchester, 1964), pp.132-70; W.F. Adams, *Ireland and Irish migration to the New World from 1815 to the Famine* (New Haven, 1932).

2. G.C. Lewis, *Report on the State of the Irish Poor in Great Britain*, H.C. 1836 (XXXIV), 429.

3. For elaboration see J.G. Williamson, 'Regional Inequality and the Process of National Development: A Description of the Patterns', *Economic Development and Cultural Change* XIII (1965), pp.3-45.

4. Cited in R.D.C. Black, *Economic Thought and the Irish Question 1817-1870* (Cambridge, 1960), pp.208-9.

5. The actual movement implies a rather low elasticity, given the huge wage differential.

6. E.H. Hunt, *Regional Wage Variations in Great Britain 1850-1914* (Oxford, 1973), pp.286-305. Since the Irish headed for the high wage areas in Great Britain, how, other things being equal, could they have increased the differential within Britain?

7. Public Record Office, Dublin, I A, 45. 27, I A, 45.28. I am grateful to the Deputy Keeper for permission to use this material.

8. $X^2 = 6.89$. However, $X^2_{.99}$ for one degree of freedom = 6.63.

9. Coimisiún Béaloideasa Éireann (Irish Folklore Commission), Ms. 1403, p.100.

10. S. Lewis, *A Topographical Dictionary of Ireland* (London, 1837), II, 142.

11. *Poor Inquiry (Ireland)*: Appendix F, H.C. 1836 (XXXIII), 139.

12. For example. K.H. Connell, 'Peasant Marriage in Ireland before the Great Famine', *Past and Present*, no.12 (1957), 76-91; 'Peasant Marriage in Ireland: its Structure and Development since the Famine,' *Economic History Review*, 2nd ser. XIV (1962), 502-23; 'Marriage in Ireland after the Famine: the Diffusion of the Match,' *Journal of the Statistical and Social Inquiry Society of Ireland* XIX (1956), 82-102.

13. C. Arensberg, *The Irish Countryman* (Gloucester, Mass., 1959); K.H. Connell, 'Catholicism and Marriage in the Century after the Famine,' in *Irish Peasant Society* (Oxford, 1968), p.117. Connell is somewhat equivocal — see *op. cit.*, pp.116, 118 — but his main emphasis is on the power of the father to decide on the 'elect', 'his worthiest son', etc.

14. R. Easterlin, 'Population Change and Farm Settlement in the Northeastern United States,' *Journal of Economic History*, XXXVI (1976), 45-75.

15. R.E. Kennedy, *The Irish: Emigration, Marriage and Fertility* (Berkeley, 1973), pp.151-2.

16. W. Carleton, *The Party Fight and Funeral* (Cork, 1973), p.20. Note that in Rosmuc in southern Connemara 'the eldest and other sons usually emigrated .. It was the youngest son who remained at home. All this was going on before 1900.' In Bearna, County Galway, 'the eldest son usually remained at home to inherit the farm — that was the custom .. unless there was a very large family with younger brothers. In that case the eldest brother might emigrate as he would have to wait a very long time until the younger brothers were all gone,

before he could take over the place and marry.' Cf. Irish Folklore Commission, MS. 1409, pp.42, 213. This account refers to a later period, though. The enumerators' reports from the 1901 census, at present being investigated by the author, promise to give us a better understanding of farm succession practices.

17. C.Ó Gráda, 'A Note on Nineteenth-century Irish Emigration Statistics,' *Population Studies,* March 1975, 143-9.

18. For a useful survey of the possibilities see D.E. Baines, 'The use of published census data in migration studies,' in E.A. Wrigley ed. *Nineteenth Century Society: Essays in the Use of Quantitative Data* (Cambridge, 1972).

19. If there was net migration inward, then AC^j_{t+1} > survivors in j, implying that $\hat{E}$ < real emigration. On the other hand, net outward migration would mean $\hat{E}$ > real emigration. There are no estimates of internal migration in our period, but the census reports provide some clues. The tables below draw together the most relevant information for 1861-71:

A. 1861

Province	Number of Persons Born in Province and Living in Ireland	Irish-born Inhabitants of Province
Leinster	1,399,311	1,422,144
Munster	1,502,364	1,495,547
Connacht	913,052	907,609
Ulster	1,905,836	1,895,263
Total	5,720,563	5,720,563

B. 1871

Leinster	1,266,010	1,294,046
Munster	1,375,600	1,367,025
Connacht	849,246	839,698
Ulster	1,815,901	1,805,788
Total	5,306,757	5,306,757

In 1861 and 1871 only Leinster was a net gainer from internal migration. However, the figures imply very small gains and losses, when compared with the $\hat{E}$'s in Table I. While internal migration was an important factor in several counties (e.g. Donegal, Cork, Dublin, Antrim) most internal migration at this time would appear to have been intra-provincial. Our use of AC_{t+1} may thus seem reasonable for analysis at provincial level, but the short-cut would be invalid for some county-level analysis. Thus for instance its use gives us an $E/\hat{E}$ of 3.77 for Antrim and 0.32 for Donegal in 1861-71.

On the assumption about death-rates we consulted A. Coale and P. Demeny, *Regional Model Life Tables and Stable Populations* (Princeton, 1966), pp.44-5, 142-3. Taking a death rate of 22 per thousand for the population as a whole implies a death rate of slightly over seven per thousand for the 5-30 years age-cohort. Twenty-two per thousand was considered 'normal' for mid-century by S.H. Cousens, 'Regional Death-rates in Ireland during the Great Famine, 1846 to 1851,' *Transactions of the British Institute of Geographers,* XXVIII (1960), 62.

20. *Commission on Emigration ..,* Table 91, p.122.

21. According to the 1871 Census Report (p.435) the average emigration rate for the whole of Ireland during the 1850s and 1860s was 17.5 per thousand per annum. However, the reported Connacht annual average was only 13.8 per thousand, while Munster's was 24.5 per thousand. The contrast with age-cohort

survival ratios for 1861-1871 is notable:

Leinster	:	0.72
Munster	:	0.64
Connacht	:	0.61
Ulster	:	0.70

22. Most relevant are S.H. Cousens, 'Emigration and Demographic Change in Ireland, 1851-61,' *Econ. Hist. Rev.,* 2nd ser. XIV (1962), 275-88; 'The Regional Variation in Population Changes in Ireland, 1861-1881,' *ibid.,* XVII (1864-5), 302-21.

23. S.H. Cousens, 'The Regional Variation ..,' p.313.

24. For a sampling see J.S. Donnelly, *The Land and the People of Nineteenth - Century Cork* (London, 1975), pp.230-1; B.M. Walsh, 'Marriage Rates and Population Pressure in Ireland, 1871 and 1911,' *Econ. Hist. Rev.,* 2nd ser. (XXIII) (1970); C. Ó Gráda, 'Seasonal Migration and Post-Famine Adjustment in the West of Ireland,' *Studia Hibernica,* no.13 (1973), 48-76.

25. For regional wage trends, see A.L. Bowley, 'The Statistics of Wages in the United Kingdom during the last hundred years: Agricultural Wages (Ireland),' *Journal of the Royal Statistical Society,* LXII (1899), 400-3. Bowley's wage data suggest that nominal agricultural wages rose by almost ninety per cent in Connacht between 1850 and 1870, and by about sixty per cent nationally.

26. Curiously enough, some of Cousens' ideas are presaged in L. Paul-Dubois' *Contemporary Ireland* (Dublin, 1908), pp.356-7. Paul-Dubois argued:

> To become an emigrant, one must first save up the price of a ticket and also the small amount of capital required of intending immigrants into America. Besides which, morally speaking, a man must have risen a degree or two above his neighbours before he feels a desire to emigrate. He must have emerged from the doubt and despair around him, and have become imbued with the wish to try his fortune. Thus even at the present day, certain districts of the extreme west, some of the most poverty-stricken in Ireland, are those from which there is least emigration. In the County of Kerry, for instance, from the districts of Dingle and Cahirciveen, there is hardly any outflow of population, whereas there is a very high average of emigrants from Kenmare and Killarney, which are more 'civilised'.

However, the census figures suggest that Paul-Dubois' claim is a non-starter. Age-cohort disappearance in the 5-30 years group was almost 39 per cent in the Dingle and Cahirciveen P.L.U.s in 1901-11, while the loss in Kenmare-Killarney was only 32 per cent.

F

PART III

INDUSTRY

6. The Irish Linen Board, 1711-1828

H. D. Gribbon

A COMMITTEE of the Irish House of Commons, appointed to inspect the state of
the linen manufacture, reported in 1709 that '... the linen manufacture is now in a
declining condition, by reason the Acts already passed for the encouragement thereof
have not fully answered the ends for which they were made.' (1) As a result, legislation
was passed in 1710 which provided, amongst other things, for the setting up of a body
of trustees charged with the management of certain funds allocated for '... the use of
the hempen and flaxen manufactures in this kingdom and to no other use whatso-
ever.' (2) The body, the Trustees of the Hempen and Flaxen Manufactures of Ireland,
otherwise the Irish Linen Board, began work in 1711.

There were 72 trustees, consisting almost entirely of members of one or other of
the Irish houses of parliament, and including representatives of the great officers of
state, the judiciary, the episcopacy and the landed gentry. Through time, as trustees
died and were replaced, adjustments were made; members of the Latouche banking
family were appointed, later the governor of the Bank of Ireland, but by and large
the original representation remained. At first sight it would be difficult to conceive
of a more unwieldy body or one less suited to supervise, regulate and promote
Ireland's staple manufacture. The Board did in fact come in for muted criticism from
eighteenth-century contemporaries and for more open criticism from nineteenth-
century bodies like the Commissioners of Public Accounts. During the Board's existence
its critics tended to be somewhat overawed by the status of its membership, but more
recently less inhibited criticism has come from Gill, Horner, Crawford and others. I
do not propose to attempt a defence, yet I doubt whether sufficient weight has been
given to all the evidence and should like to spend a little time looking at some of the
more neglected aspects.

As background, it should be pointed out that the linen industry was not introduced to Ireland by the English and Scottish settlers who came to Ulster, particularly
to south Antrim and north Down, in the mid-seventeenth century, nor by the
Huguenots who followed them. Linen had been made in Ireland from remote antiquity
in the form of narrow cloths, poorly bleached, produced on primitive looms, and
used only in Ireland. Export was confined to yarn, spun mainly if not exclusively by
distaff and spindle. (Horner suggests that the spinning wheel was not used in Ireland
earlier than the seventeenth century). (3) In other words, the native industry was
based on the minimum of capital and fixed equipment — a system which accorded
well with semi-nomadic agriculture and unsettled political conditions.

The Board's immediate task was to take over the non-commercial, instructional side of Louis Crommelin's activities, (4) to enforce the existing statutory regulations, and to encourage throughout the country, by bounties, premiums and the supply of equipment, the replacement of narrow 'bandle' linen by broader, better finished cloths already becoming predominant in Ulster. The task was not unlike that faced by a modern agricultural marketing board – the regulation of the output of a multiplicity of small producers; but the concept of such a board, with representatives of producers, wholesalers and exporters, was still two centuries in the future. Meantime the creation of the Irish Linen Board did represent some advance in thinking. Hitherto, industry had been regulated, where it attracted the attention of government, by restrictive statutes, mercantilist in aim, or by the granting of trading or manufacturing monopolies which had the object of enriching the crown, and possibly the grantee, rather than the industry; the alnage of wool, where still enforced, had long become a purely revenue raising institution. In that context, the provision of public money for the direct support of an industry was, to say the least, unusual.

The Board's income came originally from the yield of import duties on calico and linen. Amounting to about £1,600 per year, these were reinforced in 1719 by 'additional duties' on tea, coffee, chocolate and cocoa nuts which produced on average £2,500, rising in the 1730s to around £7,500 per year. In 1723 the Irish parliament began making an annual grant of £2,000, to be used specifically for promoting the growing of flax and hemp and, in 1733 a further annual £2,000 for the general encouragement of the industry in Leinster, Munster and Connaght. Later the duties on tea and coffee, which had increased enormously, were commuted for £10,350 per year; the remainder, to which were added an import duty on linseed oil and an export levy on untanned hides, were either re-allocated or produced only a few hundred pounds. Finally in 1780 the Board got £7,250 per year in lieu of a long standing bounty on imported flax-seed. The total income therefore by 1788 was £21,600 per year plus a small amount from the 'appropriated duties'. At the Union £21,600 (Irish) became the £19,938 sterling voted annually by the Westminster parliament until 1827, when it was reduced to £10,000 and then ceased. (5)

Besides regular income the Board received special sums for particular purposes – £1,060 in 1721 to restore to solvency its overspent accounts, £3,000 in 1721-23 toward the building of the Linen Hall in Dublin, £540 in 1741 for the purchase of a further piece of ground, and so on. Then there was the practice of rewarding inventors, or other people whose services to the industry were considered of particular value, not, or not only by award from Linen Board funds, but by recommendation to the favourable consideration of parliament – usually with satisfactory outcome.

Turning for a moment to legislation, the Irish parliament passed at the beginning of each session (through the 'Heads of a Bill' procedure) the money Bill necessary, amongst other things, to supply the Board's finances. In addition Bills were passed almost every other year adding to or amending the Board's powers, imposing fresh regulations on the trade, or authorising the payment, alteration or cessation of some bounty or premium. The flow of legislation was such that, according to Gill, more than twenty statutes relating to the linen industry were passed between 1780 and 1800. (6) Even at Westminster the flow continued, any diminution in volume being offset in terms of parliamentary time by the work of numerous regular and select committees.

It is evident that the Board was not cramped for finance nor deprived of parliamentary support for its legislation. In the period 1740-1763 its Bills were drafted by Baron Anthony Foster, (7) at other periods by equally able men; its membership was heavily represented on the Irish Privy Council; the lord chancellor and chancellor of the exchequer and several revenue commissioners were regularly of its number. The truth is that a body whose composition would have made it quite inappropriate for its task in the twentieth century, found that composition not only advantageous but essential in the eighteenth when influence rather than democratic orthodoxy was the key to success.

The Board needed representation for its views at least as much at Westminster as at College Green — in relation both to Irish Bills before the Privy Council and British Bills before Parliament dealing with the English and Scottish linen trade. Once again the high ranking status of the membership was useful. Not only did many English peers have Irish interests and/or Irish titles, but of the 66 Irishmen who sat for British constituencies in parliaments between 1715 and 1754, 26 were peers of Ireland. (8) In the period 1754-90 no less than 72 Irish peers sat at one time or another in the British House of Commons (9) — and these of course included members of the Linen Board. Thus, in 1764 Lord Hillsborough, an active member of the Board, wrote from London about a clause in the Irish Linen Bill of that year, '... I would at the request of the factors and drapers of London have had it left out of the Bill in Council here, had there not appeared so strong preposession in favour of it by letters from the Board to my Lord Northumberland and from him and many others to the Council on this side.' (10) In 1768 he commended the activities of John Ellis, the Board's agent in London, in connection with the Linen Bills recently passed — 'He frequently attended me and other Members who supported the Bills ...' (11) Again, in 1778 the secretary of the Board, writing to Robert Knox (who succeeded Ellis as London agent) about a desired amendment in a British Linen Bill, said, 'The Trustees ... desire you will immediately apply to Lords Hertford and Hillsborough and the other members of this Board now in London to hope for their co-operation...'(12) Of an Irish Bill in April 1782 the Board's secretary, in London to pilot it through the Privy Council, reported, 'The Duke of Leinster has taken great pains in making friends for it in the Council ... Lords Hillsborough and Fairford will do everything in their power in supporting the Bill.' (13) Most interesting perhaps is the comment in a letter of March 1779 from the secretary of the Board of Trustees for Manufactures etc. in Scotland to their agent in London, referring to a Linen Bill currently before the Westminster parliament — 'The Board has also under consideration...a clause in favour of Ireland...to be put into the Bill for renewing the bounty on linens exported, and they seemed of opinion that the admission of the clause could do little or no harm, whereas objecting to it in the present state of the Irish interest might retard or even overthrow the Bill altogether.' (14)

Nevertheless the Irish interest was not always allowed to go unchallenged. The Committee of the Privy Council appointed to consider Irish Bills had to take account of representations from Cheshire and Lancashire against the Linen Bill of 1723 (15); an Irish proposal of 1728 to continue the import duty on painted and stained muslins (the proceeds from which formed part of the Linen Board's income) met opposition from the powerful East India Company (16); during proceedings in 1749 Scottish

members in particular insisted that so long as Ireland gave bounties on the export
of sailcloth there should be an import duty on sailcloth coming into Great Britain. (17)
Significantly, Irish members of the pre-1800 Westminster parliament were said to
have been more interested in Ireland's economic welfare than her national aspirat-
ions. (18)

Despite the fact that the industries entrusted to their care were market rivals, the
Board of Trustees for Manufactures in Scotland and the Irish Linen Board enjoyed
cordial relations at both official and trustee levels. Evidence for the former is more
than adequate; evidence for the latter must rest for the moment on two pieces of
correspondence. The first is a letter written in December 1772 by Sir Alexander
Gilmore, MP for Edinburgh, to Lord Clare, for transmission to the Linen Board.
This discusses British customs duties on foreign linens, their effects on the industry,
and certain proposals for remedying their defects. The letter drew from the Irish
Board what was doubtless expected, support for Sir Alexander's views and proposals. (19)
The second is a letter of April 1771 from London to Anthony Foster about a bounty
proposed in Great Britain on the export of checked linen. There was likely to be a
divergence of interest between Ireland and Scotland on the issue. Anthony Foster's
correspondent writes, 'I have been with Lord Hillsborough and Lord Hertford ...
They are of opinion it may be proper to hear what the Scotch and Manchester agents
have to propose ... Mr Ellis ... is against having any communication with the agents
from Scotland. For my own part I can see no harm in hearing their propositions.' (20)
Evidently, whatever wariness there may have been at administrative level, at Trustee
level, and on policy aspects, there was confidence in an ability to find common
ground. It would seem that amongst the trustees there existed what it would be
irreverent but probably correct to call an 'old boy network' – an interconnection of
family, political and financial interests which, by reason of its membership, the Irish
Board was able to use to advantage.

If, on examination, the composition of the Board seems more reasonable than it
did at first sight, a similar case can be made for its size. Attendance at meetings was
notoriously bad, but the view that the number of trustees was so large as to make
the whole body unwieldy cannot be allowed to pass unchallenged, or at any rate
accepted without qualification. It must be remembered that many of the trustees
had country estates of which some, in the eighteenth century, were two or more
days' travel from Dublin. Others had public and private concerns in Great Britain.
(On one occasion, admittedly post-Union, a meeting of 23 trustees took place in
London at a time when the average attendance in Dublin would not have exceeded
a dozen.) (21) Others again who held offices of state, or members of the judiciary
on circuit, were not always free to attend; some had no interest in attending. All
this must have been foreseen in 1710 because, in the original Act, power to enter
into contracts on behalf of the whole body was given to any seven members. (22)
At various later stages and for different purposes power was given to five, seven and
twelve trustees. Attendance at meetings was entirely a matter of good will since
members received neither fees nor re-imbursement of expenses. For these various
reasons it was necessary to appoint a fairly large body initially. A reduction in numbers
would not have solved the problem of poor and irregular attendance of which most
critics complained. There are grounds for saying that membership should have been

more selective, and that it should have included men with practical experience of the linen industry, but in the climate of opinion which saw the establishment of the Dublin Society, and the direction of Dublin's many charitable hospitals and chartered schools in very similar hands it was not unreasonable to expect that a body whose membership overlapped with most of these would work at least as well as they did. The difference of course was that the Linen Board, financed solely by public money, had responsibility for Ireland's major manufacturing industry.

Another criticism of the Board requiring qualification is that it did not seek to take sufficient account of outside opinion. This is demonstrably untrue. Within a few days of its formation it was seeking advice from seven local merchants about the importation of flax and hemp seed; (23) it maintained a good relationship with Louis Crommelin who, although he somewhat exalted his sources of information — '... it was not possible for your petitioner to impart unto the whole nation the know-ledge God had given him in the said manufacture...' (24) — was nevertheless an acknowledged expert; within a few months of its formation the Board had appointed itinerant instructors and was receiving back reports from them; and it was bombarded from a variety of sources by pamphlets giving unsolicited advice. As Mr. Justice Coote, acting chairman, wrote on behalf of the Board to a London merchant in February 1712, seeking his objective view about ways in which the Irish trade and manufacture might be improved, 'The various accounts they have from people dealing in that way in this Kingdom (every man speaking according as his own private interest dictates) serves only to embarass their judgement, but does not advance the public service...' (25) Perhaps there were times when the Board got out of touch. So at least thought Sir Richard Cox of Dunmanway, co. Cork who, having developed the linen industry on his own estate, wrote in 1759, 'I am extremely rejoiced that the Trustees for those manufactures have, at length, fallen upon the method of consulting the gentlemen of the county in points essential to our welfare...' (26)

From the Board's own records and from the voluminous pamphlet material of the time there is adequate evidence of the Board having sought opinions from all sections of the trade about the legislation proposed in 1762-64, whilst from manu-script records there is similar evidence of consultation on many other occasions. The problem was that the advice which the Board received was never consistent, that is, spinners, weavers, manufacturers, bleachers and drapers, London factors and local exporters never agreed on any particular policy or action. The weavers had no objection to tighter regulation of spinners or bleachers, but the interests of independent weavers and of manufacturers who employed weavers tended to diverge. Similarly bleachers and drapers supported the Board in its efforts to impose discipline on weavers and manufacturers but raised an outcry when their own interests were affected. Bleachers who claimed to have found means of using lime or its derivatives safely were as persuasive, if not as vociferous, as those traders who deplored the disastrous effects of lime on consignments on which they had recently lost money. In general, the Board received not too little but too much advice, too many repres-entations, and not enough factual information. Whether the trustees could have made proper use of such information is of course another matter.

With its undoubted prestige and influence, with adequate finance and legislative power the Board nevertheless failed to make the most effective use of its position to foster the Irish linen industry. That at least seems to be the consensus of opinion, with the qualification perhaps that, initially, it had moderate success: during the middle period of its existence it was ineffective: toward the end a positive hindrance. Without necessarily endorsing such a broad generalisation it seems to me to contain a sufficient element of truth to require explanation. At least, the reasons why an otherwise reliable commentator like R.M. Muggeridge of the 1840 Handloom Weavers Commission (27) had such a poor opinion of the Board and its operations does merit investigation.

Any discussion of the Board's activities must distinguish between its promotional and regulatory functions. The former consisted of the gathering and dissemination of information and the distribution of looms, spinning wheels, reels and other equipment to deserving applicants, notably to spinning schools, to tenants on the estates of Trustees or to improving landlords like Thomas Adderley, co. Cork or Robert French, co. Galway. (28) Financial assistance to bleachers either for equipment or to meet the wages of skilled men was regularly provided. Bounties were given on the export of sailcloth and for a short time on exports of linen to Spain. Premiums were granted for many purposes — spinning fine yarn, making ashes for bleaching in substitution for imported potash, saving locally grown flax-seed, imitating French and German linens, and much else. There were grants to innumerable inventors of implements and equipment, for the installation of early spinning machinery, for the building of flax scutch mills and for the preparation and improving of bleaching liquids. Indeed it is difficult to think of any process or activity connected with the linen industry which did not at one time or another qualify for some measure of assistance. Sometimes efforts were misdirected or taken on inaccurate information but, generally, there was little wrong with the ideas behind the Board's promotional activities. The trouble lay in implementation. Two examples must suffice.

In the period 1806 — 1825 the Board offered bounties on sailcloth and canvas made from mill-spun yarn and sold by the manufacturer. There were claimants from a number of ports and naval bases — Cork, Dublin, Belfast and Buncrana. In order to obtain the 1½d. per yard bounty, claimants had to prove that they had manufactured or purchased mill-spun yarn (there were about a dozen small dry spinning mills in Ireland), had made it into sailcloth and sold it. The sailcloth was to be examined by the Board's inspector, invoices showing sale price and quantity had to be produced, and the whole claim was required in the form of an affidavit sworn before a magistrate or justice. For some purposes further authentication was required from the port customs officer. Despite all the precautions against abuse the Shanahan brothers of Cork managed to defraud the Board in the years 1813-15 of an amount said to have been between £5,000 and £7,000. The money was never recovered. The port inspector Bradshaw Popham, who had been in the Board's service for nearly twenty years, who had the ear of influential people and who was supposed to be under the supervision of the inspector general for the province, was subsequently dismissed. There were suggestions that the Shanahans were only one of the firms claiming bounty who found Mr Popham obliging. (29)

My second example of promotional activities going wrong relates to spinning schools, sponsored by the Board between 1715 and 1758. As a method of extending the linen industry into areas in which it was not indigenous the idea of instructing

girls in spinning, though by no means original, had much to commend it. The girls
would be taught a skill enabling them to supplement the family income; their demand
would encourage the local growing of flax and preparation of the fibre; possibly
weavers could be induced to come into the area. Under the Board's procedure a
proposal to set up a spinning school usually came from somebody of local standing –
the wife of an improving landlord or the patron of a charitable institution. The
application was considered at a meeting of trustees who could, if they thought fit,
call for a report from their local 'itinerant man' (as the inspectors were originally
called). A school having been approved, the spinning master or mistress submitted
a sworn affidavit showing how many children were ready to be taught (between the
ages of eight and fourteen years). Provided the number was between 12 and 20, the
Board issued an order for the supply to the school of an appropriate number of spinning wheels. The proprietor of a spinning school, who provided the building, a spinning
mistress, and the necessary quantities of flax was entitled to the proceeds of sale of
the yarn, plus 6s. a year for each pupil instructed (to pay the wages of the spinning
mistress), and 6d. a week for each child (to be given to the parent for its food and
clothing). To obtain these payments the master or mistress had to submit a quarterly
return sworn before the minister of the parish or a justice of the peace, showing the
number of pupils actually taught during the quarter. As a check that everything was
in order the Board arranged to instruct the 'itinerant men':

1st.   That they shall visit all spinning-schools within their respective districts, at
       least once a quarter.
2d.   That they make a roll of the names of each scholar, their age, and time of
       entrance in such schools.
3d.   That they give instructions to the spinning-master or mistress, that they keep
       a faithful account of such scholars as are absent, and on what days, which is
       to be given the itinerant man at each visitation, to be returned by him to the
       Board, that deductions may be made for the time of their absence.
4th.   That they enquire into the cause of such absence.
5th.   .... [deals with yarn quality]
6th.   That they strictly observe that the wheels and other materials are well prepared,
       and kept in good order.
7th.   That no itinerant man shall visit the schools in his district on certain days, but
       shall vary the day of the week and month.
8th.   That they take a particular account of the number and weight of the dozens
       of yarn spun in each school, between each visitation, and the value thereof.
9th.   That they keep in all points an exact account of the state of each school, which
       they are to transmit to the Board. (30)

Now, one would have thought the system foolproof but in fact it had to be brought
to an end because it had become so riddled with fraud. For instance, children were
sent to the schools who had already been taught spinning at home, or were encouraged
to remain long after there was any instructional element in their work – to qualify
for the 6d. per week. Fictitious names were added to the roll or names of children
who came to the school to spin for themselves – in order to augment the mistress's
salary; schools were set up in districts where there was little need for them. There
is also doubt whether the yarn produced in schools in the southern provinces (where
most were situated) was not too fine for local use. (31) It seems incredible that with

nearly 200 schools, and during a period of over 40 years, the 'itinerant men' should not have detected and reported frauds. One is forced to the conclusion that either the inspection system was completely ineffective or the reports received at head-quarters were ignored.

The regulatory functions of the Linen Board were an inheritance from earlier attempts to prescribe the way in which yarn should be made up for sale and to enforce minimum lengths and widths for linen cloth sold or exposed for sale. To these relatively simple regulations the Board added enormously. Toward the end of its life there were repeals and simplifications but the total volume remained formid-able. By way of illustration, a consolidating Act of 1745 contained 52 sections, an Act of 1763 97 sections and another consolidating Act of 1826 59 sections. Admittedly, about one-quarter of these sections dealt with the Board, its powers, premises and personnel; and there were sections granting privileges — weavers' exemption from service as jurors or petty constables, freedom of cities and town to weavers, flax dressers, and makers of spinning wheels — but on the whole they were regulatory and left few, if any, aspects of the industry unaffected. Not that the regulations were necessarily foolish. It was not objectionable that kelp sold for making into bleaching ashes should be free from sand and stones; (32) with no guilds to regulate apprentice-ship it was sensible that the Board's legislation should do so — length, conditions (not to be employed more than a prescribed number of days on husbandry), and so on; (33) it was doubtless a good thing from a seaman's point of view that old hempen ropes should not be covered with new hemp. (34) But there were other areas much more debatable.

In 1720, under the provisions of an Act passed the previous year, the Board appointed 'lappers' to examine white linen cloth offered for sale and to mark it with a prescribed stamp if it conformed with the current regulations. In 1733 power was taken to extend the arrangement to brown or unbleached linen. For most of the following one hundred years the Board sought in vain to make the system work. The terms 'lapper' and 'sealmaster' were sometimes distinct, sometimes synonymous; they could refer to the stamping or sealing of white linen, or brown linen, or both. There were 'white' seals and 'brown' seals, the patterns of which had to be changed regularly. Sealmasters, to adopt the single term, were appointed by the Board — on the recommendation of one or more trustees, on petition by the bleachers, drapers and traders of a district, on certification of suitability by county or provincial inspectors, or on some combination of these. Public sealmasters (35) were entitled to charge a fee of a couple of pence for measuring and stamping each web. With one or two sealmasters per brown linen market, or with one sealmaster serving an area with several bleach yards, the remuneration was small but reasonable: but if, as fre-quently, there were too many sealmasters, malpractice to obtain business quickly became rife. Equally, one or two sealmasters only in charge of a market were in a position to extort extra fees or payment in kind, commonly drink, from the weavers. Fraud and negligence seemed built into the system. Sealmasters not infrequently employed deputies even less trustworthy than themselves. The stamps of a sealmaster who died or was dismissed should have been returned to Dublin: in practice they usually passed into unauthorised hands, to be used to give an entirely spurious cachet to defective goods. Where sealmasters of better calibre were appointed, drapers

complained of their power to buy up the best webs before these reached the market.
A Newry trader in 1763 referred to sealmasters as 'protectors and encouragers of
frauds and their houses the places of meeting of jobbers'. (36) The Board's secretary,
describing the period 1750-61 said, 'The records of the Board in those years remain
an honourable memorial of their labours in striving to combat with the frauds of
the lappers; there is not a meeting that does not exhibit a numerous list of them
fined and dismissed, and others appointed in their places, the latter becoming in
their turn fit subjects themselves for similar punishment; and yet these examples
did not avail.' (37)

To ensure that lappers and sealmasters paid their fines or could be proceeded
against by those whom their negligence or malpractice had injured, the Board required
them to enter into legal bonds, supported by independent sureties: despite all of
which the Linen Hall chamberlain, writing in 1781 about recent complaints said,
'I have not yet got the account of the lappers; when I do I think I will show many
of the sealmasters are nominal names only, and their securities bubbles.' (38)

There was nothing wrong in principle with the quality marking of linen. There
were precedents in the alnage of wool and the hall-marking of precious metals; it
was practised in France, the Low Countries and Scotland; there are many modern
parallels. Rather curiously, and despite its bad reputation, the system of inspection
and stamping by sealmasters (under the control of local committees) was one of the
features of the Linen Board's machinery retained after its dissolution. C.G. Otway
observed it in operation in Lurgan, commenting, 'Most numerous are the frauds
practised on and by the seal-masters.' (39) Evidently the new brooms had not swept
as clean as had been hoped.

Another subject of concern to the Board for many years was the allegedly harmful
use of lime in bleaching, and the enforcement of the regulations against it. The point
of interest here is that, in the absence of regular and reliable inspection, the Board
seems to have relied on the severity of the legislation. For instance, an Act of 1717,
strengthened in 1745 and again in 1782, contained the provision that a bleacher
convicted of using lime (or other prohibited substances) should forfeit the value of
the cloth or yarn illegally bleached — an amount which could run into hundreds of
pounds. Moreover, the servant of a bleacher suspected of using lime could be required
to give evidence on oath against his master. If he refused to appear or to testify he
could be sent to the house of correction to be whipped and kept at hard labour for
thirty days, 'unless he do sooner submit to be examined as aforesaid'. Power of
entry, at any hour of the day, was available to magistrates, justices, the trustees, or
persons appointed by them, in searching for evidence of the use of prohibited
bleaching materials and, if such were found the workers on the premises as well as
the owners were to be subject to penalties. But a worker summoned to testify against
his master was absolved, if he complied, from any penalty for his part in the offence. (40)
As a correspondent put it in 1763, the legislation was an open invitation to any dis-
gruntled workman to incriminate his employer, even against the latter's instructions,
whilst escaping penalty himself. (41) In any age of penal legislation this was taking
things rather far!

Why, despite its suitability in many respects did the Board fall down so badly
in much that it attempted? The Irish Linen Board was created ahead of its time,

before administrative machinery had been devised to carry out the sorts of duties with which it was charged. Constituted as it was, too great responsibilities had to be delegated to the permanent officials, without adequate supervision. Almost uniformly they failed (42) — but that is another story. Given the inadequacy at administrative level it is remarkable, not so much that the Board worked badly, but that it worked at all.

NOTES

1. *H. of C. Journals (Ire.)*, III, *1703-13* (Dublin, 1782), 436.
2. 9 Ann (Ire.), c.3.
3. John Horner, *The Linen Trade of Europe* (Belfast, 1920), p.17.
4. Horner, *op.cit.,* pp.26-34; Conrad Gill, *The Rise of the Irish Linen Industry* (Oxford, 1925), pp.16-22.
5. *Precedents and Abstracts from the Journals of the Trustees etc. 1711-1737* (Dublin, 1784); Annual volumes of the *Proceedings of the Trustees etc.* 1784-1828; *Select Committee on the Laws which regulate the Linen Trade of Ireland* (Parl. Papers, 1822, VII), p.554.
6. Gill, *op.cit.,* p.198.
7. Land owner of Collen, co.Louth; MP for Louth; barrister; appointed Counsel to the Board 1740; subsequently Chief Baron of the Exchequer and member of the Board.
8. R. Sedgewick, *The History of Parliament; The House of Commons, 1715-1754* (HMSO, 1964-70), I, Appendix VII.
9. L. Namier and J. Brooke, eds. *The History of Parliament: The House of Commons 1754-1790* (HMSO, 1964-1970), I. I am indebted for the analysis to A.P.W. Malcolmson
10. P.R.O.N.I. D.562/5241. For the use of the Foster MSS and permission to quote from them I would like to thank the Deputy Keeper of Records, PRO of Northern Ireland, and Viscount Masserene and Ferrard.
11. P.R.O.N.I. D.562/5245.
12. P.R.O.N.I. D.562/1829.
13. P.R.O.N.I. D.562/5523.
14. Scottish Record Office, NG. 1/3/13, f.94.
15. 10 Geo.I (Ire.), c.2; B.M. Add. MS 21134, ff.6-21.
16. P.R.O. CO. 388/87, D.50.
17. B.M. Add. MS 21134, ff.27-8.
18. Namier and Brooke, *op.cit.,* p.163.
19. P.R.O.N.I. D.562/1831.
20. P.R.O.N.I. D.562/5276.
21. *Report of an Inquiry into the Mode of Cultivating and Treating Flax in the Netherlands, by Peter Besnard, Inspector-general for Leinster, Munster and Connaught* (Dublin, 1822), p.1.
22. 9 Ann (Ire.), c.3, s.7.
23. *Precedents and Abstracts,* p.2.
24. *Ibid.* p.3.
25. *Ibid.* p.8.
26. *A Letter from Sir Richard Cox, Bart. to the High Sheriff of the County of Cork etc.* (Dublin, 1759), p.5.
27. *Reports of the Assistant Commissioners on Hand-Loom Weavers* (P.P. 1840, XXIII), p.524. The other Assistant Commissioner, C.G. Otway, did not express an opinion but recorded the view of one of his informants — 'The Linen Board was our greatest curse. It attempted to interfere....' *Ibid.* p.492.

28. Robert Stephenson, *An Inquiry into the State and Progress of the Linen Manufacture in Ireland* (Dublin, 1757), pp.150, 182.

29. *Proceedings of the Trustees, 1815,* pp.20, 286; W. Williams, *Correspondence with the Rt. Hon. Robert Peel etc.* (Dublin, 1820); *Reply to a Recent Publication Which Has Abused the Linen Board etc.* (Dublin, 1829); P.R.O.N.I. D.207/28/588.

30. *Precedents and Abstracts,* p.19.

31. Robert Stephenson, *op.cit.,* pp.14, 196-7.

32. 2 Geo.I (Ire.), c.13, s.5.

33. 1 Geo.II (Ire.), c.11, s.11.

34. 19 Geo.II (Ire.), c.6, s.4.

35. Distinct from private sealmasters, almost entirely in Ulster, where seals were sometimes issued to registered bleachers for use on their own linens.

36. P.R.O.N.I. D.562/5234.

37. James Corry, *Report on the Measuring and Stamping of Brown Linen in Ulster* (Dublin, 1822), p.5.

38. P.R.O.N.I. D.562/5334.

39. *Reports of the Assistant Commissioners on Hand-Loom Weavers* (P.P. 1840, XXIII), p.487.

40. 4 Geo.I (Ire.), c.6, s.8-11; 19 Geo.II (Ire.), c.6, s.18-21; 21 & 22 Geo.III (Ire.), c.35, s.1-4. One would need supporting evidence that (per Horner, *op.cit.,* p.70) a clause proposed for a Bill in 1763 read, 'That any bleacher who used improper materials was to be adjudged guilty of felony and to suffer death.'

41. P.R.O.N.I. D.562/5240.

42. A conspicuous exception was the last secretary, James Corry Jun. But his period of office came too late, when both technical progress and the *laissez-faire* philosophy of the Industrial Revolution were making the Linen Board an anachronism.

7. The Scottish Linen Industry in the Eighteenth Century; Some Aspects of Expansion

Alastair J. Durie

IN AN economy hitherto mainly characterised by small advances precariously held and seldom consolidated, the growth of the linen industry stands out as one of the most impressive developments in eighteenth century Scotland. Between 1728 (the first year for which figures exist) and 1800, the output of cloth woven for sale rose in volume from 2.2 to 24.2 million yards and in value from £103,000 to £1,048,000. (1) Nor was this growth confined to the manufacture of cloth. The value of the output of the Scottish linen thread industry established in the early 1720s was estimated to be about £175,000 in 1775, £222,000 in 1784 and at no less than £485,000 in 1797. (2) The causes on the demand side of this remarkable expansion of the linen industry (or industries) have already been the subject of some discussion at least for the period up to 1775. (3) But the aim of this paper is to examine not why but *how* the industry grew, and, on the supply side, to concentrate in particular on the performance of three important factors of production, namely the supply of the raw material – flax – the provision of labour, and the sources of capital. Much of this discussion is only provisional and intended to open up some lines of enquiry.

I

We turn firstly to a consideration of the supply of flax to the Scottish linen industry during the eighteenth century. Flax was grown in many parts of Scotland but although the full extent of flax cultivation is unknown, there seems little doubt that a large proportion of the flax used in the industry was imported. Henry Home, after elaborate calculations, estimated in 1766 that 60 per cent of the heckled flax used in the industry was Scottish, whereas John Naismith reckoned that three-quarters of the flax used in 1782 was imported, an estimate with which the Board of Trustees concurred, they putting the proportion of imports to home grown at about 5:2. (4) Whatever the proportion, and none of these estimates should be taken too seriously, it is clear that imported flax was essential to the continuing growth of the industry. Imports of flax to Scotland directly from the continent, supplemented to an unknown extent by flax imported to England and then shipped coastwise to Scottish ports, rose steadily throughout the century (table 1). The rise of Dundee in the flax trade was particularly spectacular; there imports of flax from the continent rose from 150 tons or so p.a. in the mid 1740s to between 1,500 and 3,000 tons annually in the 1790s. (5)

Table 1   *Retained* imports of flax to Scotland; 1742-1799*

Tons p.a.		Tons p.a.	
1742-46	686	1775-79	4190
1755-59	2065	1780-84	4746
1760-64	2708	1785-89	4777
1765-69	3325	1790-94	6165
1770-74	3379	1795-99	7045

Sources; S.R.O., Inspector General's Ledgers of Imports and Exports for Scotland, 1755-1799, (RH 2/4 and 20/2), supplemented by a series for the years 1742-46 in NG 1/16/1, and with figures for the years 1763 and 1796 supplied from RH 2/4/549, and NG 1/60/34 respectively. The 'year' is that commencing on the 6th January except for the period 1742-46 when it is that ending on the 24th December. * Flax re-exported to Ireland has been deducted.

The dependence of the Scottish linen industry for so much of its flax on imports was a source of great concern to the Board of Trustees, and they devoted much time and money to increasing flax cultivation in Scotland. Between 1727 and 1773 the Board of Trustees spent an average of £640 p.a., or roughly one-fifth (22 per cent) of its total expenditure on the linen manufacture in a variety of ways to encourage the growth of flax in Scotland. After 1773 the Board was able to retain its normal income for other purposes and draw on the much larger resources of the so-called 'Flax Fund' solely for the purpose of stimulating flax culture: expenditure from this source ran at over £3,300 p.a. up to and beyond the turn of the century. (6) Their efforts had some effect; the acreage of flax sown (only a proportion of which was ultimately entitled to premium) rose from 510 acres in 1772 to 3,468 in 1799, and the produce of flax from 1540 stones to 55,056 (see table 2).

Table 2   *Flax raised in Scotland for the Board of Trustees' premiums (1772-1800)*

	Average No. of acres sown	Average No. of acres entitled to premium	Average Produce of flax (stones)*	(tons)
1772-1779	1486	566	36,389	260
1779-1786	3656	1006	79,375	567
1787-1793	3225	1688	81,421	582
1794-1800	3777	2335	86,370	617

* From total acreage sown, including produce from acres falling short of premium. The produce was expressed in Stones of 16 pounds *avoirdupois*. (Source; NG 1/60/35).

That there was an increase in home cultivation of flax seems evident, but even allowing generously for the unknown amount of flax raised in Scotland and not entered for the Board's premiums, it is clear how important imports were relative to domestic supplies.

The Board's efforts were given impetus by the rising price of imported flax even in peace time. Although we should beware of accepting contemporary wails at face value, particularly when the Scots were angling for government assistance, both in the 1760s and 1780s many complaints were made by Scottish manufacturers about

G

'the enormous price of Foreign Flax, which of late has been greatly advanced'. (7) Russian flax, it was said, had risen in price from £25 per ton in 1736 to £50 in 1786, and Dutch flax by a similar margin. (8) The trend of flax prices in peace time was ominous, even without the known experience of war-time fluctuations when supplies were disrupted and prices were pushed up by higher insurance and shipping costs. The freight rate per ton of flax carried from St. Petersburg to Leith rose from between 35/- to 45/- in the early 1750s to 58/- in 1758, and insurance rates more than doubled. (⁹ Dependence on continental supplies was potentially vulnerable, as David Loch and others pointed out, and the consequence of the Scottish failure 'to make their industry permanent by raising the raw materials entirely at home' was to be felt distinctly during the Napoleonic wars. In 1808 the price of St. Petersburg 12-head flax, which had been about £52 ten years earlier, jumped from £75 per ton to £125, and in February 1809 it was actually quoted in Dundee at £135-£140. (10) In some areas, the manufacture of linen was almost entirely brought to a halt by the scarcity of flax. (11)

Why then, despite the encouragement of rising prices and the subsidies of the Board of Trustees, was more flax not grown in Scotland? It could be, and was, cultivated in many parts of the country but mostly in small 'pennylots' of less than an acre. What needs explanation is why relatively few farmers chose to grow flax on a larger scale as a commercial field crop despite the incentive given by the market and the Board of Trustees. The cost of 'failure' was an annual import bill for flax of at least £250,000 by the 1780s.

Various explanations have been given and are familiar. (12) A prejudice generally held by farmers was that flax was a *scourging* crop which would rapidly exhaust the soil unless it were generously manured. It was a crop that needed constant skilled attention, and an acute sense of judgement as to when it should be pulled. Troublesome to care for before pulling and after, it was unpopular with farmers and farm servants alike. The operations of stripping off the bolls, winnowing the seed and steeping were greatly disliked, and the numerous small steps of its preparation for use tended to disrupt the other activities of the farmer. The quality of seed used for sowing was often blamed. But one feature of flax which has perhaps not received enough attention and may go a long way towards explaining the general reluctance to grow flax rather than any other arable crop, is the wide variation from year to year in *yields*. For example, between 1775 and 1778, the product in terms of dressed flax per acre sown was as high as 19.2 stones and as low as 6.6. That this is not untypical can be seen from the yields on the flax crops between 1818 and 1833 which varied from 31.75 stones per acre in 1828 to 6.9 in 1826. (13) There was no guarantee that a shortfall in the Scottish crop would be recouped through higher prices, given that there was no necessary uniformity of yield between Scotland and Russia. In short, for the Scottish farmer, flax was a risky crop, riskier than either wheat or barley, and given the availability of supplies from the continent in most years, there can have been little incentive to grow it.

This situation of continuing reliance on imported flax can be contrasted with the experience of the bleaching sector where a similar situation (with respect to the supply of bleaching ashes) existed for much of the century and likewise attracted the attention of the Board of Trustees. Despite much experimentation with home

substitutes, the importation of alkali ashes from the continent (and to a lesser extent
North America) rose steadily throughout the century. What broke this bottleneck,
with radical savings to the bleaching industry, (14) was the widespread introduction
of chlorine into bleaching from the 1790s.

II

The availability of labour was critical to the continuing expansion of the linen
industry. Nearly all the increases in output were the result of, and conditional upon,
increased inputs of labour, not mechanisation which made relatively little contribution
during the eighteenth century. The water-powered lint-mill for the scutching of flax,
first erected in the 1730s, is a development to which attention is often drawn. But
although the design was markedly improved in the early 1760s and the numbers
of these mills steadily increased thereafter from 253 in 1771 to 371 in 1782 to 408
in c.1800, (15) the bulk of flax used in Scotland continued to be scutched manually.
McLain's work suggests that in 1771 the total production of scutched flax by the
lint-mills was less than one-fifth of total raw flax imports alone, (16) and a paper
which has recently come to light amongst the records of the Board of Trustees indicates
that even in 1800 the amount of mill-scutched flax represented only about one-quarter
of the flax imported. (17) The importance of the lint-mill should not, therefore, be
exaggerated.

There is no doubt that the flax-spinning mill was to make a major impact on the
structure of the linen industry and that the decline of hand-spinning was to have
serious consequences for rural and northern household income, but the first flax-
spinning mills were not built until the late 1780s, and the output of mill-spun yarn
was probably not of much significance until the first decade of the nineteenth century.
During the Napoleonic wars, the availability of higher agricultural earnings seems to
have reduced the complementary activity of spinning in many rural areas, which in
turn led to a rapid diffusion of mill-spinning, 'occupying the vacant space of women'. (18)
Once mill-spinning had become established, demand for hand-spun yarn began to
decline — in the Dundee market, prices for hand-spun yarn were no longer quoted
after the late 1820s — and women were deflected into hand-loom weaving, a process
which contributed to the over-supply of labour in that sector after 1815. The large-
scale adoption of the power-loom, although various experiments were made in the
late eighteenth century with water or steam-driven looms, cannot be dated before
the 1820s. Mechanisation therefore made only a minor contribution to the increase
in output of the linen industry in the eighteenth century, and did little to reduce
the growth in demand for labour. Only perhaps in the finishing processes was there
any important substitution of machinery for labour with, for instance, the widespread
use of the rubbing mill and the drying house. (19) This is not to deny that there were
substantial gains in labour productivity (and therefore sharp rises in annual output)
via the substitution of the spinning-wheel for the rock or distaff, and in the continual
modification made to the hand-loom throughout the century. It is clear that the
productivity of the hand-spinner was more than doubled by the adoption of the
wheel, (20) a process which took at least until the 1790s to percolate into the remoter

parts of Scotland, (21) and it is possible that the productivity of the weaver may have risen by a similar margin. (22)

Regardless of other changes in productivity, substantial increases in output could be achieved through more efficient use of the existing labour force. In the first half of the eighteenth century, when seasonal unemployment was endemic, there was a considerable reserve of productive capacity in the textile labour force through lack of demand. William Cheap, an important Edinburgh linen manufacturer, observed in 1743 that 'the poorer sort of weavers about this place are starving for want of work at least four months in the year, and are glad of any sort of work'. (23) More regular employment for weavers and spinners alike obviously did much to raise their annual output and earnings, but the level of yarn production, however, was not solely a function of the availability of employment but also of the harvest and the cost of living. Most linen manufacturers believed it axiomatic that 'The Poor People ... decline working for any more than will barely subsist them, so that in cheap years little is manufactured and what is done, is paid for at a higher rate'. (24) The output of the cloth was also influenced by the harvest; it is probable that in 'dear' years some of the weavers in the large *'private'* (25) sector (whose cloth was made for families and not offered for sale and therefore not stamped) might sell a web or two on the market to raise the cash needed for their rent just at the time when internal demand might be falling. There was an inherent tendency for domestic supply and demand in the linen industry to be in disequilibrium because of the complex relationship between the textile industry and agriculture.

To sum up, the expansion of the linen industry's output was partially met by some increase in productivity and by the more regular employment of the existing labour force. But how far did it necessitate an increase in the numbers employed? It is beyond dispute that the numbers of weavers began to rise sharply in the second half of the eighteenth century. For instance, at Dunfermline the number of looms in the parish doubled between 1749 and 1792, and similar or greater rates of increase were reported in Forfar, Kirkcaldy and elsewhere. (26) Presumably also, the numbers of winders, hecklers, bleachers and other textile workers rose by a similar margin throughout Scotland. The supply of spinners came under the greatest pressure, not only from the linen-cloth and thread industries in Scotland, but also the demand from England and on occasion Ireland, a situation reflected in the steadily rising price of linen yarn in Scotland from the 1740s to the 1770s, and in the diffusion of linen spinning into nearly every part of Scotland, (27) from the Shetlands to Galloway, unlike cloth production, which became more and more concentrated in east-central Scotland. By the turn of the century (1798-1802) about half of all Scottish cloth was woven in just one county, Angus, and much of the rest in nearby Fife, Perth and Aberdeenshire.

The diffusion of spinning reflected the fact that at least three spinners were required to keep one weaver in yarn, plus those required to supply the thread industry and the export market. And only to a certain extent could pressure on Scottish supplies of yarn be offset by imports of German or French yarn; by the 1770s the fine linen industry in the west of Scotland used considerable amounts of the latter. The evidence, partial though it is, suggests that the Scottish linen industry was approaching a position of some crisis by the late 1770s with respect to yarn supplies. The cotton-mill may have proved the salvation of the Scottish coarse linen industry; within a decade cotton had replaced linen in the west of Scotland and led to a sharp reduction in English textile demand for Scottish yarn, thus releasing home supplies for the home industry. It appears, at least, that there was relatively little increase in yarn prices during the 1780s. (28)

An important subsidiary aspect of the supply of labour was the supply of skill. In a backward economy the only way of diffusing needed skills is through the importation of skilled workers. There was an important flow of skilled immigration to Scotland, often subsidised by the Board of Trustees, in the 1720s and 1730s to assist the improvement of various processes in the linen manufacture in which the Scots were most deficient, notably the finishing and bleaching of cloth. To Scotland came Irish and Dutch masterbleachers, English linen-printers, some brought on contract, others coming on speculation. Nor was the employment of a foreign bleacher sufficient to guarantee a bleachfield's success. Not all were good, as the Secretary to the Board of Trustees complained in particular of the Irish in 1748: 'Multitudes of such are coming yearly and none of them have the skill wanted.' Yet the contribution of some of the Irish bleachers was considerable, notably that of John Christie at Ormiston — arguably much greater than that of Dr. Cullen — who was responsible amongst other things for the invention of the drying house. As well as master-bleachers, the recruitment of Irish labour to lesser positions in the bleachfield can be traced; (29) some seem to have settled permanently, others to have come annually. But the work of the Board of Trustees, through the bleaching apprentices scheme administered at Gray's Green and later Saltoun bleachfield, did much to increase the supply of skilled Scottish bleachers in the 1740s and 1750s. By mid-century, the Scottish bleaching industry had undergone a considerable transformation; the practice once apparently common of sending Scottish brown linen to Holland for bleaching disappeared after 1754. Indeed, so much did the quality and speed of Scottish bleaching improve that by the turn of the century a fair amount of Irish linen was being sent to Scotland for bleaching.

Skilled labour was brought for purposes other than bleaching: Dutch flax-raisers, heckle and reed-makers, weavers, both Dutch and French. But the colony of French weavers brought across and settled by the Board of Trustees in 1729 was to prove one of the Board's most expensive failures. In terms of fulfilling the Board's objective of establishing the manufacture of cambric in the east of Scotland, the project was an almost complete failure, at a cost of some £9,000. In fairness to the Board, the objective was a worthy one. No contemporary voices were lifted in criticism of the project initially and once the French weavers had been brought across, the Board was morally committed to support them. The fundamental weakness was the idea that a centre of excellence be established to which labour would come for instruction, a principle that did not work either with Picardy or with the later highland stations. What was important was to station the instructors amongst the people, and far more effective were the Dutch weaving instructors recruited in the 1730s and placed with Scottish manufacturers for three years at a time to instruct and train their journeymen weavers. John Cockburn, for one, was enthusiastic about their work, (30) and they certainly assisted the establishment of several centres of fine linen weaving in the north-east of Scotland. Private enterprise also worked along similar lines; manufacturers

often recruited Dutch master-weavers for themselves. But the inflow of skilled men
began to die away after mid-century, which is yet another indication of the increasing
maturity of the Scottish industry.

III

A third factor on which the expansion of the linen industry made demands was
the supply of capital. Fixed capital investment was relatively limited except in the
bleaching and finishing processes, although the aggregate investment in lint-mills,
given their numbers, should not be overlooked. It was stated in 1788 that a lint-mill
could not be erected for less than £100 and some had cost much more. (31) But
bleachfields (and printfields) were much more costly to erect. Drying fields and
canals had to be laid out, buildings erected and machinery installed. By mid-century,
erection costs for some of the smaller fields such as Ford and Gifford came to
between £300-400, most were in a higher range of £700-800, and a few cost very
much more. To lay out and equip Saltoun bleachfield between 1747 and 1750 cost
the British Linen Company no less than £2120, and in Luncarty William Sandeman
spent in just under ten years over £4700 on his field and machinery. (32) The fixed
capital investment demanded by the expansion of the Scottish bleaching industry
from a handful of fields in the 1730s to 90 or so in the 1770s was therefore considerable, especially when allowance is made for the cost of keeping a field in repair and
technically up to date. For example, the drying-house designed to deal with cloth
during wet days, which was invented in the early 1750s, was an item speedily required by nearly every commercial bleachfield in Scotland. As the cost of construction
was not less than £90 and on occasion much more, this addition must have represented,
despite the grant generally given by the Board of Trustees to cover part of the cost,
a significant increment in the fixed capital of any bleachfield.

The capital resources required for a bleachfield had to meet not only investment
in fixed capital but also to provide working capital to pay wages and purchase
materials. Some part of the fixed capital was provided by the Board of Trustees. Their
expenditure on the bleaching sector, mostly in the form of grants which, as they
acknowledged, covered only a fraction of the costs of erection and equipment,
amounted between 1727 and 1800 to £24,784. (33) Most of this was concentrated
in two shorter periods, 1727-38 and 1747-56, when it may well have lubricated the
expansion of the sector. But the bulk of the capital required, both fixed and circulating, must have come from private sources, often by way of participation in a bleaching copartnery or company. The emergence of the company is one of the indications
of the increasing mobilisation of capital in the linen industry, and although (significantly) most common in the bleaching and finishing sector, by the 1740s they were
not confined to that alone. A factory for the weaving of fine linen was set up at
Shuttlefield in 1741 by a copartnership of Glasgow merchants concerned in the
tobacco trade. (34) There were others in the same line, and also in the manufacture
of coarse linen, notably at Arbroath (Wallace, Gardyne and Company) and at
Montrose. Manufacturing on a larger scale and for more distant markets required
more medium and short-term capital to finance the purchase of raw materials, the

payment of wages, the holding of stock, and bridge the gap till returns from sales came in.

It is easier to identify the sources from which investment in the linen industry came than to quantify the contribution, relative or absolute, of each. Prominent participants in bleaching and other concerns were merchants, often but not always active themselves in the linen industry. Tobacco merchants invested in a number of linen bleaching concerns in and around Glasgow. (35) The Falls of Dunbar held one-third of the shares in the Dunbar Bleachfield Company formed in 1766. (36) Of the Montrose Company's shares of £600 each, two were held by local merchants, and three by Scots resident at London as merchants and linen factors. (37) Many other similar examples could be given. Another major source of capital was the land. Land-owners, such as Lord Milton and Lord Deskford, helped to provide finance for the linen industry in a variety of ways. Milton made substantial loans to the British Linen Company (as well as being the largest proprietor of stock) and assisted with the erection of two bleachfields on his estate. But investment was not confined to merchants and landowners. Amongst the original proprietors of the British Linen Company were several lawyers, a jeweller, two surgeons and the Incorporation of Goldsmiths in Edinburgh. (38) The industry tapped, therefore, a wide range of sources for provision of longer and shorter-term capital and finance. In the latter respect, the banking system may have played some part through the cash credits system, and certainly the advent of the British Linen Company, in its dual role of manufacturing company and source of capital for the linen industry, with resources far exceeding those of any other Scottish company – its *paid-up* capital amounted to no less than £43,736 by 1751 (39) – did something to promote the process of growth. It is much less easy to evaluate the effect of expenditure of the Board of Trustees on the linen industry, in all, in the eighteenth century some £200,000 from normal income, and a further £89,000 from the flax fund, plus £27,000 from the highland fund, (40) but it should have contributed to easing the capital position although so much of its expenditure was wasted in unproductive ventures.

Two points remain which can be stated but perhaps not resolved. It is impossible to ascertain how much of the industry's expansion was internally financed by the retention of profits, but this must have been important. A second, and related, issue is the relative importance of circulating capital as against fixed capital investment. With most of the production of yarn and cloth organised under the domestic system, fixed capital investment was relatively limited in the industry except (as already discussed) in bleaching, and the crucial need of the manufacturer was to find the initial sources of support to purchase flax and pay wages. But once he was started, with the prevalence of credit at all stages of the productive processes, the expansion of his activities could be, and was, built on a relatively slender initial capital base and extended by the ploughing-back of profits, as long as sales (and payments) were regular. Perhaps typical of the class of linen entrepreneurs who rose in this way was John Young of Coupar Angus. A report in 1747 said 'from a very small stock to begin with he is reckoned to be worth £3-4000.' (41) Men like Young, Richard Neilson of Dundee and Walter Fergus of Kirkcaldy were the successful tip of the iceberg: the failure rate was high.

It was not perhaps unhealthy for the industry that there were frequent fluctuations

in demand, which tended to prevent an over-expansion of credit. Expansion was by
no means uninterrupted in the linen industry; there were decades of relative stagnation,
the 1730s and the 1770s, and bouts of severe depression as in 1754-5 and 1772-4. And
although the underlying trend of output throughout the eighteenth century was upwards, only on three occasions during the entire period was expansion sustained for
more than five consecutive years. Much more 'typical' was a pattern of two or three
years of growth, followed by one or two of contraction, in which those who had
over-reached themselves were thinned out. Fluctuations and instability sprang from
changes on both the supply and the demand side. There was always an inherent tendency to overproduction implicit in the structure of the linen industry, with its many
small manufacturers and independent weavers (though the numbers of the latter may
well have diminished during the second half of the century). One pamphleteer in the
early years of the eighteenth century went so far as to claim that in Scotland 'the
market does not control production ... Linen is bought and sold as an Adventure.' (42)
On the demand side, the situation was seldom stable. Markets, particularly the American
colonial market, could change quickly, and the position of competitiors could alter;
Scotland was after all only one linen-manufacturing nation amongst several. A prime
source of instability was, of course, war. It altered markets, could disrupt competitors
and the supply of raw materials alike, as in the Seven Years War.

For whatever cause, fluctuations were frequent and often the result was to check
an over-expansion of mercantile credit and debt. Bankruptcies were common during
downturns in trade, or when for any reason credit was restricted. The effect of the
American non-importation agreements in 1769 and again in the early 1770s was to
bring down several linen manufacturing firms in the east of Scotland (including that
of E. McCulloch & Co.) (43), firms which otherwise might well have come down in
the early years of the American War of Independence. Contraction, one might speculate,
in the early 1770s reduced dislocation in the later 1770s. Of course, some part of the
burden of a downturn in trade was passed on from the linen entrepreneur to his workforce through discontinuance of work. During depression and times of unemployment,
the urban worker generally suffered more severely than his rural counterpart who
might be able to draw on income from ancillary agricultural activities and produce
from his plot or pendicle of land. Wages were usually lower in the countryside than
in the towns, but so also were the risks of total unemployment and starvation, and
this feature alone goes far towards explaining the vitality of village textile economies
of east-central Scotland. But what the work force, urban or rural, could bear was
limited; if a downturn was severe or prolonged, then for many the only alternatives
might be emigration (as in 1772-4) (44) or enlistment. This also had the secondary
effect of retarding any recovery in output. A work force might be speedily scattered
but took time to recruit again. Such, at least, was the experience of the British Linen
Company after the temporary withdrawal of the bounty in 1753 had led to a contraction
in its manufacturing activities for two years. On attempting to re-start operations it
found that 'The Weavers formerly employed were dispersed; the young and healthy
having generally become Soldiers, the more elderly day-labourers and Barrowmen.
Such of them as could be collected were for some time very inexpert at their former
business...' (45)

The expansion of the Scottish linen industry in the eighteenth century was not without growing pains, but it did continue to grow. Its expansion rested to a large extent on an imported raw material, and in this respect there is an essential continuity of experience in Scottish textile history from flax to cotton to jute. In most years, however, this dependence did not greatly hinder the linen industry. Nor does it appear that the supply of labour held back growth. Considerably though employment in the industry rose, and more widely as it was diffused, not until the end of the eighteenth century did the reserve capacity of underemployment in Scotland show signs of exhaustion. The relationship with agriculture, so critical to the health of the linen industry in much of Scotland, came under stress in the 1790s and started to break down, with the two sources of income beginning to compete rather than to complement each other, so that spinners would no longer spin but weavers would no longer harvest. (46) During the century there is little doubt that the income position of the linen workforce was steadily improving. Rising wages and more regular employment combined to raise earnings sharply, and this must have assisted the growth of the Scottish economy. As to the supply of capital, the critical decade seems to have been the 1740s when the trigger for investment was the growth of demand and market opportunities. But the structure of production, the nature of demand and the narrow capital base exposed the industry to periodic crises. That it survived each to expand again is yet another indication of the increasing resilience of the industry and the economy.

NOTES

1. Figures for the year to 1st November, A.J. Warden, *The Linen Trade, Ancient and Modern* (London, 1864), p.480.

2. *Gentleman's Magazine,* LXXXVII (1787), 373; Scottish Record Office, Edinburgh (S.R.O.), Records of the Board of Trustees for Fisheries and Manufacturers (B.T.), NG 1/60/26, (1797), Abstract Account relative to Threadmakers who have received aid from the Board.

3. R.H. Campbell, *Scotland since 1707,* (Oxford, 1965), 41; A.J. Durie, 'The markets for Scottish linen, 1730-1775', *Scottish Historical Review,* LII (1973), 30-49.

4. H. Home, *The Progress of Flax-husbandry in Scotland* (Edinburgh, 1766), pp.20-21; J. Naismith, *Thoughts on Various Objects of Industry Pursued in Scotland* (Edinburgh, 1790), pp.149-150; S.R.O., B.T. Letter Book, NG 1/3/15, 27 March 1787.

5. S.R.O. B.T. NG 1/16/1, NG 1/60/30, Customs House returns.

6. S.R.O. B.T. NG 1/22/1-3, Account of moneys issued by the Receiver-General and Cashier.

7. S.R.O. B.T. Annual Report to the Crown, NG 1/6 (Xmas, 1786).

8. S.R.O. B.T. Letter Book, NG 1/3/15, 27 March 1787.

9. A.J. Durie, 'Linen, Flax and Iron: The British Linen Company and the Baltic' *Study Group on Eighteenth Century Russia, Newsletter 3* (1975), 36.

10. Warden, *op.cit.,* pp.639-42, *Dundee Weekly Advertiser.*

11. *Scots Magazine,* LXXX, (1809), 681, review of R. Kerr, *General View of the County of Berwick* (London, 1809).

12. G. Robertson, *General View of the Agriculture of Kincardineshire* (London, 1810), pp.284-7; J. Headrick, *General View...Angus* (Edinburgh, 1813), pp.333-6; J. Thomson, *General View...Fife* pp.207-15. Similar views are to be found in most of the Board of Agriculture Surveys. W.H.K. Turner, 'Flax cultivation in Scotland: an historical geography', *Transactions of the Institute of British Geographers,* LV (1972), 127-143.

13. S.R.O. B.T. NG 1/60/10, NG 1/42/8, State of Flax premiums.

14. A. & N.L. Clow, *The Chemical Revolution: A Contribution to Social Technology* (London, 1952), Ch. 9; K.H. Wolff, 'Textile Bleaching and the Birth of the Chemical Industry', *Business History Review,* XLVIII (1974), 143-63.

15. S.R.O. B.T. NG 1/7/8A. London Agents Book: copy letter to the Treasury.

16. N.E. McLain, 'Scottish Lint-mills, 1729-1770', *Textile History,* I (1970), 300.

17. S.R.O. B.T. NG 1/7/8A, 100.

18. Kerr, *op.cit.,* p.321.

19. E.E. Gauldie, 'Mechanical Aids to Linen Bleaching in Scotland', *Textile History,* I, 129-157.

20. A. Smith, *The Wealth of Nations* (Everyman Edition), I, 227. Others put the gain higher, e.g. William Alexander, *Northern Rural Life in the Eighteenth Century* (Aberdeen, 1877), p.138, considered that a three-fold increase in output resulted from the use of the wheel instead of the rock.

21. J. Mill, 'On the Spinning of Linen Yarn in Ross, Caithness, Etc.', *Prize Essays and Transactions of the Highland Society of Scotland,* I, (1799), LXV, states that the use of spinning wheels was not yet general in these counties: 'the rock, or spindle, which is a very slow method, being yet used by many, from the want of wheels'. See also J. Smith, *General View...Argyle* (Edinburgh, 1805), p.106.

22. 'No one invention revolutionised hand-loom weaving but...a number of small changes, often developed independently, greatly increased productivity'. D. Steel, *The Linen Industry in East Central Scotland, 1750-1900,* University of St. Andrews Ph.D. thesis, 1975, p.59.

23. National Library of Scotland, (N.L.S.), Saltoun MSS, box 327, Scheme for Encouraging Linen Manufacturers around Edinburgh.

24. Bank of Scotland Archives, Edinburgh (B.S.), British Linen Company (B.L.C.), Scottish Letter Book, E. McCulloch, Manager of the B.L.C., to David Flint, Secretary of the Board of Trustees, 20 November 1760.

25. The size and output of this sector are unknown, but contemporary estimates agree that it was large. D. MacPherson, *Annals of Commerce* (London, 1805), III, 336, (A.D. 1760), considered the quantity made for private use was not less than 'equal to the half of what is stamped'.

26. Warden, *op.cit.,* pp.556, 559, 563. The number of looms is strictly an index of production capacity rather than numbers employed, as weavers could and did work more than one loom.

27. Mill, *op.cit.,* p.63: 'As new manufacturers in the linen branch increased in Aberdeen, and the neighbourbood, the demand for Yarn grew in proportion: which forced the manufacturers to resort to the Highlands for additional aid'. See also A.J. Durie, 'Linen-spinning in the north of Scotland, 1746-1773', *Northern Scotland,* II (1974-5), 13-36.

28. A. Bald, *The Farmer and Corn Dealer's Assistant* (Edinburgh, 1780), gives a price series for Perthshire yarn for the years 1741-1776, which can be compared with isolated figures in Warden, *op.cit.,* pp.497, 525, etc. culled from *The Statistical Account of Scotland* (1791-9).

29. For example in 1749 the British Linen Company sent one of its servants Peter McKenzie across to Ireland to recruit some skilled hands for the Company's field at Saltoun. At least two of the field's master-bleachers were Irish, one of whom was Terence Dugan, who was later to take charge of his own bleachfield at Kevock Mill and Ford.

30. S.R.O. Clerk of Penecuik MSS GD 18/5904. Letter of John Cockburn, dated 29 Jan. 1739.

31. S.R.O. B.T. NG 1/3/15, 20 August 1788.

32. N.L.S. Saltoun MSS box 330, Account of Money expended on Luncarty Bleachfield (1761).

33. S.R.O. B.T. NG 1/42/1, Premiums for bleaching and the setting up of bleachfields.

34. Lawrence Colquhoun, William Crawford and Thomas Dunmore were named as proprietors of this manufacture, which in 1742 employed some 70 looms constantly in a large factory under supervision; the partners claimed that they had 'sunk £10,000 in stock'. S.R.O. B.T. NG 1/1/6 Minute of the Board, 3 December 1742; Glasgow Burgh Court Register of Deeds, B 10/15/5626.

35. T.M. Devine, 'The Colonial Trades and Industrial Investment in Scotland, c.1700-1815', *The Economic History Review,* 2nd series, XXIX (1976), 8.

36. D.S. Alexander, *The Falls of Dunbar — An 18th century Mercantile Family of Scotland,* University of Glasgow B.Litt. thesis, 1969, p.135.

37. N.L.S. Saltoun MSS box 328, Minute of an Agreement for Setting up and Establishing a Manufacture of sailcloth and other coarse linens at Montrose.

38. C.A. Malcolm, *The History of the British Linen Bank* (Edinburgh, 1950), Appendix 2.

39. B.S. B.L.C. Stock Journal 'A'.

40. The highland fund was a grant in 1753 of £3,000 p.a. for nine years to be used by the Board of Trustees for the encouragement of the linen manufacture in the highlands of Scotland. For further details on this point see Durie, 'Linen-Spinning', 24-28.

41. N.L.S. Saltoun MSS box 328, Letter (16 January 1747) from James Donaldson of Drumsheugh in response to an enquiry 'as to how the Makers and Coupers of Coarse Linen make so much profit'.

42. Guildhall Library, London, A 1.3, no. 14 in 64, *The Case of the Printed Linens of North Great Britain* (1719).

43. S.R.O. CS 29/732/21. McCulloch, former manager of the British Linen Company, attributed the losses of his company in 1769 and thereafter to 'the disturbances and combinations in America having totally stopped all exportation thither'.

44. Note the number of weavers and spinsters amongst the emigrants to America listed in V.R. Cameron, *Emigrants from Scotland to America 1774-1775* (Baltimore, 1965), pp.1-5, 33-4, 38-40, etc. On this point see also *House of Commons Reports,* III (1803), 'Report from the Committee appointed to Enquire into the State of the Linen Trade in Great Britain and Ireland', 25th May 1773, 102; *Scots Magazine,* XXXVI (1774), 479.

45. B.S. B.L.C. Minute Book of the Court of Proprietors, 4 July 1757.

46. See for example *The Statistical Account of Scotland,* XIV, (Parish of Kinfauns in Perthshire), 221. In many areas the relationship was unaffected or disturbed only temporarily, and harvesting continued to disrupt the manufacture of linen as late as the 1850s (Steel, *op.cit.,* pp.213-4.)

8. Aspects of the Rise and Decline of the Irish Cotton Industry

David Dickson

THE Irish cotton industry of the late eighteenth and early nineteenth centuries was by international standards fairly unimportant; not surprisingly it has attracted little outside notice. However in Ireland it has been cited by politicians, political economists and historians arguing the case for political separation from Britain; its apparent rise and decline could readily be presented as a dramatic demonstration of the benign economic effects of an Irish parliament, and of the debilitating consequences of constitutional integration. Modern historiography has long since modified, in some cases wholly rejected this simple causal relationship, and in its place the growth and contraction of the industry has been set in a wider economic context, economically and spatially: difficulties in the linen industry, and the early centrifugal tendencies of the British cotton industry have been given prominence, and it has been argued that cotton's subsequent contraction and decline in Ireland were not a function of the dismantling of protection, but only one aspect of the general concentration of the industry on Lancashire and Glasgow, in the second generation of industrialization. (2

These revisions are soundly based, but they lack detailed documentation; the chronology and the geography of the industry remain unspecific, and the importance assigned to parliamentary policy remains somewhat ambiguous. The purpose of this paper is, therefore, to look more closely at the role of official encouragement in creating the cotton manufacture; the nature of the 'southern dimension' of the industry, and the extent to which it differed from that in Ulster; and the relationship of nineteenth-century changes to the end of protection.

The old orthodoxy had it that the Irish cotton industry was born during the politically frenzied years of the American War, in the wake of the commercial concessions of 1779 ('free trade') and nurtured with bounties, aid and protection lavished by an independent Irish parliament after 1782. In fact cotton wool imports had been significant for several decades, averaging over 2,500 cwt. in the 1760s, 3,000 cwt. in the 1770s (3): certainly some of this wool was used for non-textile purposes such as candlewick, but it is quite apparent that as in England and Scotland at that time, there was an increasing local market for clothing fabrics based on a mixture of cotton and linen yarns. The British pattern was for these to develop in the areas associated with fine linen manufacture; in Ireland the early association was not with the east Ulster districts engaged in fine linen weaving, but around the centres of marketing, distribution and consumption – Dublin and Cork. Around Dublin, linen printing had become gradually more sophisticated since its introduction in the 1720s, supplying throughout the domestic market. (4) The Cork connection developed from the introduction of French artisans skilled in silk and cotton at Innishannon at the end of the 1740s, and was quickly taken up by several local manufacturers. Demand by the 1770s was sufficient for the spinning of cotton — on pre-existing worsted wheels — to become a rival rural occupation to the well established woollen and bay yarn spinning in parts of Cork and Kerry. Indeed the dominant female domestic industry in the Killarney district in the 1770s was cotton spinning, largely for Cork and Dublin mixed goods manufacturers. (5)

What of course was new to the enterprises that began to appear at the end of the 1770s was their adoption of some of the recent English innovations, at first mainly jennies and carding machines, and with them a tendency towards the greater concentration of production, insofar as the preparation and spinning of wool became at least a workshop activity, and often part of a greater village manufactory, where complementary new 'downstream' processes were established. Jennies were first introduced, as every text book notes, in a Belfast workhouse in 1777, but the most rapid diffusion was in the greater Dublin region.

The new so-called 'Manchester manufactories' appeared just at the period when there was considerable public support for an aggressive policy of import substitution. Imports of British new and old draperies, of cotton and part-cotton cloths, had grown sharply in the 1770s, while at the same time the remarkable long-run growth of linen exports had tapered off. Therefore from about 1780 official support was secured from three sources for the 'Manchester manufactories': the Linen Board gave grants of three-quarters of the purchase cost of carding machines and jennies for manufacturing mixed fabrics for a number of years; (6) the Dublin Society, the old patron of the woollen industry, gave bounties on the sale of all-cotton goods using Irish warp and weft and on cotton or mixed fabrics printed in Ireland; (7) and there was Parliament itself. Since the 1750s grants to a range of infrastructural projects and industrial enterprises, charitable, municipal and private, had been made from the surplus on revenue; in the early 1780s enlarged funds specifically to aid trade and manufactures were voted, rising from £5,000 in 1781, through £20,000 in 1783, to £96,000 in the following session, (8) and from these direct grants were made to a selection of petitioners in several industries. Over this period, these included more than twenty manufacturers claiming to be engaged in laying out substantial capital on plant for cotton or part-cotton manufacture. (9) More than half of these came from Leinster outside Dublin. Part of the 1782 grant was ear-marked to be used as a five per cent bounty on the internal sale of all mixed fabrics, and in the next session this was extended to pure cottons as well as several other manufactures. The budget allocated for this bounty fluctuated between £15,000 and £20,000 between 1783 and 1788, when it was fixed at £17,000 for a number of years. (10)

These official gestures were the response, not the cause of the new industrial departure. Only a minority of petitioners seem to have received aid. But the preferences of Parliament were to some extent to determine the next phase of the industry, because although political connections presumably influenced particular decisions, there was one condition to which all successful applicants, at least those after 1782, had to conform: they had to be based outside a ten-mile radius of Dublin. (11) On the initiative it seems of the Commons Committee of Trade, there was an attempt to redistribute as far as possible the large labour force of weavers and other workers in the woollen, silk and linen trades concentrated in the capital, mainly in the Liberties suburb. The complaints of the masters in these and other workshop manufactures about the prevalence of combinations had reached a crescendo in the 1770s, and recurring difficulties in certain trades were put down to the excessive demands and disorder of journeymen. The ineffectiveness of the first general Combinations Act of 1780, and perhaps heightened concern about the danger of urban disorder (in the wake of the Gordon Riots) led to the new policy.(12) Cotton, beginning to attract Dublin manufacturers and weavers out of older lines in silk and other fine fabrics, and with its promise of being a major employer of labour, no doubt seemed a suitable means of achieving the desired diaspora. A number of manufacturers complied by transferring at least part of their activities to rural locations, receiving additional encouragement from the fact that the disposal of the bounty on sales was similarly biassed against Dublin manufacturers. (13) However, most assistance went to new landlord-sponsored enterprises (akin to the many linen projects where attempts had been made to combine the establishment of manufacturing on an estate with the creation or extension of an estate village). In Leinster it would seem that most landlords were formally or informally in partnership with one or more Dublin master manufacturers or merchants (even before Parliament was encouraging such a move) whose function was primarily to recruit skilled labour and provide a marketing outlet for the landowners; technical know-how, the task of erecting and maintaining buildings and new machinery, was largely in the hands of English superintendents.

The most important of these enterprises in Leinster were those at Balbriggan, Malahide and Prosperous. At Balbriggan the landlord, Baron Hamilton, expanded an existing village where there was a short tradition of cotton-stocking weaving, by setting up jenny shops, distributing looms and employing a succession of Lancashire manufacturers (the majority of whom, it seemed, migrated because of financial embarrassment at home) to instal water spinning. In 1782 he encouraged a large Dublin cloth-importing partnership to extend the weaving and finishing end, and they appear to have gradually assumed control of manufacturing in the town over the next ten years. (14) Hamilton's migrants may have been the first to instal water-frames in the country, but apparently the first *successful* Arkwright mill, in Leinster at least, was at Colonel Talbot's Malahide manufactory, which was set to work in 1783. Talbot also relied on Dublin resources for weaving, and was in partnership with a major Liberties manufacturer in an attempt to transplant weavers. Both these landed proprietors received £5,000 grants from Parliament. (15) But the most remarkable enterprise was a settlement west of Dublin, christened Prosperous by its founder, Robert Brooke, c.1780; he was the second son of a Cavan landowner, and had inherited small properties including the site of his new town. On leave from service in the East India Company with £18,000 to invest, he commenced in partnership with his younger brother, a Dublin merchant, and his brother-in-law, James Kerchoffe a cabinet-maker, to develop a major manufacturing community not, he later claimed, that he had any 'inducement from an idea of profit', although thinking 'in the end it might turn out advantageously'; (16) whether by his persuasiveness or by his political connections, he secured over a five-year period unprecedented parliamentary help: by committing his own and his family's fortune in the scheme, he secured over £4,000 in direct grants and, in 1784, after claiming to have invested over £40,000, a £32,000 public loan on the security of his property. (17) Although part of the operation (the print-works) was initially sited on the edge of Dublin, his public obligation was to re-settle 2,000 city artisans over ten years in his remote and more regulated environment. In the year 1783/4, 467 individuals were enticed to move to Prosperous. (18) Most of the stages of production of a wide range of half-cottons and stockings took place around the new town, but of the 4,765 people estimated to be employed directly and indirectly by Brooke and partners c.1785, only about half resided in the immediate district. (19) With his brother-in-law he was involved in the earliest spinning mill on the Liffey at Celbridge, and in a textile-machine making factory in Dublin, which between 1781 and 1784 sold around the kingdom 361 spinning jennies (25,750 spindles). (20)

The scale of Brooke's investments caught public imagination but by 1785, when he again approached parliament, now to seek a modification of his loan arrangement, his affairs began to attract more critical scrutiny. And although his request was acceded to, the prodigality of his indiscriminate investment was becoming apparent, and the production bottlenecks, labour disputes and marketing difficulties seriously weakened his liquidity and his credit. He failed to recruit Manchester partners in 1785, and the death of his brother, the actual manager, seems to have precipitated his bankruptcy in 1786. Parliamentary trustees tried to maintain the various establishments with only partial and short-term success. Much of the massive investment had been sunk in housing and less productive aspects of the venture. Anyway, Prosperous was a totally unsuitable site; it lacked any fall of water and had only its proximity to the Bog of Allen and the Grand Canal to commend it. (21)

Direct grants from parliament, from the Linen Board, and from the Dublin Society disappeared rapidly after this episode. Even the abolition of the bounty on home sales seems to have been contemplated, but in 1788 it was guaranteed for nine years at a reducing rate. (22) Yet if such intervention was short-lived, it cannot simply be dismissed as irrelevant. The considerable migration from England in the 1780s which assisted the transfer of the new techniques – from the spinning jenny to cylinder printing (23) – was lubricated by public encouragement. The aid given to rural manufactories did help to consolidate several centres of Leinster textile activity. Bounties were credited, at the time they were being phased out, with having encouraged a manufacture of calico and muslin sufficient to supply the home market. (24) And there were positive side effects of the Prosperous fiasco: a number of those introduced to cotton by Brooke went on to become quietly successful cotton manufacturers around Dublin. (25) Most of the cotton weft across the country was probably being spun on jennies made by the partnership when Brooke, having gained a special discharge, returned to East India service as Governor of St. Helena. (26)

The legislature also influenced cotton in quite another manner: through the upward adjustment of import duties on mixed and cotton goods, with the aim of excluding British imports. The wave of agitation in 1783-4 seeking protecting duties for Irish manufactures was in part politically motivated, and although opinion among those involved in cotton was divided, this partly reflected a division of interest between those using linen warps (available at cheaper rates than in England) who had an eye to export opportunities, and those in pure cottons such as calico, whose concern was exclusively the home market. (27) In the event the old import rates remained on all but printed calico, which was raised. (28) And shortly after, Irish cotton manufacturers were faced with the unwelcome prospect of the general equalization of duties between Britain and Ireland (Pitt's Commercial Propositions) against which they lobbied. Ironically it was the alarm of the English cotton interest at the potential Irish competition, and the threats of men like Robert Peel to transfer at least part of their operations to Ireland that helped the English Opposition to defeat Pitt's measure. (29)

The import tariffs to which so much retrospective significance was attached, were in fact only fully established in 1792, at which time English muslins and printed calicoes became effectively excluded by prohibitive duties. (30) The immediate background to this move is unclear, but it was in a changing context. As Table 1 suggests, (3 the late eighties and early nineties were a climax to the first period of expansion in the industry; looms may not have expanded proportionately in that there was a considerable shift into pure cottons, as the domestic supply of cotton warp improved; this came about through the spread in the mid and late eighties of Arkwright frames, at least some taking the form of water-mills. The national total of four such mills in 1785 grew to seven in 1791; (32) this was small indeed by English or Scottish standards, (33) yet it is clear that substantial capital formation was occurring in the industry — not primarily in spinning or in weaving — but in the development of finishing and printing. This is illustrated by the case of the leading Cork cotton partnership of the period: the Sadleir brothers, starting in 1781 by importing 'machines and hands' from Manchester, commenced spinning on jennies in Cork city (operating 1,606 spindles in 1783), and outside the city at Glasheen they established loomshops for 76 weavers on their premises. As they expanded, the weaving there was restricted to finer goods, with a putting-out system adopted for coarser cotton weaving. Glasheen became primarily their finishing and printing centre; altogether they claimed to have spent £8,000 by 1783, employing nearly 1,000 people in the manufacture. (34) Between then and the mid-nineties their growing activities included a spinning and weaving factory employing at least 600 females at Mitchelstown on a site provided rent-free by Lord Kingsborough, and much more comprehensive printing facilities at Glasheen, to supply which they were actually buying in the plain cottons of other local manufacturers. (35) Henry Sadleir claimed that by 1796 £40,000 had been invested in the enterprise, then divided between at least four locations, and that it gave employment to some 4,000. (36) Yet for all this their only water-spinning mill appears, in a survey taken c.1800, to have been one of the smallest of the 16 then in the country. (37)

Similarly around Dublin by the end of the 1790s the commanding heights of the industry were occupied by those whose major investment was in the printing sector: men such as John Duffy who took over the former linen-printing works at Ballsbridge in 1791, and by 1800 calculated his capital investment at £21,000; (38) Edward Clarke, the builder of Palmerstown village who from 1788 linked up with Comerford and O'Brien's large Balbriggan enterprise, to print its calico; he survived their bankruptcy in 1793, and estimated his capital invested in 1800 at £20,000; (39) and John Orr (originally a Paisley muslin manufacturer) who had taken over the Wicklow estate

Table 1   Irish imports of cotton wool and cotton yarn in cwt.   1781-98 (three-year averages)

| | BELFAST | | | CORK | | | DUBLIN | | | NATIONAL IMPORTS |
	Wool	Yarn	% of total nat. imports	Wool	Yarn	% of total nat. imports	Wool	Yarn	% of total nat. imports	(Wool + Yarn)
1781-83*	527	1	12.9	1520	12	34.9	1934	28	44.8	4384
1784-86	701	21	9.9	2207	14	30.3	4012	109	56.2	7329
1787-89	2319	194	19.9	3326	11	26.5	6035	249	49.9	12599
1790-92	2146	638	15.8	4409	16	25.2	8268	1269	35	17591
1793-95	2694	1230	26.5	3622	231	26	4951	1202	41.5	14833
1796-98	1409	1139	18.6	3191	210	24.9	4626	2331	51	13653

Source: N.L.I. Exports and Imports of Ireland, 1763-1824.

* Year beginning 26 March until 1800, when it reverted to 6 Jan.

H

village of Stratford-on-Slaney about 1790 (which had earlier been established in imitation of Prosperous); his investment in what was mainly a print-works was put at about £20,000 in 1795, £30,000 in 1800. (40)

In that year there were about twenty-three printing works in Ireland; over half (and the more important ones) were near Dublin and Cork, the rest in east Ulster (and many of them also linen bleach-works). (41) It is one indication that the industry was by no means a predominantly Ulster phenomenon in 1800. Raw material imports also suggest that the Dublin region was the centre, with Cork and Belfast each importing about a quarter of total Irish imports. In the 1780s the growing Belfast industry was similar in organisation to that elsewhere: a few major partnerships — such as Grimshaw and Wilson; McCracken, Joy and MacCabe — investing in all stages of the manufacture. (However, by the 1790s this was changing: the expansion of the water-spinning within 15 miles of the town, and after 1789, the use of steam-power, was already ahead of other districts. By about 1800 eight of the sixteen mills in Ireland were close to Belfast (the furthest 16 miles away), and contained 54.5 per cent of national capacity. (43) Furthermore a survey c.1802 revealed that just under half the cotton looms in the country were in Ulster. (44) The apparent discrepancy between the proportions can be accounted for in two ways; firstly and most obviously, it can be assumed that spinning outside Ulster was less mechanised, that jennies and animal-powered frames were more important; secondly that a greater proportion of the manufacture in the Belfast region was becoming devoted to finer and lighter cloth (i.e. those using less cotton) than elsewhere. Muslin was introduced about 1790, largely it seems from Scotland, and was gaining on calico as the major cloth type in most of the district by the turn of the century. (45) It required finer yarns than the cords, common calicoes or other coarser cloths more prominent in the south, but it could be cheaply finished by a rapid bleach, unlike heavier fashion fabrics that normally underwent dyeing or printing.

The problem remains as to why the northern spinning sector was more advanced by 1800, for probably all the mills there were still of the Arkwright type, i.e. not producing fine enough yarn for muslin. (This was being supplied by local hand- or horse-operated mules, and from second-generation English and Scottish mills equipped with power-mules: the growth of the latter gave rise to an Anglo-Irish trade in yarn, more than half of which in the nineties was being imported at Belfast and Bangor.) (46) The greater channelling of southern investment into printing yards and weaving shops is one explanation. However, was there a differential in the supply of risk capital and of labour? Chronic liquidity problems were common to major manufacturers, north and south, as the high incidence of bankruptcy, particularly in 1792-3 and 1800-1, demonstrates. (47) The continuous pressure, particularly on manufacturers involved in all stages of production, to expand investment in order to meet English competition on the home market, was matched by the demand of warehousemen and haberdashers for credit terms as favourable as those offered by English suppliers. The experience of Nicholas Grimshaw, acknowledged leader of the Belfast industry, who was involved in bankruptcy proceedings in 1788 and 1799, and who nearly failed in 1793, had many parallels; (48) some recovered, but when the Sadleirs in Cork failed in 1801, with outstanding debts of £38,000, (49) it was a permanent injury for the whole Cork manufacture. But illiquidity and capital scarcity are of course separate problems.

The very considerable investment at this time in grain-based industries — milling, malting, brewing and distilling — in Leinster and Munster is the strongest argument against assuming capital supply difficulties. Certainly manufacturers occasionally complained of the unwillingness of other merchants to become partners in cotton ventures, (50) and indeed the rapidity of the turnover of partnerships cannot have been encouraging. It would seem however by the large outlays of capital actually made by a number of manufacturers and printers that the regular reinvestment of profits was sufficient to maintain investment momentum.

A comparison of entrepreneurial origins and textile traditions provides a more satisfactory explanation for the growing north-south contrast. The manufacture in Cork was the result of a marriage of the cotton/linen tradition with the capital and organization of merchants coming out of the declining worsted yarn trade; thus two of the leading manufacturers, Sadleirs and Thomas Deaves, had been major putters-out of wool to be combed and spun, and exporters of the yarn to England. The fitful decline of this trade — and of the local new draperies trade — over the last quarter of the century, diverted into cotton men with experience in exploiting Munster's cheap rural female labour, and in employing in manufactories combers, weavers and dyers. Their organisational experience, transferred to cotton, helped to mould its vertically-integrated, yet in most processes, labour-intensive structure; spinners were introduced to the simple cotton loom, and combers to the carding machine and the jenny. In Leinster after the early initiatives of landowners, most of the capitalised cotton manufacturers, those who developed printing and to a lesser extent spinning, had previously been importers of woollen or 'Manchester' goods: (51) their expertise lay in a knowledge of the local market for fashion goods. Under them were the small manufacturers who had moved from silk and woollen weaving to become jenny-shop and loom-shed owners. Apart from south Munster, the other district of the bay yarn trade was Queen's County and the upper Barrow valley, and there also its decline caused Dublin- and locally based dealers to transfer to cotton, so that by 1802 there were about 4,000 cotton weavers active in this area. (52) The northern manufacturers were more varied: early Belfast manufacturers came from quite disparate trades; some had been haberdashers, linen drapers and bleachers, but the role of linen was far more important in determining the type of cotton that came to dominate the district: the traditional association of the Lagan valley with the weaving of finer linen cloths provided a skilled workforce, well-equipped to transfer to muslin.

As in 1785 with the Commercial Proposition the most vociferous industrial lobby against the Act of Union and its threat of free trade were the cotton manufacturers. Now it was the heightened protection given muslin and printed calico rather than bounties that they feared to lose. (53) But their threat to the English industry as potential exporters had evaporated: rather the concession by Pitt of a gradual dismantling of duties over 21 years 'greatly discontented' Peel and his associates who sought access to the Irish market in calicoes and muslins. (54) Duties were left at their existing levels till 1808, and were gradually lowered to a rate of 10 per cent *ad valorem* in eight instalments, with a full customs union to take place five years later.

The trend of imports over the period of the dismantling of the duties (Table 2) presents a highly unstable pattern of growth:

Table 2 Irish imports of cotton wool and cotton yarn in cwt. 1799-1835 (three-year averages)

| | BELFAST | | | CORK | | | DUBLIN | | | National Imports |
	Wool	Yarn	% of total nat. imports	Wool	Yarn	% of total nat. imports	Wool	Yarn	% of total nat. imports	(Wool + Yarn)
1799-1801	3741	1095	25	3442	202	18.8	6043	3978	51.8	19333
1802-04	6132	1687	30.6	2007	434	9.6	6233	6119	48.4	25514
1805-07	12122	2585	46.4	1875	429	7.3	7865	4997	40.6	31680
1808-10	23550	2907	54.8	2423	71	5.2	13065	5326	38.1	48283
1811-13	16990	4627	46.3	4805	466	11.3	11319	4203	33.3	46675
1814-16	11426	1996	48.3	1910	356	8.2	7059	3240	37.1	27777
1817-19	13586	3391	44.9	1645	2150	10	10547	5023	41.2	37820
1820-22	19962	6272	52.5	3139	2419	11.1	10217	6183	32.8	49934
1835	17160	4018	73	360	n.g.		2944	n.g.		28833

Sources: N.L.I. Exports and Imports, 1763-1823; Second Report of the Commissioners appointed to consider and recommend a General System of Railways for Ireland (P.P., 1837-38, XXXV, 817, 819, 822, 836).

The commonly accepted picture of the post-Union industry, growing but inexorably concentrating on the Belfast region until it bowed out to linen in the 1830s, is substantially incorrect, whatever allowances are made for the import data. In the first place, the most rapid phase of growth appears in the first decade (both in Belfast and Dublin), imports reaching a level hardly surpassed in the early twenties after the recovery from the post-war recession. Secondly, while Belfast's more than five-fold growth in imports is remarkable, Dublin's from a higher base line also grew. The real stagnation occurred in south Munster, where Cork's triennial-average imports in this period only twice moved above the level of the early 1790s.

The growth in Belfast's imports from 1802 was associated with the appearance of a number of much larger mule-equipped mills, such as the two built at Bangor by McWilliams, a Scot, in partnership with Hannay, a well-established local muslin manufacturer and the landlord, Col. Ward; the first, completed in 1803, cost about £25,000 and the second, built about 1806 and certainly steam-powered, was reckoned on its completion 'more extensive than any hitherto erected in Ireland'. (55) Around the vicinity of Belfast there were 15 steam-powered mills either built or reconstructed between 1801 and 1811; a contemporary estimate of the capital thus sunk was £120,000, and the total steam horsepower was put at 212. At the same time in the Belfast area there were 12 mills wholly driven by water, and six by horse (56). Growth brought certain structural changes: prior to 1800 the town had imported most of its cotton wool from Britain and Iberia, but in most years after 1800 the greater part of its supply was shipped direct from the United States. And the spinners became more specialized, now able to supply most counts of yarn sought by the increasingly numerous small muslin manufacturers, (57) but less involved themselves by 1810 in weaving or finishing. (58)

In the Dublin region the first decade was a period of considerable if less spectacular growth. However its character was very different. Yarn imports from England and Scotland, which were relatively declining in importance in Belfast, increased markedly in Dublin until 1804 and 1805, when the actual weight of yarn, imported mainly from England, was greater than that of wool: the position was reversed somewhat towards the end of the decade, but even so the Dublin spinning sector trailed the Belfast one. The weaving of coarser cottons such as coarse cords, common calico, and checks was the major area of growth, although a number of new print-works appeared, so that there was still a buoyant market for white calico. (59)

The stagnation of Cork imports in this period was a consequence of the collapse of the large general manufacturers, working in a number of lines. One possible explanation was the changing trade pattern of the region: its early advantage of a regular trade with Iberia and the West Indies, giving it access to cotton on favourable terms, was changing by 1800 with the decline of its general Atlantic trade in provisions, and the shift in cotton supplies to mainland America. The manufacture became concentrated on the old woollen and linen town of Bandon, where two major mills (the larger costing apparently £30,000) were constructed towards the end of the decade; the staple cloth of the district was cords. (60)

The commercial crisis of 1809-11 ushered in a long period of general difficulty for the industry, with bankruptcies probably peaking in 1814-15. The crisis appeared to have been caused initially by the dumping of British cloths, particularly printed calico and muslin, on the Irish market in 1809, but this was only a precipitant. More important were the general commercial difficulties and slackness of home demand in the next decade; the intermittent appearance of cotton cloth (and yarn) in Irish exports in the 1810s was a consequence of over-capacity. Manufacturers generally claimed that exports were an unprofitable gamble, resorted to at times of domestic glut. (61) The falling level of duties cannot therefore be blamed for these difficulties; imports of the formerly protected lines from Britain only built up after 1820 at a time when the home market appears to have been recovering. (62)

Under pressure from the printers and some of the larger manufacturers, the final customs union was postponed in 1820, a decision that was reversed three years later, when immediate abolition was forced through. Prior to this *volte-face,* a parliamentary enquiry revealed a division of opinion among Irish manufacturers: the great Dublin printing firms vigorously opposed duty abolition, claiming that higher production costs arising from their large coal consumption, the limited market and dearer raw materials, would put them out of business if they had to compete on equal terms on the Irish market. But for manufacturers of middle-range goods (such as 'stout' and common calico), where cheaper Irish labour was an increasing factor, the prospect of the duty-free entry of their goods, finished or unfinished, on to the British market seemed to offer new opportunities. (63)

Absence of customs data masks the actual consequences of free trade. The 1820s were certainly a watershed, but the precise chronology is unclear. In the north, there was a recovery in investment after 1820, and the increasing cotton imports of those years were not merely taking up the slack of the previous decade; a number of new and much larger mills were constructed, such as that of Mulholland's in Belfast (64) But hard on the heels of this was the growing tendency for the muslin weaving sector to pass into the hands of Scottish agents, who put out both local and Scottish yarn; the first such agency was reportedly set up in Belfast in the year of free trade, and the practice grew rapidly in the late twenties. (65) At about the same time there were decisive improvements in flax-spinning, which caused most Belfast cotton spinners gradually to transfer operations: in 1824 there were 22 cotton mills in the Belfast region, in 1840 only 10. (66)

In Leinster and Munster, the 1820s were more traumatic. The hopes that Irish calico and cord would find a niche in the English market, or would attract English putters-out were dashed, firstly because of the recession of 1825-26 which caused the greatest run of failures in Dublin in the history of the industry, and secondly because of the fairly rapid growth of power-loom weaving in England at this time, affecting immediately coarser lines such as cords. Calico weaving continued into the 1830s, but in Queen's County rather than Dublin city itself. (67) Ironically the Dublin printing trade weathered free trade until at least the late thirties by working increasingly for the Manchester market. (68) Around Bandon, where coarse cords manufacture had thrived briefly, helped by the appearance of English agencies, the slump in the mid-twenties followed by the advent of the power-looms had a devastating effect: Bandon experienced rapid decay and emigration, probably on a scale unique by pre-Famine standards. (69)

The development of cotton in the generation after free trade was chiefly encompassed by the growing relationship with Glasgow. Muslin embroidery joined muslin

weaving as a major source of employment in a number of districts over Ulster.
Scottish agencies penetrated as far as Donegal and Balbriggan, (70) and at its peak
in the 1850s there were nearly as many looms in muslin as there had been in cotton
generally in Ulster at the beginning of the century. (71) But whereas the total labour
force in all branches of the Irish industry c.1810 may have approached 80,000, (72)
the latter-day muslin weaving trade generated little further employment.

Outside Ulster one enterprise emerged to be a lasting exception to the general
trend of contraction from the late 1820s: David Malcomson, a Clonmel Quaker
originally from the north, who had made a fortune in the grain trade and turned to
the cotton manufacture in 1825 on a virgin site, Portlaw, near Waterford. Fear for
the future of the grain trade with the prospect of foreign competition on the British
market, compounded with a measure of philanthropy inspired by James Cropper,
led him to build up a vertically-integrated complex, using power-looms from the
beginning and manufacturing plain cottons; (73) at first the Irish market seems to
have taken most of the firm's output, but later a wide range of overseas markets were
being supplied (via Liverpool). (74) The history of this firm, which expanded its
production continuously until the 1860s while diversifying into a number of discrete
fields of investment at home and abroad (ending in spectacular bankruptcy c.1874),
lies beyond this paper. However, its growth, taken together with the northern survival
of muslin weaving, is a reminder that the contraction of cotton in Ireland in the
nineteenth century was more relative than absolute: the consumption of cotton at
the Malcomson factory in the 1850s, approaching 20,000 cwt. p.a., (75) was more
than the national import in 1800. And their Portlaw investment alone, put at £100,000
in 1847, (76) was perhaps the equivalent of one-third the total fixed capital in the
Irish industry in 1800.

There is no difficulty in seeing why the Irish cotton industry failed to grow after
the 1820s: the near disappearance of Ireland's extra-British trading links, the absence
of coal, the external economies British producers enjoyed as a consequence of industrial concentration. What is in fact far less easy to assume as being inevitable is the
earlier degree of growth in the industry. It is surely reasonable to conclude that the
effect of official intervention in the period of bounties and protection was greatly
to strengthen a process that would have occurred to a more limited extent in a free
trade setting; after all, the centrifugal tendency was fairly evident in Scotland and
England in the early decades of industrialization. Yet the momentum of the industry
in Ireland was hardly paralleled in peripheral areas in Britain. The question remains
how far the level of investment in Ireland up to 1810 was related to business confidence that protection would be indefinitely continued (or that by the time it was
removed the technical and marketing advantages of British manufacturers over the
Irish would have narrowed to the point where cheaper Irish labour would more than
compensate), or whether it was simply a consequence of the high profits made in a
protected market. Free traders argued of course that the latter was the case, while
Irish manufacturers stressed the former.

The effects of the implementation of free trade can be seen in the short term to
have increased specialization in areas where Irish manufacturers enjoyed relative cost
advantages, but in the longer run to have hastened the end of parts of the industry
that with moderate protection might have lingered on another generation.

NOTES

1. I would like to thank the following for help during my research for this paper:
Mr W.H. Crawford and Mr T. Parkhill of the Public Record Office of Northern
Ireland; Prof. J.S. Donnelly, Mr J. Fitzgerald, Mr N. Gamble, Dr H.D. Gribbon, Ms
C. Mayes; also Prof. L.M. Cullen for helpful comments on an earlier draft. For the
use made of the Foster MSS I would like to thank the Deputy Keeper of Records,
P.R.O of Northern Ireland, and Viscount Masserene and Ferrard.

2. Cf. C. Gill, *The Rise of the Irish Linen Industry* (Oxford, 1925), pp.227-44;
J.J. Monaghan, 'The Rise and Fall of the Belfast Cotton Industry', *Irish Historical
Studies,* III (1942-3); E.R.R. Green, *The Lagan Valley 1800-50* (London, 1949),
pp.95-111; H.D. Gribbon, *The History of Water Power in Ulster* (Newton Abbot,
1969), pp.110-122; L.M. Cullen, *An Economic History of Ireland since 1660* (London,
1972), pp.105-8, 119-20, 122-3.

3. The customs data used in this article are the copy ledgers of Irish exports and
imports, 1763-1823, in the National Library of Ireland.

4. A.K. Longfield, 'The History of the Irish Linen and Cotton Printing Industry
in the Eighteenth Century', *Journal of the Royal Society of Antiquaries of Ireland,*
7th ser. VII (1937), 26-52.

5. *Report and Observations of Robert Stephenson made to the...Trustees of the
Linen and Hempen Manufactures for the years 1760 and 1761* (Dublin, 1762), p.36;
Report of John Arbuthnot to the... Trustees of the Linen and Hempen Manufactures
[1783], pp.36, 38-43.

6. Gill, *op.cit.,* pp.228-9.

7. P.R.O.N.I. Foster MSS, D.562/8895, Robert Brooke, Dublin to Dr Lyster,
12 Jan. 1784; H.F. Berry, *A History of the Royal Dublin Society* (London, 1915),
pp.72, 153, 204.

8. *Statutes (Ireland), 23 and 24 Geo. III c.l; 25 Geo. III c.48.*

9. *Journals of the House of Commons of Ireland,* X, 218, 232, 235, 239, 240;
XI, 40, 44, 48, 51, 54, 55, 58, 59, 65, 66, 88, 313, 318, 325, 326, 334, 339, 389.

10. *Statutes (Ire.), 23 and 24 Geo. III c.l, c.33; 25 Geo. III c.48; 26 Geo. III c.46;
27 Geo. III c.13.*

11. Manufacturers who erected water-powered machinery and employed thirty
or more people in a five to 10 mile zone were also eligible.

12. Cf. M.O'Connell, *Irish Politics and Social Conflict in the Age of the American
Revolution* (Philadelphia, 1965), pp.259-64.

13. *Statutes (Ire.), 25 Geo. III c.48.* £5,000 from the general fund was allocated
to help in the purchase of jennies for manufacturers so moving (the general Linen
Board scheme seems to have ended in the previous year), and £4,000 was provided
to fee apprentices from Charter Schools etc. Manufacturers who moved included
one Smith, an Islandbridge printer who went to Mosney, a Mrs Morgan who apparently
went from Dublin to Dundalk, and Carroll & Co., printers and manufacturers, who
went from the North Strand to Garristown.

14. *Report of John Arbuthnot...* [1782], p.5; *Report of Arbuthnot,* 1783, pp.63,
68; *J.H.C.I.,* X, 235; XI, 51, 54.

15. P.R.O.N.I. Foster MSS, D.562/8871, Col. Talbot to John Foster, 10 Feb.
[1784]; *Report of Arbuthnot,* 1783, pp.63-4; *J.H.C.I.* XI, pp.48, 334; J. Warburton,
J. Whitelaw and R. Walsh, *The History of the City of Dublin from the Earliest Accounts
to the Present Time* (London, 1818), ii, p.974.

16. *J.H.C.I.,* XI, App. dlxxviii; *Report of Arbuthnot,* 1782. For the best account
of the Prosperous venture, cf. A.K. Longfield, 'Prosperous: 1776-98', *Journal of
the Kildare Archaelogical Society,* XIV (1966-7), 212-31.

17. *J.H.C.I.,* XI, App. dlxxvii.

18. Foster MSS, D.562/8894, Newspaper cutting listing those moved to Prosperous,
c.Nov. 1784 with MS additions.

19. Foster MSS, D.562/8909, General Return of People employed in relation to
Prosperous.

20. Foster MSS, D.562/8910, 'A List of Machines...made and delivered between 1 March 1781 and 20 Jan. 1785 by James Kerchoffer'.

21. *J.H.C.I.*, XI, 389, App. dlxxviii, dccxcvi; Longfield, 'Prosperous', 223, 226-9.

22. *J.H.C.I.*, XII, 177, 179, 310; *Statutes (Ire.), 27 Geo. III c.13.*

23. For early evidence of cylinder printing, cf. Longfield, 'Irish Linen and Cotton Printing', 46.

24. *J.H.C.I.*, XVI, 177.

25. Warburton, Whitelaw and Walsh, *op.cit.*, ii, 975.

26. Longfield, 'Prosperous', 212.

27. Compare the attitudes of Brooke, committed to mixed goods manufacture and favouring free trade (*J.H.C.I.*, XI, App. dlxxviii, dccxcvi) with those of Hardman, the Drogheda manufacturer, making pure cottons and seeking protection (Foster MSS, D.562/8830, Edward Hardman to [John Foster] 9 Nov. 1783; *J.H.C.I.*, XI, pp.88, App. clii).

28. *Statutes (Ire.), 23 and 24 Geo. III c.I.*

29. Cf. *J.H.C.I.*, XI, App. dxxiv.

30. *Statutes (Ire.) 32 Geo. III c.I.* The duty levels varied over time as they were a combination of percentage *ad valorem* and flat rates per yard. The effective duty on cottons in 1800 was later calculated to have worked out at 47% in the case of printed calico, and 68% on average white calico *(Fourth Report of the Commissioners of Inquiry into the Revenue arising in Ireland* (P.P. 1822, XIII, 13).

31. There are of course several dangers in relying too heavily on raw material imports: there was a non-constant proportion of wool wasted during manufacture; a proportion of cotton wool imports was used for purposes other than textile manufacture; the figures presented in this article are gross — there were occasional re-exports to Britain.

32. Foster MSS, D.562/8854, 'Mr O'Brien's State of the Warps and Wefts used in Cotton in Ireland, Jan. 1791'; *J.H.C.I.*, XI, 334.

33. One explanation given for the slow development of mill building was the higher installation costs, when both men and machinery had (at first) to be imported (cf. *J.C.H.I.*, XI, 334).

34. *J.C.H.I.*, XI, 47; *Report of Arbuthnot*, 1783, pp.44-6.

35. *Minutes of the... Trustees of the Linen and Hempen Manufactures, 1792,* p.33; *Hibernian Chronicle,* 31 May 1792, 29 April 1793; *Cork Evening Post,* 20 Aug. 1795.

36. *Evidence taken before the Committee of the Irish House of Commons on the subject of the Legislative Union* [1800] (P.P. 1833, XXXV) pp.8-9.

37. Foster MSS, D.562/8885, Return of the Water-powered Mills spinning Cotton Twist.

38. *Evidence on the Union,* p.9; *Minutes of the... Trustees of the Linen and Hempen Manufactures, 1803,* pp.52-3. In 1822 the figure given was £50,000 (*Fourth Report into Irish Revenue,* p.239).

39. Edward Clarke to Lord Donoughmore [c. March 1800], in C. Vane, Marquess of Londonderry ed, *The Memoirs and Correspondence of Viscount Castlereagh* (London, 1849), iii, pp.483-4.

40. *Dublin Evening Post,* 4 Jan., 5 Aug. 1785, 17 March 1795, quoted in A.K. Longfield, 'Linen and Cotton Printing at Stratford-on-Slaney, co.Wicklow', *J.R.S.A.I.,* LXXV (1943), 25-7; *Evidence on the Union,* pp.1-2.

41. Duffy put the number at 23, eight about Dublin *(Evidence on the Union,* p.10); there were at least four in the Cork region. As the number around Belfast in 1809 was 12, it is presumed there were less in 1800 (cf. [H. McCall], *Ireland and her Staple Manufactures,* 3rd ed. (Belfast, 1870), pp.473-5).

42. Nathaniel Wilson at the time of his death in 1788 employed over 3,000 people in various stages of the manufacture *(Belfast Newsletter,* 24 June 1788). I am grateful to Mr N. Gamble for this reference, and for clarifying other aspects of the industry in the town prior to 1800.

43. Foster MSS, D.562/8885, Return of Mills.

44. Warburton, Whitelaw and Walsh, *op.cit.,* ii, p.972n. Probably a majority of these were in the hands of independent weavers or small manufacturers (cf. John Dubordieu, *A Statistical Survey of the County of Down* (Dublin, 1802), p.236).

45. Dubordieu, *op.cit.,* p.235.

46. It is assumed that the high imports returned for the customs district of Donaghadee refer in fact to Bangor.

47. Comerford & O'Brien of Balbriggan failed in December 1792 and in the following 12 months the bankruptcy of eight cotton manufacturers (six in the Dublin and Drogheda districts) is recorded in the *Dublin Gazette.* In the first seven months of 1801 nine cotton manufacturers were similarly recorded, six of them in Dublin city.

48. The death of his financially embarrassed partner Nathaniel Wilson was the cause of the trouble in 1788; for references to his other crises, cf. A.K. Longfield, 'Notes on the Linen and Cotton Printing Industry in Northern Ireland in the Eighteenth Century', *Proceedings and Reports of the Belfast Natural History and Philosophical Society,* 2nd ser. IV (1950-5), 59, 67n.

49. *Dublin Gazette,* 7/10 March, 12/14 May 1801.

50. E.g. Foster MSS, D.562/8861, Henry Sadleir & Co., Cork to John Foster, 28 Jan. 1785.

51. For example Carroll & Purfield, Comerford & O'Brien, Henry Crosbie, John Duffy.

52. In 1802, 2,400 looms were reported to be in King's and Queen's cos., Meath and Westmeath, and 1,500 in Wicklow and Carlow (Warburton, Whitelaw and Walsh, *op.cit.,* ii, p.972n). It is presumed these looms were geographically more concentrated than the returns would suggest.

53. Cotton dominated the Irish Commons committee hearings in 1800; nine manufacturers gave evidence. For the politics of their lobbying, cf. G.C. Bolton, *The Passing of the Irish Act of Union* (Oxford, 1966), pp.194-6.

54. Lord Auckland to Lord Castlereagh [7 March 1800], in Londonderry, *op.cit.,* iii, pp.249-50.

55. P.R.O.N.I. Beck MSS, D.1286/2/6, 'Notes on the Irish Cotton Industry', pp.51-2; E.R.R. Green, *The Industrial Archaeology of County Down* (Belfast, 1963), pp.28-9.

56. John Dubordieu, *A Statistical Survey of the County of Antrim* (Dublin, 1812), p.405.

57. The really fine yarns were still having to be imported; in 1808 Belfast spinners could not supply counts above 100 (C.H. Lee, *A Cotton Enterprise, 1795-1840: A History of M'Connel and Kennedy, the Cotton Spinners* (Manchester, 1972), p.70).

58. Among the larger spinners, there seems to have always been some who remained large employers of weavers – Robert Gemmill, for instance, a Scot who set up a mill, weaving facilities and print-works at Lambeg about 1800 (Green, *Co.Down,* p.27), and Nicholas Grimshaw's son James who maintained for a while two mills and a 110-loom 'weaving factory' in the Whitehouse neighbourhood prior to 1815 (Beck MSS, 'Notes on Cotton', p.6).

59. By 1812, there were about 15 print-works around Dublin (McCall, *op.cit.,* pp.472-3).

60. N.L.I. O'Connell MS 13629/5, Report on the Decline of Manufactures, [c.1843].

61. Cf. Orr's evidence in *Fourth Report into Irish Revenue,* pp.231, 233.

62. Cf. Duffy's evidence in *ibid.,* pp.237-8.

63. Contrast the evidence of Orr, Duffy and Osbrey against abolition (*ibid.,* pp.227-42) with that of Vance, Hayes and Pim in favour of free trade (*ibid.,* pp.200, 211-6).

64. Several technically advanced and vertically integrated mills were built in rural

locations in the early twenties, notably the Martin factory near Killyleagh (co.Down) and the Atkinson one at Glenane (co.Armagh).

65. Muslin exports from Ireland grew from half a million yards in 1822/3 to eight million yards in 1830 (Green, *Lagan Valley*, p.105).

66. *Pigot's Dublin and Hibernian Directory* (London, 1824); *Reports of the Assistant Commissioners on Hand-loom Weavers* (P.P. 1840, XXIII), p.783.

67. Cf. N.L.I. MS 13629/7, Report on the Decline of the Dublin Cotton Manufacturers, 1834.

68. W. Stanley, *Commentaries on Ireland* (Dublin, 1833), p.162; McCall, *op.cit.*, pp.472-3.

69. One of the enthusiasts in 1822 for immediate duty abolition, George Mathews, Secretary of the Manchester Chamber of Commerce, was involved with an Irish-based brother in putting out yarn for cord manufacture about Bandon (*Fourth Report into Irish Revenue,* pp.36, 253). For the decline of Bandon, cf. *Reports on Handloom Weavers,* p.658.

70. David Dickson, 'The Barony of Inishowen in the Century before the Famine' (University of Dublin B.A. dissertation 1969); *Second Report of the Commissioners appointed to consider and recommend a General System of Railways for Ireland* (P.P. 1837-8, XXXV, 754).

71. McCall claimed that there were 20,000 muslin weavers in 1860 (McCall, *op. cit.,* pp.526, 531) but the 1851 census recorded only 13,670 adult and child muslin/cotton weavers, and by the time of the 1861 census (admittedly at the beginning of the Cotton Famine) the total returned had fallen by over 42%. However, at the latter date there were 39,000 workers (nearly all female) in sewed muslin in Ulster. McCall stated that in the mid-fifties 120,000 had been so employed (*op.cit.,* p.558).

72. This estimate is a projection from Dubourdieu's calculation of 52,000 employed in all sectors of the east Ulster industry at that time (Dubourdieu, *Antrim,* pp.405-6).

73. N.L.I. Microfilm P6935, 'Notes on the Malcomson Family', *passim;* K. Charlton, 'The State of Ireland in the 1820s: James Cropper's Plan', *I.H.S.,* XVII (1971), 320-39.

74. J.F. Maguire, *The Industrial Movement in Ireland, as illustrated by the National Exhibition of 1852* (Cork, 1853), p.163. Cf. *Returns relating to Imports and Exports, 1859-63 (Ireland)* (P.P. 1864, LVIII, 191, 195).

75. Maguire, *op.cit.,* p.163.

76. Memorial of Malcomson Brothers to the Lords of the Admiralty, [1847], quoted in 'Notes on the Malcomson Family'.

9. The Scottish Cotton Industry during the Industrial Revolution 1780-1840

John Butt

ALTHOUGH the growth of the cotton industry in Scotland was most apparent after 1780, its rise and development was associated with the expansion of the fine linen and silk industries much earlier. Scottish merchants imported, mainly from the West Indies, 466,589 lb of cotton wool in 1770, an amount not again exceeded until 1785; (1) in Paisley and Glasgow there had developed 'manufactories' by the 1750s in which cotton was spun into yarn and woven with linen into fustians. (2) The expansion of Scottish demand for Indian goods — at first calicoes and later muslins — was slower in influencing technical changes than was true of the English fine linen areas such as Nottingham and Lancashire, principally because returns on assets in the established branches of silk and linen manufacture were apparently so reasonable.

This pattern began to change during the American War of Independence. I have argued elsewhere (3) that Scottish consumer demand expanded markedly in the early years of the War and was never so adversely affected later, as Ashton demonstrates was the case in England. (4) Pressure on labour resources in the central Lowlands increased, and wage levels rose. Thus, incentives to apply English textile technology were compelling. Fashion changes inevitably played an important role also: calicoes and fustians were particularly in demand for working-class and middle-class male clothing but the market for cotton stockings, handkerchiefs, shirtings, cotton dress materials and muslins greatly developed — and at a faster rate. There was a marked reaction against silk, principally because of its cost. (5) Thus, those engaged in the production of fustians and silks might well be tempted into cotton production. Linen producers faced increasing costs for flax at a time when cotton wool prices (in real terms) were falling, a process jointly aided by the influx of loyalist planters into the West Indies and the economic activities of the Armed Neutrality of the North. (6) Moreover, despite the general expansion of linen production during the War, it seems likely from the evidence of increased cotton imports that the 'fine' end of the trade did best, making transfer to pure cotton production easier for these producers as 'gluts' became apparent, as for example in 1781 and 1783. Such transfers to muslin weaving involved, at first, little in the way of organisational change and no problems over access to credit. Importers were content to take bills of exchange for raw cotton, often long-dated, and the banks provided cash credits in their customary fashion. (7) Even though West India merchants found that the War of Independence brought them untoward problems, they were committed to the expansion, *inter alia,* of cotton supplies, simply because planters sold them sugar, rum and other valuable products on condition that they also accepted quantities of cotton. (8)

Yarns produced by Crompton's mule transformed the supply position as far as the fine weavers were concerned and placed a premium on the skills available in the Paisley and Glasgow area. In consequence, the fine weaving area gradually increased its geographical range, at first without opposition from the established burgh crafts-men. (9) Added to this reservoir of labour skills was the presence of the appropriate finishing trades in established bleachfields and dyeworks, yet another legacy from the linen industry. (10) Aided by the newly established Glasgow Chamber of Commerce (1783), the spirit of innovation in finishing and weaving was locally encouraged, a vital component in any textile sector where fashion was a critical element in the structure of demand. (11)

The later expansion of the cotton industry in Scotland is now a familiar story. According to Sinclair, the industry in 1812 employed 151,300 people (mainly in their own homes), produced an output valued at £6.2 million, and possessed 120 spinning mills representing a capital of £1.4 million. (12) By 1839-40 there were over 190 mills, but the total adult labour force in spinning and weaving was only slightly more than 100,000. (13) The main burden of this present paper is concerned with entrepreneurship, capital, industrial structure and business problems, inevitably treated in summary fashion because of the exigencies of space.

I Entrepreneurship

Relatively few firms in the spinning sector were single-owner or family concerns, a definite contrast with experience in weaving, at least till the 1820s. Partnerships were easily the most common form of enterprise − from the beginning in spinning − in both sectors by 1840. This characteristic had apparently little to do with capital size in the early years: it was present in firms large and small. For instance, Strang, Davidson and Company of East Kilbride insured their assets in 1794 for £1,500 and were representative of twenty-five firms with insurance valuations of under £2,000. (14) Of eighty-one concerns with some direct interest in spinning c.1799, sixty were definitely non-family partnerships, and of the rest about a dozen had more than two partners from outside the family. (15) Thus, the functions of entrepreneurship were often dispersed between partners, although decisive voices within a partnership were commonly few.

Landowners and farmers in the early days of cotton-spinning were inclined to take an interest by joining partnerships or by providing land and/or buildings. During the boom of 1788-92 their intervention was particularly noticeable and therefore the subject of recurring comment by ministers submitting reports for the *Old Statis-tical Account*. Justice-Clerk Braxfield feued the site of New Lanark mills to David Dale; (16) James Murray of Broughton encouraged the Birtwhistles to build at Gatehouse-of-Fleet; (17) Sir John Stirling of Glorat sponsored a cotton mill at Kirkintilloch; Peter Brotherton managed to persuade Sir James Clerk of Penicuik to feu forty-five acres for the first cotton mills in Scotland; (19) Kenyon, Muir and Wheelhouse successfully approached the Earl of Bute's commissioners for lease of the site of Rothesay mills. (20) Landowners with merchanting interests, past or present, were, however, most directly concerned: Claud Alexander with David Dale at Catrine; (21) Sir William Douglas with Dale and Samuel McCaul at Newton

Douglas [Stewart]; (22) William McDowall of Garthland with George Houston and Robert Burns at Lochwinnoch; (23) Robert Dunmore of Ballikinrain with the Buchanan brothers at Balfron; (24) William Cunninghame Graham of Gartmore with the Culreuch Cotton Company. (25)

Sometimes the participants were of lower landed status. Maxwell Strang of East Kilbride was a farmer-cotton-spinner, as his fire insurance policy indicates. (26) William Robb, a Shettleston farmer, rented a building to a cotton-spinner, (27) as did John Baxter of Houston. (28) Sometimes a simple rural character permeated the style of mill architecture; John Crawford of Whitfold farm, near Paisley, owned a thatched tenement in Johnstone which in 1797 was used as a spinning mill, (29) but this was exceptional. A number of corn mills and malt barns were converted by farmers into spinning mills, usually housing jennies or mules. Nonetheless, commitment to estate or farm was paramount with landowner and farmer, and cotton-spinning was secondary.

Merchants engaged in foreign trade — not merely in the tobacco trade but rather in the West Indian trade — became partners of cotton ventures. James McDowall (d. 1808), a partner in the ill-fated West Indian house of Alexander Houston and Company, was involved in a number of industrial ventures including the handloom factory of James Renfrew established in 1789. (30) James Finlay and Company, the largest cotton firm in Scotland from 1801, could call upon the experience of a number of West Indian merchants whose firms had shareholdings. (32) Robert Owen's partners at New Lanark between 1810 and 1824 were principally concerned in trade with the West Indies. (33) One of them, Alexander Campbell of Hallyards, became principal partner in the largest Glasgow mill built in 1817. (34) The Oswalds were partners in the Linwood Cotton Company, (35) and the Denistouns had shares in Reynolds, Monteith and Company of Bridge of Weir (36) — both these families were principally engaged in the West Indian trade.

As the larger industrial concerns gradually developed their own agencies abroad for buying cotton wool or for marketing yarn or cloth, the expertise and capital of foreign merchants became less necessary. In any event they were a minority in the entrepreneurial group — much less important during the American War of Independence than later. Yet because of their connections with the Scottish banks, particularly in Glasgow, Paisley and Greenock, their support for the new cotton-spinning industry went beyond direct participation in partnerships.

The most numerous group of entrepreneurs came from established textile or finishing business — from fine linen and yarn merchants, wool and silk manufacturers and wholesalers. David Dale was the prime example of the flexibility of the existing economic structure, beginning as a weaver's apprentice and ending as the outstanding cotton capitalist of the first phase of the factory age. (37) Apart from New Lanark, Newton Stewart and Catrine, he was involved for a time in partnerships at Blantyre and Spinningdale and provided funds for a transfer of ownership of Stanley Mills to James Craig of Glasgow. (38) But Dale was merely the greatest of a substantial line of entrepreneurs which had its origins in the linen industry and its associated trades. Wright, Mellis and Company of Cromwell Park, Perth, turned to cotton spinning from flax-broking; (39) Todd, Shortridge and Company, Glasgow merchants and fine linen printers switched both to printing calicoes and producing yarns for muslin-weaving; (40) Lindsay, Dalrymple and Company were spinning both flax and cotton as late as 1800 at Duntocher. (41) At Dunbar, Kinghorn, Dundee, Kirkland, Montrose and Aberdeen mills were switched to cotton, and new mills built. (42)

In Paisley and the county of Renfrewshire mills to take Arkwright's water frame as well as 'jeanie' houses for Hargreave's jenny and Crompton's mule were commonly built for merchants concerned in the production of fine silk, linen and woollen goods. Jenny houses were often built by relatively small firms such as Dundas Smith and Company, a Paisley firm established by three weavers and a tailor in 1789 to manufacture muslins, which floated John Dalziel and Company with a capital of £900 in November 1792. (43) The larger mills produced coarser yarns, principally for warps, and were established by partnerships in which yarn merchants or cloth finishers were important. The McKerrels of Paisley turned from manufacturing silk to producing cotton yarns (44) as did the Houstons of Kilbarchan and Johnstone. (45) These families were also owners of bleachfields. At Fereneze printfield over one thousand people were employed in the early 1780s by the Fultons of Paisley, and they found little difficulty in transferring also into cotton yarn production. (46) Thread production, well established in this area since the 1730s, also stimulated demand for fine cotton and encouraged a transfer of entrepreneurship into jenny-house partnerships.

Glasgow yarn merchants, 'domestic-system' entrepreneurs, calico printers and finishers were found in cotton partnerships in many parts of the same area. In Mearns parish (Renfrewshire) William Ferguson acquired the lands of Newmilns in 1780 and built a cotton mill containing 1,200 spindles. (47) At Dovecothall Samuel Ramsay, John Leviston and John Love combined with Jonathan and William Houghs, local manufacturers, and John Clewdsley from 'near Proud Preston' to establish an Arkwright-type mill with 2,464 spindles. (48) At Bridge of Weir, Black, Hastie and Company were building in 1793 a large cotton mill and still continuing their established weaving business. (49) Campbell, Spiers and Company, cotton brokers and importers, established a mill at Johnstone c. 1795. (50) Alexander and James Crum, manufacturers and calico printers, also added cotton spinning to their business empire at Thornliebank in 1793. (51) Generallly these firms were controlled from Glasgow and were managed on the spot by 'technical' men, sometimes recruited from within the kinship group.

Shortage of good, experienced managers, a long recognised problem for the cotton industry in the expansive days of the 1780s, necessitated recruitment from England and also improvement of the manager's status. A minor place in the entrepreneurial group was often set aside for the able manager. Robert Burns, who introduced Arkwright's water frame into Renfrewshire c. 1781, combined both machine-making and managerial skills; this *rara avis* contributed no capital but was assigned a partnership in three concerns simultaneously. (52) Henry Houldsworth was recruited from Nottingham by John Freeland and William Gillespie of Glasgow c. 1799, became managing partner and then, with the aid of capital provided by his brothers in Manchester, was launched into mill ownership c. 1804. (53)

Southern involvement was also provoked by two further circumstances. The Glasgow-Paisley area was an excellent market for Manchester fine yarns, (54) and thus, Lancashire capital might follow its products. Furthermore, Scots fabrics, warps and thread soon acquired markets in England and on the continent, and wholesalers

and exporters based elsewhere were prepared to participate north of the Border.
Robert Owen and his partners, who bought New Lanark from David Dale in 1799,
exemplify the first trend, (55) as do James Doxon (56) and Robert Twyford. (57)
Gideon Bickerdike, (58) a Manchester merchant of German origin, and his nephew,
Benjamin Flounders, (59) a Quaker from Yarm (North Yorkshire) are representative
of the second.

Occasionally, entrepreneurial teams were inspired by exceedingly complex social
and economic dynamics; a good example of this was the Twigg family. Attracted
by regional cost advantages, several members of this family had moved from Derbyshire to Paisley and established themselves by the 1780s as silk merchants with their
principal market in London. By 1803 they were involved in four different co-partner-
ies: Joseph, William and Samuel Twigg of Paisley, silk and muslin merchants; William
Twigg and Company, cotton-spinners of Paisley; Twiggs and Ashby and Richard
Burton and Company, both of London. There were several other English partners
in these firms, mostly from London and Derbyshire, and the firms were intimately
associated. William Twigg and Company supplied yarns for muslin manufacture to
Joseph, William and Samuel Twigg; once the muslins were woven, they were sent
for sale to the two London firms. (60) This degree of integration (masked by the
number of copartneries) was quite unusual.

Perhaps more surprising, the continuation of partnerships for longer than a
decade was also rare. Partly, this is explained by business mortality and partly by
mercantile convention which commonly prescribed the period of the partnership.
A few firms did, of course, exist for many years with reorganisation arising naturally
when partners died — James Finlay, for instance — but a comparison between the
insurance policies *c.* 1795-1800 and cotton firms listed in *Pigot's Directory* (1825)
showed a survival rate of less than ten per cent. These were difficult years, of course,
particularly up to 1820.

New recruits to entrepreneurship tended to follow the pattern already outlined.
They came increasingly from native firms engaged in cotton-broking, weaving, print-
ing and dyeing. Moreover, Glasgow exerted greater control over the whole industry.
Entrepreneurs in outlying areas such as Galloway and Fife tended to leave the industry;
Aberdeen witnessed the same phenomenon in the late 1840s and early 1850s.

II   Capital

Contemporary estimates of capital formation in the British cotton spinning
industry vary considerably as far as credibility is concerned. Patrick Colquhoun
believed that total fixed capital in 1787 was about £1 million; (61) Watts, ten years
later, considered £2 million reasonable; (62) Isaac Hodgson (63) of Manchester
estimated that in 1812 between £10 million and £13 million represented the fixed
capital, and Archibald Buchanan felt that £11-12 million was a fair estimate for
1818; (64) Edward Baines, following McCulloch, thought £20 million reasonable
for 1834. (65) Dr. Stanley Chapman, using a variety of evidence — but especially
insurance records — has revised some of these estimates, and for the Scottish spinning
mills gives us a target of £292,280 for *c.* 1795. (66)

Andrew Brown in his *History of Glasgow* (1795) calculated 'sunk capital in

building and machinery' for cotton spinning at £490,200, but probably underestimated the number of jenny houses and certainly missed three water mills revealed by insurance policies. He thought the water mills, on average, cost £10,000
each, making a total of £390,000 (for 39), Hargreaves jennies £7,200, mules £18,000
and housing for them £75,000. (67) Dr Chapman believes Brown's estimates of
capital are too high but perhaps has undue faith in insurance valuations. Thomas
Billing, a London silk merchant, who appeared in the Court of Session as assignee
for William Twigg, was prepared to state that 'insurance cover on the building
[cotton mills in general] is not more than one half or one fourth of the true value
of the property'. (68) Whether Billing's judgment was correct or not, it is the case
that where it has been possible to check the firm's capital valuation of its assets
with the insurance valuation, the latter is invariably lower. The worst example refers
to Woodside Mills (Aberdeen) where the firm claimed to have spent £100,000 on
buildings, machinery and stocks in 1815, but the insurance valuation was only
£12,500.

Table 1   *A comparison of capital values with insurance valuations 1796-7*

Firm	Year	Insurance Valuation (£)	Capital (£)
Corse, Burns & Co	1796	9,000	16,000
Houston, Burns & Co	1796	6,900	18,000
Gillespie, Freeland & Co	1796	6,200	10,000
Crosslee Cotton Company	1797	4,300	10,000
John White & Co	1797	6,700	12,303 15s 8d
Totals		33,100	66,303 15s 8d

Sources: Sun Fire Insurance Company Policy Register; Court of Session Records.

Under-insurance possibly affected larger firms more significantly than smaller
ones, but if the evidence of Table 1 was representative of the industry as a whole,
then Brown's estimate seems not too unreasonable. Nor if one takes account of the
average cost per spindle (including housing) does Brown's arithmetic seem untoward:
water frame spindles, according to his estimate, cost £3.125 each and mule and jenny
spindles £0.54 each. The latter, of course, were certainly much less productive and
much less expensive.

For later periods a combination of approaches was found necessary because of
data deficiencies. Sinclair valued the spinning sector at £1.4 million in 1812 and
certainly had access to excellent data. Wilson, (69) writing of Renfrewshire the
same year, believed that £300,000 represented the capital employed for slightly less
than 30 per cent of the industry's capacity, but the differing geographical weightings
of water frame spindles to mule spindles made any attempt to compute accurately
an aggregate figure for cotton spinning impossible. Nonetheless, a figure of £58 per
employee in spinning (calculated from Wilson's data) does not seem outrageously
high, and if this were applied to the spinning sector as a whole, Sinclair's estimate
would suggest a labour force of about 24,000, not at all unreasonable.

Actual valuations of machinery and buildings were used to give a capital figure
per 1,000 power looms or 1,000 spindles for later periods. Generally handlooms

J

were estimated at £10 per loom (for building, machinery and accessories). The
results are embodied in Table 2:

Table 2 *Capital Formation Estimates (£000) 1790-1840*

Year	Spinning	Handlooms	Power looms	Finishing	Aggregates
1790	166	390		100	656
1795	500	400		200	1,100
1803	1,000		10	400	
1812	1,400			560	
1830	1,700	420	500	800	3,420
1840	1,900	450	900	1,200	4,450

Inevitably, these estimates must be treated with caution, and they are offered without
any firm belief in their certainty.

We can be more positive about the sources of capital and, as the previous section
on entrepreneurship suggests, the cotton industry was most dependent on internal
financing for fixed capital. The switches from the other textile sectors were at first
most important, but some banks became involuntarily committed to long-term
lending: the Royal Bank in the case of David Dale's involvement at Stanley Mills, (70)
Bertram, Gardner and Company of Edinburgh (failed 1793) at Penicuik, (71) and
Watsons of Glasgow (failed 1832) in the case of a number of power loom ventures. (72)
Bankruptcy records reveal that loans on bond for working capital were quite common
before 1810, as were cash credits at the banks.

Technical development enforced changes in the quality of capital. Despite water
power resources (which in many cases were inadequate), Scottish firms took an early
interest in the application of the steam engine, but James Watt's many friends in
Glasgow prevented the pirating of his invention which was so general in other textile
centres. (73) After Watt's patent lapsed, locally made engines increased the horsepower available, but in many country mills steam power remained an auxiliary. The
concentration of the industry on Glasgow, steadily apparent after 1800, was steam-
based, and Baines's figures for 1835 mildly under-estimate steam horsepower in use:

Water and Steam power in 1835

No. of Mills	Steam hp	Water hp	Total
125	3,200	2,480	5,680

Source: E. Baines, *History of the Cotton Manufacture* (1835), p.390

Throstles and mules played an increasing part in spinning output after 1805, and
the power loom was applied relatively speedily in Scotland. Wilson estimated that
Renfrewshire alone had *c*.500 by 1811, and Baines calculated that Scotland had
15,000 by 1834. (74) Yet totally integrated firms remained few.

III Industrial Structure

Table 3 summarises data derived from insurance valuations about size of spinning
firms *c*.1795:

Table 3 *Sizes of firms in spinning c.1795*

Insurance Valuation	Number of Firms
Up to £1,000	17
£1,001-2,000	8
£3,000	4
£4,000	6
£5,000	5
£6,000	4
£7,000	4
£8,000	5
£9,000	4
£10,000	4
over £24,000	2

Even allowing for the possibility and extent of under-insurance, it is still certain that small firms were very numerous. Although before 1840 Scottish factory returns are very defective, there is little doubt that few small firms survived in spinning, and that the generality employed more than 150 people by the latter year. (75) There were many casualties in the credit crises provoked by the French Wars, and already by 1815 the pattern of relatively large firms was set. (76) A few, such as James Finlay and Company, owned more than one site and compared reasonably with Owen's New Lanark in employing more than 1,000 workers. (77)

The weaving firms tended also to increase in capital size, usually at the social cost of dispensing with labour. Nonetheless, they rarely employed more than 100 workers in power loom factories before 1830; it was much more usual to employ more than a thousand handloom weavers.

IV   Business Problems

Under-capitalisation was a common initial problem, partly because capital resources of some partnerships were plainly inadequate. For instance, William Caldwell of Lochwinnoch (bankrupt in July 1793) began cotton spinning with a capital of £200 and raised working capital by heritable bonds, by loans from his relatives and by bills drawn on Paisley manufacturers against future yarn deliveries; in the adverse trading circumstances of 1793 he had little chance of survival. (78) Often profits proved disappointing or non-existent, as with the first co-partnery at Rothesay; (79) even wealthy partners were discouraged from increasing their investment but preferred to cut their losses.

Capital flow problems were very common before and during the French Wars. Owen, as recent work has shown, was hard-pressed to meet his commitments in the period between 1812 and 1814. (80) The Buchanans ran into difficulties in the crisis of 1788, because their liquid funds did not match their liabilities, although total assets were much more than their debts. (81) Bad debts were a very general cause of failure. Markets for yarn and cloth were often very volatile, and price falls could be of ruinous proportions. David Pullar of Paisley (bankrupt in 1835), for example, had no bad debts but acquired a deficit of over £3,570 principally through a fall in the price of goods. (82)

When financial crises struck, the banks generally adopted hard money policies to protect their deposits and refused to discount bills. The resulting restriction of credit saved the banks but slaughtered small and medium-sized cotton firms. This process was apparent in 1793, 1803, 1809-12, 1815, 1819 and 1826. (83)

Machine-making capacity often lagged behind demand. Many firms produced their own machinery, but the larger mills sometimes took years to acquire a full complement of up-to-date machines. This made it difficult for even the best managers to reduce overhead costs. Relative to total costs machinery costs remained high throughout the period, and specialist machine production might have reduced these.

Management skills were relatively scarce, and many firms suffered through poor management. Some partnership disputes arose through inefficient management by members of the kinship group; these were unlikely to restore or to increase profitability. For example, John Buchanan, nephew of Robert Corse, who was the principal partner in Corse, Burns and Company, proved an unacceptable manager to Corse's colleagues but proved impossible to dismiss in Corse's life-time. (84) Henry Houldsworth predecessor with Gillespie, Freeland and Company, Thomas Milligan (also recruited from Nottingham), apparently reduced a very profitable concern to tiny profit levels before his dismissal, and even then he sued for breach of contract. (85)

Labour relations varied considerably from firm to firm. Generally, employers were faced from 1810 with a relatively strong, but often disunited, spinners' union. They responded by strengthening their association and by a policy of joint wage reduction when suitable opportunities occurred. The militancy of the cotton-spinners has been commonly stressed, but there were long periods of industrial peace, for example between 1826 and 1836. (86)

Contemporaries commented upon a declining level of profitability. Kirkman Finlay thought the high-point for profits was c.1802 and that afterwards there was a steady decline. (87) This has yet to be proven. However, capacity did tend to expand in fits and starts, and this may have posed marketing problems not readily solved as Europe's cotton industry — and that of the United States — developed and as Lancashire exerted its regional advantages. Energetic entrepreneurs sought alternative markets: in the course of the 1830s, for instance, Asia became a more significant market for the Scottish industry than any other continent. (88)

V

In conclusion, the Scottish cotton industry's progress between 1780 and 1840 was not perpetual nor inevitable. One strength was the common use of the partnership to raise capital which came from several social groups but principally from those with already established textile businesses. Assessing the quantity of capital involved in all stages of production remains a problem fraught with difficulties, but it seems that about a seven-fold increase occurred between 1790 and 1840. Such estimates require further refinement which only more research can produce. The weeding of small firms out of the industrial structure was a more certain process for it seems that only larger firms could deal satisfactorily with the business problems outlined — and not always all of them. (89)

NOTES

1. Public Record Office (P.R.O.), Customs, 14.

2. This is apparent from insurance policies taken with the Sun Fire Insurance Office. Policy registers deposited in the Guildhall Library, London (G.H.) include references to cotton yarn, e.g., G.H. 11936/90, 7 Sept. 1750, Policy for John Bruce's factory at Graham's Hall, Glasgow insures linen and cotton yarn for £300. Cf also *Glasgow Journal,* 24 Feb. 1765 and 11 Sept. 1766.

3. J. Butt, 'The Scottish Economy during the American War of Independence' (Paper presented to the Scottish Universities Bicentennial Conference, June 1976).

4. T.S. Ashton, *Economic Fluctuations in England 1700-1800* (Oxford, 1959), p.164.

5. M.M. Edwards, *The Growth of the British Cotton Trade 1780-1815* (Manchester, 1967), pp.34-37; Senex [Robert Reid], *Glasgow Past and Present* (Glasgow, 1884), III, 374 ff.; G. Unwin, *Samuel Oldknow and the Arkwrights* (Manchester, 1968), pp. 7ff.

6. I have been unable so far to construct a good time series for flax prices, but qualitative sources such as *The Scots Magazine* comment regularly on the increased costs of flax. Cotton prices, according to the Foreign letter-books E and F of Alexander Houston & Co (National Library of Scotland), ranged from 18-21d per lb in October 1776 to 13-14½d in 1778, the period during which the investment decisions about the first two spinning mills were made. Seymour Shapiro, *Capital and Industry in the Industrial Revolution* (New York, 1967), pp.260 and 265 shows a substantial fall of 11 per cent in the 1770s in average real cotton prices.

7. S.G. Checkland, *Scottish Banking, a History, 1695-1973* (1975), p.230.

8. T.M. Devine, 'Transport Problems of Glasgow West India Merchants during the American War of Independence, 1775-83', *Transport History,* IV, (1971), pp.266-304. I have gained greatly from discussions with Dr. Devine about the transfer from fine linen production to cotton.

9. Apart from Perth and Edinburgh, where fine weaving was long established, the principal counties for this specialisation were Renfrewshire, Lanarkshire and Ayrshire.

10. Cf. A. and N. Clow, *The Chemical Revolution* (1952), pp.165-233.

11. Mitchell Library, Glasgow Chamber of Commerce Correspondence 1783-1808 has many references to aid given to weaving and finishing.

12. Sir John Sinclair, *General State of Agriculture* (1814), III, 317-20.

13. Factory Returns in BPP Accounts and Papers, 1839 XLII, 296. Good child labour statistics are difficult to get, but probably there were at least 50,000 children working mainly in handloom weaving in 1840.

14. G.H. 11937/4, Policy No. 623982.

15. These figures are derived from insurance valuations and court records.

16. *Old Statistical Account (OSA),* edited by Sir John Sinclair (1795), XV, 22-3.

17. J. Butt, 'The Industrial Archaeology of Gatehouse-of-Fleet', *Industrial Archaeology,* III (1966), 127-37.

18. Scottish Record Office (S.R.O.), RH 15/1362, Journal of William McCormick; S.R.O. UP Adams Mack, Mc8/10, McCormick v. Stirling, 1802; *OSA,* II, 279.

19. Signet Library (S.L.), Edinburgh Court of Session Records, Vol. 449; 23, Information for John White and Company v. Richard Hotchkis, 19 Feb. 1803, p.l.

20. S.L., 411; 62, Answers for Carrick and Brown, 25 Nov. 1800, p.4; J. Eaton Reid, *History of the County of Bute and Families connected therewith* (Glasgow, 1864), p.104.

21. W.H. Marwick, 'The Cotton Industry and the Industrial Revolution in Scotland', *Scottish Historical Review,* XXI (1924), 208; Mitchell Library MS 63 19 ALS, Dale-Alexander Correspondence, 1787-97.

22. G.H. 11937/11, Policy No. 648860, 21 Nov. 1795; S.R.O. RH 15/1304, Wage Book of Douglas, Dale and McCall [sic].

23. S.L. 264; 2, Matthew Burns v. Houston, Burns and Company, 16 Jan. 1812.

24. S.L. 368; 21, Petition of Robert Dunmore, 5 July 1796.

25. S.R.O. Cunninghame Graham Muniments, G.D. 22/1/219.

26. G.H. 11937/11, Policy No. 648673, 13 Nov. 1795.

27. G.H. 11937/12, Policy No. 651349, 21 Jan. 1796.

28. G.H. 11937/32, Policy No. 701323, 7 April 1800.

29. G.H. 11937/17, Policy No. 664619, 23 Feb. 1797.

30. S.R.O. RH 15/814, Sederunt Book of the creditors of John Renfrew, 1798.

31. S.R.O. UP Currie Dal Seq R1/34 Rothesay Spinning Company, 1812.

32. Anon., *James Finlay and Company, 1750-1950* (Glasgow, 1951), p.7.

33. J. Butt, 'Robert Owen as a Businessman' in *Robert Owen Prince of Cotton Spinners* (Newton Abbot, 1971), pp. 174 ff; S.R.O. GD 64/1/247, Campbell of Jura Muniments, Articles of Co-partnery of New Lanark, 1810.

34. Mitchell Library, MS 79/10, Papers relating to the trust of Alexander Campbell of Hallyards.

35. S.R.O. Particular Register of Sasines, Renfrewshire, Vol. 48, f. 29.

36. Ibid., Vol. 42, f. 217. I am grateful to Dr. T.M. Devine for these two references.

37. W.G. Black, 'David Dale's House in Charlotte Street', *Proceedings of The Regality Club*, 4th series, part second, pp.93-121; G. Stewart, *Curiosities of Glasgow Citizenship* (Glasgow, 1881), pp.45-64.

38. Senex, *Glasgow Past and Present* (Glasgow, 1884), II, 51-3; III, 371 ff.; *OSA*, VIII, 383; S.R.O. GD 64/1/247, Campbell of Jura Muniments, Copy Memorial relative to the action at the instance of the Royal Bank against Dale's trustees, 1818.

39. Insurance policies over time demonstrate this.

40. *Glasgow Journal*, 13 Nov. 1766; *Glasgow Mercury*, 23 March 1780; G.H. 11937/11, Policy No. 648658, 13 Nov. 1795.

41. G.H. 11937/29, Policy No. 698451, 20 Jan. 1800.

42. Dunbar: G.H. 11937/11, Policy No. 648801, 14 Nov. 1795, Robert Fall & Co; Kinghorn: G.H. 11936/395, Policy No. 615756, 15 June 1793, Fergus & Russell; Dundee: G.H. 11936/395, Policy No. 615780, 15 June 1793, Jobson, Millard & Co; Kirkland: G.H. 11937/1, Policy No. 620859, 1 Nov. 1793, Aislabie, Neilson & Co; Montrose: G.H. 11937/14, Policy No. 653332, 8 March 1796, Lyall, Petrie & Co; Aberdeen: G.H. 11937/12, Policy No. 648723, 17 Nov. 1795, Leys, Brebner and Hadden; G.H. 11937/9, Policy No. 644260, 23 July 1795, Gordon Barron & Co. This list is incomplete and merely serves to exemplify.

43. S.L. 455; 2, Petition of Peter Millar, 23 Nov. 1803.

44. G. Crawfurd, *The History of the Shire of Renfrew*, ed. Wm. Semple (Paisley, 1782), pp.74ff; S.L. 632; 6, Petition of the creditors of William McKerrel, 21 Jan. 1814.

45. G. Crawfurd, *op.cit.*, pp.114 and 256-7; G.H. 11937/14, Policy No. 651776, 5 Feb. 1796.

46. G. Crawfurd, *op.cit.*, p.172; S.R.O. Bill Chamber Processes II, 5493, Bond of Caution by John Cochrane, 1806.

47. G. Crawfurd, *op.cit.*, p.207.

48. *Ibid.*, p.172.

49. G.H. 11937/2, Policy No. 622759, 17 Dec. 1793.

50. G.H. 11937/7, Policy No. 636268, 3 Jan. 1795.

51. G.H. 11937/2, Policy No. 622167, 11 Nov. 1793.

52. S.R.O. Bill Chamber Processes I, William King and others v. Buchanan, 1798.

53. G.H. 11937/35, Policy No. 710220, 31 Oct. 1800.

54. C.H. Lee, *A Cotton Enterprise 1795-1840: A History of McConnell & Kennedy fine cotton spinners* (Manchester, 1972), pp.23-46; R. Owen, *Life by Himself* (1971 edn), ed. J. Butt, pp.44 ff.

55. R. Owen, *op. cit.*, pp.51 ff.

56. S.L. 394; 4; J. Aiken, *The Country from Thirty to Forty Miles round Manchester* (1795), pp.448, 476-7.

57. G.H. 11937/4, Policy No. 629340, 27 June 1795.

58. S.L. 368; 21, Petition of Robert Dunmore, 5 July 1796.

59. S.L. 500; 89, Benjamin Flounders v. Stirling 1817.

60. G. Crawfurd, *op.cit.*, p.323; G.H. 11937/17, Policy No. 666655, 22 April 1797, S.R.O. UP Currie Dal Seqn. T1/13, 1803.

61. P. Colquhoun, *An Important Crisis in the Calico and Muslin Manufactory... Explained* (1788), p.4.

62. cf. S.D. Chapman, *The Cotton Industry in the Industrial Revolution* (1972), pp.28-30. I have benefited considerably from conversations with Dr. Chapman.

63. *House of Lords Committee on the Cotton Factories Bill,* P.P.1818, Vol.XCVI, 203.

64. *Ibid.,* p.63.

65. E. Baines, *History of the Cotton Manufacture in Great Britain* (2nd edn. 1966), p.401.

66. S.D. Chapman, 'Fixed Capital Formation in the British Cotton Manufacturing Industry', in *Aspects of Capital Investment in Great Britain, 1750-1850* (1971), edited by J.P.P. Higgins and S. Pollard, pp.102-3.

67. A. Brown, *History of Glasgow* (1795), p.241.

68. J.P.P. Higgins and S. Pollard, *op.cit.,* p.115; S.R.O. UP ISH/A/7/49, Arkwright v. Twiggs, 1815.

69. J. Wilson, *General View of the Agriculture of Renfrewshire* (1812), p.250.

70. S.R.O. GD 64/1/247, Copy Minutes of Mr. Dale's trustees, 25 Oct. 1816.

71. S.L., 449; 23, Information for John White and Company v. Richard Hotchkis, 19 Feb. 1803.

72. Senex, *op.cit.,* I, p.504; S.R.O. RH 15/404, Copy of the Sederunt Book of the creditors of Watson and Lennox, 1828.

73. This is apparent from correspondence in the Boulton and Watt collection (Birmingham Reference Library). I am grateful to Dr. Jennifer Tann for drawing my attention to Scottish material in this collection.

74. E. Baines, *History of the Cotton Manufacture* (1835), p.236.

75. Cf. the miscellaneous information given in *Reports from Select Committee on the Act for the Regulation of Mills and Factories* P.P.1840, Vol.X.

76. Cf. Henry Houldsworth's return to the *Select Committee on the State of Children Employed in Manufactories,* P.P.1816, Vol.III.

77. *House of Lords Committee on Cotton Factories Bill,* P.P.1818, Vol.XCVI, p.65.

78. S.R.O. UP Currie Dal Seqn C1/8; S.L. 360; 12, Petition of John Stein, 13 May 1794.

79. S.L. 209; 34, Petition of William Scott and others, trustees of deceased Charles Scott of Woodbank, 1800.

80. A.J. Robertson, 'Robert Owen and the Campbell Debt 1810-12', *Business History,* II (Jan. 1969), 23-30; R. Owen, *op.cit.,* xi-xxiii; J. Butt, 'Robert Owen as a Businessman', *Robert Owen, Prince of Cotton Spinners* (Newton Abbot, 1971), pp.173-87.

81. S.L. 360; 16, Petition of George Buchanan, 10 March 1794.

82. S.R.O. RH 15/404, Sederunt Book of the creditors of David Pullar, 1835.

83. An increase in the number of bankruptcies is most marked in these years. Cf. also C.H. Lee, *op.cit.,* pp.38 ff; *Report on the State of Commercial Credit, 1793* (reprinted) P.P. 1826, Vol.III, pp.124 and 129; *Report on the House of Lords Committee on Circulation of Promissory Notes,* P.P.1826-7, Vol.VI, p.248; S.G. Checkland, *op.cit.,* pp.213-25; W. Smart, *Economic Annals of the Nineteenth Century, 1801-20* (1910), pp.263-4.

84. S.R.O. Bill Chamber Processes I, 59,801, William King and Others v. J. Buchanan, 1798.

85. S.R.O., UP Innes Mack, G 19/4, Gillespie, Freeland & Co. v. Milligan, 1796.

86. Glasgow City Archives, Minute Book of the Association of Master Cotton Spinners; Mitchell Library, Chamber of Commerce Correspondence 1824-5; cf. the forthcoming article by W.H. Fraser, 'The Glasgow Cotton Spinners, 1837'.

87. *Select Committee on Manufactures, Commerce and Shipping,* P.P.1833, Vol. VI, Qs.648-662.

88. Mitchell Library, Chamber of Commerce statistics, Jan.-Feb. 1840, Exports of Cotton Yarn from Scotland, 1835-9.

89. I am grateful to the Social Science Research Council for sponsoring the research upon which this paper is based.

10. The Patent Still Distillers and the Role of Competition

R. B. Weir

I

THE treatment of their respective distilling industries by Scottish and Irish economic historians provides an interesting historiographical contrast. Although the subject of a large number of popular histories, the Scotch whisky industry has received less attention from academic historians and is normally accorded little comment in the standard textbooks on Scottish economic history. (1) Hamilton in his study of eighteenth-century Scotland provided more generous discussion than later writers. He argued that the whisky industry was of considerable importance at the end of the century, basing his argument on the direct and indirect employment generated by the industry, its share of Scotland's capital resources, and its links with agriculture. (2) In subsequent studies the industry has only received a fleeting glance and with growing interest in the social consequences of economic change rather greater notice has been taken of the heavy drinking patterns that became evident in industrial society than of the economics of the supplying industries. (3) This emphasis would doubtless have been applauded by the magistrates of late eighteenth century Edinburgh who worried about 'the pernicious consequences arising from the baneful practice of dram drinking.' (4) It would also have delighted the Rev Dr Thomas Martin, a contributor to the *Statistical Account,* who believed that:

> Had all the fabled ills emitted from Pandora's box been realised, they could not have produced more deplorable consequences, than when whisky, of all other liquors the most subversive of the health, the industry and the morals of the people, became so cheap and so common as to supersede the drinking of beer, the good old whole-some beverage of our fathers. Religion, morality, health and industry are the dreadful sacrifices ... (5)

This has not, however, been the only factor which has limited discussion of the whisky trade's place in Scottish industrialisation. An adequate account of the industry involves the need to include explanatory material relevant largely only to the industry rather than to the industrial revolution as a whole. (6) This is particularly true of the bewildering variety of excise systems under which the distilling industry operated between 1784 and 1823 and which did so much to determine pace and direction of change. The scarcity of useful nineteenth-century studies of the industry and, until recently, the problems surrounding access to business papers increased the difficulty of establishing the development of the industry. (7) There is, though, another and more important reason; one which is well reflected in the contrasting treatment of the industry in the *Statistical Account* and the *New Statistical Account.*

The *Statistical Account* is replete with references to the industry. In the 1790s few parishes lacked a still, the industry was embroiled in controversy, and the market-creating potential of a local distillery for farming was widely appreciated. The great Lowland distilleries with their steam engines, prodigious fuel consumption, canals, large labour forces and stock fattening units were, if not quite oases in an industrial desert, one of the few points of contact for many parishes with industrial change. (8) The *New Statistical Account,* on the other hand, contains far fewer references even though the Scottish distilling industry was well on the way to becoming the largest in the United Kingdom. It was, though, much less controversial than in the 1790s: the excise reforms of 1823 had encouraged a large licensed distilling industry, the illicit distilling problem was much diminished, and the accepted links between distilling and agriculture attracted little comment. (9) Above all there was a plethora of industrial developments in textiles, mining and transport for contributors to describe: distilling was only one feature on the new industrial landscape of Lowland Scotland.

Authors face difficult decisions in selecting their material and with a wealth of industrial change, especially the emergence of a flourishing heavy industry sector, Scottish economic historians have rightly determined their priorities accordingly. In this way features of the subsequent history of the Scotch whisky industry such as the role of the grain distillers in curbing competition within the U.K. spirit trade (from 1865 to 1888), the expansion of export sales, the lead given by the Distillers Company in the 'consolidation' of the trade (after 1900) and its search for new products in the industrial uses of alcohol and alcohol derivatives, have gone unnoticed. (10)

With a less bountiful industrial panorama, historical study of the Irish whisky trade has been significantly different. Illicit distilling was the subject of a brilliantly perceptive essay by the late Professor Connell and, in 1972, a full scale study of the trade was produced by E.B. McGuire. (11) Brewing has also fared better, being the subject of a major business history which sired the dual economy controversy. (12)

In the interpretation of nineteenth-century Irish economic history the distilling industry has been accorded a substantial role. For Professor Beckett, writing in 1965, brewing and distilling were 'the notable exceptions' to the decline of manufactures outside the North-East of Ireland. Decline, Beckett argued, was an inevitable result of industrial development elsewhere. As manufacturing became more specialised and concentrated, small local manufacturers found their markets invaded by cheaper goods from more highly developed areas. (13) In 1969, Professor Lee saw brewing, distilling and milling – 'the three most important industries in the interior of the country' – as instances of trades which were seriously affected between 1850 and 1880 by this tendency. (14) Reductions in transport costs achieved by the railways removed protection from competition whilst rural prosperity increased the local market sufficiently to attract Dublin and English manufacturers. Such competition, Lee argued, became 'especially keen' after 1873 as English manufacturers sought to offset depression at home with increased sales in Ireland. (15) A similar explanation but one which also stressed factors peculiar to the distilling industry, such as Father Mathew's temperance crusades of 1839-42 and the increase in spirit duties after

1853, was argued by Professor Cullen. (16) Like Professor Lee, he emphasised the repercussions on Irish industry of the ending of the worldwide industrial boom allied with the effects of the agricultural crisis on rural purchasing power. After the 1860s, however, the distilling industry provided the prime evidence for the thesis that only by developing export markets could industrial firms 'reach a scale of production which would make their costs competitive and hence enable them to survive on the home market against foreign competition'. Distilling was thus 'the most striking instance of how exports could alter the fortunes of an industry'. Contraction at home was offset by exports:

> Exports doubled between the 1860s and 1870s, doubled again by the 1890s and yet again by the first decade of the twentieth century. Output rose from 5½ million gallons in 1865 to over 12 million gallons; exports, rising from a million gallons in the 1860s to 8½ million gallons in 1907, came to account for about two-thirds of output. By 1907 the industry accounted for a quarter of the United Kingdom output; allowing for the higher per capita consumption of whiskey in Scotland, it seems that the Irish industry exported a higher proportion of output than the Scottish distilleries ... (17)

Cullen also pointed to the domination of exports by a few large firms and the association, in the 1890s, between the growth of exports and the expansion of blended whisky. (18)

To sum up: the Irish distilling industry is seen as being in decline between 1840 and the mid 1860s; faced with keen competition in common with other Irish industries in the 1870s; but, unlike other Irish industries which were swamped by severe competitive pressures, staging a remarkable export-based recovery. It is parts of this record, in particular the role of competition, which will be examined against developments in the Scottish distilling industry.

II

The depression in the spirit trade during the early 1860s provides a convenient starting point. Despite the use of 'universal and general competition, to prevent monopoly and combination ..' (19) as a guiding principle in excise reform as early as 1816, it was not till 1858 that full internal free trade in spirits within the United Kingdom was achieved when the duty on spirits was harmonised at 8s. per proof gallon (p.p.g.). Unfettered access for foreign distillers to the U.K. spirit market came two years later when the last remaining props of the old mercantilist structure surrounding imported spirits were dismantled. (20) In the 1860s, therefore, the distilling industries of England, Scotland and Ireland moved into a new competitive environment.

The environment was not particularly inviting, as spirit consumption was hard hit by the series of duty increases necessary to secure harmonisation and by a further increase of 2s. p.p.g. in 1860. Falling spirit consumption occurred throughout the United Kingdom but the depression was deepest in Ireland and Scotland where the increases in duty had been greatest. The position can be summarised by comparing spirit consumption in each national market for the year of peak consumption after 1823 with the position in 1860/64:

Table 1   *Spirit Consumption (Million proof gallons)*

	England	Scotland	Ireland
	England	Scotland	Ireland
Excise Duty in 1823	7/- *	2/4¾	2/4¾
Year of Peak Consumption	1860	1852	1838
Consumption in Peak Year	12.904	7.172	12.296
Average Spirit Consumption			
1860/64	11.207	4.706	4.432

* For England, 1825
(Source: G.B. Wilson, *Alcohol and the Nation* (1940) App.C, p.318, Table 3, pp.336-9)

Ireland, which in the 1830s had been the largest spirit market in the U.K. was, by the early 1860s, the smallest: a result of the activities of the energetic Father Mathew, duty increases, a resurgence of illicit distilling and loss of population. The Scottish spirit market was also much reduced and only marginally larger than the Irish market. By contrast, the English market was only slightly down: a consequence of the increase of duty in 1860 and not fiscal harmonisation. From being the smallest market in the 1820s, consumption had grown and by the early 1860s it was the largest and most buoyant market in the United Kingdom.

Subsequent trends in spirit consumption confirmed the importance Irish and Scottish distillers attached to the English market. For home-produced spirits (that is, gin and whisky) it is possible to establish the changes in demand in individual countries. Fig. 1 shows the movements of per capita consumption of home-produced spirits between 1860 and 1910. (21) Peak per capita consumption was reached in Scotland in 1875 and the following year in Ireland. After 1876, with a falling population Irish distillers faced a prolonged contraction in demand, whereas in Scotland demand stagnated until the boom at the end of the 1890s. In England, however, consumption did not peak till 1900 and the gradual rise in per capita consumption after 1887 exerted a buoyant influence on the spirit market. England thus provided the main source of demand in the last quarter of the nineteenth century. Expansion in England was accompanied by a marked shift in consumer preference from gin to Scotch and Irish whisky. (22) In 1834 gin dominated the English market and consumption amounted to 7.369 m.p.g. By 1890, when English spirit consumption at 16.9 m.p.g. was more than double the level of 1834, only 6 m.p.g. of gin were consumed. Seventeen years later, with English spirit consumption over 22 m.p.g., only 1.5 m.p.g. of gin were consumed. In absolute terms, therefore, gin consumption fell only slightly between 1830 and 1890 but relatively it was losing ground to whisky. The most dramatic shift in preference came in the 1890s and by 1907 the once mighty gin occupied a relatively insignificant place in the spirit market. The struggle between the Irish and Scotch whisky trades to increase their respective shares of this growing market was one of the most striking features of the spirit trade after 1860.

No separate national figures for the consumption of imported spirits (that is, brandy, rum, and 'other' spirits) exist till 1891 but fig. 2 shows the consumption of

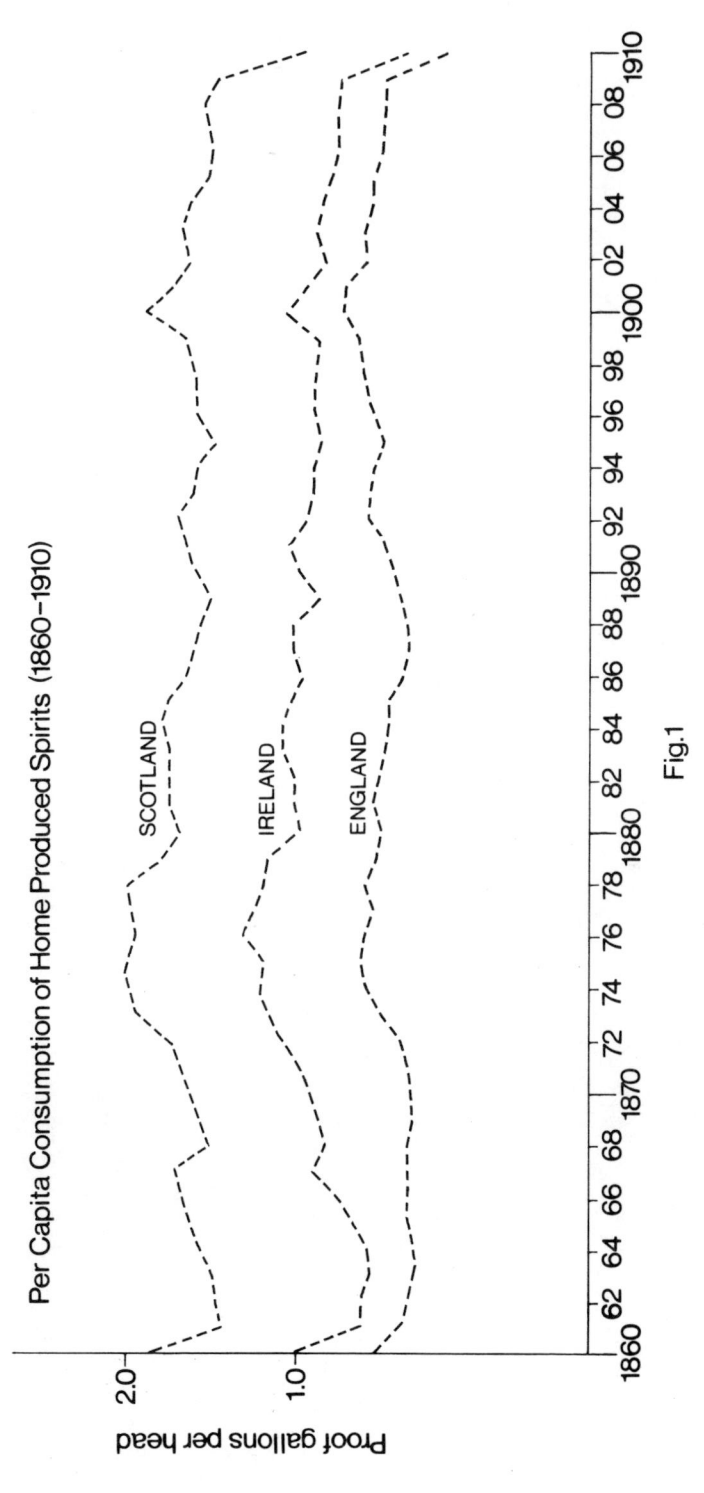

Per Capita Consumption of Home Produced Spirits (1860–1910)

SCOTLAND

IRELAND

ENGLAND

Proof gallons per head

2.0

1.0

1860 62 64 66 68 1870 72 74 76 78 1880 82 84 86 88 1890 92 94 96 98 1900 02 04 06 08 1910

Fig.1

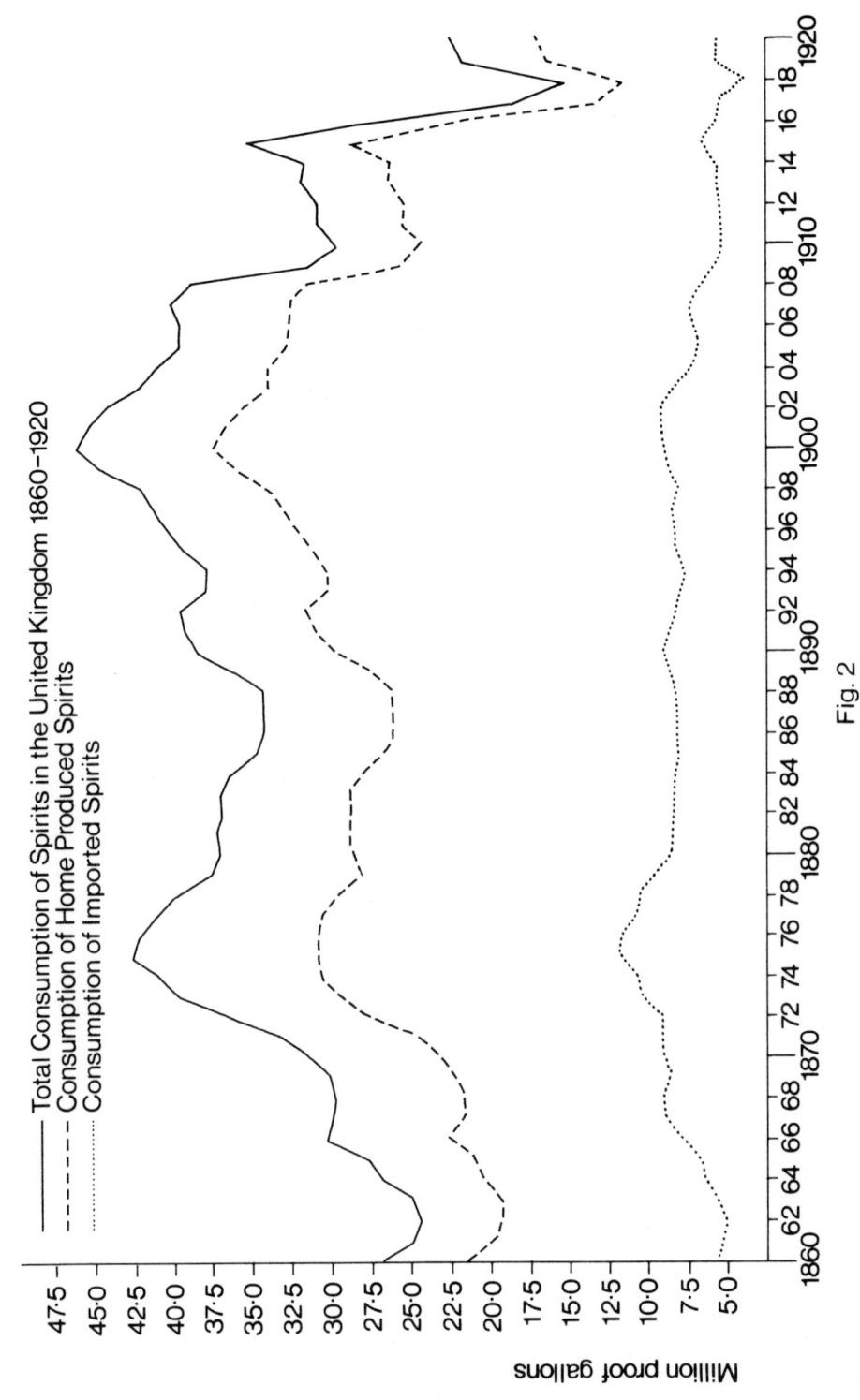

Million proof gallons

—— Total Consumption of Spirits in the United Kingdom 1860–1920
---- Consumption of Home Produced Spirits
········ Consumption of Imported Spirits

1860 62 64 66 68 1870 72 74 76 78 1880 82 84 86 88 1890 92 94 96 98 1900 02 04 06 08 1910 12 14 16 18 1920

Fig. 2

home and imported spirits in the United Kingdom between 1860 and 1920. The period was dominated by two large waves of spirit drinking in the 1870s and 1890s. At the start of the twentieth century spirit consumption was in decline. The other noticeable feature was the growth in the share of the U.K. market held by imported spirits from 21 per cent in 1860 to 28 per cent in 1875, the peak year of consumption. External competitive pressures were also a feature of the distilling industry.

III

Central to what the Inland Revenue delicately described as 'the special causes' (24) that kept the level of duty in Scotland and Ireland below that in England until the 1850s was the fact that:

... while the business is carried on by the licensed manufacturers at so extraordinary an expense of machinery and capital, spirits may also be produced by the most simple and accessible means, and at the most trifling expense ... (25)

Both the excise system and the desire of the excise officials to achieve internal free trade had to be tempered to meet the requirements of the small-scale peasant-distiller. Thus the 1823 Distillery Act in Scotland and Ireland deliberately sought to encourage 'men of little capital to set up small distilleries'. (26) It was much more successful in Scotland than in Ireland (27) and by the early 1830s the industrial structure in Scotland encompassed producers as diverse as John McDonald of Caithness, who distilled a trifling 166 gallons of malt whisky, and James Haig whose distillery at Lochrin, the largest in Scotland, produced over half a million gallons. (28) The Act made licensed distilling more accessible to small-scale producers but it could not guarantee their survival. Reform '... raised a competition in the trade ...' and it was soon apparent that the future lay with the large-scale distillers. (29) Between 1833 and 1864 the number of licensed distillers in Scotland declined from 160 to 115, the total output of the industry rose from 9.1 to 13.7 m.p.g. and the average scale of production increased from 35,000 to 119,000 proof gallons per annum. (30)

Like the Irish industry, therefore, the Scottish industry underwent structural change. Those eliminated from the trade in the greatest numbers were the small-scale farmer-distillers operating in the Highland counties. (31) Transport improvements, however, seem to have played a different part in this process in Scotland. Highland malt distillers, especially in the north-east, were amongst the most enthusiastic supporters of railway development, regarding the railways as a means of escaping from an impoverished local market; an opportunity to be seized rather than to be feared.

IV

Another feature of structural change and one which has not been sufficiently distinguished in the history of the Irish distilling industry was its association with a new method of distilling spirits. In 1850, Aeneas Coffey, a retired Irish exciseman, patented his design for a still which worked continuously. (32) Coffey ended the long search of the European distilling industry for a continuous still but the adoption of his patent created a sharp divide within the distilling industry between the patent still distillers and those who continued with the traditional pot still. The Coffey or patent still radically altered the economics of spirit production and profoundly altered competitive relationships within the U.K. distilling industry. It is therefore worth explaining its features in some detail.

Until 1830 the most widely used distilling vessel was the pot still. In Scotland it was used to produce two types of spirit: malt whisky, distilled from a mash entirely composed of malted barley, and grain whisky, made from a mixed mash of malted and unmalted or raw grain. In Ireland, except in the North, there was little demand for malt whisky and Irish distillers produced a whisky very similar to Scots grain whisky.

Malt whisky, said by the Parnell Commission in 1834 to be 'long established by the prevailing taste as the national beverage' of Scotland, (33) was more expensive than grain whisky because of the additional expense of malting, the loss of spirit in an all-malt mash, and the excise duty on malt. In the Lowlands, where before 1823 the excise system was more effective than in the Highlands, malt whisky was regarded as a luxury and consumed 'by the better sort of people'. (34) Malt whisky was, however, also the traditional product of Highland distillers and regarded more as a 'necessity' than a luxury. To lower the cost of malt whisky and stimulate its legal production, a drawback of malt duty was introduced in 1821 and maintained until 1855 when the duty on all raw materials used in distilling was ended.

Grain spirits were sold as whisky but they also provided the base for a wide range of additives and mixtures, including mixtures of malt and grain whisky. Being cheaper, they were 'chiefly drunk by the Dram Drinkers, who wish to get drunk at the cheapest rate, and whose corrupted stomachs prefer the harshest spirits'. (35) Both Irish and Scottish grain distillers sold large quantities of grain spirit to English rectifiers for gin production, despite a number of obstacles created by the differences in the excise systems of the three countries. This trade remained unrecorded on a regular basis until after 1860 but the odd statistics that do exist suggest that the Scottish distillers gained the lion's share of the English trade. In 1834, for example, English distillers produced 4.653 m.p.g. Imports from Scotland were 2.575 m.p.g. and from Ireland 420,000 gallons. Of the Scottish and Irish spirits just 279,000 gallons were made from malt, the remainder being raw spirit for rectification. (36)

The English distilling trade was quite different: 'the prevailing taste of the principal consumers is still in favour of gin' and 'there is scarcely any demand for whisky in the purer state in which it is prepared for consumption in Scotland and Ireland'. (37) English distillers did not produce a spirit which was immediately pot-able. Instead, using large-sized stills and a high gravity wash they turned out a harsh, undrinkable spirit. (38) This was sold to rectifiers who re-distilled it in the presence of flavouring ingredients such as juniper berries and coriander seeds. This consumer preference contributed to an industrial structure quite unlike Scotland and Ireland.

The pot still, if worked slowly and carefully, employing good quality raw materials, could be made to produce a well-flavoured spirit. For the ambitious, cost-cutting distiller seeking a wider market it had obvious limitations. Pot still distillation was

Table 2   *The structure of the distilling industry (1832/33)*

	England	Scotland	Ireland
Number of Distillers	12	260	87
Number of Rectifiers	108	11	19
Duty Paid (£)	£1.42mn	£1.33mn	£1.54mn

(Source: 7th Report, p.29; A.W. Slater, 'A London Firm of Still Makers', *Business History 1965/66,* Vol. VII/VIII, pp.48-59.)

(and is) a discontinuous or batch process. The first distillation produced a weak concentration of alcohol and a second or even third distillation was needed to raise the alcoholic strength. Redistillation increased the cost of fuel and labour. Securing a proper fractionation of the spirit so that it did not contain too large a proportion of secondary constituents was a difficult task. With inadequate concentration and fractionation poor quality raw materials gave the spirit an unpleasant flavour. The still was heated by fire. Raising the contents of the still to boiling point was a slow process. Wear and tear from repeated heating and cooling were high, and there was the ever present danger of spoiling the flavour of the spirits by charring the solid matter in the wash. (39)

Coffey's still broke away entirely from the traditional pot still design. The still was heated by steam and the exchange of heat within the still between steam and wash cut the cost of fuel. With extraordinary efficiency the still produced a concentrated spirit containing between 86 per cent and 96 per cent alcohol.

Descriptions of the product of the Coffey still have ranged from: '... a bland grain spirit ... the product of a technological process rather than a craft ...' to '... surgical spirit ...' (40) What the still produced was a very pure grain spirit relatively low in secondary constituents. (41) It produced a much thinner-flavoured spirit quite unlike malt whisky but a cheaper substitute for pot still grain whisky. The proportion of secondary constituents could be varied but only within relatively narrow limits compared to the pot still. Unlike the pot still where the quality of spirit could vary widely not only between different distilleries but even within the same distillery from one year to another, the quality of patent still spirit was much more uniform. The distinguishing feature of patent still spirit was, paradoxically, its lack of a distinguishing feature. Thus it came close to being a homogeneous commodity. As the internal and external barriers to competition crumbled and as transport improvements widened the market that could be reached by individual patent still distilleries, the potential for severe competition in patent still distilling was very high. There were, however, other characteristics of the Coffey still which unlike its homogeneous product did not belong to the much loved model of perfect competition and which ensured that the patent still distillers' response to competition was very different from their brethren in pot still distilling.

What was striking about the diffusion of the Coffey still was the small number of distillers who actually adopted it (see Table 3). Their share of output was, however, out of all proportion to their numbers (see Table 4).

K

Table 3   *The number of distilleries using patent stills*

Year	England	Scotland	Ireland	Total
1830	-	1	2	3
1840	4	2	13	19
1850	10	13	16	39
1860	8	12	8	28

(Source: *Royal Commission on Whisky,* P.P.1909, App. T, Table VII)

Table 4   *Total spirit distilled by pot and patent stills (m.p.g.) and percentage of
the total distilled in patent stills*

	England		Scotland		Ireland	
1830	4.604	0%	9.738	1.5%	8.701	1.2%
1840	5.866	55.6%	8.944	7.5%	8.851	20.7%
1850	5.747	100.0%	11.609	45.3%	8.612	37.9%
1860	8.012	100.0%	12.590	53.7%	6.421	35.9%
1870	7.569	100.0%	14.572	59.1%	7.345	42.6%
1880	9.828	100.0%	16.357	60.3%	9.903	41.1%
1890	9.556	100.0%	20.576	62.4%	12.461	51.2%
1900	12.581	100.0%	30.816	66.3%	14.527	71.5%

(Source: Wilson *op.cit.,* Table 5, p.319)

In 1860, for example, the 12 patent still distilleries in Scotland had a combined
output of 6.9 m.p.g. Pot still distilleries numbered 111, a fall of 57 in the previous
fifteen years, and they shared an output of 5.7 m.p.g. The 8 Irish patent still distilleries
were in a less dominant position but their combined output of 2.3 m.p.g. still contrasted
sharply with the 4.1 m.p.g. shared by 27 pot still distilleries. In the United Kingdom
as a whole, 27 m.p.g. of spirit were distilled; 63 per cent came from patent stills and
these were concentrated in a mere twenty-eight distilleries.

There was no wave of new distilleries built around the patent still process. Most
of the distilleries which adopted the patent still were already established and the
nature of their investment decision was either to convert their premises for patent
still production or to extent their distilling capacity by adding a patent still. (42) In
Scotland it was the largest of the Lowland distilleries serving a growing, urban market
which converted to the patent still. The same seems to have been true of Ireland
where the eight patent still distilleries in existence in 1833 were located as follows:
2 in Dublin, 2 in Cork, and one each in Belfast, Kilkenny, Enniscorthy and Londonderr

Traditionally the advantage of the patent over the pot still has been explained in
terms of its lower variable costs, in particular the lower fuel costs arising from the
interchange of heat in the operation of the still. This hardly seems consistent with
the observation that large-scale producers adopted the patent still: lower variable
costs would surely have been equally attractive to all distillers. Although the patent
still did lower variable costs, the attainment of this benefit involved a sizeable fixed
capital investment. Not only was the still itself costly, but to gain the full benefit
from continuous production larger boilers, pumps, mash tuns, maltings and other
ancillary equipment were needed. This put fixed investment on a totally different

level from pot still distilling. Because the patent still was expensive its use was confined to the large-scale distillers. Its greatly enhanced productive capacity meant,
however, that unit costs of production and the capital/output ratio in patent still
distilling were lower than in pot still distilling. In other words, high costs of entry
restricted the number of patent still distillers but those who could afford the entry
fee gained a lower cost of production.

These results explain most of the features of the diffusion of the Coffey still. The
lower cost of production and the lower price of grain spirit (in 1857, Scottish malt
whisky prices ranged from 3s.9d. to 4s.6d.; the price of grain spirit was 2s.6d.) explain
the dramatic rise in patent still output at the expense of pot still. Although the price-
reducing effects of the Coffey still were offset by increases in spirit duty, the competitive position of the pot still distillers was more seriously affected. After Coffey,
pot still distillers stood out as high cost producers. On the other hand, for the patent
still distillers the increase in their numbers during the 1840s and 1850s when consumption in Ireland and Scotland was falling posed a serious threat. One additional
Coffey still meant a larger proportional increase in output than one additional pot
still. Attempts to control the output of patent still spirit therefore became crucial
to the grain distillers, and, because the high costs of entry kept the numbers of patent
still distillers relatively small, combination was a more feasible proposition. Another
response to the depressed conditions of the early 1860s, in addition to casting envious
glances at the English market, was therefore possible.

V

The first attempt to restrict competition occurred in October, 1856, when six
Lowland grain distillers agreed to restrict their sales. The agreement covered too few
distilleries (there were another eleven grain distilleries in Scotland) and too small a
percentage (45 per cent) of Scottish patent still output to be effective. (43) The
agreement lasted only a year and it was not till 1865, after a period of intense competition, during which profits were squeezed between falling spirit prices and rising
barley prices, that a further attempt was made at combination. Six of Scotland's
seventeen patent still distilleries went out of business between 1856 and 1865, providing an object lesson in the dangers of uncontrolled competition for the survivors.
Thereafter, from 1865 to 1888, the history of patent still distilling was largely the
history of two trade associations, The Scotch Distillers' Association (1865-1876)
and The United Kingdom Distillers' Association (1878-1888). (44) The latter organisation
was mainly the work of the Distillers Company Ltd. (D.C.L.), a new firm formed in
1877 from six Lowland distilling firms. Tables 5 and 6 show the membership of the
two Associations. The original participants in the D.C.L. were the first five firms in
Table 5, along with Alexander Stewart & Co. of Kirkliston distillery.

This is not the occasion to present a detailed account of these attempts, lasting
for almost a quarter of a century, to restrict competition, but some general remarks
can be made.

The ultimate aim of both Associations was to control sales and prices in the United
Kingdom whilst leaving distillers free to compete in the export trade. At 8 per cent of

Table 5 *Membership of the Scotch Distillers' Association*

Firm	Distillery
Scottish Distillers:	
John Bald & Co.	Carsebridge
McNab Bros. & Co;	Clenochil
Robert Moubray	Cambus
Daniel Macfarlane & Co.	Port Dundas
John Haig & Co.	Cameron Bridge
Menzies, Bernard & Craig	Caledonian
Robert Harvey & Co.	Yoker
Irish Distillers:	
The Cork Distillers Co.	Midleton, Co.Cork
Malcolm Brown & Co.	Dundalk
David Watt	Londonderry
English Distillers:	
Archibald Walker & Co.	Vauxhall Distillery, Liverpool
The London Distillers	(Number of firms and names not known but see Table 6)

(Source: W.H. Ross, *op.cit.,* pp.15-17)

Table 6 *United Kingdom Distillers' Association: Original Membership 1878*

Firm	Distillery
Scottish Distillers:	
Distillers Company Limited	Six Grain Distilleries One Irish Pot Still Distillery: Phoenix Park, Dublin
Menzies & Co.	Caledonian, Edinburgh
J. & W. Harvey	Yoker, Glasgow
J. Calder	Bo'ness
Archibald Walker	Loch Catrine, Glasgow
Irish Distillers:	
Archibald Walker	Limerick
Cork Distillers Co.	Midleton, Co.Cork
D. Watt & Co.	Londonderry
Malcolm Brown & Co.	Dundalk
English Distillers:	
R.W. Preston & Co.	Bankhall, Liverpool
Archibald Walker	Vauxhall, Liverpool

Members by Supplementary Agreement (from 1882)

London Distillers' Association:	
John Currie & Co.	Bromley
C.H. Smith & Co.	Thames Bank
John Watney & Co.	Wandsworth
H. & J. Haig	Hammersmith
J. & W. Nicholson	Three Mills, Bromley
Thomas Board	Bristol
Firm not known	West Ham
William Higgins & Co.	Avoneil, Belfast

(Source: compiled from the minute books of the UKDA)

the total demand for home produced spirits in 1865 and 11 per cent in 1890, exports were too small to absorb excess production. For all patent still distillers it was home demand that mattered most.

What underlay both Associations was a growing awareness of mutual interdependence. This owed much to the fact that patent still spirit served more than one type of market but it was also increased by foreign competition. By the mid-1860s three main markets existed for patent still spirit. The first and probably the most important was the sale of grain spirit for consumption as whisky, either on its own or, as was increasingly the case, after blending with pot still whiskies. The second was its use in England for gin rectification. The last and newest was the methylated spirit market created by the Act of 1855 which allowed the duty-free use of denatured spirit. (45) In 1860 a mere 149,000 gallons of spirit were methylated, amounting to 0.1 per cent of total U.K. patent still output. It was not, at this stage, an important factor in the formation of the Associations.

In neither a technical nor an economic sense were the first two markets separate. Recognition of this created a constant pressure to recruit as many patent still distilleries as possible into the ranks of the Associations. Recruiting incentives not infrequently included the use of subsidised prices to undercut firms outside the Associations. During the Scotch Distillers' Association, Irish and Scottish firms selling in the English market were subsidised from the higher prices prevailing in Ireland and Scotland to persuade English distillers to agree to raise their prices to the Association level. Later, in 1883, Irish members of the U.K.D.A. were subsidised in an effort to destroy the challenge posed to the Association by a new entrant to the industry, William Higgins of Avoneil. Belfast was 'the field where Higgins would be met' and after three months Higgins agreed to join the Association with a sales quota of 200,000 gallons, well below the 850,000 gallons productive capacity of his distillery. (46)

Such actions were at odds with the prevailing economic ideology, but so too was the competition distillers faced from imported spirits. In world terms, the United Kingdom was not a large producer of alcohol but it was a free-trade nation with an open market for the surplus output of other nations. London, described by one distiller as 'the spirit market of the world', bore the brunt of foreign competition but the repercussions were felt throughout the entire patent still industry. (47) Imports of low-priced German and American spirit reached 11.5 per cent of U.K. patent still production in 1875. German spirit was being offered for 8½d. to 1s. p.p.g. between 1870 and 1875 when home-produced grain spirit was selling at between 2s. and 2.6d. German spirit was made mainly from the Prussian potato crop and the State fostered alcohol production in the interests of agriculture. There was little the distillers' combinations could do to stem this inflow beyond petitioning the Government, unsuccessfully, for protection. American spirit, too, formed part of a surplus deliberately exported to Europe at loss by the American whisky pool. Changes in the supply conditions in the countries of origin rather than the actions of the Associations – or the British Government – led to a diminution in imports. In 1887, the members of the American pool formed 'The Distillers and Cattle Feeders Trust' based on the model of the Standard Oil Trust. Instead of exporting at a loss, the Trust concentrated production on a small number of distilleries and used cost savings from this rationalisation to lower prices and crush outside competitiors. In Germany, also in 1887, the State lowered the export bounty and began to encourage the use of alcohol for non-potable purposes in the production of heat, light and power. (48)

Both Associations gained members as a result of a deep-seated feeling of insecurity created by the internationalisation of the spirit trade. In their turn, though, they created insecurity amongst their customers, particularly in the early 1880s when the U.K.D.A. trading regulations were accepted by every patent still distillery. The response of this took the form that the U.K.D.A. most feared: the foundation of new patent still distilleries by whisky merchants alarmed at the Association's control over grain whisky supplies for blending. In 1885, two new patent still distilleries, The Irish Distillery at Connswater near Belfast and The North British Distillery in Edinburgh, were established. (49) The former was financed by three Belfast blending firms and the latter was a co-operative promoted by whisky blenders in Edinburgh and Leith. (50) Competition from these distilleries and the disenchantment of the Distillers Company with the trade association as a means of governing the trade, finally destroyed the U.K.D.A.

In the boom of the 1890s patent still distillers continued less formal consultations about prices but with the upsurge in demand there was little anxiety about competition. After 1900, in very different circumstances, it was the Distillers Company which applied the lesson learnt from the experience of the U.K.D.A. that grain distilling could only be controlled by full amalgamation. By 1922, the D.C.L. was to control all but one patent still distillery in Scotland (North British), all but one in Ireland (Midleton) and all but two in England (Three Mills and Wandsworth).

VI

In recent years considerable effort has gone into re-interpreting Irish economic history and rescuing it from the nationalist mould which emphasised the harmful effects of British economic policy on Irish industry. In the process the key factor in explaining nineteenth-century Irish economic history has become the role of competition between two countries at different levels of economic development. The history of the patent still distilling industry suggests the need to qualify that interpretation and to re-examine the view that the survival of Irish industries depended on their ability to export. Competition was not a blind force, unforeseen and impossible to impede. Competition in patent still distilling produced deliberate attempts to restrict it. Attempts which, like competition itself, were made possible by improvements in communications that in the 1860s and 1870s enabled the representatives of the English, Scottish and Irish patent still distillers to meet fortnightly to discuss affairs in their industry.

NOTES

1. Studies of the industry with a historical content include: R. Bruce Lockhart, *Scotch* (1951); S.W. Sillett, *Illicit Scotch* (Aberdeen, 1965); D. Daiches, *Scotch Whisky* (1969); R. Wilson, *Scotch: The Formative Years* (1970). The industry has been the subject of two doctoral theses: I.A. Glen, 'An Economic History of the Distilling Industry in Scotland 1750-1914' University of Strathclyde Ph.D. thesis,

1969, and R.B. Weir, 'The Distilling Industry in Scotland in the Nineteenth and Early Twentieth Centuries', University of Edinburgh Ph.D. thesis, 1974. See also R.B. Weir, *The History of the Malt Distillers' Association of Scotland* (Elgin, 1974).

2. H. Hamilton, *An Economic History of Scotland in the Eighteenth Century* (Oxford, 1963), pp.103-10.

3. See e.g. R.H. Campbell, *Scotland since 1707: The Rise of an Industrial Society* (Oxford, 1971), pp.200-2.

4. Two *Reports from the Select Committee on the Distillery in different parts of Scotland, and on the best mode of levying and collecting the Duties upon the Distillation of Corn Spirits in Scotland,* P.P. Vol.XI, 1803, App.26, p.388.

5. *Statistical Account,* XVIII, 603.

6. Though aspects of the reforms such as the emphasis on competition and the discussion of the principles of taxation have a general interest.

7. The main problem here was the need to obtain access to the archives of the Distillers Company, the firm which came to dominate the industry by the 1920s.

8. References to these features include: *Statistical Account,* I, 361; II, 38, 85, 206; V, 9; VIII, 293; XIV, 623.

9. *New Statistical Account,* VIII, 49, 150; IX, 226; XIII, 137.

10. 'Consolidation', i.e. the elimination of excess distilling capacity.

11. K.H. Connell, 'Illicit Distillation: An Irish Peasant Industry', *Historical Studies,* III (London, 1963); E.B. McGuire, *Irish Whiskey: A History of Distilling in Ireland* (Dublin, 1973).

12. P. Lynch and J. Vaizey, *Guiness's Brewery in the Irish Economy 1759-1876* (Cambridge, 1960).

13. J.C. Beckett, *The Making of Modern Ireland 1603-1923* (Glasgow, 1966), pp. 291, 363.

14. J. Lee, 'The Railways in the Irish Economy' in L.M. Cullen, ed, *The Formation of the Irish Economy* (Cork, 1969), p.85.

15. Lee, *op.cit.,* p.86.

16. L.M. Cullen, *An Economic History of Ireland since 1660* (London, 1972), pp.145-7.

17. Cullen, *op.cit.,* pp.157-8.

18. Blending is the mixing of different whiskies. Many of these points were also raised by F.S.L. Lyons, *Ireland since the Famine* (London, 1971), pp.55-6.

19. *Fifth Report of the Commissioners ... for inquiring into the Collection and Management of the Public Revenue arising in Great Britain* P.P. Vol.VII, 1823, App.83, p.252.

20. Full details of these changes can be found in J. Scarisbrick, *Spirit Manual* (Burton-on-Trent, 1891), pp.72-83, 116-25.

21. Sources: G.B. Wilson, *Alcohol and the Nation* (1940), Table 4, pp.341-8 and B.R. Mitchell and P. Deane, *Abstract of British Historical Statistics* (Cambridge, 1962), Table 3, pp.8-10. There is an important assumption underlying these figures, namely that few transfers of duty-paid spirit took place within the United Kingdom. For a discussion of their reliability see R.B. Weir, 'The Development of the Distilling Industry in Scotland in the Nineteenth and Early Twentieth Centuries', University of Edinburgh Ph.D. thesis, 1974, II, 453.

22. There is no direct way of establishing the market shares of gin and whisky, as the sole description used by the Excise for home-produced spirits was 'British Plain Spirit'. The figure for gin consumption in 1834 comes from *The Seventh Report of the Commissioners of Inquiry into the Excise Establishment and into the Management and Collection of Excise Revenue throughout the United Kingdom* P.P. Vol.XXV, 1834, 30. For 1890 and 1907 the figures are the quantities of raw spirit being rectified, i.e. undergoing the process for gin making. Sources: Report from the *Select Committee on British and Foreign Spirits* P.P. Vol.XI, 1890-91, v; *Royal Commission on Whiskey and Other Potable Spirits* P.P.1909, Cd. 4797, QQ. 14144-7.

23. In 1891 the consumption of foreign spirits was distributed as follows: England, 6.956 m.p.g.; Scotland, 0.799 m.p.g.; Ireland, 0.666 m.p.g. Source for Graph 2: Wilson, *op.cit.,* Table 10, pp.356-8.

24. Report of the Board of Inland Revenue to the Treasury, 28th February, 1865 on the Rate of Spirit Duty   P.P. Vol.XXXI, 1865, 20.

25. *The Seventh Report,* p.37.

26. *The Seventh Report,* p.56.

27. For the reasons see Connell, *op.cit.,* pp.72-3.

28. *The Seventh Report,* pp.229-32.

29. *Report from the Select Committee on the effect of allowing a Malt Drawback on Spirits* P.P. Vol.VII, 1831, 130.

30. Production figures from Wilson, *op.cit.,* Table 3, pp.336-8. Number of Distilleries from *The Seventh Report,* p.29 and *Report from the Board of Inland Revenue* P.P. Vol.XXXI, 1865, 20.

31. For details see Weir, *op.cit.,* I., 196-209.

32. A. Coffey, *British Patent 1830,* 5974.

33. *The Seventh Report,* p.48.

34. *Select Committee on the Distillery in Scotland,* evidence of Abraham Newton, spirit dealer in Edinburgh, pp.74-5.

35. *Select Committee on the Distillery in Scotland,* App. I(A), p.60.

36. *The Seventh Report,* pp.29-30.

37. *The Seventh Report,* pp.30-31.

38. A high gravity wash gave a large yield of spirits.

39. This discussion of pot and patent stills relies on three main sources: Slater, *op.cit.,* pp.48-59; A.J.V. Underwood, 'The Historical Development of Distilling Plant', *The Transactions of the Institution of Chemical Engineers,* 13, (1935), pp.45-62; and R. Wilson, 'The Evolution of the Patent Still', *The Wine and Spirit Trade Record,* 18th October, 1962, pp.1392-6; 16th November, 1962, pp.1538-44; 17th December, 1962, pp.1742-46; 16th January, 1963, pp.48-50.

40. I.A. Glen, Introduction to A. Barnard, *The Whisky Distillers of the United Kingdom* (first published 1887; new edition Newton Abbot, 1969); D. Diaches, *Scotch Whisky* (1969), p.60.

41. Grain spirit is not a neutral spirit, i.e. pure ethyl alcohol, but it contains less of the higher alcohols and traces of raw materials which give malt whiskies distinctive characteristics. For a modern account of the chemical analysis of Scotch grain whisky see M. Pyke, 'The Manufacture of Scotch Grain Whisky', *Journal of the Institute of Brewing,* LXXI, (1965), 3.

42. For discussion of this see Weir, *op.cit.,* I, 268-88.

43. The only source for the trade agreement of 1856 and The Scotch Distillers' Association of 1865-1876 is W.H. Ross, 'History of the Company', *D.C.L. Gazette,* January, 1923, pp.12-17.

44. The minute books of the United Kingdom Distillers' Association have survived. Subsequent reference cited as U.K.D.A.M.B.

45. Denatured spirit: spirit rendered unfit for potable purposes by the addition of a noxious substance. Originally crude wood naptha was used.

46. U.K.D.A.M.B. No.I at 20th September, 1883.

47. *Royal Commission on Whiskey,* Q. 8599.

48. The above discussion is based on two main sources. For America the source is J.W. Jenks, 'The Development of the Whiskey Trust', *Political Science Quarterly,* IV (1889). For Germany it is C. Simmonds, *Alcohol: Its Production, Properties and Applications* (1919), pp.107-110. Much of Simmonds' material was drawn from E. Kremers, *Agricultural Alcohol: Studies of its Manufacture in Germany,* Abstract of United States Department of Agriculture, Bulletin No. 182 (Washington, 1915).

49. Their productive capacities were 2.0 m.p.g. and 1.3 m.p.g. respectively.

50. The blenders were Kirker, Greer & Co., Messrs. Mitchell & Co., and James Wilson & Son.

PART IV

TRADE

11. A Comparative Study of the Irish and Scottish Livestock Trades in the Seventeenth Century (1)

Donald Woodward

An Englishman: 'Pharaoh's lean kine will feed upon our full pastures'. 1606. (2)
An Irishman (by adoption): 'Great good will come to this kingdom by transporting
    cattle ... into England'. 1616. (3)
And a Scotsman: 'Better sell nowte (nolt or black cattle) than sell nations'. c1707. (4)

I

IN BOTH Ireland and Scotland terrain and climate tended to dictate the predominance
of pastoral agriculture over much of the land and countless contemporary writers
and later historians have borne witness to that bias. The first goal of peasant economic
activity was to provide a sufficient supply of grain for the family but thereafter economic well-being depended on the production of a livestock surplus. For many, cattle
constituted the only readily realisable form of wealth and, moreover, tended to
determine an individual's social standing. (5) However, until the end of the sixteenth
century political and social constraints in both countries prevented the export potential
which flowed from this predominantly pastoral bias from being fulfilled. (6)

Perhaps the major constraint on economic development in sixteenth-century
Scotland was the 'lack of good government, lack of universal justice, and the threat
of war'. (7) Much the same was true for Ireland, only there war was often real enough.
During the century the English crown made repeated attempts to extend its power
in Ireland and replace Gaelic law and customs by their English counterparts. (8) This
process, which included periods of devastating conflict, was complicated by the
existence of domestic rivalries often no less destructive. In Scotland more than a
century of weak government was ended by the majority of James VI who strove,
with increasing success, to extend his control. But ancient animosities could not be
ended overnight and feuds continued to be actively pursued until the end of the century
and beyond. (9) Feuds in both countries often involved a degree of economic opportun-
ism, as when war parties suddenly descended and carried off valuable herds of cattle. (10)
In addition to the widespread lawlessness the system of landholding in neither country
was designed to facilitate large-scale production for the market. Large sections of the
population were on a war footing and the aim of chiefs in the more turbulent areas
was to maximise fighting power rather than economic production. Such a situation,
in which many 'regarded themselves as so many cavaliers or men-at-arms, rather than
as the peasantry of a peaceful country', (11) was infertile soil in which to plant the
seeds of economic development.

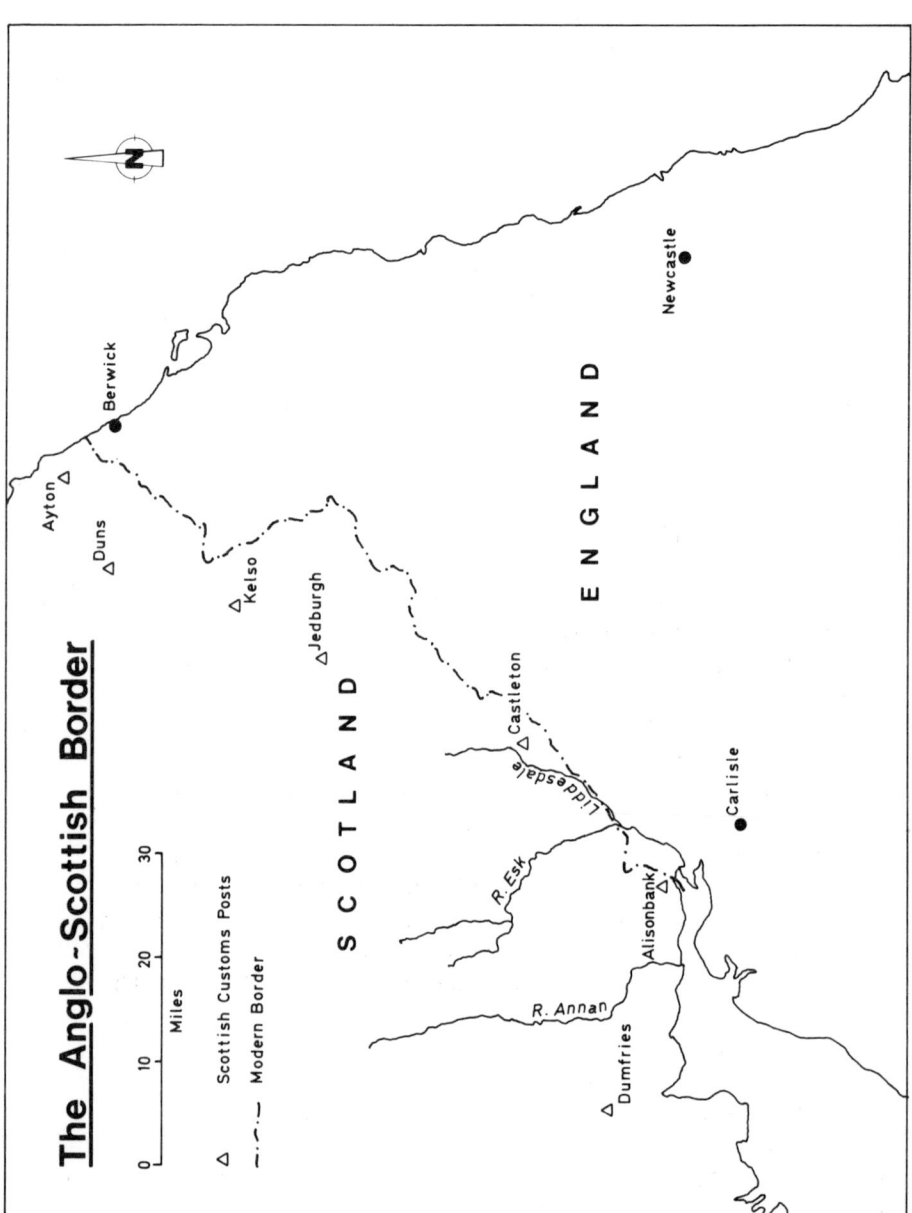

The Anglo-Scottish Border

Miles

0   10   20   30

△   Scottish Customs Posts

—··—   Modern Border

S C O T L A N D

E N G L A N D

Ayton △

△ Duns

△ Kelso

△ Jedburgh

Berwick ●

Newcastle ●

△ Castleton

Liddesdale

△ Alisonbank

R. Esk

R. Annan

△ Dumfries

Carlisle ●

Map by D. Waite, University of Hull.

However, it is important not to exaggerate the barriers to development. Although both countries were economically backward compared with England and most other countries of Western Europe, they were not simple subsistence economies. By the sixteenth century important inter-regional trades had emerged in Scotland – the most important of which was the exchange of Highland cattle for Lowland grain – and the merchant communities of both countries had trading contacts with other countries as well as with each other. (12) The presence of towns also implies the existence of a market economy. By the later sixteenth century the population of Edinburgh had reached about 30,000 and Dundee, Aberdeen and Perth contained between five and eight thousand inhabitants. (13) Most other towns were considerably smaller although Scotland contained 'many royal boroughs yoked on end to end'. (14) Town development in Ireland was less impressive but the countryside provided a surplus for the country's port towns including the thriving port of Dublin.

The early seventeenth century witnessed the development of more settled conditions in both countries. In Scotland the Lowlands enjoyed peace for much of the century and by the 1630s the restless Borderers no longer participated in large-scale raids but had become increasingly litigious or dabbled in petty crime. (15) The Highlands took longer to change; the last pitched battle between two clans took place as late as 1680 and raids on the Lowlands continued until the end of the century. (16) But even the Highlands were more settled than in previous centuries. In Ireland peace was not achieved overnight although with the Tudor conquest the whole country, for the first time in its history, was open to English administration – including Ulster, that 'receptacle and very den of rebels and devouring creatures'. (17) Some sections of Gaelic society continued to resist English control – during the 1610s and 1620s wood-kernes stole and destroyed cattle – but not sufficiently to disrupt economic progress. (18) With the coming of peace trade was able to flourish as never before.

II

During the seventeenth century most of the cattle and sheep produced in Ireland and Scotland found their way into native cooking pots but they have left few traces for the historian to follow. But some animals were traded over longer distances and, fortunately for the historian, some of the animals considered fit enough to tramp to English markets (having survived an awkward sea crossing in the case of the Irish contingent) caught the attention of customs officials who recorded their movement. It is with these Celtic exports, once 'seen creeping like moles in size and slowness of motion on the broad face of the moor', (19) that I shall be concerned mainly in this paper.

During the sixteenth century occasional consignments of cattle were sent to England from Ireland and Scotland but even the more important Scottish branch of the trade remained 'spasmodic and interrupted'. (20) Then during the first four decades of the following century Irish livestock exports expanded considerably although the size of the trade is uncertain because of deficiencies in the customs data. However, by the late 1630s annual cattle exports probably exceeded the 20,000 mark, possibly by a large margin. Sheep exports seem to have been at a rather lower

level. (21) There is hardly any evidence relating to the Scottish trade for the period
before 1640 except the solitary suggestion for the early 1610s that 'great quantity'
of cattle and sheep were 'transported by land daily'. (22) We may guess that the
trade grew, but we can do no more than guess.

For both countries the 1640s and 1650s were difficult decades. Political disturbances and war played havoc with trade and economic life in general especially in the
years around 1650. (23) The flow of beasts from Ireland was reduced to a trickle
and may have stopped altogether in some years. No doubt the same was true for
Scotland. But in both countries total economic collapse was avoided and recovery
set in at some point during the 1650s, as is suggested by the high level of livestock
exports from both countries during the early 1660s.

Irish livestock exports to England were at record levels during the 1660s; the
rather disjointed information available suggests that 50,000 or more cattle and over
100,000 sheep were shipped from Ireland each year in the mid 1660s. (24) Some
of the Irish cattle arriving in England came via Scotland; the customs book for the
border customs point at Alisonbank records that 7,287 Irish cattle marched to
England from Scotland between 30 May and 13 July 1666. (25)

Unfortunately less information is available for the Scottish trade during this
period. Only the Alisonbank customs book has survived and it records that 1,050
cattle, 6,003 sheep and 622 lambs crossed to England during 1665-6. In the absence
of customs data it is necessary to fall back on contemporary estimates and calculations
although it is recognised that they can be highly misleading; thus it would seem that
the estimate, voiced in the English House of Commons in 1663, that more than
80,000 head of Scottish cattle were sold yearly in England was a typical piece of
parliamentary rhetoric. (26) Another estimate, for 1662-3, placed the number of
Scottish cattle customed at Carlisle at 18,364 (27) although a later estimate – probably
belonging to 1664 – put the trade at a rather higher level. (28)

Table 1   *An estimate of Scottish livestock exports, c1664.*

	Cattle	Sheep
Carlisle	30,961	9,402
Berwick (Eastern & Middle Marches)	16,932	c 2,000
Total	47,893	11,402

Source: P.R.O. 30/24/4/112.

Thus it seems that livestock exports from both countries were running at a fairly
high level during the early 1660s, although figures for the Scottish trade are problematical. Indeed, Celtic cattle and sheep were arriving in England in such large numbers
that old English fears about the effect of large-scale imports on price and rent levels
were revived. In 1663 the English parliament addressed itself to the problem and
the 'act for the encouragement (sic) of trade', which closed the trade for some months
each year, was passed. This measure, which came into force in 1664, prohibited the
import of Irish cattle between 1 July and 20 December and Scottish cattle between
24 August and 20 December. The sheep of both countries were banned between

1 August and 20 December. (29) This act was not designed to stop livestock imports altogether but just to remove the competition from Celtic fatstock and force the Irish and Scots to send lean beasts to England. This act does not seem to have reduced the total volume of Irish livestock shipments to England although it did, as was intended, force landowners to get their beasts to market rather earlier than they would have liked. (30)

The 1663 act was soon superseded by the 'act against importing cattle from Ireland and other parts beyond the seas' which received the royal assent on 18 January 1667 and came into force two weeks later. (31) As the title suggests, Scottish livestock were exempt from the new provisions and the Scots quickly followed the English lead by prohibiting the import of Irish cattle with effect from 1 March 1667. (32) Regular shipments of Irish stock were stopped by these measures although some consignments managed to evade the customs officials; if the volume of complaint is a realistic index, the Scots had more trouble than the English with illicit Irish imports. (33)

It is reasonable to assume that the closure of the English market to Irish livestock would provide a congenial environment for the further development of Scottish live-stock exports to England. Unfortunately there is very little evidence for the period immediately after 1667 with which to test such a suggestion. Only two border customs books for the 1670s have survived and they reveal a low level of traffic passing through Kelso and Jedburgh. (34)

Table 2   *Scottish livestock exports via Kelso and Jedburgh*

	Cattle	Sheep	Lambs
Kelso 1673	213	112	0
Jedburgh 1672			
(Aug to Oct only)	219	350	120

Source: S.R.O. E72/14/2,3; 13/2.

Much more information is available for the 1680s. With the exception of the years 1687 and 1688, for which customs books have not survived, it is possible to reconstruct almost the whole of the southerly traffic in livestock that came under the scrutiny of the Scottish customs officials. This information, presented in Table 3, needs to be studied together with the more detailed data provided in the Appendix because not all the customs posts are represented each year in the global figures given in the table. Thus the figures for cattle and sheep exports in 1681 and 1691 are depressed by the absence of Castleton although the absence of Ayton and Duns in some years is less serious. However, cattle exports for 1686, apparently a 'good year' according to the table, are probably seriously under-represented because of the absence of infor-mation for Dumfries. There was also some under-recording of the trade at Ayton and Kelso because of the practice of listing the duty paid at fairs on beasts destined for England rather than the number of livestock on which the duty was paid. (35)

Despite deficiencies Table 3 demonstrates that the legal trade in livestock was indeed 'that species of commerce ... liable to sudden fluctuations'. (36) Given the present state of knowledge it is not easy to explain these fluctuations; perhaps they were in part connected with climatic or harvest fluctuations in Scotland or, as in the

Table 3 *Scottish livestock exports to England 1681-6, 1689-91*

	Cattle	Sheep	Lambs	Pigs
1681[a]	10,942	6,374	569	221
1682	16,491	20,910	3,769	365
1683[b]	27,294	31,857	4,585	193
1684[b]	14,015	19,652	587	295
1685[b]	20,564	14,398	1,313	239
1686[c]	25,100	25,156	4,644	564
1689	16,278	9,780	1,108	400
1690[d]	12,367	11,570	3,019	92
1691[ad]	11,591	11,935	2,857	15

Source: As in the Appendix

Notes: a Excluding Castleton
              b Excluding Duns
              c Excluding Dumfries
              d Excluding Ayton and Duns

last years of the decade, with political uncertainty.

Historians of the Scottish livestock trades have generally followed contemporary observers in believing that cattle were the only animals to be moved across the border in significant numbers during the seventeenth century. However, as Table 3 demonstrates, there was a lively market in England for Scottish sheep, as indeed there was for Irish sheep. In some years more sheep than cattle were driven to England during the 1680s although in value terms cattle remained more important. (37) Smaller numbers of lambs also made the crossing each year as did a few score pigs. Perhaps the most bizarre part of the livestock trades was the export of 'roasting geese' via Ayton and Duns (38) and the sixteen chickens exported from Jedburgh in 1682.

There was also a small trade in dead-stock to England mainly across the eastern section of the border. The customs books for Ayton and Duns are full of references to small consignments of dead sheep and other stock and this is illustrated by Table 4. (

Table 4 *Dead-stock exports, 1682*

	Cattle	Sheep	Calves	Lambs	Pigs
Ayton	227½	704	8	120	149
Duns	236	1,401	53½	469	99
Total	463½	2,105	61½	589	248

Source: As in the Appendix. The unit is single animals.

From 1691 until the start of the English Ledgers of Imports and Exports in 1696-7 the only customs data available for the livestock trade come from the 1695 customs books for Alisonbank, Castleton and Jedburgh. The first book, which gives entries for Alisonbank and Castleton, lists 13,090 cattle, 2,734 sheep and 28 lambs which crossed the border into England. The Jedburgh book lists 484 cattle, 13,361 sheep and 386 lambs. (40)

In 1705 John Spreull, a Glasgow merchant, suggested that Scotland sent between 24,000 and 30,000 cattle to England a year. (41) This was not a bad guess; it seems to have been much more realistic than many earlier estimates of the Irish trade and some estimates of the Scottish trade. Details of the Scottish livestock trade at the end of the century are laid down in Table 5.

Table 5   *Scottish livestock exports to England 1696-1707*

	Cattle	Sheep	Lambs
1696-7	20,615	1,180	0
1697-8	59,701	0	0
1699	18,132	210	0
1700	39,261	0	140
1701	13,839	0	0
1702	11,314	0	0
1703	14,767	15	0
1704	0	0	0
1705	-	-	-
1706	0	0	0
1707	0	0	0

Source: P.R.O. Customs 3/1-10, 81.

Unfortunately the reliability of the data presented in Table 5 is open to question on two counts. Firstly, the figures for sheep exports are suspiciously low compared with those for the 1680s (Table 3). Secondly, it is difficult to accept that livestock exports ceased altogether in 1704, 1706 and 1707 despite the political uncertainties of those years and the problems connected with the mooted anti-Scottish legislation of 1705. Historians of trade have been inclined to accept the figures of the Inspector General of Imports and Exports, but at least in relation to Scottish livestock exports they remain in some doubt. (42)

It is difficult to establish the overall trend of Scottish livestock exports from the fragmentary information presented in this paper and it must be stressed that the establishment of trends is bedevilled by uncertainty as to the relative size of the illegal branch of the trade and its possible variation over time. The data presented here suggest that a high level of exports was achieved in particular years — such as 1664, 1683, 1686, 1697-8 or 1700 — although this may have been at the expense of exports in subsequent years. For what it is worth, the average annual export of cattle during the 1680s was 18,873 head (Table 3) compared with an average export of 25,518 at the turn of the century (Table 5, 1696-1703 only). These tentative and problematical figures suggest that Scottish livestock exports did not expand significantly during the second half of the seventeenth century.

It could be argued that the major problem facing the Scottish producer in this period was a stagnant English market. English population grew little in the later seventeenth century and the changes taking place in English agriculture probably involved a gradual increase in the size of the national flock and herd. But such a facile explanation of postulated Scottish export performance runs counter to the Irish experience. As we have seen, Irish exports were banned in 1667 although this

L

was not a permanent measure. The ban ended during the spring of 1679 and almost immediately Irish stock were shipped across for the English market. During 1680 24,116 cattle and 83,452 sheep were landed at the west coast ports south of Cumberland. But the trade did not last. A new bill to ban Irish livestock was rushed through parliament and in January 1681 livestock shippers were hurrying once again to beat a 1 February deadline. (43)

The brief interlude of 1679-81 during which Irish stock once again found a ready sale in England gives us an illuminating insight into the development of the two economies. It has often been suggested that the Irish reacted to the 1667 ban by developing the provisioning trades. However the redevelopment of the livestock trade during 1679-81 suggests that provisioning had taken up only a part of the slack although the relatively low cattle exports of 1680 compared with the level achieved during the 1660s does suggest that provisioning had made some significant progress. The Irish performance of 1679-81 also suggests that English demand for meat was not totally satisfied by home production together with additional supplies from Scotland and Wales. (44) Thus it seems that Scottish producers failed to take advantage of favourable market conditions created by the 1667 ban on Irish stock. However, the hypothesis that the inability of Scottish producers to expand output dramatically was not due to market conditions in England cannot be proved conclusively in the absence of detailed information relating to production costs, droving costs, and selling prices for English, Irish and Scottish beasts.

III

One of the greatest problems in dealing with the Irish and Scottish livestock trades is knowing exactly where the beasts came from and were going to. It is generally assumed that in England the long-distance livestock trades were set in a southerly direction, designed essentially to feed the rapidly growing population of London. According to John Houghton's estimate of 1692, London consumed some 88,400 cattle yearly. (45) If this is a realistic guess, the Irish and Scottish cattle moving to England in the early 1660s could have more than satisfied London's demand. But some stock was sold and consumed elsewhere and the overall pattern of these trades in England is likely to remain a mystery. So far only fragments of data about the two trades have emerged. The accounts of the Tokes, who farmed in Kent and specialised in fattening beasts for the London market, contain only a single reference to both Irish and Scottish stock; likewise the banker Edward Backwell dabbled in the Irish trade during the 1660s but he soon dropped it after getting his fingers burnt and concentrated on buying English stock to fatten on his Buckinghamshire estate. (46)

Unfortunately it is no easier to establish the origin of the beasts moved to England. At the moment the extent of cattle and sheep farming in the different parts of Ireland is not at all clear (47) although some slight assistance can be gained from the English port books. Throughout the century Dublin was the greatest centre of the trade, sending cattle and sheep mainly to Chester and Liverpool. Unfortunately, little is known about the extent of Dublin's hinterland except that cattle were moved a long way to the port; thus Sir George Rawdon and the Earl of Conway regularly sent cattle to Dublin for export from the Lisburn area, near Belfast. (48) The export of stock, especially sheep, from southern ports — mainly Waterford, Youghal and Cork in the 1660s (49) — indicates the flourishing nature of livestock production in Munster.

For the Scottish trade the point at which beasts crossed the border gives some clue as to their origin. The 1680s customs books show that the bulk of the cattle were funnelled through the west coast plain while sheep tended to cross more easterly parts of the border.

Table 6 *Proportion of stock passing through the different customs posts, 1681-5 inclusive*

	Cattle %	Sheep %
Kelso and Jedburgh	6.9	51.4
Castleton	10.8	28.0
Alisonbank	38.9	18.6
Dumfries	42.8	0.5

Source: As in the Appendix

There is little doubt that the bulk of the sheep sent to England were produced in the Border region. This was sheep country *par excellence,* in part a legacy of the medieval monastic estates. (50) As John MacKy remarked of the hills of Tweeddale, which he likened to the Sussex Downs, 'they are all green, and it's hardly credible the number of sheep one sees upon them'. (51) Sheep moving to England via Kelso, Jedburgh and Castleton probably came from the Borders and it seems likely that many of those customed at Alisonbank were of similar origin. Hardly any sheep paid duty at Dumfries, which underlines the accepted notion that the south-west was devoted mainly to cattle production. Finally, the relatively early movement of sheep to England each year suggests that they could not have been brought from the Highlands in time. Monthly stock movements are presented in Table 7.

Table 7 *Monthly stock movements from Scotland to England, 1681-5*

	Jan.	Feb.	Mar.	Apr.	May	June	July	Aug.	Sep.	Oct.	Nov.	Dec.
Cattle[a]	0	0	0	2.0	7.1	8.0	6.6	20.0	36.2	13.8	5.6	0.7
Sheep[b]	0.2	0	0	0.6	7.8	50.6	10.3	4.6	5.3	9.3	6.4	4.8

Source: As in the Appendix.
Notes: a Alisonbank, Castleton and Dumfries only.
       b Alisonbank, Castleton, Kelso and Jedburgh only.

The origin of the cattle sent to England is less easy to establish. It is tempting to interpret Table 6 by suggesting that some 18 per cent of the cattle came from the Border region (via Kelso, Jedburgh and Castleton), nearly 43 per cent from the south-west (via Dumfries) and 39 per cent from further north (via Alisonbank). But such an interpretation is fraught with difficulties. Perhaps a high proportion of the cattle customed at Dumfries were originally from the Highlands and merely fattened in the south-west. Conversely, it may be that the bulk of those cattle were bred locally and also that many of the beasts customed at Alisonbank were from the south-west rather than from the Highlands.

The Scottish customs books give the names of the men who controlled the stock moving to England and at first glance it seemed that these names could provide clues about the origin of the cattle. But once again there are substantial problems of interpretation. To begin with, the role of the man (it is never a woman) listed is not always clear; sometimes a drover is specified but on other occasions the man can be identified as a substantial landowner who may or may not actually, have been with the drove. In addition only a few of the books regularly give the men's domiciles (52) and when they are given there is then the problem of identification. Little Park, the home of Patrick Herron who sent 1,000 or more cattle to England via Dumfries in each of the years 1689-91 inclusive, (53) is in Kirkcudbrightshire: but it occurs in no gazetteer, and only the local knowledge of Professor Butt at the seminar enabled us to identify it. A cursory examination of surnames suggests that Highlanders did not feature prominently in the trade. In the customs books of the 1680s English and Border names predominate, although some Highlanders controlled large herds; the 1681 Alisonbank book lists John McLeod along with 570 cattle. But even in a case like this is it legitimate to assume that he was controlling a herd of Highland cattle?

Did Scottish cattle exports come predominantly from the Highlands during the seventeenth century as is often assumed? The tentative data presented here suggest that, as Professor Smout suspected, the south-west played a crucial role in the trade in the later seventeenth century. (54) It has long been recognised that David Dunbar of Baldoon, with his famous cattle park, was a lively improver in those parts and that he was followed by others. (55) Some names could be added to the list by a careful study of evidence provided in the customs accounts and they would include Sir Patrick Maxwell of Springkell in Dumfriesshire. In 1682 he sent two droves totalling 680 cattle to England and a later drove of 420 cattle in conjunction with a certain Duncan McDugall. (56) In suggesting that the south-west may have been the chief source of cattle for the English market (57) I am not denying the southward movement of Highland cattle. During the seventeenth century the Scottish burghs — and especially Glasgow — grew in size and it may be that Highland producers geared their efforts towards delighting Lowland rather than English palates.

IV

Both Ireland and Scotland benefited substantially from the development of the livestock trades, which in the case of both countries sprang predominantly from native enterprise. (58) It has been suggested that in Ireland 'cattle fairs drew business interests together and gave to the country its first semblance of effective economic unity', and the same was probably true for Scotland. (59) Certainly the resulting cash and credit flow was of immense value to both countries and fluctuations in the livestock trades often determined the rate of exchange with sterling. (60) But by the end of the century the paths of the two economies had diverged somewhat. By 1700 Ireland, temporarily depressed by the 1667 ban, had developed the more labour-intensive provisioning trade, whereas Scotland was still committed to the traditional livestock trade. In the seven years ending 1703 cattle exports amounted to 40.2 per cent of total Scottish exports to England and it was this trade which gave the northern kingdom a favourable balance of trade with her southern neighbour. (61) Despite the loss of the livestock trades, Irish exports to England were valued at more than three times the level of Scottish exports to England. (62)

For much of the seventeenth century Ireland and Scotland (and Wales also) produced a livestock surplus which helped to satisfy growing demand in England. Down to 1667, and especially during the 1660s, Irish landowners seem to have responded more readily to this stimulus. If the Scottish data can be relied on, and that is by no means certain, the Scots did not expand their sales to England appreciably after 1667. Unfortunately much of the information needed to examine this hypothesis of relative unresponsiveness to the English market is not available. We know little about the relative costs of delivering Irish and Scottish stock to English markets although they would vary according to the particular market involved. Assuming that many of the beasts were destined for the London area, Irish cattle arriving at Chester or Minehead would have only about half the distance to travel overland, compared with cattle from Dumfriesshire and even less compared with Highland cattle. But to offset this advantage Irish merchants had to pay for shipping their charges across the Irish Sea. This was not always an easy operation, for beasts were often kept waiting for a favourable wind for days or even weeks on end and had to be driven, often considerable distances, to the point of embarkation. (63) All things considered, it seems likely that the relative costs of moving Irish and Scottish cattle to the south of England did not seriously disadvantage the producers of either country.

It seems plausible to suggest that the differential rate of exploitation of natural resources in the two countries was caused by the degree of social change in rural society. During the seventeenth century there were massive upheavals in Irish land-ownership. The Tudor conquest destroyed the old social order and was followed by plantation. The Cromwellian settlement resulted in an even greater upheaval and put much of the land under a new colonial landowning class. (64) One result of these changes was increased production for the market. Not only did livestock exports flourish, other aspects of economic life quickened during the century; wool and linen yarn exports to England rose dramatically and there was a rapid exploitaion of timber resources. (65) Over much of Scotland change occurred more gradually. The coming of peace did not involve the arrival of an army of new landowners; with the exception of the settlement of Kintyre, plantation proved a failure in Scotland. (66) In the Highlands land might change hands but traditional modes of social organisation survived largely intact into the eighteenth century. Highland society was not static — declining produce rents and rising money rents in some areas suggest the increasing penetration of market forces (67) — but the pace of progress remained slow until the later eighteenth century. Thus it seems that the introduction of a new landowning class in Ireland was largely responsible for quickening the tempo of economic life, whereas in Scotland the absence of major change among landowners meant that, especially in the Highlands, export potential was not fully realised. (68)

Appendix   *The export of livestock from Scotland to England, 1681-91*

A. CATTLE

	1681	1682	1683	1684	1685	1686	1687	1688	1689	1690	1691
Ayton	11	14	-[a]	87[b]	-[a]	58	-	-	70[b]	-	-
Duns	135[c]	299	-[a]	-	-	1,322[d]	-	-	211[b]	-	-
Kelso	116[f]	284	1,522[e]	607	199	1,106[f]	-	-	132[b]	63	67
Jedburgh	11[f]	351[g]	1,101[h]	621	752	1,919	-	-	240	231[k]	150
Castleton	-	1,784	3,156	2,473	1,083	4,944[m]	-	-	-	1,101[k]	-
Alisonbank	3,565	5,012	10,752	5,366	9,382	15,751[m]	-	-	7,916	5,536	3,888
Dumfries	6,204	8,747	10,763	4,861	9,148	-	-	-	7,709	5,436	7,486
Total	10,042	16,491	27,294	14,015	20,564	25,100	-	-	16,278	12,367	11,591

Notes: a   Included in the Kelso account
b   Plus 5 calves
c   Plus 22 calves
d   Plus 20 calves
e   Plus 3 calves
f   February to October only
g   Plus 1 calf
h   Plus 2 calves
k   March to October only
m   November to September only

B. SHEEP

	1681	1682	1683	1684	1685	1686	1687	1688	1689	1690	1691
Ayton	666[b]	153	-[a]	184	-[a]	120	-	-	424	-	-
Duns	945[b]	1,012	-	-	-	1,089[c]	-	-	260	-	-
Kelso	371	4,120	6,078[b]	2,654	949[d]	3,106	-	-	563	323	80
Jedburgh	2,344	7,888[e]	14,396[f]	6,510	1,988	10,358	-	-	3,993	3,492[g]	6,235
Castleton	-	5,019	7,720	6,010	5,529	5,750	-	-	-	2,549	-
Alisonbank	1,387	2,678	3,663	4,034	5,772	4,733	-	-	4,200	5,206	5,430
Dumfries	661	40	0	260	160	-	-	-	340	0	190
Total	6,374	20,910	31,857	19,652	14,398	25,156	-	-	9,780	11,570	11,935

Notes: For customs books that do not cover a full year see Appendix A.

a Included in the Kelso account
b Including 60 'ewes and lambs'
c Including 11 'ewes and lambs'
d Including 20 'ewes and lambs'
e Including 289 'ewes and lambs'
f Including 40 'ewes and lambs'
g Including 180 'ewes and lambs'

C. LAMBS

	1681	1682	1683	1684	1685	1686	1687	1688	1689	1690	1691
Ayton	0	1	-[a]	0	-[a]	0	-	-	84	-	-
Duns	9	60	-	-	-	736	-	-	62	-	-
Kelso	0	862	1,208	220	93	790	-	-	109	40	0
Jedburgh	398	462	436	0	100	934	-	-	165	830	180
Castleton	-	1,716	520	0	400	0	-	-	-	283	-
Alisonbank	0	478	1,439	327	720	2,184	-	-	688	1,652	1,735
Dumfries	162	190	982	40	0	-	-	-	0	214	942
Total	569	3,769	4,585	587	1,313	4,644	-	-	1,108	3,019	2,857

Notes: For customs books that do not cover a full year see Appendix A.

a   Included in the Kelso account

D. PIGS

	1681	1682	1683	1684	1685	1686	1687	1688	1689	1690	1691
Ayton	14	7	-[a]	4	-[a]	97	-	-	87	-	-
Duns	23	31	-	-	-	128	-	-	11	-	-
Kelso	184	327	193	291	239	339	-	-	302	92	15
Total	221	365	193	295	239	564	-	-	400	92	15

Notes :   a   Included in the Kelso account.

Sources: Ayton and Duns, S.R.O. E72/4/1-6, 9-10, 12-15, 17, 19; Kelso, S.R.O. E72/14/4-11, 13, 15, 18, 20, 23; Jedburgh, S.R.O. E72/13/3-13, 15-17; Alisonbank and Castleton, S.R.O. E72/2/6-7, 10-14, 17-18, 20-1, 23; Dumfries, S.R.O. E72/6/4, 6-10, 12, 14, 19, 23.

NOTES

1. I am indebted to Dr K.R. Andrews for his most helpful comments on an earlier draft. I have also benefited from discussions or correspondence with Dr J. Chartres, Mr D. Dickson, Dr C.L. Horricks, Mr A.R. Mitchell, Mr P.D. Richardson, Dr P.W.J. Riley and Professor T.C. Smout. For the purpose of this article livestock means cattle, sheep and pigs but not horses.

2. Sir Christopher Piggot in the English House of Commons quoted in S.G.E. Lythe, *The Economy of Scotland in its European Setting 1550-1625* (Edinburgh, 1960), p.205.

3. Sir Oliver St John, *C.S.P. Ireland,* 1611-14, pp.501-2.

4. R. Chambers, *Domestic Annals of Scotland,* 3 vols (Edinburgh, 1858-61), III, 338. This quotation is attributed to Patrick Ogilvie; it was a comment made to his brother the Earl of Seafield who was involved in the Union settlement. The story was told to Chambers by Sir Walter Scott, whose mother received part of her education in the Ogilvie household. Scott used the story with a twist in *Rob Roy*, (Everyman Ed., 1975), p.206; 'better stealing nowte than ruining nations'.

5. A.R.B. Haldane, *The drove roads of Scotland* (Edinburgh, 1952), pp.45-6; D.B. Quinn, *The Elizabethans and the Irish* (Ithaca, N.Y., 1966), p.14.

6. However, both countries exported large quantities of skins. Lythe, *op.cit.,* pp.11, 159-60, 220; A.K. Longfield, *Anglo-Irish trade in the sixteenth century* (1929), pp.58-76; D.M. Woodward, *The trade of Elizabethan Chester* (Hull, 1970), pp.7-8.

7. Lythe, *op.cit.,* p.25.

8. See G. Morton, *Elizabethan Ireland* (1971) for a good, clear narrative. See also N.P. Canny, *The Elizabethan conquest of Ireland: a pattern established 1565-76* (Harvester Press, Hassocks, Sussex, 1976) which arrived too late to be used in the present article.

9. T.C. Smout, *A history of the Scottish people 1560-1830* (London, 1972 ed.), pp.94-105.

10. J.A. Symon, *Scottish farming past and present,* (Edinburgh, 1959), pp.123, 130-3; S.O. Domhnaill, 'Warfare in sixteenth-century Ireland', *Irish Historical Studies,* V (1946-7), 30.

11. Sir W. Scott, *The two drovers* (Westwood, New Jersey, 1971 ed.), p.34.

12. Lythe, *op.cit.,* pp.4-5, 70; Smout, *Scottish people,* p.123.

13. Lythe, *op.cit.,* p.117.

14. *Rob Roy,* p.132.

15. Lythe, *op.cit.,* pp.22-3, 198; P. Williams, 'The northern borderland under the early Stuarts', in H.E. Bell and R.L. Ollard, eds. *Historical essays 1600-1750 presented to David Ogg* (1964 ed.), pp.14-15; T.I. Rae, *The administration of the Scottish frontier 1513-1603* (Edinburgh, 1966), pp.232-3.

16. Smout, *Scottish people,* p.205.

17. T. Blenerhasset, *A direction for the plantation in Ulster* (1610), p.23.

18. T.W. Moody, *The Londonderry Plantation, 1609-41* (Belfast, 1939), pp.329-31, 345.

19. *The two drovers,* p.24.

20. Haldane, *op.cit.,* p.13; Longfield, *op.cit.,* pp.107-8, 223.

21. Based on D. Woodward, 'The Anglo-Irish livestock trade in the seventeenth century', *Irish Historical Studies,* XVIII (1973), 489-523. This article contains substantially more information about the Irish branch of the trade than is possible in the present paper.

22. Quoted in T.C. Smout, *Scottish trade on the eve of Union 1660-1707* (Edinburgh, 1963), p.206.

23. Smout, *Scottish people,* p.107; L.M. Cullen, *An economic history of Ireland since 1660* (London, 1972), p.9.

24. Woodward, 'Irish livestock', pp.497-8, 515-17.

25. Scottish Record Office, Edinburgh (S.R.O.) E72/2/1. For a list of Scottish customs books for the 1680s see the Appendix; no further references to these books are given in the text of this article.

26. C. Edie, *The Irish cattle bills; a study in restoration politics, Trans. of the American Phil.Soc.,* n.s., LX, pt. 2 (Philadelphia 1970), 12.

27. Imports of Scottish and Irish cattle at Carlisle in 1662-3 were put at 26,440 head, while imports of Scottish cattle only were put at 18,364. Public Record Office, London (P.R.O.) S.P.Dom., Charles II, 78/11; 79/3. The incorrect figure of 18,574 is given in *C.S.P.Dom, 1663-4,* p.226. The number of Irish cattle is approximately 8,000 and not 9,000 as given in Woodward, 'Irish livestock', p.497.

28. P.R.O. 30/24/4/112. For a discussion of the problems relating to the document which contains this estimate see my paper 'Anglo-Scottish trade and English commercial policy during the 1660's', forthcoming in *The Scottish Historical Review.*

29. 15 Chas II, cap.7.

30. Woodward, 'Irish livestock', 499-500.

31. 18 Chas II, cap.2.

32. R. Steele, *A bibliography of royal proclamations,* 3 vols (1967 ed.), III, no. 2305; *Register of the privy council of Scotland, 1665-9,* pp.253-4.

33. Woodward, 'Irish livestock', pp.500-1 and the many references in the *Register of the privy council of Scotland.*

34. Most of the customs books cover a year from November – e.g. Nov. 1680 to Nov. 1681; in such cases a single year is given, viz. 1681.

35. Ayton 1684, duty on corn, sheep, cattle, eggs and dead-stock £99 8s 8d; Kelso 1685, duty on stock £164, on stock and linen cloth £56, on stock and corn £179; Kelso 1686, duty on stock £475 14s 0d, on corn and cattle £263 10s 0d; Kelso 1690, duty on stock £128; Kelso 1691, duty on stock £428 12s 0d. The duty on stock at that time was 10s 0d (Scots) per head of cattle and 2s 0d (Scots) per sheep.

36. *Rob Roy,* p.397; this statement is in Scott's introduction.

37. Cattle were valued at five times the value of sheep; see note 35 above.

38. Geese – Duns 1681, 51; 1682, 25; 1689, 23; Ayton 1681, 6; 1682, 17; 1689, 6; 1690, 10.

39. Dead-stock was occasionally exported at other places; at Kelso on 23 Sept. 1681 three carcases of beef were intended for England although one was sold 'after it was laid on the horse'.

40. University of Edinburgh Library, La II 491/2/1; 10/2.

41. J. Spreull, *A accompt current betwixt Scotland and England ballanced* (sic) (1705) in J.W. Burns ed. *The miscellaneous writings of John Spreull* (Glasgow, 1882).

42. For further critical comments on this source see D. Woodward, 'The portbooks of England and Wales', *Maritime History,* vol.3 (1973), 160-1.

43. Woodward, 'Irish livestock', 502-4.

44. For Welsh droving see P.G. Hughes, *Wales and the drovers* (1943); H.R. Rankin, 'Cattle droving from Wales to England', *Agriculture,* LXII (1955-6), 218-21; C. Skeel, 'The cattle trade between Wales and England from the fifteenth to the nineteenth centuries', *Transactions of the Royal Historical Society,* IX (1926), 135-58). Dr R.J. Colyer is about to produce a book on Welsh droving in which there will be some discussion of the pre-1700 period.

45. J. Houghton, *A collection for improvement of husbandry and trade* (1969), II, no.118 (2 Nov. 1694).

46. E.C. Lodge ed. *The account book of a Kentish estate 1616-1704* (1927), pp.265, 381; Williams and Glyn's Bank Ltd., Backwell Ledgers; L, ff.14, 57-8, 403; M, ff.405, 560, 588.

47. H.F. Kearney, *Strafford in Ireland, 1633-41* (Manchester, 1959), p.130.

48. Woodward, 'Irish livestock', 510 and many references in *C.S.P. Ireland.*

49. Dungarvan and Kinsale were also important for sheep shipments during 1679-80. Woodward, 'Irish livestock', 498, 521.

50. Haldane, *op.cit.*, p.151; Lythe, *op.cit.*, p.10; Rae, *op.cit.*, p.4.

51. J.MacKy, *A journey through Scotland* (1723), p.17.

52. Most of the Alisonbank books give the domiciles of some men; this information is fullest in the 1695 book.

53. 1,273 in 1689; 1,000 in 1690, 1,100 in 1691. He also dispatched 600 head through Dumfries in 1684 and 220 in 1685. In 1685 the 'Laird of Little Park' sent 82 sheep to England via Alisonbank.

54. *Scottish trade*, p.214; *Scottish people*, p.123; T.C. Smout and A. Fenton, 'Scottish agriculture before the improvers – an exploration', *Agricultural History Review*, XIII (1965), 80.

55. *Ibid.*, pp.80, 85; Chambers, *op.cit.*, III, 151-4; Haldane, *op.cit.*, p.126; Smout, *Scottish trade*, p.214; Symon, *op.cit.*, pp.110, 116, 323. On 3 September 1681 David Dunbar moved 300 head of cattle to England via Dumfries.

56. Also two droves totalling 465 cattle via Alisonbank in 1683 and one drove of 160 cattle via Dumfries in 1685. He may have been active in other years for which I do not have detailed information.

57. Smout, *Scottish people*, pp.126, 128. On the importance of cattle production in the south-west see also T. McGrouther, 'The cattle trade with England', *Falkirk Archaeological and Natural History Society*, III (1938-9), 45-51; W. McDowall, *History of the burgh of Dumfries* (Edinburgh, 1867), pp.838-9.

58. As is evident from the English and Scottish customs records.

59. Cullen, *op.cit.*, p.11; Haldane, *op.cit.*, pp.133-6.

60. Smout, *Scottish trade*, p.213; P.R.O. S.P. 30/24/30/65; 63/339/62; B.M. Add. Mss., 47020 ff. 272-4; 47021 f.215.

61. According to the Ledgers, Scotland's balance of trade with England was unfavourable in 1697-8 but this was because cattle were valued at only £1 a head compared with between £1 10s 0d and £2 in other years. If cattle exports for 1697-8 are revalued at the higher level the balance again becomes favourable. In 1704 and 1706 when there were no cattle exports the Scottish balance was unfavourable. P.R.O. Customs 3/1-10, 81.

62. *Ibid.* During the six years 1697-8 to 1703 average annual exports were valued as follows – Scotland £93,850; Ireland £308,750.

63. Woodward, 'Irish livestock', 511-13. For further details on shipping see D.M. Woodward, 'The Overseas trade of Chester, 1600-1650', *Trans. of the Hist. Soc. of Lancs. and Chesh.*, CXXII (1970), 32-8.

64. See especially Moody, *op.cit.*, and K.S. Bottigheimer, *English money and Irish land; the 'Adventurers' in the Cromwellian settlement of Ireland* (Oxford, 1971).

65. L.M. Cullen, *Anglo-Irish trade 1660-1800* (Manchester, 1968), pp.35-6; E. McCracken, *The Irish woods since Tudor times* (Newton Abbot, 1971).

66. Smout, *Scottish people*, pp.104-5; A. McKerral, *Kintyre in the seventeenth century* (1948).

67. C.L. Horricks, 'Economic and social change in the Isle of Harris 1680-1754', University of Edinburgh Ph.D. thesis, 1974, pp.154-61, 187-8. I am grateful to Dr Horricks for allowing me to consult her valuable thesis. She is currently preparing articles for publication based on the thesis which will question many traditional views about the Highlands.

68. On landlord conservatism in seventeenth-century Scotland see Smout and Fenton, *op.cit.*, pp.86-7.

12. Merchant Communities Overseas, the Navigation Acts and Irish and Scottish Responses

L.M.Cullen

THE rapid growth of Irish and Scottish foreign trade was reflected in the rise in the number of Irish and Scottish merchants overseas. Merchant communities overseas were essentially the same in nature for both nations, the links with the homeland being close, kinship ties characteristic and personal mobility very evident. London, too, as the main centre of the exchange business of the two islands had substantial Irish and Scottish communities. A somewhat impressionistic conclusion would see the Irish overseas as the more numerous, more dominant as well as more cosmopolitan in the first half of the century, a fact reflected dramatically in the role of the Fitzgeralds in the tobacco trade (1), the key element in Scottish re-exports. The Fitzgeralds reflected a powerful Irish presence in London, starting with the houses of Kirwan and Trant, already active from the 1680s. London attracted many Irish: Willes, in 1760, wrote that 'an imagination that London is a kind of paradise and that England in general is very much like it, is the occasion of such numbers of my countrymen as swarm in London in all occupations.' (2) Some like Laurence Sullivan, who became chairman of the East India Company in 1758, (3) followed non-mercantile careers, but many were merchants. A directory count suggests at least nine Irish houses in 1736 (4), but the records of Mediterranean passes in the Public Record Office in fact reveal a larger Irish mercantile presence in the 1720s and 1730s, and by 1758 the merchant community consisted of a certain 15 houses and a possible 10 others. (5)

The Jacobite element of the early decades in London was represented by the Arthurs and the Cantillons, both with Paris interests and both connected by marriage (6); the non-Jacobite element consisted of the Cairnes and the Nesbitts, both related by marriage to the Goulds, one of the houses in 1736 being Gould and Nesbitt. Other important houses included the Gurnells whose Irish affiliation consisted of one of the Cork Hoares who moved to London in 1744, and the Dillons. The Galway mafia were well represented in London, not only by the Kirwans continuously from at least the 1680s to the end of the eighteenth century, but by a succession of Galway families closely related by family ties, and all with business interests in the West Indies and in Europe. Blake and Lynch were in partnership in the 1740s; the Blake partnership with Isidore Lynch was dissolved in 1748 (7), Isidore Lynch and son being prominent into the 1770s after which the Frenches, apart from the Kirwans, became the dominant Galway house in London. However, there was no Irish group whose collective weight in the London market approximated to that of the principal Scottish houses including the Coutts and Herries. The Nesbitts, drawing successively on close family and business ties with the Cairnes, Goulds and Colebrooke, were the only Irish house who were comparable in stature. The Nesbitts (Nesbitt and Stewart after 1784), plantation owners in Jamaica and Grenada, West India merchants and having banking and exchange business with Ireland, had become the major Irish house in London in the 1780s. (8) They were closely involved in the Irish congerie revolving around the still largely obscure activities of Sir George Colebrooke in the London market. Colebrooke's introduction to the Irish mafia may be dated to his marriage to the heiress daughter of an Irish planter, Peter Gaynor, which brought him three estates in Antigua. He opened a bank in Dublin in 1764, the only London financier to do so, himself visited Ireland in the course of his business activities; and the Nesbitts incurred some £30,000 of the total loss of £100,000 in a speculative venture involving Sir George Colebrooke and others in or around 1772, the crucial year in his affairs. (9) In contrast to the Scottish houses from Glasgow and Edinburgh, the Irish houses represented business families from the periphery rather than the centre. Cork and Dublin were poorly represented in London, a reflection ultimately of the fact that both ports were poorly represented overseas generally. The house of Digges La Touche, based in London and Jamaica, the O'Connors, a branch of a Dublin house closely linked to the Galway interest, and John Pim, a Quaker, who moved to London around 1770, were the only Dublin houses in London, none of them of major importance; and the marriage of Samuel Hoare of Cork into the London Gurnells led to the sole significant Cork connection with London.

The pattern of colonies overseas affords an interesting contrast. The Scots were already well-established and dominant in north-west Europe; the Irish in France and south-west Europe. Even before 1705 or 1689 the Scots were few in France, and their trade by comparison with the Irish trade with France negligible. On the far side of the Atlantic, the Scots were not numerous in the West Indies in contrast to the Irish, who were already a considerable element in St. Christopher's by 1643 (10). In Montserrat in 1678 there were 1,869 Irish and 52 Scots; in Antigua 610 Irish and 98 Scots. (11) On the other hand, the Scots had already penetrated the colonies in mainland America. Already in 1700 tobacco in Philadelphia was 'engrossed by the Scots (as almost all other trade here is)', and from Philadelphia the Scots had already made contact with Maryland, carrying goods overland to exchange for tobacco. (12) Scottish emigration in the eighteenth century and their hold on the tobacco trade were an accentuation of an already emerging phenomenon. At the same time, the Scottish presence in the West Indies, so limited in the seventeenth century, grew. The Scots were the main developers of the lands recovered from the French in St. Kitts after 1713 (13); they accounted for 13 family dynasties 'of some consequence' in Antigua (14); and they also held a prominent place in the belated exploitation of Jamaica: one quarter of the landholders in 1754, they accounted for 40 per cent of the inventories after death of above £1,000 in 1771-5 (15). In 1771-5 Irish and Jews accounted for only ten per cent of the total.

The West Indies are particularly relevant to the present study because they are the only area (London and Rotterdam apart) where Scots and Irish were simultaneously numerous. The Scots role in the British West Indies was undoubtedly the greater; behind the Irish in 1707, they caught up and surpassed them, the Scottish role being particularly evident in Jamaica which by the 1770s produced as much sugar as all the other British islands combined. In the other islands the Irish and Scottish roles

were closer. The Irish interest was paramount in Montserrat; in the 1729 census, 15
of the island's 30 larger plantations were Irish including the six largest. (16) In
Antigua, where, according to Sheridan, the Scots contribution was out of proportion
to their numbers, of 18 post-1707 dynasties only two were Irish, 11 Scots (pre-1707,
six Irish, two Scots) (17). But the criterion of important dynasties is arbitrary, and
overstates the relative importance of the Scots. There are prominent Antiguan families
not listed by Sheridan, notably the Blakes. Martin Blake held plantations both in
St. Christopher's and Antigua; his uncle Patrick had plantations in Montserrat and
St. Christopher's, being at the time of his son's marriage to a Trant in 1742 'one of
the most considerable persons in the island of St. Christopher's'. (18) Others who
held estates in Antigua were Bodkin, Butler, Bolan, French, Galway, McCarthy,
Murray and Trant.

The Irish were numerous in all the islands, Jamaica apart, of which it was reported
in 1762 in contrast to all the other islands that there were few Catholics. (19) Individual
Irishmen held plantations in several islands; there was considerable inter-island mobility,
a mobility which was unique moreover because it also embraced the foreign islands in
the West Indies. The Lynches as well as being in Antigua, Montserrat and Barbados
were already in Martinique before 1689. The Kirwans appear in Martinique and Saint
Croix in addition to Antigua. The war-time extension of families was dramatic. The
Blakes, firmly established in Antigua, Montserrat and St. Christopher's, appeared as
merchants in Saint-Domingue in 1762 (20) and in St. Eustatius where in 1761 Joseph
Blake was 'a nominal man'. (21) The major example is that of the Stapletons of
Thurlesbeg, Co. Tipperary. Sir William Stapleton, governor of the Leeward islands
from 1672 to 1685, held two estates in Nevis and one in Montserrat; members also
moved to the French islands, prelude to Richard Stapleton's career in privateering
in the 1690s and the establishment of the family at Nantes. (22) Stapleton's daughters
married members of the Walsh and MacNamara families, the three families representing
the major, though not the sole, Irish plantation interest in Saint-Domingue (23). One
of the most interesting features of Irish colonisation in the West Indies is the Irish
settlement of the Danish island of Saint-Croix from 1749, illustrating both the movement of Irish families already established within the West Indies and accentuated
war-time mobility. The first Irish planter in Saint-Croix was Nicholas Tuite of Montserrat who established a plantation there in 1749. (24) The major Irish influx took
place from 1755 when, with hostilities beginning, the advantages of a neutral island
were enhanced. Tuite claimed that he settled 700 families, probably an exaggeration,
but by 1760 there were 250 Catholics, twelve Irish plantation owners and 100 Irish
overseers. (25) The Irish were, therefore, far more cosmopolitan within the West
Indies even without taking into account Irish activities in the Spanish empire reaching
from the islands to a Macarthy sugar plantation near New Orleans as late as 1795. (26)

Moreover, the West Indies served as a prelude to investment or settlement in
London and Europe. This was especially evident in London with the establishment of
members of colonial families as early as the 1680s. London houses arising from the
colonial trade include those of the Blakes, Lynches, Kirwans, Hussey, Burke, Tuite,
French, Skerrett, Digges La Touche, Nesbitt, Delap, Browne and Meade. The West
Indies gave a fillip to settlement in Europe too, although as European centres did
not play the role that London did in the exchange and trade of island families, the

purpose is not as clear-cut, especially as some of these families through their Irish relatives at home had direct trade links from Ireland with Europe and hence independent reason to settle there. But colonial money, the network of connections that colonial trade created, and the stimulus of prospering family involvement in colonial business, helped in many cases. Francis Delap who had settled in Antigua before 1715 left bequests in his will of 1775, to his first cousin Samuel of Bordeaux and 'my good old master and uncle', Thomas Barton of Bordeaux. (27) As Samuel Delap settled in Bordeaux in 1736 and Barton in 1725, the West Indian success of Francis Delap may have helped to strengthen the family involvement in trade. West Indian money certainly helped to put younger relatives on their feet in European ports. The absentee Nevis planter, James Tobin of London, in his will of 1732, left money for one of his Irish nephews 'to be educated a merchant and to go to Cadiz'. (28) Monica Lynch in a Chancery commercial debt case in 1759 in the Isle of Man represented that 'she had a son at age and that she had an expectancy of a large sum from some of the West Indian islands.' (29) Andrew French of London invested money in East Indies ventures from France (30) when the French East India company was wound up: in turn this link with Gallic houses associated with such ventures may have helped to account for the growing prominence of the London house in the 1770s and 1780s. The Meades, McCarthys, and Galweys were almost the only Cork families to settle extensively in the West Indies: it is almost certainly no accident that they were at a later date among the very few Cork houses to open in France in the course of the eighteenth century. The Bordeaux McCarthys like the Bordeaux Delaps in time developed remarkably close American connections, conceivably a reflection of their West Indian background. Apart from the Arthur/Cantillon family grouping, the Fitzgeralds and the Dillons, all the significant Irish houses in London were established by families intimately involved in plantation ownership.

One of the most striking features of the colonial trade was the absence of Dublin houses among the colonial families. The Delaps, a co. Donegal family, are atypical because their Dublin and London houses followed rather than preceded their colonial and Bordeaux settlement. Several of the Galway families had Dublin houses — Lynches Bodkins, Frenches, Kirwans, Blakes — but the houses were fewer and more modest than the London houses of the same families. They were a relatively modest part of the Dublin mercantile community, more the consequence of the ability of cosmopolitan families to serve local banking needs than an important link in holding their widespread overseas trading network together. However, the Dillons, the Dublin banking house of the early 1750s, were from the west of Ireland, and they did extensive business with the two contemporary Galway banks. The O'Connors, powerful in Dublin in the second half of the century, and with a branch in London, were from the west of Ireland and already related at mid-century to the Lynches. Significantly, Dublin sugar refining, one of the largest branches of the industry within the British Isles, drew its capital and skill not from the West Indies but from Bordeaux. Bordeaux sugar refiners went to Dublin in the 1720s (31) and by the 1750s between 50 and 60 per cent of Dublin sugar houses bore French names, (32) the powerful Bordeaux family of Nairac even being represented among the city's refiners. Contrary to statements by both Sheridan and Pares, little French sugar came to Ireland; the French origins of the capital and techniques in Dublin sugar refining — and the corresponding absence of the Irish colonial families — illustrate how little direct impact the colonial trade had on the city.

While the Scots were dominant in the north-west of Europe, the Irish greatly outnumbered the Scots and English alike in the two greatest and most rapidly growing centres in the south — Cadiz and Bordeaux, both of which reached their peak in the second half of the century. The number of Irish houses in Bordeaux, seven at the beginning of the century, rose to about 20 by the early 1750s with several lesser houses to follow. In 1721, in the 'English factory' in Cadiz there were 13 or 14 Irish merchants, in 1775 27 Irish surnames divided between 19 houses, (33) not taking into account Irish houses in the French colony. Within Europe the brandy trade of the Barcelona branch of the Herries had its Irish counterpart in the Benecarlo house of Patrick White who also supplied the Isle of Man. At a later date, the Hennessys at Cognac and the Boyds in Bordeaux (34) played a pioneering role in the growth of the quality trade in brandy, which had suffered during the earlier boom in rum. The Blacks of Bordeaux had a branch in the Isle of Man in the partnership of Ross, Black and Christian, (35) whose clerk was a Park of a Belfast rum importing family. There were other houses on the island, Thomas Arthur, Francis Deane, Hugh Connor, Patrick Creagh, the Lynches, a larger presence than the Scottish one on the island. When the island was closed in 1765, the Connors set up a Dublin house which continued to have relations with smugglers and may have financed them behind the scenes; Arthur may have opened the Dunkirk house of the same name, which emerged around this time and the Parks set up business in both Nantes and Roscoff. As far as the East Indies trade is concerned, Scottish prominence in Scandinavia inevitably meant a prominent Scottish role in the Swedish East India company, but in other companies the Irish were dominant. James Tobin was even reported to have financed the first venture from Ostend to the east, before the short-lived Ostend company was set up. (36) In his will Tobin left bequests to several nephews; the earliest Tobin to settle in Nantes was in 1736, the Tobins there in the early 1770s helping to finance East Indies ventures by Rothe and Sutton de Clonard, Irish directors of the disestablished East India company. (37) Of the role of Irishmen in this company it has been said: 'ils se sont assurés dans la seconde moitié du siècle une sorte de monopole sur l'empire colonial'. (38) Through France, Irishmen also provided assistance to the Spanish East India Company, one of whose directors in 1732 was Stephen Roche, 'an Irishman bred in France, of known conduct'. (39)

There are three discernible major axes in Irish merchant communities overseas, the main ones being Galway and Waterford family groupings, the lesser one the Limerick grouping. In addition there was a small Meath/Westmeath grouping starting with the Nugents, owing its pull perhaps to the success of Peter Gaynor (whose three plantations were inherited by Sir George Colebrooke) and including the Tuites, Husseys and Penthenys. The Limerick grouping included Kerry and Clare families. Its original nucleus was the Trants, Sarsfields, Arthurs, and Cantillons, but it also included MacNamaras, Rice, Woulfe, Creagh, Stritch and Clancy. The Waterford and Galway groupings were, however, by far the more important in numbers and geographical diffusion. The difference between the Galway and Waterford networks was essentially that the Galway network spread from the colonies back to Europe,

M

the Waterford merchants followed existing but prospering direct trade routes from Ireland to France. All the Galway houses first settled in the West Indies, the first European venture in the modern era seemingly being that of the Lynches in Bordeaux in 1698, and the Joyces in Nantes almost contemporaneously. Their West Indian connections compensated in part for the decline of Galway itself as a port, but John Kirwan of Galway probably paid about one fortieth of the duties on the country's foreign trade, a reflection of the concentrated strength of the largest of the Galway houses. (40) Rich, cosmopolitan, owning land in two counties, the landed Galway merchant oligarchy, reluctant to lose their all in the Williamite wars, were less committed to resistance than their Limerick and Waterford counterparts, and fared well in the peace in holding or regaining their lands, many also conformed to the established church then and later. By contrast, Waterford's merchant representation overseas was linked to European trade, its merchants appeared in European ports at an earlier date, and the dynamics of their appearance in those ports was different. Waterford families appeared in La Rochelle, Nantes and Saint-Malo both before and during the Restoration period. Very few of them reached the West Indies, (the only major exception was the Tobins and the Walshes); a few early representatives apart, they largely by-passed Bordeaux, but from Saint-Malo and La Rochelle they came to dominate the Irish merchant communities of Spain and Portugal. Lees, Lincolns, Geraldins (and Fitzgeralds), Hores, Walshes, Butlers, Murphys, Stranges, Shees, Byrnes, Tobins, Ryans, Farrells, Waddings, Powers, Sweetmans and Whites came from Waterford city and the adjoining counties of Tipperary, Kilkenny and Wexford.

The Galway and Waterford families were long-established families; merchants purchased land; younger sons of landed houses were apprenticed to trade. There was an alliance between town and country, most striking in the case of Galway where landed and mercantile families were indistinguishable, where greater continuity in landownership made the link more effective than in Limerick, Waterford or Cork and where intermarriage had produced a complex relationship between families across two counties. Their rental from land, said to have been £30,000 in the 1680s, was estimated at £140,000 around 1760. (41) Galway families held land before and after 1691. Catholics continued to hold it, some conformed, some relied on trustees. It is misleading to see Catholics as having been driven by the loss of land into trade, or by the closure of professional outlets consequent on the operation of the penal laws. In fact, if land through the wealth it created or the rich dowries it attracted helped to finance younger sons in trade, it is likely that land resettlement and the penal laws, far from having driven Catholics into trade or encouraged them to seek outlets in trade, had quite a contrary result: by limiting Catholic profits in land and the professions they held Catholic investment in trade and plantation below the level it might otherwise have attained. What is surprising is the limited circle of families which sustained mercantile initiative in France or in Spain, (still more so in the West Indies), the relatively early date at which most of the families made their establishment overseas, and the very limited subsequent diversification, much of it itself accountable by marriage ties (e.g. in the case of the Moores of Alicante intermarried into several Galway 'tribes'). Most of the diffusion of Irish families in the West Indies came from existing families; the opening up of Jamaica which attracted so many Scots drew comparatively few Irish settlers whose surnames were not already known in the West Indies: a handful of Belfast men as planters or over-seers. In other words success was confined to families already enjoying access to wealth or land. Interestingly, a few Catholic landed families with no previous tradition of overseas trading settlement entered trade as the eighteenth century wore on: the Galway Bellews and the Cork Nagles.

Land was therefore favourable to involvement in trade rather than the reverse. An associated factor in limiting Irish participation was the relative paucity of the Catholic Irish in the professions. A remarkably high proportion of Scottish plantation owners came from medical doctors and lawyers. (42) The profits of colonial office — from which Catholics were debarred — also helped to finance colonial enterprise. While successful families like the Blakes could (on the evidence of their papers) provide rather generously even for nephews at home, all Irish planters seem to have complained about the presence of relatives without trade or profession arriving with little more than 'a few letters of recommendation and a general transportation'. (43)

The effects of the navigation acts can be exaggerated as far as Ireland is concerned. It is true of course that Irish merchants had occasion to resent restrictions on trade with Ireland or, if resident in the West Indies, on trade between the English and foreign islands, a factor which helped to ensure, religion apart altogether, that the interests of Irish and English settlers did not coincide. However, the obvious immed-iate effects can be exaggerated. In the case of tobacco the effect on the consumer was mitigated. Tobacco was generally in excess supply, numerous merchants were in competition in consigning it to Ireland, and merchants in the larger ports like Cork selling on the account of English principals were in competition with merchants in smaller ports like Limerick importing on their own account, for the custom of the hinterland. (44) In sugar, as French or Spanish sugar never reached Ireland in quantity, prices in Britain were above the world level. Moreover, the refiners had a monopoly in the Irish ports, (45) and combination among them probably ensured that in contrast to the highly competitive tobacco trade, sugar prices remained high. Turning from consumer to merchant, the Irish merchant was of course deprived of a re-export market, *de jure* to Britain, *de facto* to Europe. But a re-export trade was never feasible in sugar as British sugar was above world prices, and in tobacco a re-export trade would have been relatively short-lived. Moreover, even if Ireland had advantages for re-export, the Scottish monopoly of the trade was ethnic as well as legal, and Ireland could only have played a large role in tobacco purchases in the Chesapeake if there had been an Irish migration to parallel the Scottish (in fact, the middle colonies, not the south, was the pole of attraction for the first movement in the 1750s of Ulster-Scots mercantile initiative into the new world). It is possible to argue that had an entrepot trade existed, its profits would have been ploughed back into industry. But Ireland lacked the mineral wealth of Scotland, and the coincidence between the rise of domestic exports and re-exports underlines the need not to overstate Scottish tobacco profits or their role.

The real loss to Ireland consequent on the navigation acts was less tangible. The lack of a direct colonial trade and of a re-export trade reduced the need for sophis-ticated financial institutions. Jacobite bankers and banking had certainly been more Irish than Scottish, but much of it in the case of the Arthurs and Cantillons was non-mercantile. (46) Although the Dillons were the most mercantile of Irish banks, their dealings with the Paris houses of Waters and Woulfe were modest, (47) and the notarial records of Nantes and Bordeaux amply confirm how limited was the role of the Paris houses in the financing of the Irish merchant communities in the seaports. Moreover, the Woulfes who had more mercantile dealings than the others were on a small scale: at their failure in January 1770 their liabilities amounted to a mere 600,000 *livres*. (48) The trade from Chesapeake, unlike the sugar trade from the West Indies, was in no way financed by the outflow of colonial capital and personnel to London. The absence of colonial capital was responsible for the quickened growth of Scottish banking including the emergence of Glasgow banking when the tobacco trade took off in the 1740s and 1750s. On the other hand, Dublin, lacking a mart for colonial products, had a less pressing need for banking facilities, and Cork's export trade, increasingly on foreign account, was responsible for Cork banking, formerly mercantile, becoming increasingly mixed in its composition. Even if Ireland was cut off from direct or entrepot trade, Irish merchants in London were of course free to play a prominent role in financing trade from their London base. This was the case of the Fitzgeralds. But it is significant that after the Fitzgerald failure in 1759 the tobacco re-export trade, reflecting the increasing sophistication of the Scots, became an entirely Scottish affair. In sugar, declining British re-exports were hardly a sound base for a comparable initiative, but in any case the large number of London sugar merchants ensured that there was no shortage of adequate finance, and even in re-exports to Ireland there is no evidence of a conspicuous role by the Irish houses in London, despite their multiple family ties.

One of the effects of the navigation acts was to quicken the shift of trade from the periphery to the centre. Cork had dominated direct imports of tobacco in the 1680s, and Belfast and Galway had imported almost as much as Dublin; Belfast and Cork imported more sugar than Dublin. Belfast, Cork and Galway traded on their own account. The effect of the navigation acts was to strengthen both the position of Dublin, which already dominated exports from England, and commission dealings in Dublin and Cork on English account. Galway's decay from 1685 was uninterrupted, Belfast entered into a real but temporary decline halted only when novel traffics — flax seed and emigration — gave it a new dynamism in the 1730s, and Cork's involvement was conspicuously passive.

The decline of peripheral centres and the growth of imports on British account meant the absence of pressures on financial institutions. What is striking is the sophistication of Galway, although its commodity trade had become negligible, in consequence of its far-flung merchant network. Lynch's bank is as early as any outside Dublin, Galway's two banks in the 1750s were matched in number outside the capital only by Cork, and a French of Frenchpark (a family already intermarried into the highly mercantile Blakes) (49) was a partner in the Dublin bank of Lennox and French. There was a well-defined Galway community in Dublin and more importantly in London. Within Ireland, Kellys and Tierneys moved to Limerick, Kellys, Joyces and Lynches to Cork. By the 1790s the Galway firms of Joyce and Lynch had opened two discount houses, the two houses combining to open a bank in 1802. The Blakes were involved in a bank opened by a second Joyce, (50) and the Frenches opened one at Tuam. Galway, poor in commodity trade and peripheral, is an interesting example of what colonial trade did for its trading methods. Dublin

and Cork lacked similar complex relationships with the outside world, and Waterford's were less diffuse. Despite the wide network of the Walsh and Fitzgerald
families, much of the city's enterprise in the eighteenth century was new, and all
its banking came from new families — Congreve, Weeks, Newport, Hayden, and
Rivers. The distinctive combination of wide merchant involvement overseas and
of a numerous resident gentry gave Galway the essential base for its banking role.

In Ireland at large the demand for banks came from gentry. The abortive campaign in 1719 for a national bank was gentry-inspired, gentlemen were active partners
in many banks in the 1720s and 1730s, when mercantile banks failed in 1754-5 the
response — the prohibition of involvement in banking by active merchants in the
act of 1756 — was distinctly anti-mercantile and was followed by the absurd aristo-
cratic banking experiment of Malone, Clements and Gore in 1758. The Bank of
Ireland founded in 1782 was merchant-dominated in its management, (although
not in its proprietary), but it was a rediscount business handling first-class bills,
rather than a bank actively expanding the discount facilities available. The 1754-5
bank failures (five banks in all) were the Irish equivalent of the Scottish crisis of
1772, coming at the end of an expansionary boom. The crisis was triggered off by
the failure of the Rotterdam member of Dillon's bank, and the five banks that
failed were all mercantile. The effects of the failure were to be seen in the slowness
of the recovery of banking, and the limited movement from trade into banking.
Whereas the assets of the Scottish banks rose six-fold between 1750 and 1770, (51)
the Irish note issue had probably not exceeded the 1754 level at the outset of the
1790s. The lack of stimulus to growth, caused by the absence of colonial trade
combined with a gentry demand for a remitting rather than a discounting banking
system, had together ensured that banking expansion was rudimentary. The opening
of 'discount houses' in the 1780s and 1790s by merchants in several centres both
illustrates the merchant urge to move towards banking and the obstacle created by
the 1756 act which effectively prevented merchants who chose to remain in trade
from issuing bank notes.

Galway, like Saint-Malo and La Rochelle on the French side, was increasingly
peripheral to the main centres of advance in foreign trade in the eighteenth century,
and its relatively sophisticated financial institutions did not in any way help to
arrest its decline. If anything, they reflected the established lines of communications
which helped Galway's younger sons to move out of Galway to trade in the colonies
or European centres. If the navigation acts had not discriminated against Ireland,
Ireland might on the analogy with Scotland, whose colonial trade prospered after
1707, have fared better economically. But even if relaxation of the acts had permitted growth and even if land confiscation had not taken place to impair Catholic
ability to engage in trade, diversification would have been limited, and the boom
would in the absence of mineral wealth have had little follow-through. Financial
institutions would have been less dominated by the gentry, and more sophisticated
than they actually were; they would have been geared more directly to the requirements of trade and industry. As it was, only war-time inflation — necessity as much
as opportunity consequent on the suspension of convertibility in 1797 — brought
about a growth in banking beyond the arrested state in which it still remained in
the 1790s. The navigation acts may well have stunted the growth of institutions,

and certainly it is striking that the limited banking growth of 1760-1793 was more evident outside Dublin than in it (six full-blown banks in the provinces, only three in the capital excluding two institutions largely revolving around rent-remitting exclusively). No private bank was opened in Dublin in the quarter century before 1793 despite the fact that in that time several banks in the capital went out of business. The lack of a colonial trade limited the scale of the main financial centre to the financing of those aspects of domestic trade not financed locally. In such circumstances, central dominance in banking was limited. All Britain's foreign exchange was cleared through London; although (and ultimately because) Ireland's needs were relatively smaller, Belfast and Cork conducted at least part of their exchange business with London without the interposition of Dublin. Ireland's situation was more similar to France's than Britain's. In such a situation it is not altogether surprising that while the country's financial institutions were dominated by the requirements and the legislation of the gentry, the periphery showed some elements of vitality lacking at the centre. The gentry involved in trade were old Anglo-Norman (and sometimes Irish) rather than immigrant English, minor rather than great (Galway's gentry for instance was both numerous and enjoyed a novel continuity in land ownership), and peripheral rather than central. Such an economy affords a striking contrast with Scotland, whose strength lay in a rich agricultural region deeply penetrated by the towns, and in a growing financial dominance by Glasgow and Edinburgh unparalleled in Ireland.

NOTES

1. J.M. Price, *France and the Chesapeake* (Ann Arbor, 1973), 2 vols., especially I, 557-562.
2. Public Record Office of Northern Ireland (P.R.O.N.I.), letters from Baron Willes, c.1760 (microfilm).
3. L.S. Sutherland, *The East India Company in eighteenth-century politics* (Oxford, 1952), p.59.
4. *The directory containing an alphabetical list of the names and places of abode of...merchants...* (London, 1736) in Guildhall Library, London.
5. *A complete guide to all persons who have any trade or concern with the city of London,* 1758, in National Library, Dublin.
6. On the Arthur/Cantillon marriage link, see Cantillon genealogy in the O'Connell Papers, Archives Department, University College, Dublin, P12/2A/209. On the London Gould relationship to Cairnes and Nesbitt, see Genealogical Office, Dublin Castle, Ulster's Office vol. 170, pp.57-66; Will Pedigrees, vol.3, f.155.
7. National Library of Ireland (N.L.I.) MS 827, letter book of Kelly, merchant, Limerick, 30 July 1748 to Isidore Lynch, London.
8. Public Record Office of Ireland, Dublin (P.R.O.I.), CAV 18, Lucas Clements papers, which contain some business and legal documents of the Nesbitt and Nesbitt and Stewart firms including the articles of the 1784 partnership of Nesbitt and Stewart, CAV 18/3/36.
9. P.R.O.I. Lucas Clements papers, CAV/18/4/1, letter book headed 'executors of Thos. and Wm. Nesbitt', p.4, Cheltenham, 8 July 1822.
10. R. Sheridan, *Sugar and Slavery: an economic history of the British West Indies 1623-1775* (Barbados, 1974), p.151.
11. Sheridan, *op.cit.,* pp.171, 189.
12. *Calendar of State Papers, America and West Indies,* 1700, pp.107, 634.

13. Sheridan, *op.cit.*, p.158.

14. Sheridan, *op.cit.*, p.197; 'The rise of a colonial gentry: a case study of Antigua, 1730-1775', *Economic History Review*, 2nd series, xiii, no.3 (April 1961), 355-7.

15. Sheridan, *op.cit.*, pp.369-70.

16. Sheridan, *op.cit.*, p.175. The Wyke plantation belonged to the Stapletons. See Vere Langford Oliver, *The history of the island of Antigua*, vol. III (London, 1899), 101.

17. Sheridan, *Economic History Review, loc.cit.*, 355-7.

18. P.R.O.I. Blake papers; Vere Langford Oliver, *op.cit.*, I (London, 1894), 53.

19. Hugh Fenning, 'The mission to St. Croix in the West Indies: 1750-1769', *Archivium Hibernicum*, xxv (1962), 108.

20. Archives Départementales de la Loire Atlantique, Nantes, E" 761, 8 Nov. 1762.

21. Fenning, *loc. cit.*, p.99.

22. Vere Langford Oliver, *op.cit.*, 3, 100-101., R. Hayes, *Biographical dictionary of Irishmen in France* (Dublin, 1949), pp.291-2. The common assumption that the Stapletons settled directly in France from Ireland is incorrect. For instance, the privateer [Richard] Stapleton under commission from Saint-Malo was said to be 'of an Irish family and born at Montserate'. B.M.Add. MS 9764, f.103.

23. Archives Départementales de la Loire Atlantique, Nantes, notarial archives, various acts in the *étude* Boufflet.

24. Fenning, *loc. cit., passim;* P.C. Yorke ed. *The diary of John Baker* (London, 1931), pp.62-3n.; Sheridan, *op.cit.*, p.445.

25. Fenning, *loc.cit.*, 84-5.

26. Jean Baptists de Macarthy. His portrait is in the Louisiana State Museum, New Orleans.

27. Vere Langford Oliver, *op.cit.*, I, 196.

28. Vere Langford Oliver, *op.cit.*, III, 137.

29. Isle of Man Record Office, Chancery Court, 11 Nov. 1759, Francis Dean for Peter Fox of Rotterdam v. Hugh Connor.

30. H. Luthy, *La banque protestante en France* (Paris, 1961), II, 445.

31. Archives Départementales de la Gironde, Bordeaux, série C. There is fleeting reference in the Chambre de Commerce archives to the movement of Bordeaux sugar refiners to Dublin in the 1720s.

32. I am indebted to my student Miss Aideen Graham for establishing this point.

33. P.R.O. S.P. 94/250, 25 February 1776; S.P. 94/213, 11 August 1721.

34. L.M. Cullen, 'The smuggling trade in Ireland in the eighteenth century', *Proceedings of the Royal Irish Academy*, LXVII, Section C (1969), p.153n. The Park participation in the firm comes out in various references in the Chancery Court Records, Isle of Man Record Office.

35. Archives Départementales de la Gironde, Bordeaux, 7 B 1169 – 7 B 1186, 1785-1789.

36. Vere Langford Oliver, III (1899), p.137.

37. Archives Départementales de la Loire Atlantique, Nantes, E"770, 26 March 1771; E"771, 23 September 1772.

38. J. Chaussinand-Nogaret, 'De l'exil religieux aux affaires: les Jacobites au XVIIIᵉ siècle', *Annales: économies, sociétés, civilisations*, Sept.-Oct. 1973, p.1104.

39. P.R.O. S.P. 94/220, Cadiz 15 July 1732. See also letter of 12 Oct. 1732, Cadiz.

40. L.M. Cullen, 'Tráchtáil is baincéaracht in Gaillimh san 18ᵘ céad, *Galvia*, V (1958), 60n.

41. *A discourse concerning Ireland and the different interests thereof in answer to the Exeter and Barnstaple petitions* (London 1698), p.8; P.R.O.N.I. Willes Letters (microfilm), C.1760.

42. Sheridan, *Economic History Review, loc.cit.*, 349-50; *op.cit.*, pp.197-200, 369-73.

43. Irish Manuscripts Commission, *Analecta Hibernica,* vol. XIV (October 1944), 53. See also P.R.O.I. Blake papers, M6936/5, Martin Blake, Antigua, 25 June 1738. Andrew Blake struck his eldest son out of his will 'because of his undutifulness to me and following the advice of a parcel of Irish knaves who meant nothing but to plunder him' (Vere Langford Oliver, *op.cit.,* I, 53).

44. N.L.I. MS 827, Kelly letter book, especially letter of 7 Dec. 1744 to Percivall and Co., Chester.

45. Cork Archives Council, letter book of Richard Hare, Hare to Bairds, 2 Aug. 1771.

46. Archives Nationales Paris, inventory of Paris Notarial étude LXVI.

47. N.L.I. N3142 (microfilm), bill book of Dillon and Co., 1750-52.

48. Archives départementales de la Gironde, Bordeaux 7 B 1706, Jean Bodin, 24 Jan. 1770.

49. C.M. Tenison, 'The old Dublin bankers', *Journal of the Cork Historical and Archaeological Society,* III, no.36 (Dec. 1894), p.222; H. Dutton, *A statistical and agricultural survey of the county of Galway* (Dublin, 1824), pp.418-9. On the French-Blake family relationship, see P.R.O.I. Blake papers, paper A enclosed with no.28, 'extracts and remarks taken from antient family papers and books found at Ballyglunin, the 1st December 1803'.

50. P.R.O.I. Blake papers, M6934(9), 1,2,3.

51. Smout, *A history of the Scottish people,* p.228.

13. Colonial Commerce and the Scottish Economy, c.1730-1815

T. M. Devine

WITHOUT question the most dynamic factor in eighteenth-century Scottish commerce was the dramatic rise of the colonial trades linking the Clyde with North America and the Caribbean. In 1762, one commodity, tobacco, accounted for 40 per cent of all Scottish imports and 50 per cent of overseas exports; by 1770, the total value of all produce shipped from the New World to Scotland comprised 58 per cent of all cargoes landed. There is less certainty, however, on the more important issue of the relationship between this booming trade sector and the domestic economy. (1) Victorian commentators, bathing in the full glow of their country's economic prosperity, had no doubts. To them, Scottish hegemony in the Atlantic trades was the first fruit of the Treaty of Union of 1707 which guaranteed access to England's transatlantic empire and, in turn, produced the capital and the enterprise that eventually led to the industrial transformation of the later eighteenth century. (2) This thesis, albeit in less crude form, remained influential and attractive until the 1950s (3) when opinion began to shift markedly towards a more sceptical interpretation. Increasingly, the 'enclave theory', which contended that foreign trade affected only a small part of the economy in a minor fashion and left the rest largely untouched, commanded support. (4) Partly this new interpretation was a reaction to the unproven assumptions and *simpliste* claims of the old orthodoxy but, perhaps more fundamentally, it was related to the absence of convincing evidence of extensive linkages between the home and overseas sectors. In the last few years, however, some of these gaps in knowledge have been partially filled, and the time now seems ripe to attempt a tentative re-assessment and to provide a brief guide to current scholarly thinking on this problem. (5)

The eighteenth-century Scottish tobacco trade was, in its early phase, an example of partially exogenous growth. As a re-export trade, with over 98 per cent of imports sold in foreign markets, it was not necessarily stimulated by, nor was it a reflection of, domestic economic expansion. But while it was not propelled by indigenous demand there remains the alternative possibility that its success induced increases in Scottish production. For unlike the sugar and slave trades of Bristol and Liverpool, (6) Glasgow's initial commercial development was not based on an urban economy which could, of itself, sustain the flow of commodities required in the first half of the eighteenth century. (7) Yet the 'store system', the characteristic business method of the great Glasgow houses, depended upon the exchange of consumer goods and plantation equipment for the primary produce of the Americas. It therefore necessitated the development of close relationships between merchants and industrial producers. (8)

177

Much care was taken to select suitable articles for marketing purposes because returns from retailing such goods were often as great as those from selling tobacco itself. (9) Furthermore, as the number of store outlets expanded rapidly after c.1740 and as the Clyde trade became dominated by a handful of very large enterprises, it was more vital to buy in bulk and at attractive prices. The Glasgow system depended on shaving costs to a minimum. Only thus could the merchants sustain profit levels and at the same time achieve rapid turnover of capital. The Scottish firms, as owners of the tobacco they supplied to Europe could not afford the lengthy bargaining of the London consignment houses who were merely selling agents. Since the main income of the Londoners came from commission on tobacco sales, they wanted to hold out for the highest possible price. The Glasgow companies, on the other hand, compensated for their lower returns by cutting operating costs. (10) One method of doing so was by vertical integration involving the production of store goods.

Table 1   *Gross total of industrial units with some element of Glasgow colonial merchant capital in stock, c.1700-1815*

Manufacture	Total No. Units	No. outside Glasgow	No. outside West-Central Scotland
Textiles (silk, linen, wool)	23	2	-
Textiles (cotton-spinning)	12	10	1
Textiles (finishing processes)	9	4	1
Iron (malleable)	2	-	-
Iron (pig)	3	3	-
Mining (coal)	14	8	1
Mining (other minerals)	2	-	2
Sugar-houses	7	2	-
Rope/Sailcloth manufactories	3	2	-
Leather manufactories	4	-	-
Glassworks	3	2	-
Breweries	2	2	-
Soapworks	2	-	-
Tobacco – Spinners	1	-	-
Potteries and Delftworks	1	-	-
	88	35	5

Source: Devine, *op.cit.,* (1975), Appendix II
Notes: (1) Each unit refers to a 'new' venture. Alterations of partnership over a
firm's life were not included.
(2) Where a particular company comprised different industrial activities,
e.g. operated both in linen weaving and printing, it was listed under one
of those activities.

This was one reason why, as Table 1 illustrates, there was a considerable employment of commercial capital in the economy of west-central Scotland in the decades after c.1730. Over the seventy years, 1660-1730, only 9 'manufactories' were funded by colonial traders, but between 1730-50 a further 18 were established and from 1780-95 an additional 21.

Moreover, it was the typical, not the exceptional trader, who had industrial connections, well over half of the merchant community between 1770 and 1815 holding shares in manufacturing and a considerable number retaining multiple investments. Of the 163 merchants of partnership status involved in the American trades between 1740 and 1790, eighty-five had a share in one 'industrial' company. Between 1770 and 1815, 21 traders held capital in one firm, 19 in two, 11 in three and 9 in four. Of the remainder, three individuals had money in six units, one in seven, three in eight, one in nine and two in ten. One individual had shares in no less than 17 different partnerships. (11)

The trend towards diversification was encouraged by the increasingly oligopolistic structure of the merchant community which, linked with the speedy growth of Atlantic commerce, helped to ensure the rapid accumulation of savings among the élite. These could then be deployed elsewhere. Of course, the very complexity of the mercantile investment portfolio meant that not all surpluses represented net profit from the colonial sector and the precise proportion so derived will probably never be known. Nevertheless, since those merchants considered here were primarily committed to tobacco and sugar, it is reasonable to conclude that a substantial part of their investment funds did come from those trades. (12)

The impact of this flow of capital on the western regional economy was very significant. Merchant finance was not only available to industries ancillary to port and shipping services but was also dominant in a number of other manufacturing activities. The two malleable ironworks in the west were funded by colonial merchants. (13) The entire sugar and glass industries were under their control. In linen production, their role was most crucial in the capital-intensive finishing processes. (14) In brief, merchant enterprise created a new diversity in Scottish manufacturing. Specialised products, such as sugar mills, were evolved in the nascent iron industry and this relationship formed one of the bases of the west's engineering supremacy in the nineteenth century. (15) Again, several of the pioneering firms in textile finishing (such as the Prestonpans Vitriol Co., the Pollockshaws Printfield Co. and The Glasgow Cudbear Co.) were founded and funded by members of the trading elite. (16)

It would be no exaggeration to say, therefore, that this capital outlay markedly affected employment and income in the regional economy. One indication of a multiplier effect was the parallel rise of coalmining in the area, mainly financed by the merchants, and reflecting increments to domestic or manufacturing demand. A second is the evidence that money wages in west central Scotland after c.1750 were substantially higher than the Scottish average. (17) An associated development was the creation of a new economic infrastructure. Between 1760 and 1800 the work of Golborne, Smeaton and Rennie transformed the Clyde from an unnavigable waterway to a ship canal. The Forth and Clyde Canal, Glasgow's route to the east, was related to the tobacco men's need to link quickly with European markets, while the Monkland Canal was financed by the same group to relieve the city's fuel crisis by exploiting the mineral-rich parishes of Lanarkshire. (18)

Merchant membership of industrial partnerships, while the most obvious, was not necessarily the most important factor in the movement of funds from the commercial sector to the domestic economy. Several traders with limited formal company associations yet lent considerable sums on bond to manufacturing ventures.

Three examples of this process must suffice. James Somervell, the great West India merchant, had a single £200 share in the Rope Manufactory of Glasgow, but a further £7,700 out on loan to a range of other industrial concerns. (19) Robert Dinwiddie in 1818 had £4,000 outstanding from Prestonpans Vitriol Co. and another £3,000 lent on bond to the Clyde Ironworks and the St Rollox Chemical Works. (20) Richard Oswald, between 1762 and 1780, lent out a total of £72,000. (21) The important regional capital market in personal and heritable bonds is still imperfectly understood and it cannot be insisted that colonial merchants formed the only, or indeed, even the most influential group within it. (22) But equally, in the west of Scotland, one is impressed by the number of wealthy overseas traders whose names persistently appear in registered bonds. (23) It is very possible, therefore, that their role in capital provision in this area gains even greater significance if seen in the context of the traditional financial limitations of the Scottish economy.

Better known, though arguably of less basic importance, is the fact that the tobacco trade gave birth to a formal credit structure in Glasgow. The city's first three banks were founded by merchant enterprise in the 1750s and 1760s and the extant records of two of these do indicate that they not merely provided ancillary services to foreign trade but also to a variety of business and social groups in the western lowlands. (24) In the east, the Royal Bank's liquidity was also crucially influenced by earnings from the tobacco trade. (25) The evidence suggests, therefore, that some proponents of the 'enclave theory' have overstated their case. In another sense, however, modern research has helped to substantiate the claim of this school that there was less direct connection between *later* eighteenth-century economic growth and merchant investment patterns. For one thing, there is no indication of a prolonged acceleration in industrial funding by traders in the crucial period 1780-1815. Between 1795 and 1815 they took up shares in only 9 partnerships compared with at least 21 in the period from 1780 to 1794, despite the fact that the aggregate formation of industrial ventures probably increased in the later phase. Furthermore, of these 9, four were but renewals of partnership contracts rather than wholly fresh foundations. (26) Again, there is some evidence that the role of colonial merchants diminished at this time in a number of companies which they had helped to establish and had long dominated. (27) All this, therefore, implies that, by the last two decades of the century, indigenous industry proved more capable of producing its own resources for future expansion and that accelerated growth at that time is to be explained in terms of factors within the domestic structure. The old supposition that colonial trade represented a kind of *deus ex machina* in the process of change must then be largely discounted.

The basis of the overseas merchant's supremacy at an earlier period had been that he, almost alone, had the resources and motivation required to invest in 'factory' industry at a time when most production typically took place in the home and on the farm. The merchant group had also performed a variety of functions relevant to the needs of the domestic economy as well as foreign commerce. They were insurers, bankers, builders and providers of industrial capital. Gradually, however, and particularly from the early nineteenth century, these several functions were fragmented and undertaken by other groups, a trend indicative of the new wealth in society and of the more complex needs of a rapidly growing economy. In short,

the Scottish Industrial Revolution was not caused by an increase in merchant investment. Rather social and economic change brought the era of mercantile dominance
to an end. This fact is plainly reflected in the recruitment patterns of Glasgow
burgesses. Between 1766-70, 158 'merchants' were enrolled in the burgh guild, a
figure which then more than doubled to 381 between 1786-90. At the same time,
the number of colonial merchants declined as a proportion of the general group
from 10.1 per cent of those gaining burgesships between 1766-70 to 2.1 per cent,
1801-5, and to 0.4 per cent from 1811-15. (28)

Modern opinion is surely correct too when it asserts that the dramatic growth
of the cotton industry was not related, as was once thought, to a 'transfer of resources' from the tobacco trade. That manufacture's rapid rate of progress was
mainly financed and organised from the existing linen industry in general and by
yarn and cloth merchants in particular. (29) Several colonial merchants did invest
in cotton, as their predecessors had always invested in earlier industrial ventures,
but there was no special concentration on the new sector as such and most known
linkages were with Caribbean rather than with North American trade. (30) Indeed, it
would have been surprising if such a close relationship had developed. Tobacco
commerce did not 'collapse' during the American War. After 1783 Glasgow houses
once again ventured to dominate the Chesapeake and to do so granted generous
credit to planters starved of finance during hostilities. There was thus no sudden
access of spare resources available for re-deployment in other sectors. (31) The
most impressive characteristic of these years was rather the new strength of the
Scottish economy which made possible both a renewal of the American link and
substantial progress in the domestic sphere.

The debate over *late* eighteenth-century industrial investment seems therefore
to be resolved in favour of the more sceptical interpretation espoused in recent
years. But there were a number of other important interconnections between trade
and economic development, and to neglect these would be to supplant the old
discredited orthodoxy by an equally unbalanced revisionism. The first phase of
rapid growth in cotton until c.1800 was based on raw materials from the Caribbean
and this was partly associated with changes in the overseas sector. The West Indies
had long been familiar to Scottish merchants (32), but during the American War existing
contacts expanded as Glasgow houses started to use the area as the centre of a
clandestine tobacco trade with the rebel colonies. (33) One consequence of this
was a new Scottish interest in the West India commodity trade in sugar, rum and
cotton. Merchant correspondence suggests that importers were concerned primarily
with sugar but were required to take the less desirable cotton as a condition of
securing business with some of the planter class. (34) As a result there was a considerable fall in the price of raw cotton imports to the Clyde from 18d-21d per lb in
October 1776 to 13d-15d per lb in April 1778 and to 11d-12d per lb in August
1780. (35) This trend may have been relevant to entrepreneurial calculations at a
time when the new cotton technology was becoming available and the price of
fine linen yarn rising. In the longer term, cotton's crucial advantage over linen was
that raw material prices fell as demand and production expanded. This could not
easily have happened if Glasgow (like Liverpool in relation to the English industry)
had not had a developing link with the Caribbean.

But possibly of even greater significance in economic growth was the role of colonial trade in the Scottish financial system *before* the period of structural change. The economy could not have emerged to the threshold of industrialisation without a widening of the cash base, the restriction of which in the early eighteenth century earned Scotland its reputation as one of the poorest countries in western Europe. One factor which helped to alter this image was changing agricultural productivity over time, since a key element in international liquidity was the net surplus/deficit in grain. (36) The expansion in the linen and cattle business to England may have been equally relevant. Nor should the function of colonial earnings be neglected. The most recent historian of Scottish banking has claimed that the tobacco trade's vital function lay in 'bringing an element of liquidity to Scotland'. (37) Undoubtedly domestic activity and the overseas sector could not proceed along independent lines. For example, when tobacco markets were dull, the important linen industry suffered through prolonged payments. (38) Furthermore, Scotland was partly spared some of the consequences of the commercial crisis of 1772 (despite the well-known failure of the Ayr Bank) because tobacco sales to France remained buoyant and, as a result, the liquidity of the Glasgow houses and their industrial suppliers was not fundamentally impaired. (39) Ultimately, of course, the precise importance of the tobacco business in this respect cannot be decided until the thorny issue of Scotland's balance of payments position has been thoroughly explored. (40)

It may be objected that the colonial sector itself tied up a considerable amount of capital. But there is little evidence that the tobacco trade starved indigenous activity of precious funds because most of its capital was generated within the trade itself or raised through bills of exchange drawn on the London market. Further, the mechanism was lubricated by the concentration, in the quarter century after c.1750, on the French market. The French bought in bulk, in cash and in easily discountable bills of exchange. Therefore, since the Glasgow firms disposed of their cargoes in huge sales to the French buyers (rather than on the hogshead by hogshead basis characteristic of the London consignment houses) they were able to turn over their capital more quickly and diminish the possibility of major liquidity crises in the economy. (41)

Most of the personal profits reaped by individual merchants from this lucrative commerce were laid out on land purchase. Between c.1770-1815 at least sixty-two tobacco and sugar merchants acquired a 'landed estate' and some obtained several properties in a number of counties. As Table 2 reveals, almost all of these were located in west-central Scotland:

Table 2   *Number and location of estates owned by Glasgow tobacco and West India merchants, c.1770-1815*

Area	No. of Merchant Landowners	No. of Estates
Barony of Glasgow	34	40
Lanarkshire	22	37
Renfrewshire	19	36
Dunbartonshire	11	11
Stirlingshire	6	10
Ayrshire	8	11

Source: Devine, thesis, II, 590-608.

It would be wrong to assume, however, that the majority of merchant-landowners withdrew from trade and embraced the life of the country gentry. In fact they aspired to an equilibrium between a series of different but complementary types of investment among which land was important. Even the greatest (such as Speirs, Glassford, McDowall, Ritchie and Dunlop) trained their sons in business and, while giving them a gentlemanly education, encouraged them in a commercial career. (42) The 'haemorrhage of capital' thesis, which proposes that merchant land purchases resulted in a transfer of funds from more productive sectors (commerce and industry) to a less productive one (agriculture) does therefore require qualification. (43) Most families continued their association with overseas trade long after buying an estate and did not regard the source of their wealth and their new status as incompatible. Most who owned land had town houses or tenement flats in Glasgow; some spent half the week there, looking after their business interests, and stayed the remainder at their country estates, which would normally be situated a short horse-ride from Glasgow. (44)

Whether merchant land-purchase should be regarded as a fundamental force in Scottish agrarian change is open to debate. The tobacco lords and sugar princes comprised only one section of the group of 'new' landlords who penetrated rural society in the eighteenth century. Their estates were regionally concentrated and, even in the west-central zone, they were inferior both in numbers and size to those of the older landed families. (45) Often indeed a merchant's desire for land was satisfied by a very small property extending to no more than a few hundred acres on which he could build an elegant villa in rural surroundings. (46) It is true that merchants had more plentiful sources of capital than other landlords. But this encouraged expenditure on stately homes and fine furnishings as well as enclosures and drainage schemes. Indeed, the very fact of their greater wealth occasionally allowed some to employ funds in highly speculative projects which excited the humour of their more canny but less opulent neighbours. (47) Adam Smith contended that merchants were often 'the best of all improvers', yet in the later eighteenth century 'improvement' was a commonplace activity, and a good head for business was not the sole prerogative of the professional trading community. Andrew Wight, in his detailed survey of Scottish agrarian change between 1778-82, was as much impressed by the performance of long-established families as by the activities of enterprising burgesses in the counties around Glasgow. (48) The movement of colonial traders into land was therefore, at best, but a part of the process of commercialisation of Scottish agriculture.

Their main contribution to agricultural development was probably made in a more oblique fashion. The growth of Glasgow's population from over 12,000 in 1708 to 83,000 in 1801 was paralleled by a similar expansion of other Clyde towns such as Greenock and Port Glasgow. This was partly a consequence of developments associated with the colonial trades, and the net increase in non-food producing groups widened the market and increased incentives for the district's farmers. (49) Furthermore, the vitality of the land market implied a penetration of commercial profits into rural society in the western lowlands. It was one means by which non-mercantile elements shared in the gains of colonial trade and it helped to limit the dangers of capital shortage in Scottish agriculture at a time of increasing investment. The associated relationship was that land purchases by successful merchants encouraged the diversification of estate economies since they were sometimes linked to existing contacts in the coal and textile industries, together with potential interests in road and canal development. The movement of rich traders into the mineral-rich Monklands area of Lanarkshire in the 1780s and 1790s, for example, was related to their involvement in the Monkland Canal and their investments in Glasgow coal-mining. (50)

In the final analysis, the significance of colonial markets for Scottish producers is at once among the most crucial questions of this discussion and the one least capable of a wholly satisfactory solution. There are three main problems. In the first place, although the colonies, because of their high labour costs and the constraints of mercantilist regulation, represented rapidly growing markets for all kinds of commodities, not all exports on Scottish account to these markets originated in Scotland. Secondly, there is the obvious difficulty of assessing the *relative* importance of colonial markets for Scottish industry. Finally, the thorny issue of the extent to which the colonial sector may have exerted an indirect, though important, influence on Scottish production through the re-export of Scottish goods from London merits investigation. Inevitably, not all of these obstacles can be entirely overcome and therefore a wholly satisfactory assessment at this point in time is not possible.

Certainly Scottish merchants only found a proportion of the goods they required in Scotland itself. Rum was sent from the Caribbean to the thirteen colonies. Ireland, especially after 1783, became an important source of provisions for the West Indies trade. Woollens, ironmongery and cottons were ordered from English sources and sent out via London. (51) Thus the value of exports to the colonies from Scotland was always much less than colonial imports to Scottish ports. In 1770-74, Scottish imports from the thirteen American colonies were 29.2 per cent of the British total, while Scottish exports direct from Scotland to that area formed 9.77 of the same total. (52) Nevertheless, Scottish exports to the New World did rise, albeit more slowly than imports, over the period c.1740 to 1775. Exports to the thirteen colonies at official sterling values (which thus denote changing volume rather than current values) averaged £97,962 per annum in 1740-44, £153,835 in 1745-49, £145,069 in 1750-54 and £128,265 from 1755-59. Thereafter, there was more rapid growth to £197,277 per annum in 1760-64, £224,497, 1765-69 and £298,922 from 1770-74.

The second point at issue is whether 'Scottish exports' were necessarily all produced in Scotland rather than simply shipped from Scotland. Merchant correspondence does indicate that goods ordered from English suppliers in the 1750s and 1760s were normally dispatched from English ports on Scottish account. (53) Also, it is unlikely that re-exports from Europe comprised a sizeable proportion of 'Scottish exports' since, in the second half of the eighteenth century, most manufactured articles shipped to the British colonies were made in the British Isles. Dutch and German linens were the only exceptions. (54) But from 1747 to 1768 between 72 per cent and 75 per cent of linen exported from Scotland was Scottish-made, the remainder being Irish or German. (55)

It is worth adding here that data on American trade alone obviously understate the value of Scottish exports to the colonial sector as a whole. The Caribbean and the Canadian region, which such figures do not take into account, while not of great importance before mid-century, eventually became significant. The West Indies in particular was very relevant to the expansion of the Scottish coarse linen trade and was well-nigh vital to the growth of the Clyde-based herring fishery which distributed income and employment throughout the western Highlands and Islands. (56)

The relative share of Scottish production absorbed by colonial markets, the most vital problem of all, is also the most controversial. As a preliminary, however, it should be stressed that most industrial case-studies which have been completed indicate that the U.K. market took the biggest proportion of Scottish goods in the eighteenth century and that, thereafter, the competitive edge of Scottish industry allowed its products to penetrate European and South American markets as well as those in the colonies. (57) In aggregate terms, therefore, the colonial sector was almost certainly subordinate though, as will be seen, not necessarily unimportant. For instance, it is probable that the many manufactories which emerged in the west central area of Scotland between 1730 and 1790 catered mainly for transatlantic trade. The small local population could not have supported such a growth on its own. The malleable iron industry in the same period was equally dependent on American and Caribbean markets but, it should be added, quickly achieved access to consumers outside Scotland. (58)

It is in the history of the linen industry, however, that an ambitious attempt has been made recently to gauge the role of overseas markets in the growth process with more precision. This has been made possible by the survival of production data which can be used in combination with trade statistics to give approximate measurements of the relative importance of the home and foreign markets. (59) This is of consider-able value for two reasons. First, linen represented the most significant single manu-factured item in cargoes shipped to the colonies. (60) Secondly, it was Scotland's staple manufacture throughout most of the eighteenth century and the progenitor of the cotton industry.

Dr Durie's investigations show that the colonies before 1775 were easily the most important overseas market for linen with about 90 per cent of all linen exported from Scottish ports between 1750 and 1775 going to America and the Caribbean. (61) This was a figure equivalent to around 20 per cent of 'total production' (i.e. linen stamped for sale by the Board of Trustees for Manufactures and Fisheries). More importantly, since most Scottish linens were sold in London — contemporary estimates suggest the capital took between one-half and four-fifths of all cloth produced — an unknown proportion of this was later re-exported to the Americas. Durie himself estimates that, as a result, the final total of Scottish-made linen exported from Britain to the colonial area seldom dropped below 20 per cent to 30 per cent between 1750 and 1775 and on occasion reached 35 to 40 per cent of total production. While it must be admitted that these figures are arrived at on the basis of assumptions with which not all would agree, the fact remains that colonial demand was clearly very relevant to the coarse linen industry as a whole and to the linen areas of eastern Scotland in particular. There, growth was sustained, not by productivity gains, but by access to transatlantic markets buttressed by bounty legislation and British protective tariffs.

It is possible to conclude, then, that neither the old orthodoxy, which viewed the colonial trades as the vital engines of economic growth in the later eighteenth century, nor some versions of the more modern 'enclave theory' are wholly satisfactory. Struct-ural change in the last two decades of the century was not directly related to trans-atlantic commerce nor was it financed by merchants from that sector. Equally, however, the interdependence between foreign trade and the domestic economy over the period

N

c.1730-c.1780 has surely been underestimated in recent writing. The tobacco trade was clearly not, as a modern general history of Scotland has insisted, 'a self-contained matter of purchase and re-export, locking up a lot of money, and with little effect on industry and labour'. (62) Rather, in terms of demand pressures and investment links, the relationship was close, intimate and of mutual benefit to overseas commerce and indigenous manufacturing alike. The latter was fructified by capital and enterprise while the former gained in the supply of cheap goods. While not directly responsible for accelerated growth in the later eighteenth century, Scottish success in the transatlantic sector was among the series of influences which helped to raise the impoverished economy of the early 1700s to the threshold of industrialisation fifty years later.

Above all, the expansion of transatlantic commerce was crucial to the emergence of the west-central region to a dominating position in the Scottish economy. The tobacco business raised Glasgow from the status of a provincial centre to that of a great international port with developed links throughout the nexus of European and Atlantic trade. The area's economic infrastructure of waterways, docks, warehouses and canals was similarly inherited from the tobacco age. But perhaps, ultimately, the achievements in colonial commerce ought to be regarded as much a symptom as a cause of growing sophistication. The ingenuity and sheer business skill which formed the basis of Scottish success in the colonies were to be again among the nation's prime assets in the later period of industrial growth and penetration of world markets. It follows therefore that one of the fundamental tasks confronting Scottish economic historians is to discover why such qualities flourished in the eighteenth century. Only by doing so can they hope to provide a comprehensive exposition of the country's economic growth.

NOTES

1. For the expansion of the tobacco grade see Jacob M. Price, 'The Rise of Glasgow in the Chesapeake Tobacco Trade, 1707-1775', reprinted in P.L. Payne, ed. *Studies in Scottish Business History* (1967), pp.299-318; Jacob M. Price, *France and the Chesapeake* (Ann Arbor, 1973); J.H. Soltow, 'Scottish Traders in Virginia, 1750-75', *Economic History Review,* 2nd ser., xii (1959); T.M. Devine, *The Tobacco Lords* (John Donald Publishers Ltd., Edinburgh, 1975). For the rise of the Caribbean trades see Anon, 'The Rise of Glasgow's West Indian Trade, 1793-1818', *Three Banks Review,* XXXVIII (1958); T.M. Devine, 'Glasgow Merchants in Colonial Trade c.1770-1815', University of Strathclyde Ph.D. thesis, (1971), I, 99-172. I am very grateful to Professors J. Butt, R.H. Campbell and S.G. Checkland for kindly reading an earlier draft of this paper and providing several valuable comments.

2. A.E. Gordon, *The History of Glasgow from the earliest times to the present time* (Glasgow, 1872), 2 vols.; J.O. Mitchell, *Old Glasgow Essays* (Glasgow, 1905); 'Senex' (J.M. Reid), *Glasgow Past and Present* (Glasgow, 1884), 3 vols. This view had an even longer pedigree, see W. Fullarton, *General View of the Agriculture of the County of Ayr* (1793), p.130; J. Denholm, *History of Glasgow* (Glasgow, 1804), p.408; David Macpherson, *Annals of Commerce, Manufactures, Fisheries and Navigation* (1805), III, 593.

3. H. Hamilton, *The Industrial Revolution in Scotland* (1932), p.121; L.J. Saunders, *Scottish Democracy, 1815-40 : the Social and Intellectual Background* (Edinburgh, 1950), p.98; J. Cunnison and J.B.S. Gilfillan, eds., *The Third Statistical Account of Scotland : Glasgow Region* (Glasgow, 1958), p.103.

4. M.L. Robertson, 'Scottish Commerce and the American War of Independence', *Economic History Review,* 2nd ser., ix (1956), 130; K. Berrill, 'International Trade and the rate of Economic Growth', *Economic History Review,* 2nd ser., xii (1960), 351-59; R.H. Campbell, 'An Economic History of Scotland in the Eighteenth Century', *Scottish Journal of Political Economy,* xi (1964), 19. Professor Campbell's theories are also developed in 'The Anglo-Scottish Union of 1707 : II The Economic Conse- quences', *Economic History Review,* 2nd ser., xvi (1964), 472; *Scotland since 1707* (1965), p.40; 'The Union and Economic Growth' in T.I. Rae, ed. *The Union of 1707 : Its Impact on Scotland* (1974), 63-4. See also T.C. Smout, *History of the Scottish People, 1560-1830* (1969), p.245 and Rosalind Mitchison, *A History of Scotland* (1970), p.328.

5. See, *inter alia,* S.G. Checkland, *Scottish Banking : A History, 1695-1973* (1975); T.M. Devine, 'Glasgow Merchants in Colonial Trade, c.1770-1815', University of Strathclyde Ph.D. thesis, (1971), 2 vols; *The Tobacco Lords* (Edinburgh, 1975); 'The Colonial Trades and Industrial Investment in Scotland, c.1700-1815', *Economic History Review,* 2nd ser., xxix (1976), 1-13. Alistair J. Durie, 'The Scottish Linen Industry 1707-1775, with particular reference to the early History of the British Linen Company', University of Edinburgh Ph.D. thesis, (1973); 'The Markets for Scottish Linen, 1730-1775', *Scottish Historical Review,* LII (1973), 30-49. Clifford Gulvin, *The Tweedmakers* (Newton Abbot, 1973); Jacob M. Price, 'New Time Series for Scotland's and Britain's Trade with the Thirteen Colonies and States, 1740 to 1791', *William and Mary Quarterly,* XXXII, 2 (April, 1975), 307-325.

6. For the situation in Bristol see W.E. Minchinton, 'Bristol-Metropolis of the West in the 18th Century', *Transactions of the Royal Historical Society,* 5th ser., iv (1954); for Liverpool, Paul G.E. Clemens, 'The Rise of Liverpool, 1665-1750', *Economic History Review,* 2nd ser., xxix (1976), 211-225.

7. J.H. Burton, ed. *Autobiography of the Rev. Dr. Alexander Carlyle containing Memorials of the Men and Events of his Time* (Edinburgh, 1860), p.13. This point is verified in Mitchell Library (M.L.), Glasgow, Bogle MSS, George Bogle's letter book, 1725-31 and Glasgow City Archives (G.C.A.), Burgh Court Register of Deeds, B.10/15.

8. See Scottish Record Office (S.R.O.) GD247/58/0, Correspondence of James Robinson, 1768-1774.

9. Devine, *op.cit.,* (1975), p.61.

10. *Ibid,* pp.67-8.

11. T.M. Devine, 'The Colonial Trades and Industrial Investment in Scotland, c.1700-1815', *Economic History Review,* 2nd ser., xxix (1976), 1-13.

12. See Devine, *op.cit.,* (1971), I, 4-14 where this point is discussed.

13. S.R.O. GD237/151/3, (Copy), Continuation of Copartnery among the partners of Muirkirk Company (1793); G.C.A. Register of Deeds, B.10/15/7460, Contract of Copartnery betwixt the Glasgow Iron and Steel Manufactory.

14. Devine, thesis, II, 362-374.

15. R.H. Campbell, *Carron Company* (Edinburgh, 1961), p.105; J.Butt, 'The Scottish Iron Industry before the Hot Blast', *Journal of West of Scotland Iron and Steel Inst,* xxiii, 6 (1965-6).

16. *Glasgow Mercury,* 19 January 1790; S.R.O. Register of Deeds, 295/143 DAL; Signet Library, Edinburgh, Court of Session Process 438/18.

17. Valerie Morgan, 'Agricultural Wage Rates in late Eighteenth-Century Scotland', *Economic History Review,* 2nd ser., xxiv (1971), 181-201.

18. G.C.A. Register of Deeds, B10/15/7368; Signet Library, Court of Session Process 457/6; *Glasgow Mercury,* 2 August 1781.

19. G.C.A. Sederunt Book of James Somervell (uncatalogued when examined).

20. G.C.A. Memorandum Book containing copies of documents concerning Capt. W. Lockhart of Germiston (uncatalogued when examined).

21. S.R.O. Register of Deeds, 271/583 DUR, Commission, Alexander Houston to John Campbell.

22. For some evidence on the nature of this market see T.M. Devine, 'Sources of Capital for the Glasgow Tobacco Trade, c.1740-c.1780', *Business History,* XVI, July 1974, 113-129.

23. This view is based on an examination of G.C.A. B.10/15, Burgh Court Register of Deeds for the period c.1710-90 and G.C.A. B.10/12, Burgh Court Register of Sasines. See also S.R.O. Register of Deeds, c.1760-1800.

24. G.C.A. Ship Bank Balance Book, 1751-61; Ship Bank Ledger, TD 161/3, Part I, 1769-72; TD 161/2, Thistle Bank Journal, 1778-9. Less well known is the merchant role in the formation of the Greenock Banking Co. and the Renfrewshire Banking Co. See Signet Library, Edinburgh, Court of Session Paper 400/21; S.R.O. Commissariat of Wills and Testaments (Glasgow), CC9/7/78/181; *Glasgow Herald and Advertiser,* 12 June 1809.

25. Checkland, *op.cit.,* p.66.

26. Devine, thesis, II, 320-409.

27. For instance, the Dumbarton Glasswork Co (S.R.O. Adams Mack Misc., 22, Day Book, Minute of Meeting of Partners, 25 February 1802) and the Dalnottar Iron Co, which left mercantile control in 1813 (G.C.A. B.10/15/10244, Bond by Dennistouns and McLachlan, 19 December 1813).

28. G.C.A. Records of the Merchants House of Glasgow, Matriculation Book, 1768-1830; J.R. Anderson, ed. *The Burgesses and Guild Brethren of Glasgow, 1751-1846* (Edinburgh, 1935).

29. Based on unpublished data kindly supplied by Prof. John Butt.

30. Devine, *loc.cit.* (1976), pp.11-13.

31. Price, *op.cit.,* pp.728-31. Devine, *op.cit.,* pp.161-8.

32. S.R.O. GD237/151/3, State of Mr Dunmore's subjects. National Library of Scotland (N.L.S.), MS8800, Journal of William McDowall (1729). M.L. Bogle MSS, George Bogle's letterbook, Bogle to Matthew Bogle, 11 September 1731.

33. Library of Congress, Washington (L.C.), James Dunlop Family Papers, Hugh Wylie to James Dunlop, 22 December 1779; G.C.A. Speirs Papers, TD131/9, Letterbook of Alexander Speirs, Speirs to Robert Burton, 28 February 1782; T.M. Devine, 'A Glasgow Tobacco Merchant during the American War', *William and Mary Quarterly,* Third ser., xxxiii (July 1975), No.3.

34. N.L.S. MS8793, Letter book 'E' of Alexander Houston and Co, *passim.*

35. *Ibid.,* MSS 8793-4; S.R.O. GD247/58/0, Cunninghame - Robinson correspondenc

36. R.H. Campbell, 'The Union and Economic Growth' in T.I. Rae, ed. *The Union of 1707* (Glasgow, 1974), pp.65-6.

37. Checkland, *op.cit.,* p.66.

38. Durie, *op.cit.,* pp.242-3.

39. Arthur Lee letters, 1763-1774 (microfilm in possession of Colonial Williamsburg Foundation, Williamsburg, Virginia), William Lee to Frances Lightfoot Lee, 23 June 1772; Price, *op.cit.,* pp.640-1.

40. See H. Hamilton, 'Scotland's Balance of Payments Problem in 1762', *Economic History Review,* 2nd ser., V (1953).

41. Devine, *loc.cit.* (1974), 115; Price, *op.cit.,* pp.660-1.

42. Devine, *op.cit.,* (1975), p.26.

43. For this see H.J. Habbakuk, 'The English Land Market in the Eighteenth Century', in J.S. Bromley and E.H. Kossmann, eds. *Britain and the Netherlands* (1960), pp.55-65.

44. Devine, *op.cit.,* (1975), p.26.

45. Andrew Wight, *Present State of Husbandry in Scotland* (Edinburgh, 1778-84), III, pt.I, *passim.*

46. See, for example, S.R.O. Particular Register of Sasines (Renfrewshire), 1780-90.

47. There are a number of instances. See James Gourlay, *A Glasgow Miscellany* (privately printed, n.d.), pp.45-6. G.C.A. Speirs Papers, TD131/5, Ledger C; TD131/1, Cash Book, 1760-1778; TD131/13, Sederunt Book of the Trustees of Alexander Speirs, 20-1; A. Martin, *General View of the Agriculture of the County of Renfrew* (1794), pp.8, 13. The McDowalls (of Alexander Houston and Co., the greatest West India house in Glasgow) spent over £5,000 in attempting to drain the loch of

Lochwinnoch in Renfrewshire, despite the advice of their fellow lairds, only to see it fill in again after a few years. See S.R.O. GD237/139, Notebook of work done at Castlesemple, 1770-78; Bill Chamber Process, I, 75, 756, Dunlop versus McDowall (1801).

48. Wight, *op.cit.*, III, pt I, *passim.*

49. John Naismith, *General View of the Agriculture of the County of Clydesdale* (Glasgow, 1798), pp.43-4; *Transactions of the Glasgow and Clydesdale Statistical Society,* vol.I.

50. S.R.O. Particular Register of Sasines (Lanark), 25/138; 164-166; 27/87; 29/189; General Register of Sasines, 32/171; G.C.A. Dunlop Papers, State of the Funds of James Dunlop, 23 March 1793.

51. S.R.O. RH15/1179, James Lawson's Letter book, 1758-62; GD247/59/Q/2, Dunmore-Cunninghame correspondence, 1774-82; M.L. Bogle MSS, George Bogle of Daldowie's Letter book, 1729-42.

52. Subsequent details on Scottish trade to the thirteen colonies are based on 'An Account of the Values of Exports and Imports to and from North America and England [and Scotland] from Christmas 1739 to Christmas 1773, distinguishing each Colony and Year', House of Lords Record Office, Main Paper, 20 November 1775: The 'Account' has been reprinted in D.I. Fagerstrom, 'The American Revolutionary Movement in Scottish Opinion, 1763 to 1783', University of Edinburgh Ph.D. (1951), pp.23-4 and, more recently, together with a valuable analysis, Jacob M. Price, 'New Time Series for Scotland's and Britain's Trade with the Thirteen Colonies and States, 1740-1791', *William and Mary Quarterly,* 4th ser., XXXII, 2 (April 1975), 307-325. Figures are given in 'official values'. As Professor Price comments, 'The most likely hypothesis is that Scottish values were drawn up when the Scottish series started in 1755 and represent prices of ca. 1754-1756'. Price, *loc. cit.,* 317.

53. S.R.O. RH15/1179, James Lawson's Letter book, 1758-62; G.C.A. Oswald Account Book, TD188; Letter book of Alexander Henderson, 1758-64 (xerox copy, original in C.G. Lee Collection, Alexandria Public Library, Virginia, U.S.A.).

54. Ralph Davis, 'English Foreign Trade, 1700-1774', *Economic History Review,* 2nd ser., XV (1962), 185-303.

55. Durie, *loc. cit.,* 39.

56. On one calculaton, some 89 per cent of crew members of herring 'busses' receiving bounty at Greenock in the 1780s were Highlandborn. See R.D. Lobban, 'The Migration of Highlanders into Lowland Scotland c.1750-1890 with particular reference to Greenock', Edinburgh University Ph.D. thesis (1970), p.33. For the growth of Canadian trade see David S. Macmillan, 'The 'New Men' in Action: Scottish Mercantile and Shipping Operations in the North American Colonies' in D.S. Macmillan, ed. *Canadian Business History* (Toronto, 1972), pp.44-143.

57. R.H. Campbell, *Carron Company* (Edinburgh, 1961), 105; Gulvin, *op.cit.,* 32-3; Durie, *loc.cit.,* 30-49; Alistair G. Thomson, *The Paper Industry in Scotland* (Edinburgh, 1974), pp.79-80; P. Caddell, *The Iron Mills at Cramond* (Edinburgh, 1973), p.12. There was a similar market bias in the brewing industry. (I am grateful to I.L. Donnachie of the Open University for this information from his research.)

58. Campbell, *op.cit.,* (1961), 105; Caddell, *op.cit.,* 12; *Glasgow Mercury,* 1 January, 30 December 1784; 8 June 1786.

59. Durie, *loc.cit.,* 30-49.

60. In the early 1760s annual average orders for stores in Virginia belonging to John Glassford and Co. were of the order of £1,000. Textiles of various kinds comprised about 80 per cent of this total and about 50 per cent, by value, consisted of linens alone. See G.C.A. Letter book of Alexander Henderson, 1758-64 (xerox copy, original in C. G. Lee Collection, Alexandria Public Library, Virginia, U.S.A.).

61. This paragraph is based on an analysis of Durie, *op. cit., passim* and *loc. cit.,* 30-49.

62. Rosalind Mitchison, *A History of Scotland* (1970), p.328. A similar opinion is voiced in Smout, *op.cit.,* p.245, though in a more restrained fashion: 'Glasgow's entrepot trade, important though it was, brought prosperity mainly to a group of merchants and financiers in that city. Of course, some of that prosperity spilled over from the enclave when orders were placed in the Borders for shoes, or in Dunfermline for linen and in Musselburgh for woollens...'

PART V

LAND

14. The Influence of the Landlord in Eighteenth-century Ulster

W. H. Crawford

ANY discussion of landlord-tenant relations evokes the topic of Ulster tenant right. The very name suggests that in that society the tenants had managed to secure important concessions from their landlords in the age-old struggle. It raises a host of questions. What were the origins of Ulster tenant right? What combination of events occurred to provide the tenants with such a strong bargaining position? How did they manage to maintain their gains in changing economic circumstances? The answers to these questions are very complicated and it is easier to appreciate the situation from the point of view of the landlords and to assess their influence at any given time by examining their handling of certain problems. This paper will examine the circumstances in which Ulster landlords found themselves in the eighteenth century and explain how little room for manoeuvre they really had in altering their relations with their tenants. A discussion of the main issues illustrates how both sides benefited from the balmy economic climate of the mid-century and that civil disturbances were not the product of tenant grievances. The final section attempts to discover the real expression of landlord influence in the community. (1)

I

The landlords of seventeenth-century Ulster were a motley collection of adventurers who secured estates for themselves in the chaos that followed the collapse of the Gaelic aristocracy. After the flight of the Gaelic leaders in 1607 the English crown had parcelled out six of the nine counties of Ulster to new landowners under the scheme for the plantation of escheated lands. All of the land at the disposal of the crown was granted to a new group of landlords composed of 'servitors' who were officials of the Dublin administration, and soldiers; institutions such as the Irish Society, the Church of Ireland, Trinity College Dublin, and the royal schools; 'undertakers', the new colonists; and those among the Irish chiefs and gentry who were likely to prove loyal to the crown. Some of the institutions and servitors managed to obtain extensive holdings, especially in Londonderry and the neighbouring counties of Antrim and Down, but to the undertakers and the Irish on the escheated lands were granted small, compact estates comprising only one thousand, fifteen hundred or two thousand acres of profitable land. (2) Such estates were too small to attract the interest of casual speculators from Britain and so generally grants were taken up by the poorer element among the applicants for land. Those among them who did not relish the prospects on their arrival or soon realised that their incomes would represent a poor return on the outlay required, sold their properties to neighbours. The crises of the 1640s and 1688-91 produced further upheavals in land ownership, forcing estates on to the market. As long as land sold at ten years' purchase, and even in especially bad times at seven years, it was a good, if speculative, investment and those who could command ready money were able to secure estates of potential value. (3) Prominent among their number were representatives of the families of soldiers, churchmen, lawyers, and merchants. (4)

Yet the authority of this new landlord element was not as unconstrained as many people have believed: above all it was trammelled with the heritage of the seventeenth century. The theory of the plantation scheme had presumed that the undertakers would bring tenants with them from Britain and to this end the royal patents to the undertakers provided them with the powers essential to regulate the conduct of their tenants. The reality of the situation was different. Because the immigration of colonists was both slow and sporadic the landlords had great difficulty in securing and retaining tenants. To the British they had to offer attractive terms, then nurse them during hard times, and even acquiesce when tenants abandoned leases. (5) They often took native Irish tenants whom they found more reliable and amenable, if less civilised in their husbandry. So it is likely that on the eve of the 1641 rising the settlers were in a minority of between 1:2 and 1:3 with the natives and that the pre-plantation pastoral economy still predominated. (6) Although the 1641 rising almost destroyed the colony, there was in its aftermath considerable immigration from Scotland and the North of England. The consequent improved prospects for the landlords were dampened by the cattle acts of 1667 and 1681, which subsequently placed Ulster at a serious disadvantage with the development of an alternative provision trade, and by recurring economic crises. (7) Not until the great Scottish immigration of the 1690s did the balance of population begin to swing towards the British so that their settlements were able to penetrate many districts hitherto dominated by the Irish. (8) Substantial settlers were given leases over the heads of the Irish who were often reduced to the rank of undertenants. The original plantation scheme had stipulated that tenants should have leases and because settlers had been so difficult to obtain the granting of leases to tenants had become common practice. By the early eighteenth century, when tenants had become sufficiently plentiful to create competition for holdings, landlords found that they could not deny leases to prospective tenants or even use the covenants in them as a means of exercising control over their tenants' conduct. As early as 1718 they witnessed groups of tenants complaining about the behaviour of their landlords when they were leaving for America, a country which offered more land and opportunities than Ulster, and they realised that emigration could endanger the British colony. (9) Any landlord who treated his tenants with lack of consideration soon found too that there were other landlords in Ulster itself keen to attract tenants.

Landlords required British tenants to introduce British husbandry practices to supplant the traditional Irish pastoral economy. Tenants who were prepared to undertake improvement covenants requiring them to build a dwelling to certain minimum standards, to plant an orchard, and to ditch and mear the outbounds of their holding as well as emparking it with whitethorn quicksets, were granted leases for a term of three lives (or in the eighteenth century in the case of Catholics, of thirty-one years) at a rent based on the current value of the holding. Capital for development was scarce but in this unimproved countryside the plentiful labour of the farmers and their undertenants was soon converted into rising land values. For his part the farmer was guaranteed the enjoyment of his improvements throughout the remainder of his lease. When his lease expired he would hope by his claim that he had behaved as a good tenant and made substantial improvements, to persuade his landlord to renew the lease of the property – or at least part of it – at a new rent based on the current value of the land. Marginal land was leased to men who could guarantee the landlord his rent. Sometimes this was an individual who encouraged poor men to settle on the land to improve it: he became the middleman. In other cases groups of small farmers combined to take partnership leases: the fact that they were jointly bound for the rent could act as an inducement for the more progressive of them to seek separate leases when the original lease became due for renewal. (10)

These developments in settlement and land-holding in Ulster reflect its colonial character throughout the seventeenth century. In the eighteenth century the character of that economy came to be dictated more and more by the expanding linen industry. As early as 1740 Ulster linens had secured a firm foothold in the London market against their continental rivals, (11) while the mechanisation of several bleaching and finishing processes was about to bring about a radical re-organisation of local linen markets and stimulate a great increase in output to cope with rising demands from Britain and the colonies. (12) Although there were commentators who believed that the industry should be confined to the towns, it spread rapidly through the countryside, especially during the second half of the century. Good prices for webs induced many small farmers to concentrate more of their energies on the loom and gave them a reliable income to supplement their incomes from farming. Their small farms provided them with accommodation and some physical relief from the loom. Because their rents were paid by selling webs of linen rather than by farming, it was practicable for weavers to sub-divide their holdings among their children even over several successive generations. The domestic linen industry provided labour for all the family and therefore a premium for large families. As early as 1740 there were comments on the high density of population in the main weaving district in mid-Ulster and by the 1760s the demand for holdings near the important linen markets was forcing up rents. (13) Throughout the province the number of houses paying hearth tax almost doubled between 1753 and 1791 from 115,539 to 222,879, whereas the 1712 figure had been 102,625. (14)

The demand for small holdings by weavers with enough income to pay regular rents encouraged farmers to sublet portions of their farms: the returns were much more substantial than income from farming. The landlord who watched this happening on his estate realised that he could exploit this situation to the greater increase of his rentroll. When a lease expired the landlord could grant a new lease to the sitting tenant for only that portion of his land that he actually occupied and lease the re-mainder of the property directly to the occupying subtenants. In the districts where

fine linens were woven (in the triangle of country between Dungannon, Lisburn
and Armagh) the weavers obtained such leases from the landlords and as a result the
class of substantial farmers disappeared. Such a conclusion depended on the ability
of the weavers to outbid the farmers for small holdings. Elsewhere farmers continued
to exploit the weavers who for their part concentrated on trying to obtain security
of tenure. In some parts of the province they were successful in obtaining sub-leases
granting them definite terms in the property, but in other places their efforts were
repelled and they remained cottiers holding at the will of the farmer in return for
weaving, for performing essential work on the farm, or breaking in marginal land.
In a countryside with so much land still requiring reclamation, cottiers were essential
and easily paid in potato ground and access to turbary (to the manifest annoyance
of the landlords). This class grew rapidly throughout the late eighteenth century,
stimulated by putting-out of yarn by small manufacturers, and was especially significar
in Cavan and Monaghan. (15) Not until the Napoleonic Wars is there any mention of
farmers expelling cottiers in order to use their land for growing grain. (16) The cottier
problem grew to dominate Ulster and Irish rural life until the Great Famine. (17)
Historical hindsight reveals the vulnerability of the Ulster economy but the eighteenth
century commentator saw rather a landscape of intensively cultivated small holdings
reaching out into the bogs and up into the mountains, thronged by an industrious
peasantry enjoying a higher standard of living than elsewhere in rural Ireland. (18)
Landlords were well rewarded for a minimum outlay of capital. As one landlord wrote
in 1784: 'I am just returned from the North where I have been setting between three
and four thousand acres. The populousness of that county owing to the linen manufacture enabled me to set the lands to much better advantage than I can set lands of
the same quality in Munster, I may reasonably say twenty-five per cent better, though
I have set my lands lower, I believe, than any in the neighbourhood.'(19)

II

The relationship between landlord and tenant in Ulster was reciprocal and well-
understood on both sides although there were local differences of emphasis. A good
tenant improved his farm, kept the covenants in the lease, paid his rent when it was
due, and did not quarrel with his neighbours. A good landlord appreciated the efforts
of his tenants, understood and sympathised with their problems and disasters;
championed them against interference from other landlords, clergy, magistrates
and government officials; and was not too strict in exacting his rents and dues,
especially in hard times. The success of both parties in maintaining good relations
was reflected in the reputation or 'character' of the estate. (20) Every estate observed
its own individual code of practice which had evolved to protect the interests of the
landlord while encouraging the tenant. It had to take account of local concepts of
natural justice. Legal practice adopted this attitude and therefore the lease, the
written agreement between the two parties, tended to guarantee security for the
tenant while it required the landlord to prove any case against the tenant. A claim
by the landlord that the tenant had broken covenants in his lease had to be tried
before a jury, almost inevitably composed of other tenants. (21) As a result tenants
were often able to take advantage of any lapse by the landlord and alter the

interpretation of estate practice to suit their own interests. The most notable examples of this were the use of obstructionist tactics to break the monopolies of the manorial mills and the undermining of the authority of manorial courts. (22) In this context it should not be overlooked that the administration of justice in Ireland was dominated by English judges who exasperated Irish landlords by their readiness to punish them for breaches of judicial regulations and to give judgments against them in the courts. (23)

The most serious potential areas of conflict between landlord and tenant in the eighteenth century were tenure and rents, and they became interlinked. It had for long been assumed on many estates that a good tenant should have the right of renewal of his farm (or at least part of it) at the termination of the lease if he was prepared to pay the new rent. Only when the tenant vacated the property would another man be prepared to open negotiations with the landlord for it. This practice had prevented friction between the tenants, but in the second half of the eighteenth century it began to generate friction between some landlords and tenants. By that time the number of tenants on the estates was increasing rapidly, chiefly as a result of subdivision within families, for, as an agent wrote in 1784, 'they seldom make any other provision for son or daughter than the land.' (24) In bad years more and more tenants got into difficulties and it was a problem for the landlord to decide how much rent he should allow a tenant to owe. The law permitted the landlord under the terms of the lease to distrain or seize crops or livestock from the tenant equivalent in value to the rent he owed and then after a fixed period, if the money was not paid, to sell them towards payment of the debt. A good landlord would wish to employ this legal weapon sparingly but on some estates it did become the practice for tenants not to pay the rents until the bailiffs appeared. (25) When a tenant was found to be hopelessly in debt the practice was to convince him that he should sell his interest in the farm. Until he agreed to sell no one else would bid for the farm and so it was necessary for the landlord to put pressure on him. He could send the tenant to gaol until the rent was paid, but this might not compel surrender of the lease, and as long as the tenant refused, the landlord could not do anything with the farm. The last resort was eject-ment which was both cumbersome and expensive: sometimes months elapsed before the landlord could regain possession and the tenant had yet a further six months to redeem the property by paying the debt with costs. (26) Even then the landlord's problem was not solved because unless he could find a new tenant he would have to work the farm at his own expense. (27)

It might be argued that such initiatives by landlords were bound to provoke retaliation from tenants. In general, however, these powers were used sparingly and in the last resort. It is significant that throughout the century there was not widespread con-frontation between landlords and tenants. Ulster society was relatively stable and integrated until the mid-1780s. Its backbone was the very large number of lease-holders who had a stake in the community and security to make a living. For them rents were not exorbitant. Prices for grain and livestock were improving in a period of gentle inflation. The linen industry was continuing to expand geographically into neighbouring counties and socially by putting out yarn for weaving to the cottier class. Many landlords and agents not only dealt sympathetically with the tenants on their estates but also helped to settle disputes between tenants. Emigration to America provided escape for the ambitious, the impatient and the discontented. Although there were no police of any kind to keep order, the army was rarely needed to keep the peace. The Volunteers who performed the peace-keeping functions of the army during the American War of Independence were never extended: the fact that they were 'the armed property of the nation' had been a stabilising influence during a difficult period. (28)

It has been asserted that the Oakboys in the early 1760s, the Steelboys in the early 1770s, the Orange-Defender disturbances and the United Irish risings in 1798 were all symptoms of bad relations between landlords and tenants. (29) The attribution of these troubles to bad landlord-tenant relations alone would require a major distortion of the evidence. The Oakboys protested mainly against the enforcement of the ancient obligation to provide six days' work annually on the roads. In a period of economic development the burden of providing unpaid labour on the roads became too onerous for the small farmers, especially after an act of 1759 had exempted day labourers. In 1765 the demands of the Oakboys were met by the abolition of the six days' labour and the adoption of a uniform county rate or 'cess' of a few pence per acre to hire labourers for the construction and repair of main roads. (30) The Steelboy disturbances were sparked off by the re-leasing of the Earl of Donegall's estates about Belfast. The setting of all of such a vast estate at one time caused much excitement which was itself a potential source of troublesome incidents, and the situation was made worse by the decision of the Earl to set a few of his many townlands to wealthy Belfast merchants for the sake of obtaining lump sums by granting reduced rents. The excitement was intensified when tenants of the neighbouring Upton estate invaded Belfast and secured the release from prison of one of their members. (31) Elsewhere, in county Armagh, the grand jury decided to employ military aid to enforce the payment of cess in one barony after no one had dared to collect it for more than five years. This provoked some of the more lawless elements, who broadened their appeal by condemning high rents and tithes and the landlord's control over turbary rights. Nevertheless, after some skirmishes the agitation suddenly fizzled out. (32) Just over twelve years later, in 1785, trouble broke out again in Armagh where the Orange-Defender disturbances should be traced to the development of an emancipation movement among the Catholics that upset society in south Ulster. In the late 1780s the more responsible landlords were successful in damping down the unrest but repercussions from the French wars made it more serious and encouraged some of the minor gentry to assume an active role in Orange societies. (33) The United Irish movement in Ulster had its origins in urban radical politics in Belfast and when it did try to proselytize the countryside it continued to concentrate its main attack on the Church of Ireland establishment. It took care, however, not to attack property rights, mainly because the moving spirits were urban professional men more interested in sharing power with the landlords, and substantial farmers who were not prepared to extent to their subtenants the privileges conceded to them by their landlords. (34)

III

Much of the antipathy of the United Irishmen had been directed against some '750 squires nominated by an officer of the Crown' sitting on the several grand juries throughout the country. (35) The grand jury was the stronghold of the landlord interest in each county. It also reflected the pecking order of the local landlords. (36) The most influential families represented the county in Parliament in Dublin or effectively decided the nomination. Below them ranked the gentry according to their influence, their rentrolls, their abilities, and their characters. Their standards were those of Dublin society, for Dublin was capable both of translating London ideas and generating its own. The grand jury helped to disseminate these fashions at the county level. As one English judge on tour in the mid 1760s remarked: 'The spirit of improvement is gone forth and I can perceive by dining with the grand juries that a man makes a figure in his country in proportion to the improvements that he makes. You hear him complimented on his having encouraged any branch of manufacture, or draining and reclaiming so much bog or mountain, sowing so much flax, tilling so many acres of wheat, planting so many trees, etc ...' He added: 'Gentlemen of large estates are almost the only people who can afford or who think it worth their while to improve the land, and as all gentlemen in the country have large and extensive demesnes in their own hands their improvements are frequently confined to their own demesne, so that although it beautifies a country it does not extend to a general improvement of it'. (37)Although this comment is an accurate assessment it does not really take account of the attempts of landlords to develop and exploit the natural resources of their estates. The seventeenth century had seen most of the major stocks of timber exploited and little provision made for the future. (38) Since the early days of the Plantation, searches had been made in Ulster for minerals. The patents of the Ulster landlords had secured for them the right to exploit whatever minerals might be found beneath their properties and they were well aware of their value. Commentators were alert to phenomena that might indicate their presence, whether they were traces found in springs or streams or even the mal-functionings of a compass. Local supplies of iron had fed the forges in the Lagan Valley and south-east Londonderry since early in the seventeenth century. Many attempts were made to find coal. Richard Dobbs in his 'Brief description of the county of Antrim' of 1683 claimed that he had bored and sunk for coal on his own property at a cost of forty or fifty pounds and mentioned that other trials had been made in the neighbourhood of Carrickfergus. (39) About 1694 coal was discovered near Dunganon in south-east Tyrone on the lands of the Archbishop of Armagh and by 1703 a project was afoot to construct a canal so that the coal could be delivered by water to Dublin. (40) Dublin's complaints against the monopoly enjoyed by the English and Scottish coalowners in supplying the city compelled the Irish government to promote the mining of coal in Ireland. Its grants subsidised another significant coal-mining venture with the opening of new mines at Ballycastle in north Antrim and their development by a minor landowner, Hugh Boyd, who secured a lease of the property from the Earl of Antrim. (41) The relative although minor success of these mines has obscured the attempts of other landlords such as Stewart of Ballintoy, the Earl of Abercorn in the Foyle Valley, and the Earl Bishop of Derry at Magilligan, to locate and develop seams on their own property. (42) The Registry of Deeds in Dublin contains memorials of leases to work mines for coal or for other minerals. (43) Most of these ventures ended in failure while the success of the others was too slight to inspire confidence, but attempts continued into the nineteenth century. To many landlords in eighteenth-century Ulster it seemed that the natural resource most in need of development and exploitation was not minerals but property. Therefore they concentrated on developing their towns and the infrastructure of their estates. The heart of every estate was its town where the landlord could provide a market house with all necessary facilities and promote it by giving premiums to those who would come to buy and sell in it; he could encourage people to settle by granting them building leases (if he were shrewd he himself would not build the houses); and he could enrich the community by endowing and supporting churches, schools, the poorhouse and infirmaries. Around the middle of the century a great surge of activity following the construction of the Newry canal (which opened up the Lough Neagh basin direct to the sea) led to the expansion of several villages and the creation of others throughout the southern part of Ulster — such as Clones in Monaghan; Aughnacloy, Cookstown and Moy in Tyrone; Keady and Newtownhamilton in Armagh; and Saintfield, Rathfriland and Castlewellan in Down. (44) Linked with this urban renaissance was a great improvement in communications. Landlords used their influence in the grand juries to promote the construction of roads and bridges, while some of them served on turnpike trusts and others had themselves elected 'overseers of the highways' in the parish vestries so that they could direct work on the roads. (45) That the enthusiasm of the landlords for road construction did sometimes exceed that of their tenants was demonstrated in the Oakboy disturbances of the early 1760s: some individual landlords were waylaid and compelled by the mob to swear that they would never again 'be aiding or assisting in laying on any tax or cess for building useless bridges and making highways (the King's highways excepted) ...' (46) There was no such opposition to the construction of the first canal, the Newry Navigation completed in 1742, because the Dublin government financed it. (47) Later in the century the Earl of Donegall provided the initial impetus for the construction of the Lagan navigation while the Earl of Abercorn sponsored the Strabane canal. (48) A further impressive achievement was the construction of Derry Bridge in 1791 as the result of a campaign conducted by the Earl Bishop of Derry since 1768. (49)

The quality of social leadership that the landlords provided was in itself a response to pressures within society. The landlords did not supply the dynamics of the Ulster economy: that role belonged to the linendrapers and the merchants. Although the spiritual home of the landlords and the fount of social and political advancement was in Dublin, no landlord who valued the political influence of his family could afford to neglect his county constituency. He had to measure the effect of his actions on the freeholders. In the preliminaries to the 1768 election William Stewart, the sitting member for County Tyrone, confided to the Earl of Abercorn that he had had to withdraw his nomination in favour of his own son because he himself was considered to have given offence to the lower class of freeholders by his application to the government in 1763 to send the army to put a stop to the Oakboy disturba even though the sheriff and the grand jury had voted him their thanks for his action. (50) An even more significant incident was the success of the Presbyterians in 1776 in securing the repeal of an act passed two years earlier to prevent Dissenters from voting in parish vestries: their threat to run independent candidates induced Thomas Conolly, a very powerful figure in the Commons and the member for County Londonderry, to introduce the repeal bill. (51) The Presbyterian influence in the Commons had been strengthened by the passage of the Octennial Act in 1768 to limit the life of parliaments: support to secure full civil rights for Dissenters had been organised through their congregations. (52) In 1778 the Volunteer movement sprang up to defend the country against possible French invasion and it soon developed, both politically and socially, democratic tendencies which the landlords sought to counteract from within. They succeeded only after the radical element failed to coerce the Dublin government in 1783. In the late 1790s they had the support of the army in suppressing the more extreme Presbyterian element which comprised the United Irish movement in Ulster, but they failed to subdue the sectarian strife that had broken out among the lower orders in County Armagh. (53)

This sectarian strife reflected the antipathy of Protestants, both Episcopalian and Presbyterian, to the growing confidence of the Catholics (soon to be demonstrated in the Catholic emancipation movement). Orangeism soon secured leaders among the minor gentry and permeated Ulster in the aftermath of the '98 rebellion. It has been observed that 'a major factor in the loyalty to it of the uninfluential is that its meetings have an explicitly egalitarian ethos that makes it easier for them to talk bluntly to their leaders'. (54) That trait can be traced to the eighteenth-century origins of the societies when the colonial atmosphere, the structure of landholding, and the prosperity of the domestic linen industry, combined to strengthen the strong democratic traditions that had been imported from Scotland.

NOTES

1. I am grateful to Mr David Dickson, Dr Anthony Malcomson, and Mr Sean McMenamin for their comments on this paper. My thanks are also due to His Grace the Duke of Abercorn for permitting me to quote so extensively from his family papers.

2. The most useful books on the Plantation are G. Hill, *The Plantation of Ulster* (Belfast, 1877); T.W. Moody, *The Londonderry Plantation, 1609-41* (Belfast, 1939); and M. Perceval-Maxwell, *The Scottish Migration to Ulster in the Reign of James I* (London, 1973).

3. R. Lawrence, *The Interest of Ireland in its Trade and Wealth Stated* (Dublin, 1682), p.7; Public Record Office of Northern Ireland (hereafter P.R.O.N.I.) Waring Papers, D.695/10B, Draft of letter from William Waring [Waringstown, County Down] to Mr Layfield, Spring 1675.

4. Many Ulster landed families could trace their descent to the original grantees. Among those descended from soldiers were the families of Caulfield, Creighton, Clotworthy, Clements, Chichester, Brooke, Blacker, Audley, and Magill. Among those descended from churchmen were Colvill, Echlin, Conyngham, Montgomery of Fivemiletown, Leslie of Glaslough, and Young of Culdaff. The families descended from merchants were Knox (later Lords Ranfurly), Corry (later Lords Belmore), and Cairnes (later Lord Rossmore). Among the families descended from legal men were Conolly, Madden, Ward, and Forde.

o

5. W.H. Crawford, 'Landlord-Tenant Relations in Ulster 1609-1820', *Irish Economic and Social History*, II(1975), 10.

6. For a fuller discussion see L.M. Cullen, 'Population Trends in Seventeenth Century Ireland', *The Economic and Social Review*, VI(1975), 152-4.

7. L.M. Cullen, *An Economic History of Ireland since 1660* (London, 1972), pp.10-17; Donald Woodward, 'The Anglo-Irish Livestock Trade in the Seventeenth Century', *Irish Historical Studies*, XVIII(1973), 501 and 504.

8. Cullen, 'Population Trends', 157; W. Macafee, 'The Colonisation of the Maghera Area in South Derry during the Seventeenth and Eighteenth Centuries', *Ulster Folklife* (forthcoming).

9. R.J. Dickson, *Ulster Emigration to Colonial America, 1718-1775* (London, 1966), ch.2.

10. Crawford, 'Landlord-Tenant Relations', 8-9.

11. N.B. Harte, 'The Rise of Protection and the English Linen Trade, 1690-1780' in N.B. Harte and K.G. Ponting, eds. *Textile History and Economic History* (Manchester, 1974), pp.94-6.

12. H.D. Gribbon, *The History of Water Power in Ulster* (Newton Abbot, 1969), pp.81-5; C. Gill, *The Rise of the Irish Linen Industry* (Oxford, 1925), p.341; W.H. Crawford, 'The Market Book of Thomas Greer, A Dungannon Linendraper, 1758-9', *Ulster Folklife*, XIII(1967), 54-60.

13. W.H. Crawford and B. Trainor, eds. *Aspects of Irish Social History 1750-1800* (Belfast, 1969), p.92; P.R.O.N.I. 'Hints towards a natural and topographical history of the Counties of Sligo, Donegal, Fermanagh and Lough Erne by Rev. Wm Henry ... 1739', Mic.198.

14. I am indebted to Mr David Dickson for providing me with these figures collected for his paper 'Irish Population in the Eighteenth Century: Some Reconsiderations', read to Irish Historical Society on 13 Nov. 1973: an abstract of the paper appears in *Bulletin of the Irish Committee of Historical Sciences*, 3rd Series, No.1 (1974).

15. C. Coote, *Statistical Survey of the County of Cavan* (Dublin, 1802), pp.41-2; C. Coote, *Statistical Survey of the County of Monaghan* (Dublin, 1801), pp.43-4.

16. J. Hall, *A Tour Through Ireland* (London, 1813), p.118.

17. W. Greig, *General Report on the Gosford Estates in County Armagh, 1821* (Belfast, 1976), pp.146-62.

18. P.R.O.N.I. Willes MSS, T.2368; D.A. Beaufort, *Memoir of a Map of Ireland* (Dublin, 1792), pp.18, 20, 23, 25, 27, 34, 38.

19. Letter from Henry Cavendish to Robert Stephenson, 12 August 1784, quoted in Stephenson, *Observations on the Present State of the Linen Trade of Ireland* (Dublin, 1784).

20. Greig, *General Report,* pp.166-70.

21. P.R.O.N.I. Barrett-Lennard Papers, T.2529/6/200, Brabazon Noble to [the Right Hon. Lord Dacre], 24 April 1760.

22. P.R.O.N.I. Abercorn Letters, T.2541/IA1/1/10, Jo Colhoun, Corncamon, to Lord [Paisley], 21 August 1736; T.2541/IA1/6A/26, J. Sinclair, Holyhill, to Richard Nelson, Dublin, 26 February 1760; T.2541/IA1/8/36, James Hamilton, Strabane, to [Earl of Abercorn], 13 March 1768; Greig, *General Report*, p.145.

23. P.R.O.N.I. Tennent Papers, D.1748/28, John Tennent's journal, entry for 8 April 1790; Abercorn Letters, T.2541/IA1/19/26, Rev. Thomas Pemberton, Taughboyne, to Marquess of Abercorn, London, 22 March 1793.

24. Abercorn Letters, T.2541/IA1/14/35, James Hamilton, Strabane, to [Earl of Abercorn], 9 July 1784.

25. Crawford and Trainor, *Aspects*, p.24.

26. Abercorn Letters, T.2541/IK/8/2/105, [James, Earl of Abercorn], London, to James Hamilton, [Strabane], 2 November 1769; T.2541/IA1/13/1/8, James Hamilton to Earl of Abercorn, 25 January 1780.

27. Abercorn Letters, T.2541/IA1/13/1/6, James Hamilton, Strabane, to [Earl of Abercorn], 21 January 1780.

28. Abercorn Letters, T.2541/IA1/13/1/29, James Hamilton, Strabane, to [Earl of Abercorn], 5 May 1780; T.2541/IA1/18/7, James Hamilton, Strabane, to Marquess of Abercorn, London, 1 February 1791.

29. M. Wall, 'The Whiteboys' in T.D. Williams, ed. *Secret Societies in Ireland* (Dublin, 1973), p.25.

30. W.H. Crawford, 'Economy and Society in South Ulster in the Eighteenth Century', *Clogher Record* (1975), pp.251-2.

31. Crawford and Trainor, *Aspects,* pp.37, 42-3.

32. *Ibid.,* p.38.

33. *Ibid.,* pp.171-4; H. Senior, 'The Early Orange Order 1795-1870' in T.D. Williams, ed. *Secret Societies in Ireland,* pp.36-41.

34. W.H. Crawford, 'Change in Ulster in the Late Eighteenth Century' (forth-coming).

35. Crawford and Trainor, *Aspects,* p.181.

36. *Ibid.,* pp.122-4.

37. *Ibid.,* p.2.

38. E. McCracken, *The Irish Woods Since Tudor Times* (Newton Abbot, 1971), chs.1 and 2.

39. G. Hill, *The Macdonnells of Antrim* (Belfast, 1873), pp.378-9, 388.

40. W.A. McCutcheon, *The Canals of the North of Ireland* (Dawlish, 1965), p.17.

41. J.E. Mullin, *The Causeway Coast* (Belfast, 1974), pp.161-76.

42. *Ibid.,* pp.151-2; Abercorn Letters, T.2541/IA1/5/23, Nathaniel Nisbitt, Lifford, to [Earl of Abercorn], 20 April 1758; T.2541/IA1/8/113, James Hamilton, Strabane, to [Earl of Abercorn], 27 January 1769.

43. Registry of Deeds, Dublin, Book 22, Page 454, Number 12560, Earl of Donegall to T. Caulfield and A. Jones, 22 January 1718/9; Book 186, Page 481, Number 125545, Sir Archibald Acheson to several, 1756.

44. S. Lewis, *A Topographical Dictionary of Ireland* (2 vols, Dublin, 1837), I, 313; II, 34, 438; [W. Harris], *The Ancient and Present State of the County of Down* (Dublin, 1744), pp.83, 95, 100; G. Camblin, *The Town in Ulster* (Belfast, 1951), pp.78, 81; Crawford and Trainor, *Aspects,* pp.92-3; Royal Irish Academy, Charlemont MSS, I, letter 26, Thomas Adderley to Charlemont, 28 January 1755; Barrett-Lennard Papers, T.2529/6/236, Thomas Noble to Lord Dacre, 5 January 1771.

45. J.T. Fulton, 'The Roads of County Down, 1600-1900: The Evolution of the Road System of an Irish County', Queen's University Belfast Ph.D. dissertation, (1972), chs 2-4; Abercorn Letters, T.2541/IA1/18/9, James Hamilton, Strabane, to Earl of Abercorn, 11 February 1791.

46. Crawford and Trainor, *Aspects,* p.36.

47. McCutcheon, *Canals,* p.18.

48. *Ibid.,* pp.42-55; Abercorn Letters, T.2541/IA1/3/118, Nathaniel Nisbitt to Earl of Abercorn, London, 15 December 1755; T.2541/IA1/8/105, John Hamilton, Strabane, to [Earl of Abercorn], 27 November 1768.

49. Abercorn Letters, T.2541/IA1/8/88, Frederick, Bishop of Derry to [Earl of Abercorn], 11 September 1768.

50. Abercorn Letters, T.2541/IA1/8/27, William Stewart to [Earl of Abercorn], 25 February 1768.

51. Crawford and Trainor, *Aspects,* pp.164-5.

52. P.R.O.N.I. Downshire Letters, D.607/159, Robert Ross, Rostrevor, to Earl of Hillsborough, 7 September 1778.

53. Crawford, 'Change in Ulster in the Late Eighteenth Century'.

54. R. Harris, *Prejudice and Tolerance in Ulster* (Manchester, 1972), p.xiii.

15. The Scottish Improvers and the Course of Agrarian Change in the Eighteenth Century

R. H. Campbell

THE exceptional famine conditions at the end of the seventeenth century highlighted the precarious nature of Scottish agricultural sufficiency. Dearth returned from time to time in the eighteenth century, but in general the age-old spectre of widespread famine was removed. The contribution of the improvers to the transformation has been recognised by many writers, who have provided detailed studies of the work of a few leading proprietors, studies of individual initiative as much as of a movement. (1) The case for that emphasis is strong. Landowners dominated the social structure of Scotland in the eighteenth century. Political power, national and local, was in their hands, and the national power was increased through legal peculiarities, whereby the large landowners were able to create a string of dependent voters. Thereby the political life of Scotland could be so managed that great magnates continued to occupy a leading role in Scottish society even when their power and influence was declining elsewhere. (2) The political power of the landed interest remained throughout the century, even though its exercise fell into different hands: sometimes by powers being delegated, when the greater landowners were so absorbed in the political life of London that they had to leave much responsibility and initiative to their agents in Scotland, (3) or, later, especially after the death of the 3rd Duke of Argyll in 1761, when the power of political management passed into other, socially inferior, hands.

In such a society those who aspired to positions of influence, whatever their origins, did so through landownership. The two chief sources of recruits were the successful lawyers, especially around Edinburgh, and the successful merchants, especially around Glasgow. The move was never complete. The law or merchanting remained their prime activity. (4) Landownership was the path to a position of social prestige, but not, as was perhaps the case elsewhere, or even in Scotland in the nineteenth century, the path to another way of life altogether. Since there was no need to discard the old on entry to the new, landownership was likely to be infused with ideas brought from elsewhere. (5)

The landowners also enjoyed an impregnable legal position. Apart from the Highlands, where the old military tenure of ward-holding persisted until 1747, tenurial rights were clearly defined. Enclosure in Scotland was therefore an operation which could not be arrested, provided the desire to act was there. Opposition was possible if land was held in runrig, or where proprietors were unwilling to share the costs of enclosure. Legislation of the seventeenth century provided remedies: acts of 1661, 1669 and 1685 provided for the sharing of expenditure on the enclosure of land,

and an act of 1695 provided for the coercion of recalcitrant owners of land lying
in runrig. One other important legal change came later: an act of 1770, applicable
to the third of the land of Scotland which was estimated to be entailed, authorised
longer leases, if tenants agreed to certain improvements, and allowed proprietors to
charge to their heirs three-quarters of the costs of enclosure and other agricultural
improvements.

Opposition by such powerful landowners would have inhibited agrarian change,
but mere absence of opposition was inadequate. The landowners, with apparently
little need to countenance agrarian change to maintain their position in society, had
to become its positive agents of change. Explanations of such positive initiative
centre on the non-economic, and uniquely Scottish, effects of the Union of Parliaments in 1707, and of the intellectual life of Scotland in the following century.

It may be suggested that the removal of government to London, and the rapid
subsequent demise of even the vestiges of a separate Scottish administration, deprived the Scottish landowners, with all their political potential, of any active means
of exercising it. In brief, there was little left for them to do, hence they turned to
agricultural pursuits and followed English examples. (6) Even such a simple explanation of a complex psychological reaction may not be easily sustained. To some the
Union gave opportunities. The greater magnates, who had savoured an enticing
exercise of power free from the worst curbs of royal authority after 1688, found
prospects for further action in the wider, political sphere of Westminster attractive.
They countenanced agrarian change, but through agents, and for that indirect source
of initiative towards agrarian change, some further explanation is required. Though
the Westminster stage was not open equally to the lesser landowners, possibilities
of political, or at least of official, action remained, particularly for the exceptionally
able and exceptionally unscrupulous, who exploited new-found opportunities which
enabled them to exercise authority and influence. Significantly, the management
of Scotland, in the hands of the House of Argyll in the early part of the century,
was in the hands of Henry Dundas at the end. Government intervention in a number
of fields, especially the economic, increased openings for placemen, or for substitute
political action in a variety of official and semi-official bodies. The opportunities to
exploit the openings were greatest for the lawyers, but they were not alone. The
names of merchants also begin to appear on the rolls of membership of official
bodies. Hence, the vacuum left by the Union is less evident than may be assumed,
and the possible contribution of the intellectual life of the eighteenth century to
the landowners' positive desire to improve agriculture is correspondingly increased.

Whatever explanations may be offered of the intellectual achievements of
Scotland in the eighteenth century, two — each with some validity — may be offered
of its influence on Scottish landowners.

The first suggests that intellectual thought in Scotland surrendered its obsession
with matters ecclesiastical and theological and so released effort and energy for new
activities, a view which does not provide an explanation of positive action. The
second interpretation, needed to supplement, and possibly to dispense with the
first, is that, whatever the cause of the intellectual changes of the eighteenth century,
their nature was conducive to the solution of secular, including agricultural, problems.
The view of man's relation to his environment changed, from one where the link was

considered chiefly theological, and where the individual had little control over his environment, to one where the link was secular, and so could be understood and controlled. The attempt to cast all knowledge into systematic form was as applicable to agriculture as to any sphere of human endeavour. (7)

The social structure of Scotland not only required that the landlords accept the new approach to agricultural methods; it ensured that they did so. Society was closely knit with no gulf between the intellectuals and landowners, especially as the ranks of the landowners were infiltrated by merchants and lawyers. Similarly, since the magnates handed much of their power to their agents, the links with the ideas of the Enlightenment became direct. The power of the magnates was wielded by those who were part of the Enlightenment themselves.

If the acceptance of an intellectual analysis of the physical and social world which no longer regarded the hazards of agricultural operations as divinely ordained was a pre-requisite in the successful onslaught on the hazards of agricultural change, then it becomes possible to hold that the motivation for change was not economic necessity but patriotism, fashion, social control, (8) factors which operated in a social environment which was uniquely Scottish, and which render Scottish experience less comparable with events elsewhere. But it is doubtful if Scottish experience was so unique, because at the deepest level economic factors were probably still the most important agents in change. That would be so if the fundamental motivation lay in the demand for higher rents, and there is evidence that it was so. The move of the greater magnates to London increased their economic needs, and ensured that they became active promoters of agrarian change. Montrose made an apt complaint to Sunderland in 1708 that 'London jornys dont verie well agree with Scots estaits', (9) and Annandale was alleged to be the only Scottish peer who could keep himself in London without a subsidy. If some unfortunate person of quality, and of old family, had no resources, his position was indeed desperate, as with the poor Earl of Home, who had to borrow for his journey to London in 1711, though 'it was with the greatest difficulty imaginable that he could get credit for one hundred pounds or two'. (10) The need to transmit rents was a common topic of complaint by commentators throughout the century, from Patrick Lindsay in the 1730s to John Knox fifty years later. (11)

Lavish living and political objectives required additional resources or led to increased debt. The need for increased rent, even in the case of the House of Argyll, is emphasised by Mr. Cregeen: 'The [5th] Duke's interest in improvement was to a great extent controlled by the need for revenue ... [He] had the experience of his predecessors to guide, and, at times, to warn him. They had long led the field both in the magnificence of their expenditure and in the development of the resources of their estate, most notably, of course, the 3rd Duke's development of Inverary, activities which in some years absorbed almost the whole of the property rents of the Argyll lands'. (12) Examples can be increased to provide support for the view that the demand of an absentee landlord for the fruits of his land may have been the most powerful force making for agrarian change and, though the influence of Scotland's institutional and intellectual position in the eighteenth century may have been unique, the demand for higher rents was certainly shared by other societies. Even the ideals of the Enlightenment needed higher rents for their expression, and an interesting combination of incentives is expressed in a letter from an adviser to the Earl of Stair in 1778: '... as for improvements considering the rise of waiges, horse, in short every thing needed, is byyond Measoure, but when land is improven is equally high, besydes theres imense pleasoure in embeleshing the country employing the laborer by much more solid pleasour than in vain show, etc. which at present prevail byyond measoure'. (13)

The private needs and the desires of the landowners for agrarian change were evident early in the eighteenth century. By the later part of the century the social need for agrarian change became increasingly pressing, as agricultural productivity was supporting economic progress on a wider front. The early phases of economic growth often ended in liquidity crises, as reserves fell and the rate of exchange on London worsened. A major factor straining liquidity was the need to import grain, both in the long-run as a growing population became less self-sufficient, and in the short-run as poor harvests precipitated a sudden need to import. From the 1760s the long-term trend, evident since the Union at least, of net exporting switched to net importing. Equally significant, increased imports accompanied periods of financial stringency and crisis and increased exports, or decreased imports, accompanied increased economic activity. Even when agrarian change removed brakes on expansion in the aggregate, a similar problem remained for some regions. (14)

The need for change was there; and the forces making for change were operative, but agrarian change was uneven by the last decade of the century. Its nature is evident in the pages of the *Old Statistical Account.* A survey of parochial accounts of the Lowlands leaves no doubt of the existence of improvements, and these favourable comments have greatly coloured the writings of many historians. The improvements noted were orthodox; rotations were common, though their exact form varied; turnip husbandry had been introduced; trees had been planted. The qualifications are more interesting, especially in parishes which possessed those characteristics which the writers themselves considered appropriate stimuli to improvement. Markets were critical, though indirect access, by coastwise shipping, was adequate. (15) At Duddingston 'the greatest medium of improvement is the manure of Edinburgh'. (16) Given the desirability of being adjacent to a centre of population, parishes near Glasgow and Edinburgh should have provided evidence of change. They do, (17) but with qualifications. Old practices were perpetuated, usually in parishes less well-endowed naturally, and with less easy access to larger centres of population. (18) Change was recent, within a generation or so before the accounts were written in the 1790s. (19) Examples of desirable improvement are cited, (20) particularly enclosure, its application limited by the difficulty of obtaining adequate supplies of necessary materials. (21)

The ministers wrote as agrarian change was increasing rapidly. The sixth edition of Kames' *The Gentleman Farmer* (1815) commented pertinently: 'there never were greater agricultural improvements carried on in any country than there have been in Scotland during the last thirty years'. (22) The motives and knowledge of much of the eighteenth century were inadequate to ensure change rapidly. Impediments were too great and counterbalanced the powerful forces making for improvements. Two stand out: the conservatism of the tenants and the cost of agrarian change. The former has been readily recognised by many writers. One quotation,

as early as 1732, stands for all: 'Husbandry, till of late, was intirely managed in
Scotland by the Vulgar, who, like Moles, blindly ran on in the Tract their Fathers
had made before them'. (23) Even though the Duke of Argyll embodied all the
favourable forces making for change, his estates provided an example of the problem.
In 1737 Duncan Forbes visited the old Duart lands in Mull, Morvern, Coll and
Tiree to eliminate the tacksmen and lease lands directly to the subtenants. (24)
The opposition was virtually complete. Eventually Forbes leased the lands directly,
but victory was hollow. The increase in rents proved illusory as arrears accumulated.
Consideration was given to the possibility of restoring the tacksmen, and sub-letting
was permitted. (25) Perhaps most interesting of all, while initially no special preference was given to Campbells, the '45 led to the modification of policies to ensure
political loyalty. (26) If Argyll modified his plans, even reviving sub-letting to avoid
emigration, (27) it is not surprising that others did likewise. (28) The motives behind
the landlords' attitudes towards tenants were various: feelings of kinship, humanitarian
concern, a residual belief that greatness, personal or national, was ensured by retaining large numbers on the land — these were mixed with new economic motives. Modification of plans for improvement was often accepted because of a lingering acceptance of the old social structure by landlords, especially when the dispersal of tenants
was at stake. It is not wholly misleading to hold that when the question of emigration
arose 'everyone wrote against it'. (29) Not quite everyone, for the desire to keep
people on the land was not necessarily interpreted as a policy which was socially
desirable, but as an example of feudal victimisation, a possible cause for radical
critics, as when Burns denounced Breadalbane's attempt to prevent emigration. (30)
But it was considered chiefly a means of perpetuating a social structure which the
improvements were tending to destroy. Some landlords were as reluctant as their
tenants to see that order disappear.

The cost of improvements was also recognised widely as the other major impedi-
ment in the path of an improver. Not all improvements were expensive; even more
so, not all had to be implemented on a large scale, but frequently the more expensive
were also socially the more disruptive, and so were doubly unattractive, even when
they held the greatest promise of increased productivity. The financial difficulties
of extensive improvement are obvious in the emphasis in the *Agricultural Reports*
of the 1790s on the continued need for action over enclosure, the abolition of runrig, and drainage. In Midlothian enclosure had 'been but lately introduced'. (31)
Drainage, technically less easily and satisfactorily achieved, had made even less
progress. In Banff, scene of the work of the Earl of Findlater, 'the drainage of the
land seems to be a mode of improvement very little known or practiced here'. (32)
In Fife 'the drainage of the land ... is ill understood and often improperly executed'. (33)
Since enclosure and drainage were costly operations the responsibility for action fell
heavily on the proprietors. The adequacy and generosity of their help may be
questioned. In an area where it was remarked that there was 'much Dycking going
on', the allowances paid to tenants of hill farms in the 1780s were small. (34) When
capital was provided, some at least thought the rate of interest charged was excessive. (35) The landlords were not without excuse. Their desire for higher rents indicated
that their capital resources were often strained, so they borrowed, from unorthodox (36)
as well as orthodox sources. The banks helped, particularly in financing cattle droving, (3

and from the 1760s when landed estate was an acceptable form of security. (38) But
from the evidence of the banks and of the estates, it seems that the help was often
intermittent, varied and sometimes quite small. One illustration of the need to borrow
and of the attractions of a ready supply of funds, whatever its source, is in the unfortunate experience of the Ayr Bank. In his *Report* on Ayrshire, Fullarton remarked
that '... no tenant could command money to stock his farm, and few landholders
could raise the means of improving their estates. Indeed, when a laird wished to raise
money, he was obliged to sell his property, perhaps for 20 years purchase, or accept
of loans on wadset'. (39) Hence the Ayr Bank and its policies were attractive to the
landowners of the south-west. Its legacy was a mixed blessing. George Robertson,
who had factored in the county, dated enclosure in Ayrshire from the Bank's foundation in 1769 and explained: 'Most of the great landed proprietors were connected
with it, and all had a very ready accomodation from it; and though it turned out to
be a curious concern to the copartnery, it was, nevertheless, the means of improving
the county'. (40)

The two impediments of social opposition from the tenantry and the need for
capital expenditure limited improvement to areas where landowners exerted complete
social control and where relatively little capital expenditure was required. In effect
action was limited to the policies and to the home farm, and no further. At Monymusk 'it was there that Grant carried out his experiments in the new ways of farming', (41) and yet even as late as 1774 'the estate of Monymusk was a picture of
violent contrasts'. (42) In Banff, 'notwithstanding Lord Findlater's unwearied exert-
ions, it was many years before fallow and sowing grass seeds, turnip, and other green
crops, came into general use, even in that corner of his estate where he himself
resided.' (43) Smith's cynical comment on the large proprietor was not inaccurate:
'He embellishes perhaps four to five hundred acres in the neighbourhood of his house,
at ten times the expence which the land is worth after all his improvements; and finds
that if he was to improve his whole estate in the same manner ... he would be a bankrupt before he had finished the tenth part of it'. (44)

Stress on the impediments provides a possible explanation of why the powerful
motivation of the Scottish improvers failed to achieve widespread agrarian change
quickly. But the improvers may not have been so well endowed with the qualities
requisite for agrarian change as is usually assumed. In particular the criticism of the
recalcitrant tenantry by the landowners, and by later writers, (45) may need qualification. James Anderson defended tenants directly in his *Report* on Aberdeenshire
in 1794: '... however slow the progress of improvements may be among the tenantry
in Aberdeenshire, it is not to be attributed to the ignorance or obstinacy of the
people, nor to the bigotted prejudices in favour of old customs; but that it must be
ascribed to the operation of other causes ... I know of no bigotry so great as that of
those, who ... still ... exclaim against the obstinacy of country people, and their
attachment to old customs'. (46) The desire for higher rents, and some of the reasons
behind it, show that the landowners themselves were not wholly enlightened.

Two critical appraisals of their contributions are in the abstract reasoning of
Adam Smith and in the more practical views of farmers and factors, such as George
Robertson. Smith considered that landowners, especially the larger among them,
had the potential for improvement. They had greater capital than the tenant and so

could afford to run the risks of experiment. (47) But they suffered great defects. Specific legacies of feudalism were harmful; primogeniture, (48) entails, (49) modes of conveyancing, all retarded agriculture. (50) Even their removal would not eliminate all the defects of the large proprietor, since he attended more 'to ornament which pleases his fancy, than to profit'. (51) Hence 'it seldom happens ... that a great proprietor is a great improver'. (52) Smith's judgement, based on philosophical principles, may seem extreme. The more practical view of George Robertson, advanced as late as 1829, held that 'the great mass of improvements arising from a better mode of tillage, and system of rotation in cropping, has been owing almost entirely to the farmers themselves, with very little example set them by the proprietors'. The reason was that agriculture required more 'attention, and so much laborious industry, that few men who are in the independent circumstances of an opulent landholder can bring themselves to dedicate to it their whole talents and time'. (53) Robertson limited his definition of an 'agricultural improver'. Many given the title did not engage in his narrowly defined practical agricultural activities. They concentrated on the administrative reorganisation of their estates, and on their policies and home farm. Whether the landowner was one of the great, as Argyll, or of lesser importance, as Monymusk, the same stream of instructions flowed out explaining what was required, the instructions being directed at some intermediary factor. Such a stream of orders can be accepted too readily as warrant for admission to the ranks of the improvers, but it should be accepted only as an endorsement of Professor Habakkuk's much narrower view that 'supervision of estate management rather than the promotion of agricultural improvement was their characteristic contribution'. (54)

Even in the field of administration, the action of the landowners was not without criticism. Again Smith provides the general, and rather cynical, analysis: 'If the landlords should ... be tempted to farm the whole of their own lands, the country ... would be filled with idle and profligate bailiffs, whose abusive management would soon degrade the cultivation, and reduce the annual produce of the land'. (55) A specific example of the possible harmful influence of the new administration lay in the granting of leases. Long leases were of ancient origin in Scotland, (56) but their beneficial effects were offset by other legislation and practice. The nub of Smith's criticism was that many feudal provisions had to be removed before further action was possible. The improving landlords are frequently commended for going further and for imposing leases which positively encouraged improvement. The practice was unexceptional in general, but the detail was sometimes extreme, and not necessarily appropriate for a locality or time. (57) For successful agrarian practice some provisions had to be ignored. Smith, once again, wrote of the 'foolish' practice, whereby 'some leases prescribe to the tenant a certain mode of cultivation, and a certain succession of crops during the whole continuance of the lease', a condition which he attributed to 'the effect of the landlord's conceit of his own superior knowledge (a conceit in most cases very ill founded)'. (58) There is practical confirmation of his view in the 1794 *Report* on Perthshire, which pointed out that 'leases have been written, by persons better acquainted with law and account, than with economy' and held that 'no estate can possibly be improved, let the regulations in leases be ever so good, and the restrictions ever so well detailed, unless the landlord shall either superintend his own property, or his factor be acquainted with husbandry, and submit to the arduous

task of directing agricultural improvements'. (59) This specific complaint was sub-
stantiated by other *Reports* of the 1790s, which, while generally prescribing longer
leases, and crediting some of the landlords with prescribing rotations, were generally
against ordering them. (60)

When to the impediments of social opposition and lack of capital is added the
possibility that the landlords contributed only narrowly to the improving movement,
and not always competently at that, it is not surprising that success was not easily
achieved. Even Argyll encountered difficulties, but Argyll's problem was limited to
the failure of earlier experiments under Duncan Forbes. Success came later under
Forbes' successor, Lord Milton. For those landowners, possessed of less social prestige
and power, or of more limited financial resources, the need for capital expenditure
spread over a period, lengthened by the time needed to overcome the resistance to
social change, led frequently to strained and straitened resources at best, and, at
worst, to bankruptcy. The best known example of technical success and of private
economic failure is John Cockburn of Ormiston. Those who survived, and earned a
lasting reputation, did so often because they did not do too much too quickly. Some
of the improvers operated on a minute scale. Sir John Clerk of Penicuik wrote in
January 1741 that he had continued his improvements 'as I have done constantly
above 30 years, and for that end had 7 or 8 men always imploied to drain, ditch, or
hedge, especially in the spring seasons'. Earlier, in 1728, he explained his highly
limited method of operation in describing the building of a bridge: 'This wou'd have
been an expensive job to me if it had not been that I bestowed 8 years upon it, and
finished it with my own Men and carts, except what related to the Lyme and Mason
Work, which came altogether to no great sum'. (61) And the time-scale was protracted.
At Monymusk, after sixty years of improvement, 'there were still many parts ... not
very different from what they had been at the beginning of the century'. (62)
Improvements there lasted over four generations, and were completed only a century
after they were started, when an absentee acting for an insane baronet first incurred
claims against subsequent heirs under the provisions of the Entail Act, 1770, and
drained with government aid. (63) Even in estates with the advantages of ready access
to markets improvement was delayed. In 1800 the estate of Cardross was reported
to be still 'in that situation which many Estates of the kind in Scotland has been in
previous to their being improved'. (64)

The impediments in the path of an improver limited the scale and delayed the
timing of his activities, but did not alter his objectives; one force, derived from the
fundamental desire for higher rents, did so. A landowner was unlikely to incur the
risks attendant on improvement if he could achieve higher rents with minimum
change. An opportunity to do so was provided by the cattle trade, which is frequently
cited as an example of successful agrarian change, but the success of which depended
more on the expansion of demand, chiefly from English markets, and less on structural
changes or improvements in the quality of supply. Changes in arable cultivation to
provide better grazing and winter fodder, (65) and perhaps even a change in the form
of livestock enterprise, (66) required capital expenditure and ran the risk of social
opposition. Apart from some well-known examples of attempts at structural change,
as in Galloway as early as the 1720s, (67) the possibility of increasing returns from
livestock husbandry still further could be ignored. No other changes were required
to achieve the basic objective of increased incomes. (68)

The improving movement was far from being a general and widespread force in eighteenth-century Scotland, and agrarian change was not some automatic and common response to it. If the basic attraction to the improvers was the possibility of higher rents, then, since agrarian change involved many risks, the alternative of obtaining higher rents through limited action, if available, was attractive to many. Where the prospects of agrarian change were least favourable, as in areas of limited endowments and remote from markets, the attraction of limited action was greatest. Such was the case in the Highlands, and explains why change was often least when, as during the Napoleonic Wars, increased demand, prices and income were making conditions otherwise favourable to improvement. (69) Even where hazards and impediments were less, they were adequate to limit the attractions of improvement until the risks of doing so were reduced by favourable market conditions, and such was not the case in Scotland until late in the eighteenth century, or early in the nineteenth. The pattern of the trade in grain indicated the need for agrarian change; it also indicated that agrarian change held out prospects of higher rewards late in the century. Significantly, Lord Kames asked rhetorically in 1776: 'Can greater encouragement to industry be wished, than a ready market for every thing the soil produces? how different from the condition of Scotland, not more than forty years ago!'. (70)

Hence much work in recent years has moved against the older fashion of a semi-biographical case study approach to the explanation of the connection between the improving movement and agrarian change towards stress on the movement of economic variables, especially of population and prices, providing opportunities for easier economic conditions. With that change of emphasis has come a later dating for many of the large-scale agrarian changes, these being associated with the price rises of the Napoleonic Wars. That was certainly the period when rentals rose. It was also the period which witnessed the appearance of some of the technical changes, especially mechanical, which were essential for further Scottish agricultural improvement. Agrarian change has therefore to be linked less along the traditional lines to the improvers of the eighteenth century and more to the pattern of demand and supply of a wider area and later period.

NOTES

1. For example, '... the smaller lairds ... turned Scottish agriculture from a clumsy medieval craft into a modern science'. James Fergusson, *Lowland Lairds* (London, 1949), pp.17-18.

2. P.W.J. Riley, 'The Structure of Scottish Politics and the Union of 1707', in T.I. Rae, ed. *The Union of 1707* (Glasgow, 1974), pp.21f.

3. J.M. Simpson, 'Who Steered the Gravy Train?' in N. Phillipson and R. Mitchison, *Scotland in the Age of Improvement* (Edinburgh, 1970), p.66.

4. T.M. Devine, *The Tobacco Lords* (Edinburgh, 1975), p.172.

5. 'The habits ... of order, economy and attention, to which mercantile business naturally forms a merchant, render him much fitter to execute, with profit and success, any project of improvement': Adam Smith, *The Wealth of Nations* (1776) ed. Campbell, Skinner and Todd (Oxford, 1976), p.412 (III.iv.3). See also Adam Smith, Lectures on *Justice, Police, Revenue and Arms,* ed. Cannan (Oxford, 1896), p.228.

6. Cf. J. Clive, 'The Social Background of the Scottish Renaissance' in Phillipson and Mitchison, *op.cit.,* p.235.

7. Henry Home, Lord Kames in his preface to *The Gentleman Farmer* (Edinburgh, 1776), xii: 'I pretend only to have reduced the theory of agriculture into a sort of system, more concise at least, and more consistent, than has been done by other writers'.

8. T.C. Smout, *A History of the Scottish People, 1560-1830* (London, 1969), p.297.

9. Quoted in G. Holmes, *British Politics in the Age of Anne* (London, 1967), p.393.

10. *Historical Manuscripts Commission, Portland MSS,* v (London, 1899), 121. See also *Portland MSS,* x (London, 1931), 406-7.

11. Patrick Lindsay, *The Interest of Scotland* (Edinburgh, 1833), pp.101-2; John Knox, *A View of the British Empire,* third edn. (London, 1785), p.97.

12. E.R. Cregeen, *Argyll Estate Instructions, 1771-1805* (Edinburgh, 1964), Scottish History Society, I (fourth series), xi-xii.

13. Scottish Record Office GD 135/Box 42, letter from John Macadam, 28 December 1778.

14. A useful synopsis of the grain trade is in George Chalmers, *Caledonia* (London, 1810), iii, 33. Annual figures from 1770 to 1803 are in *Parliamentary Papers,* 1803-04. VII. 487 and 507, and for occasional years in Treasury: Accounts, Scotland. (Public Record Office T.36).

15. *O.S.A.,* v, 339 (Cathcart); *O.S.A.,* x, 166 (Athelstaneford).

16. *O.S.A.,* xviii, 365. See also viii, 142 (Carluke).

17. See, for example, *O.S.A.,* xviii, 200 (Eastwood); v, 252 (Cambuslang); xiv, 452 (Corstorphine).

18. *O.S.A.,* xviii, 191 (West Calder); xiv, 58 (Heriot); xviii, 162 (Carmunnock); ii, 191 (Hamilton).

19. *O.S.A.,* ii, 352 (Whittinghame).

20. *O.S.A.,* x, 603 (Fala and Soutra); ix, 409 (Kirknewton).

21. *O.S.A.,* xiv, 110 (Dolphinton).

22. p.537.

23. *An Essay on the Husbandry of Scotland with a Proposal for the further Improvement thereof* (Edinburgh, 1732), p.5. For the views of one of the earliest improvers, Sir Archibald Grant of Monymusk, on his tenants in 1716, see *Miscellany of the Spalding Club,* ii (Aberdeen, 1842), 96-7.

24. Forbes' report to Argyll is reprinted in *Report of the Royal Commission on the condition of the Crofters,* 1884 (Napier Commission), Appendix A (LXXV), 387-94.

25. Cregeen, *op.cit.,* p.xv.

26. Simpson, *op.cit.,* p.163. The memory of the tenants' alleged lack of initiative remained. In 1883 the then Duke of Argyll wrote to the Napier Commission that not only the first step 'towards a more civilized condition ... [but] all subsequent steps were taken, by the proprietor, and not by the people'. *Report of the Royal Commission on Crofting,* 1884. Appendix A, 381.

27. *O.S.A.,* xiv, 189 note (Kilfinichen and Kilvickeou).

28. On Assynt the tutors to the young Countess of Sutherland 'showed no eagerness of any kind to encourage emigration' and in the 1770s switched from the leasing of farms to single tacksmen to the leasing of them conjointly. R.J. Adam, ed. *John Home's Survey of Assynt* (Edinburgh, 1960), Scottish History Society, LII (third series), xxxiii. The reaction was not confined to the Highlands; for an example of similar concern in the Lowlands, see R.H. Campbell and J.B.A. Dow, *Source Book of Scottish Economic and Social History* (Oxford, 1968), pp.2-3.

29. A.J. Youngson, *After the 'Forty-Five* (Edinburgh, 1973), p.66.

30. In his *Address of Beelzebub.* See also Margaret M. McArthur, ed. *Survey of Lochtayside, 1769* (Edinburgh, 1936). Scottish History Society XXVII (third series), lxxiii.

31. George Robertson, *General View of the Agriculture of the County of Midlothian* (Edinburgh, 1793), pp.34f. and p.80.

32. James Donaldson, *General View of the Agriculture of the County of Banff* (Edinburgh, 1794), p.40.

33. Robert Beatson, *General View of the Agriculture of the County of Fife* (Edinburgh, 1794), p.16.

34. S.R.O. GD 135/Box 42, letter from Quinten Macadam, 19th July 1769. *Factors' Accounts* (Box 40) shows allowances frequently in single figures.

35. Robertson, *Midlothian*, p.34 note.

36. As from a Professor of Moral Philosophy by the Duke of Gordon. R.S. Walker, ed. *James Beattie's Day Book, 1773-1798*. Third Spalding Club. (Aberdeen, 1948), p.14.

37. B. Johnson, *General View of the Agriculture of the County of Dumfries* (London, 1794), pp.108-112; A.R.B. Haldane, *The Drove Roads of Scotland* (Edinburgh 1952), pp.46f.

38. S.G. Checkland, *Scottish Banking: A History, 1695-1973* (Glasgow, 1975), pp.227-8.

39. W. Fullarton, *General View of the Agriculture of the County of Ayr* (Edinburgh, 1793), p.13.

40. George Robertson, *Rural Recollections* (Irvine, 1829), p.585.

41. H. Hamilton, ed. *Monymusk Papers, 1713-1755* (Edinburgh, 1945), Scottish History Society, XXXIX (third series), xiii.

42. T.P. Soper, *Monymusk, 1770-1850*. University of Aberdeen Ph.D. thesis (1954), p.27.

43. Donaldson, *Banff*, p.15.

44. Smith, *Wealth of Nations*, p.386 (III.ii.7). See also *Lectures*, p.228.

45. As in D. Daiches, *The Paradox of Scottish Culture* (London, 1964), p.7.

46. James Anderson, *General View of the Agriculture of the County of Aberdeen* (London, 1794), pp.72-3.

47. *Wealth of Nations*, p.832 (V.ii.c.15).

48. *Lectures*, p.120.

49. *Lectures*, p.124.

50. *Lectures*, p.228.

51. *Wealth of Nations*, p.385 (III.ii.7).

52. *Wealth of Nations*, p.385 (III.ii.7). Also *Lectures*, p.228. For a very different view of the small proprietor, see *Wealth of Nations*, p.423 (III.iv.19).

53. Robertson, *Rural Recollections*, p.352.

54. H.J. Habakkuk, 'Economic Functions of English Landowners in the Seventeenth and Eighteenth Centuries', *Explorations in Entrepreneurial History*, vi (1953). Reprinted in W.E. Minchinton, *Essays in Agrarian History* (Newton Abbot, 1968), p.192.

55. *Wealth of Nations*, p.832 (V.ii.c.15).

56. See *Acts of the Parliaments of Scotland*, ii.35 (1449).

57. G.E. Mingay, *English Landed Society in the Eighteenth Century* (London, 1963), pp.160-171.

58. *Wealth of Nations*, p.831 (V.ii.c.13).

59. James Robertson, *General View of the Agriculture of the County of Perth* (London, 1794), p.24.

60. See also Sir John Sinclair, *General Report of the Agricultural State and Political Circumstances of Scotland* (Edinburgh, 1814), iii, 384.

61. J.M. Gray, ed. *Memoirs of the Life of Sir John Clerk of Penicuik* (Edinburgh, 1892), Scottish History Society (First Series), 160 and 134.

62. Soper, *op.cit.*, p.iv.

63. *Ibid.*, pp.131, 138 and 143.

64. S.R.O. GD 15/41 Report regarding the Estate of Cardross, June, 1800.

65. *Wealth of Nations*, p.239 (I.xi.l.3).

66. M.L. Ryder, 'Sheep and the Clearances in the Scottish Highlands: a Biologist's View', *Agricultural History Review*, XVI (1968), Part II, 155f.

67. S.R.O. GD 18/J6/5246(1) and (5), 5288, 5272, 5301 and J7/5750. Some Galloway estates were leased comprehensively on long leases in the 1720s but apparently without significant changes in tenants or holdings.

68. Cf. Cregeen, *op.cit.,* pp.xvi, xxxii.

69. Cf. Sir James Steuart, *Considerations on the Interest of the County of Lanark* (1769) in *Collected Works* (London, 1805), p.307.

70. Kames, *op.cit.,* p.x.

16. Landlord and Tenant Relations in Ireland between the Famine and the Land War, 1850-1878

W. E.Vaughan

IN THE 1930s two books on landlord and tenant relations in Ireland were published: John E. Pomfret, *The struggle for land in Ireland, 1800-1923* (Princeton, 1930) and Elizabeth R. Hooker, *Readjustments of Agricultural Tenure in Ireland* (Chapel Hill, 1938). From the 1930s to the 1960s thinking on the subject of landlord and tenant relations between the Famine and the Land War was dominated by these two books, in which was enshrined the picture of a peasantry oppressed by high rents, insecure in its holdings and goaded into violence by its grievances. This interpretation rested on four statements about landlord and tenant relations, each apparently true and each leading logically to its successor. First, the law of landlord and tenant in Ireland permitted landlords to increase rents as often as they pleased, to evict even tenants who paid their rents punctually, and to confiscate permanent improvements made by tenants. Secondly, Irish agriculture was backward because the landlords did not improve their estates and insecurity of tenure prevented tenants from improving their holdings. Thirdly, the countryside was plagued by agrarian crime provoked by landlord oppression. And fourthly, a reform of the law, giving tenants security of tenure and fair rents would have released the productive capacity of Irish tenants while improving social relations. This picture of landlord and tenant relations began to be questioned in the 1960s and the work of the small group of historians and economists who began the questioning has now advanced so far that it is possible to put forward an alternative interpretation. (1) This paper will examine, in the light of recent research, the main arguments of the traditional interpretation: that rents were high and rent increases frequent, that evictions were common, that rural society was endemically disordered by landlord-tenant disputes and that the landlord system discouraged investment in agriculture. (2)

It was often alleged by contemporaries that rents in Ireland were high and frequently increased but an examination of the movement and level of rents, based on the surviving rentals of individual estates, suggests that such statements were exaggerated and applied, at most, to isolated cases which received publicity. In the period from the early 1850s to the late 1870s, rents lagged behind rising agricultural prices to such an extent that there occurred a significant re-distribution of the relative shares of total agricultural income received by landlords and tenants. From the early 1850s to the mid-1870s, agricultural prices, with some exceptions, rose steadily, coinciding with the great wave of mid-century prosperity in Great Britain. The prices of livestock and of livestock products rose dramatically. The prices of store cattle, beef, butter and pork in the period 1851-5, when compared with prices in the period 1871-5, show increases of over 100 per cent for store cattle, over 50 per cent for beef, 40 per cent for butter, and 14 per cent for pork. (3) Calculations of the value of gross agricultural output for every year between 1850 and 1881, based on the Irish agricultural statistics which were published annually, show more precisely the course and magnitude of the effects of price increases. From the 1850s the value of output rose steadily and decisively until the late 1870s when it was 40 or 50 per cent higher than it had been twenty-five years before. (4) Progress was not, of course, uninterrupted, a decline in the early 1860s, for example, preceding a dramatic peak in the mid-1860s.

If the traditional picture of rack-renting landlordism has any validity, one would expect rent increases in excess of 40 or 50 per cent. But an examination of the rentals of over fifty estates showed that rents were increased by more than 40 per cent on only a handful of estates. While there were very high rent increases on two estates (the estates of the Earl of Leitrim in Counties Donegal and Leitrim whose rents were increased, on average, by 53 and 60 per cent), most increases were moderate, most rents being increased only once in the thirty-year period. Taking the group of over fifty estates as a whole, rents were increased by only 20 per cent between the 1850s and the 1870s. (5) Rents, therefore, lagged behind increases in the value of agricultural output, allowing tenants' incomes to increase at a greater rate than agricultural output itself and implying, therefore, that a significant re-distribution of landed income took place between the Famine and the Land War.

These results are so decisive that, even allowing for errors which might have minimized rent increases while exaggerating increases in the value of agricultural output, they contradict the picture of a tenantry impoverished by rack-renting. But if rents lagged behind the rising value of agricultural output and if tenants were prosperous, why were there so many complaints about rents and why was there a growing, if somewhat erratically pursued, demand for legislation to curb the powers of the landlords?(6) There were, I believe, three possible explanations for the phenomenon of apparent prosperity accompanied by discontent. First, while the burden of rents as a whole was moderate, individual rents were often high and the whole system of levying rents was riddled with inconsistencies. Secondly, the very fact that rents lagged behind increases in the value of agricultural output gave tenants a vested interest in securing legislation which would prevent them from ever catching up. Thirdly, it is possible that the smaller farmers were unable to take advantage of rising livestock prices.

Of the three explanations for discontent over rents, the third explanation does not take the argument very far because an examination of increases of agricultural output on farms of different sizes showed that even the smallest farms shared in the increases. But rents bore more heavily on small farmers because rent, even a low rent, was a large proportion of the income remaining to them after they had provided for the subsistence of their families. On Irish estates, furthermore, rents were not graduated according to the size of farms and small farmers paid as much for their land as large farmers. Also, small farmers suffered from diseconomies of scale, notably in the use of horses, which further reduced their net incomes. The very existence of numerous small farms (those between one and five acres numbered 62,000 in 1881), (7) the net incomes of the occupiers of which probably did not exceed the wages of landless labourers, was a potential source of chronic discontent, especially

P

in bad years, when a fall in prices would erode their small incomes or bad weather destroy their vital supplies of turf and potatoes. But the collective plight of the smallest farmers was serious only in bad years and does not, in itself, entirely account for complaints about rents which were perennial and came as frequently from the larger, comfortable farmers as from the smallest ones.

The explanation of discontent over rents must be sought in the inconsistencies of rent increases and rent levels and in the fact that the lowness of rents as a whole was a source of agitation. Of the unevenness of rents and the inconsistencies of estate management an examination of surviving rentals leaves little doubt. Rent increases, even on the same estate, varied greatly in amount and rent levels, when compared with the official tenement valuation, showed great differences and individual estates often recorded high coefficients of variation. (8) The timing of rent increases, too, was unpredictable. Sometimes the rent was increased when a new tenancy began but, frequently, rents were increased without warning and, apparently, arbitrarily. Irish landlords did not follow the practice of Scottish landlords whose rents were allowed to fluctuate annually with the prices of agricultural commodities. (9) All of this made it easy for critics of landlordism to discover and publicise examples of unfairness, which could be found even on well-managed estates. The presence of a handful of vigorous landlords, such as the Earl of Leitrim whose management was vigorous to the point of extortion, merely strengthened the critics' case by dramatising it. (10)

Although it was easy for the critics of Irish landlordism to construct and present a powerful case in newspapers, pamphlets and in the evidence given to parliamentary inquiries, the real power of their case for legislation to secure fair rents lay not in the catalogue of high rents discovered and publicised but in its appeal to the great mass of tenants whose rents were not high and who did not want to pay higher rents. Also, since rents lagged behind increases in the value of agricultural output, landlords did not exploit their estates to the full, leaving tenants in the enjoyment of a sort of equitable interest in the land similar to that of the landlords. When such a situation exists, the practice of buying and selling tenancy rights is, if not an inevitable development, a predictable one. Such a practice, known as 'the custom of tenant right', existed in the north of Ireland and conferred even on yearly tenants the right to sell or transfer their holdings. But rents in Ulster were not lower than rents in the rest of Ireland. Tenants in the south of Ireland, therefore, enjoyed the same equitable interest in their farms as tenants in Ulster did, but they did not enjoy the same customary rights of disposal. The frustration of tenants, enjoying an equitable interest in their holdings but unable to realize its value by selling it or mortgaging it, lay behind the agitation for legislation which would limit landlords' power to increase rents and give legal recognition to the existence of 'tenant right'.

The desire of tenants to secure permanently the advantages of low rents, the inconsistencies of many rent increases and rent levels, added to the existence of numerous and economically vulnerable small farmers, were the chief ingredients of the controversy about Irish rents. Examples of high rents and arbitrary rent increases created the impression of rack-renting in spite of the general lowness of rents. Rents, however, although controversial, were not the most emotive aspect of landlord-tenant relations. More public attention was probably devoted to evictions and agrarian

outrages than to rents, with arbitrary evictions forming the *gravamen* of the case
against landlordism. Evictions and agrarian outrages were dramatic incidents which
often received much publicity of a blatantly sensational kind. (11) This and the fact
that some evictions were carried out with an atrocious unscrupulousness, which even
sensational publicity could not exaggerate, created the impression that rural society
was chronically disordered. To some extent, of course, the impression of disorder
was artificially strengthened by the government assiduously compiling statistics
(which had no equivalent in other parts of the United Kindsom) of evictions and
agrarian outrages. A close look at evictions and agrarian outrages, however, suggests
their importance was exaggerated by contemporaries.

After 1854 the annual number of evictions returned by the police did not exceed
2,000 until the crisis year of 1880 and, in most years, the total was less than 1,000,
which means that less than 20 tenants in 10,000 were removed annually. (12) The
annual fluctuations of evictions suggest, moreover, that evictions were caused by
arrears. When the value of agricultural output increased as in the mid-1850s, for
example, arrears fell and evictions also fell. The opposite happened when the value
of output fell, as in the early 1860s and late 1870s, when arrears and evictions increased. The connection between arrears and evictions is further strengthened by
the evidence of the judicial statistics, published annually from 1863, and of the
rentals of individual estates. The judicial statistics and the rentals of ten estates
examined show that processes for the recovery of arrears exceeded those processed
on notices to quit, that most of the tenants processed on the ten estates were in
arrears and that threats of eviction greatly exceeded actual evictions. (13) It seems,
therefore, that the most numerous victims of eviction were not solvent, improving
tenants as was often alleged (and whose lot it was the intention of Gladstone's Land
Act of 1870 to improve) but tenants who had fallen hopelessly into arrears in bad
times. Threats of eviction, furthermore, were more common than actual evictions
because landlords and agents used them, in the form of the notice to quit, not to
remove tenants but to secure some other end by threatening removal. The notice
to quit was the estate agent's maid-of-all-work, being used to collect arrears, to
force tenants to pay increases of rent, to settle quarrels between tenants and to
discourage bad farming.

The versatility of the notice to quit as a method of controlling tenants is illustrated
in detail in the ejectment books of the estate of Lord Fitzwilliam in County Wicklow. (14)
These books, covering the period 1845-86, give the number of notices served annually
and the reasons for their service. Most notices were served on tenants who had not
paid their rents but some were served to prevent the dividing of farms without the
landlord's consent, the harbouring of squatters, sub-letting, non-residence and bad
farming. The supervision of farming on the estate seems to have been strict because
in 1867, for example, tenants who had sold their hay were served with notices. Other
reasons for service were more eccentric, reflecting the views of a paternal agent. One
tenant was threatened for 'beating his wife and drunken rows'. Another because he
'practised snaring hares' and another because he was 'not thought to be steady'. Most
of the tenants served with notices to quit were not evicted and some names appeared
regularly in the ejectment books which suggests that threats of eviction were not
taken seriously by a small knot of rural recidivists.

Although the clearances which succeeded the Famine and the occasional clearances which took place in the 1850s and 1860s gave the very word eviction a terrible significance, tenants enjoyed practical security of tenure on most estates and, even when threatened with eviction, showed considerable powers of survival and resistance. (15) Lord Fitzwilliam's estate was not an isolated case. On the Dungannon school estate near Stewartstown in County Tyrone, for example, one family of tenants tormented and defied for nearly thirty years, with virtual impunity, a quiet well-meaning agent. (16) The tenants' recalcitrance occasionally passed beyond insolence and legal obstruction to actual crime. In Ireland, such crimes, known as agrarian outrages, were returned by the police separately from ordinary crime. (17) Like evictions, agrarian outrages were prominent in debates about landlord-tenant relations, often causing bitterly exaggerated debates in the newspapers. But like evictions, the importance of agrarian outrages was exaggerated. (18)

Agrarian outrages were even less numerous than evictions. Between 1850 and 1880 the annual number of agrarian outrages exceeded 500 in only seven years (in 1850, 1851, 1852, 1869, 1870, 1879 and 1880) and in some years the total was very low, for example, only 87 in 1866. Serious outrages, such as murder and manslaughter, were included in the totals with many trivial offences, the occasional murder giving a touch of distinction to a whole range of offences including arson, ham-stringing, sending threatening notices (the most frequently committed offence) and firing at the person. The last offence, given the poor quality of rural assassins' fire-arms, could often have been returned more accurately as attempted suicide than as attempted murder. But when they were all added up and published in parliamentary papers or reported (often over and over again) in newspapers, the impression was created of an endemically violent society in which, according to one well-informed contemporary, poor seasons led to arrears, arrears led to evictions, and evictions led to outrages. (19)

The connection between agrarian outrages and evictions was, superficially, convincing. The number of outrages in any year tended to respond to the number of evictions, which, as has already been observed, tended to respond to fluctuations in the value of agricultural output and arrears. For example, outrages declined in the mid-1860s, coinciding with an increase in the value of agricultural output and a decline in evictions. Likewise, they increased in the early 1860s and the late 1870s when the value of output declined and evictions increased. But the great wave of outrages in 1869-70 (767 in 1869 and 1,329 in 1870) was not related to evictions. An analysis of the relationship between evictions and outrages in individual counties gave less decisive results showing that, while association was stronger in bad years when evictions and outrages were relatively numerous than in more peaceful years, association was not decisively strong even in bad years. The statistical evidence does not, therefore, prove an automatic connection between evictions and outrages. It proves conclusively only that not all outrages were caused by evictions and not all evictions caused outrages. The incidence of agrarian violence is inexplicable if the only cause sought is harsh behaviour on the part of landlords. The existence of turbulent groups amongst the tenantry prepared to make trouble on any pretext was equally important. The same agent, managing two different estates, would find one peaceful and the other turbulent and be puzzled by the difference. As William Wann, who managed Lord Gosford's estate in County Cavan and the Dungannon school estate in County Tyrone, mournfully reflected after a long row with tenants on the latter estate:

> I may now tell you that the perpetual worry and annoyance which I so long endured in Gartlaney's case had a very bad effect on my health, so much so that I was obliged to put myself into the doctor's hands.... I receive from the *same number* of tenants in Cavan as in the school lands over £4,000 a year for Lord Gosford and for the last twenty years the trouble I have had from the *entire estate* would fall far short of what I experienced in Gartlaney's case. (20)

The elusiveness of the connection between agrarian outrages and evictions and, indeed, other acts of provocation becomes even greater when the causes of individual outrages are examined. An examination of the causes of over one hundred homicides, committed over a twenty-year period, revealed that the majority of them had nothing to do with disputes between landlords and tenants; 30 per cent were the result of disputes between tenants, another 30 per cent the result of family disputes and 5 per cent the result of disputes between tenants and sub-tenants. Only the remaining 35 per cent were directly or indirectly caused by disputes between landlords and tenants. But homicide is an intimate crime likely to result from quarrels within families or between neighbours, and an analysis of homicides is likely to show a high incidence of crimes caused by domestic quarrels. Cases of firing at the person, on the other hand, when analysed in the same way, showed that landlord-tenant disputes accounted for 59 per cent of the incidents. This analysis of serious agrarian outrages, suggesting that less than 50 per cent were caused by disputes between landlords and tenants, reveals the treacherous ambiguity often found in official statistics. The term 'agrarian outrage' was applied to all crimes committed in relation to the occupation of land and, if accepted uncritically, would lead one to believe that it referred only to landlord-tenant disputes. Only an analysis of its components revealed its wider meaning, embracing even quarrels within families about inheritance. The fact, too, that all crime was divided into two classes, ordinary crime and agrarian outrages, implies that agrarian outrages were as numerous as ordinary crime. But only 5 or 6 per cent of all crime was agrarian and if five or six agrarian homicides a year sounds serious, it sounds less serious when one discovers that there were about fifty or sixty homicides of all kinds every year. To some extent, the impression of a disordered society was created by the way in which crime statistics were compiled. If homicides and assaults in the English countryside, caused by affrays between poachers and gamekeepers, had been classified separately from ordinary crime, it is probable that the English game-laws would have emerged as a greater waster of human life than landlordism in Ireland.

If contemporaries exaggerated the importance of agrarian outrages, evictions and high rents, did they also exaggerate the effects of insecurity of tenure on agricultural investment? Although there was much exaggeration, the fact remains that there were a few harsh landlords, that some tenants were capriciously evicted, that some rents were high and that the law, before 1870, did permit landlords to confiscate tenants' improvements. The great majority of tenants enjoyed security of tenure and were not rack-rented, but did they feel secure? The argument of the landlords' critics, therefore, that landlords did not invest in the improvement of their estates and that the law, by permitting landlords to increase rents when they

pleased or to evict tenants and to confiscate their improvements, prevented tenants
from investing in their holdings, may have a validity which is not challenged by the
fact that most landlords behaved reasonably. The allegation that landlords did not
invest large sums in the improvement of their estates is certainly true. An examination
of the accounts of nine estates showed that landlords spent only about 5 or 6 per
cent of their rent-receipts on improvements. (21) Only one of the nine, a Scottish
absentee who owned an estate in County Donegal, spent a substantial amount, about
16 per cent, comparable with the expenditure of English landlords, whose lavish
expenditure was held up as a norm of landlord investment by critics of Irish landlordism. (22) There were sound reasons for the parsimony of Irish landlords, including the impossibility of building houses and out-offices on a multitude of small
holdings and the fact that Irish agriculture provided many outlets for cheap, trifling
improvements whose apparent usefulness was gratifying to the pride of great landlords.
A gate here, a fence there, a short stretch of road or a pedigree bull bought in a fit
of enthusiasm and then sold when his appetite for oil-cake became burdensome, was
the usual erratic pattern of landlord investment in Ireland.

   If landlords did little to improve their estates, and if the tenurial system discouraged
tenants who wanted to improve their holdings, was Irish agricultural prosperity impeded
by the difficulties of landlord-tenant relations? Sir John Gray, in a speech in 1869,
claimed that if all Ireland were brought to the same food producing capacity as Ulster,
where tenants enjoyed virtual security of tenure under the custom of tenant right,
the value of the gross output of Ireland would increase by 40 per cent. (23) Sir John's
argument rested on two assumptions: that Irish agriculture could be dramatically
improved and that tenants would carry out the necessary improvements if they had
security of tenure. It is, unfortunately, impossible to examine tenants' investment in
detail because few farm records survive but, although a precise estimate of the effect
of the law on tenants' improvements is impossible, Sir John's assumptions are amenable to indirect ànalysis. Implicit, for example, in his argument is the assumption
that Ulster was more prosperous than the other provinces and that its prosperity was
based on security of tenure.

   There was much to be said in favour of the argument that Ulster was more prosperous and peaceful than the other provinces, Ulster having better housing in its
rural areas, fewer evictions and fewer outrages than the other provinces. When, however, individual Ulster counties were compared with individual counties in the south,
the contrast became less decisive. A survey in 1854 of the extent to which farms
were kept free from weeds showed, furthermore, that Ulster, in this vital aspect of
farming, was better than only Connacht, coming behind Leinster and Munster. (24)
To have excelled only Connacht was hardly an achievement for Ulster farming! Even
if it could be proved decisively that the difference between Ulster and the rest of
Ireland was more significant than, for example, the difference between the east and
west of Ireland, there is no reason to believe that Ulster's prosperity was caused
solely by security of tenure. Some contemporaries were ready with other explanations,
for example, the cultivation of flax in Ulster, which was labour-intensive, giving a
high gross income per acre and, therefore, ideally suited to the economy of small
farmers. An estimate of the value of the flax crop, made by the agent of an estate
in County Cavan, showed its great importance in the economy of small farms: flax

grown on only one eleventh of the area of the estate not only paid the whole rent
of the estate but left a handsome balance in the tenants' pockets. (25)

The argument that Ulster was prosperous because of security of tenure and the
custom of tenant right was, on the whole, more important as a polemical device
than as a practical demonstration of the effects of security of tenure on tenants'
investment. But the argument put forward by Sir John Gray was probably at its
weakest, not when it assumed that Ulster was prosperous, but when it assumed that
Irish agriculture was capable of dramatic improvement. This was an argument which
was taken seriously by contemporaries, including Gladstone when he was preparing
the bill which became the Irish Land Act of 1870. (26) There was no doubt that
Irish agriculture was backward when compared with, for example, Scottish agriculture.
A comparison of Irish and Scottish agricultural production in the 1870s showed that
the input of labour per person engaged in Irish agriculture was only half of that in
Scotland and that Irish farm horses were less efficiently used than Scottish ones.
The survey of weeds in 1854, furthermore, showed that, on 50 per cent of farms
in Ireland, the work of keeping down weeds was largely or wholly neglected. Irish
agriculture was backward when compared with the very advanced agriculture of
Scotland but such a comparison, though useful, is misleadingly inappropriate. When
compared with continental agriculture, on the other hand, output per head and
yields of crops in Ireland compared very favourably. (27) Also, the actual performance
of agricultural output between the 1850s and the 1870s was a not unimpressive performance, implying that Irish farmers reacted intelligently to rising prices. (28)

It is doubtful if Irish agriculture was capable of the dramatic improvement
imagined by Sir John Gray even if tenants had security of tenure. The practical
openings in Irish agriculture for improvement along conventional lines were probably
exaggerated by contemporaries. The house-feeding of livestock, steam ploughing,
fancy gates, neat fences and all the other accoutrements of high farming were, perhaps,
profitable in the Lothians but they were unsuitable in Ireland where the production
of store cattle did not lend itself to intensive investments of that kind. (29) After all,
bullocks do not grow faster simply because their pasture is enclosed by a neat fence
and an iron gate. In Ireland improvement was more likely to take the form of increased
dealing in livestock and the taking of more land. As an explanation of the apparent
unwillingness of Irish farmers to carry out improvements, insecurity of tenure was
probably less important than the unprofitability of some of the improvements
suggested at a time when farmers were doing well by reacting to the rising prices of
livestock (a form of investment often ignored by contemporaries). The fact, too,
that agricultural production did not expand dramatically after 1881, when tenants
received full security of tenure, and the long continuance of the eleven-month 'conacre
setting', a form of tenure more wretchedly insecure than the system which prevailed
before 1881, strengthen further the case for saying that insecurity of tenure did not
decisively influence economic development before 1881.

This examination of rents, evictions, agrarian outrages and agricultural investment
suggests strongly that the traditional interpretation of landlord and tenant relations
was strongly biased in spite of its plausible coherence and sustained longevity. A
possible explanation of the contrast between traditional and new interpretations
seems, at first sight, to lie in the nature of the sources used. Pomfret and Hooker

relied mainly on parliamentary papers and other official publications which tend
to emphasize the contentious aspect of landlord and tenant relations, but some of
those who have questioned the traditional interpretation have relied on estate papers
which tend to emphasize the difficulties of landlords. There is, of course, some
strength in this argument but it is not entirely conclusive because some of the modern
works, for example, B.L. Solow's *The land question and the Irish economy, 1870-
1903* (Cambridge, Mass., 1971), use no source which was unavailable in the 1930s.
The power of the traditional interpretation, as well as its bias, lay not only in its
sources and methods, but in its assumptions about human behaviour and its attitude
to recent history. The assumption, for example, that positive law influenced economic
behaviour, once accepted, tends to concentrate the attention on those who exercised
to the full their legal rights but ignores the practical, as opposed to moral, restraints
on those who did not. But above all, the traditional interpretation seemed to enshrine
the verdict of history. A system of land tenure which vested the ownership of all
land in a few thousand individuals, crowded the majority of tenants on to 25 per
cent of the available land and then allowed the owners to exploit the tenants was
demonstrably unjust. Successive British governments, furthermore, accepted the
tenants' view of their landlords and abolished, slowly and reluctantly but irrevocably,
the whole landlord system. The tenurial successor of landlordism, peasant proprietary,
was successful (in social and political terms, at least) and became one of the most
distinctive and best established institutions of the new Irish community which
emerged after the First World War. In the 1930s, therefore, landlordism was an
institution which had been successfully indicted, decisively convicted and enthusiastic-
ally condemned at the bar of history. Nothing, it seemed, remained for the historian
but to make a short résumé of the defendant's most conspicuous iniquities. But
assumptions have changed since the 1930s and historians no longer believe that
positive law exercises a strong influence on economic behaviour and a few, at least,
no longer believe that discontent and agitation are always founded on actual oppression. (30) The idea, too, that a sense of property in the occupiers of the soil would
make the desert rejoice and blossom as a rose, while still strong, is not without its
critics. Changing assumptions, therefore, as well as new methods of analysis and
new sources have contributed to a revision of the traditional interpretation of landlord and tenant relations.

NOTES

1. The amount of published and unpublished material is now considerable. See
R.D. Crotty, *Irish agricultural production* (Cork, 1966); James S. Donnelly Jr, *The
land and the people of nineteenth-century Cork. The rural economy and the land
question* (London, 1975); Cormac Ó Gráda, 'Post-Famine adjustment : essays in
nineteenth-century economic history', Columbia University Ph.D. thesis (1973),
'Pre-Famine and post-Famine rents', *Economic and Social Review,* vii (1974), 385-92.
'The investment behaviour of Irish landlords 1850-75 : some preliminary findings',
Agric.Hist. Rev., xxiii (1975), 139-55, and 'Supply responsiveness in Irish agriculture
during the nineteenth century', *Econ. Hist. Rev.,* 2nd ser. xxviii (1975), 312-17;
Olive Robinson 'The London Companies as progressive landlords in nineteenth-
century Ireland', *Econ. Hist. Rev.,* 2nd ser. xv (1962-3), 103-18, and 'The London
Companies and tenant right in nineteenth-century Ireland', *Agric. Hist. Rev.,* xviii

(1970), 54-63; B.L. Solow, *The land question and the Irish economy, 1870-1903* (Cambridge, Mass., 1971); and W.E. Vaughan, 'A Study of landlord and tenant relations in Ireland between the Famine and the Land War, 1850-78', Trinity College, Dublin Ph.D. thesis, (1974).

2. Most of the material for this paper was taken from Vaughan, *op.cit.*

3. See the index of agricultural prices in Thomas Barrington, 'A review of Irish agricultural prices', *Journal of the Statistical and Social Inquiry Society of Ireland,* xv (1927), 249-80.

4. For the methods used in calculating the value of agricultural output, see Vaughan, *op.cit.*, pp.336-58.

5. See also Donnelly, *op.cit.*, pp.187-200; Ó Gráda, 'Pre-Famine and post-Famine rents', *Economic and Social Review,* vii (1974), 385-92; and Solow, *op.cit.*, pp.57-77.

6. The most compendious source of examples of tenants' complaints was the evidence presented to the Bessborough commission. See *Report of H.M. commissioners of inquiry into the working of the Landlord and Tenant (Ireland) Act, 1870, and the acts amending the same*, (P.P. 1881, xviii, xix).

7. The most comprehensive survey of agricultural holdings in this period was included in the census of 1881. See *Census Ire., 1881, general report* (P.P. 1882, lxxvi), pp.165-214.

8. For the principles on which the tenement valuation was based see Sir Richard Griffith, *Instructions to valuators and surveyors appointed under 15th and 16th Vict., cap. 63* .... (Dublin, 1853). The Irish valuation, unlike the Scottish one, was not revised to take account of the increases in the value of land which occurred after its completion in the 1860s.

9. For a description of such rents, see Peter Cowan, *Corn rents* (London, 1857).

10. For an insight into the quality and tone of Lord Leitrim's estate management, see Agents' and bailiffs' reports on the administration of Lord Leitrim's estates in County Donegal (N.L.I., MS 13,339).

11. See, for example, the press cuttings in the Larcom papers (N.L.I., MSS 7632, 7633).

12. See *Return, by provinces and counties, of the cases of eviction which have come to the knowledge of the constabulary, in each of the years 1849-80* (P.P. 1881, lxxvii), pp.3-23.

13. See, for example, *Judicial statistics (Ireland), 1867* (P.P. 1867-8, lxvii), p.197.

14. Ejectment books of the estates of Lord Fitzwilliam, 1845-86 (N.L.I., MSS 4972, 4992).

15. For an example of the great clearances which occurred after the Famine, see *Reports and returns relating to evictions in the Kilrush union* (P.P. 1849, xlix), pp.3-57.

16. For numerous examples of the difficulties encountered by this agent, see Copy letter books of William Wann, 1846-1881 (P.R.O.N.I. D. 1606/5/3-6).

17. See *Irish crime records, 1848-93* (S.P.O.I., VIIIB. WP2/1-2).

18. For a systematic statement of the argument that rural Ireland was in a state of chronic disorder, see G.L.T. Locker-Lampson, *A consideration of the state of Ireland in the nineteenth century* (London, 1907).

19. Mountifort Longfield, 'Address by the president, Hon. Judge Longfield', *Journal of the Statistical and Social Inquiry Society of Ireland,* iv (1865), 135.

20. William Wann to W.C. Kyle, 12 Feb. 1873 in Copy letter book of William Wann, 1870-81 (P.R.O.N.I. D. 1606/5/5).

21. For a lower estimate, see Cormac Ó Gráda, 'The investment behaviour of Irish landlords 1850-75 : some preliminary findings', *Agric. Hist. Rev.,* xxiii (1975), 153.

22. For estimates of English landlords' expenditure on improvements, see Richard Perren, 'The landlords and agricultural transformation 1870-1900', *Agric. Hist. Rev.,* xviii (1970), 36-51.

23. Sir John Gray, *The Irish land question speech of Sir John Gray, delivered at the Free Trade Hall, Manchester, on 18 October 1869* (London and Dublin, 1869), p.34.

24. *Agricultural statistics of Ireland, 1854* (P.P. 1856, liii), p.223.

25. Rentals, accounts and agents' reports of the estate of Sir George Hodson bt, in County Cavan, 1861-7 (N.L.I. MS 16,419, p.114).

26. E.D. Steele, *Irish land and British politics. Tenant right and nationality 1865-1870* (Cambridge, 1974), pp.207, 243.

27. See contemporary estimates in Michael G. Mulhall, *Dictionary of statistics* (London, 1892), pp.18-37.

28. For an estimate of the economic performance of Irish farmers, based on modern methods of analysis, see Cormac Ó Gráda, 'Supply responsiveness in Irish agriculture during the nineteenth century', *Econ. Hist. Rev.*, 2nd ser. xxviii (1975), 312-17.

29. See R.D. Crotty, *Irish agricultural production* (Cork, 1966), pp.61, 70.

30. See, for example, Samuel Clark, 'The political mobilisation of Irish farmers', *Canad. Rev. Soc. & Anth.*, xii (1975), 483-99.

17. Highlanders, Irishmen, and the Land Question in Nineteenth-century Prince Edward Island (1)

I. R. Robertson

MOST studies of Scottish and Irish immigrants in North America focus upon their adaptation to a new and different environment. But in nineteenth-century Prince Edward Island these Celtic immigrants faced a problem which most had encountered previously, and which indeed had forced many of them to leave their ancestral homes: a neo-feudal system of land tenure. Their responses were no doubt conditioned by their Old World experiences, yet were complicated by the ethnic and religious mixture in their new setting. This paper examines the roles of Scottish and Irish immigrants in nineteenth-century Prince Edward Island, with particular reference to the 'land question', as it was locally known, and to their relations with each other.

I

More than anything else, the land question was the distinguishing characteristic of colonial Prince Edward Island. (2) A leasehold system of land tenure had been established following the transfer of the island from France to Great Britain by the Treaty of Paris in 1763. The island was surveyed, and divided into 67 lots or townships of about 20,000 acres each. In 1767 a lottery was held, and each township went to a favourite or group of favourites of the crown. After the Seven Years' War, the government had been besieged by retired officers and other persons who had ingratiated themselves. They were in search of offices, titles, and land in compensation for their services, and the island land lottery was one means chosen to satisfy their appetites. There were several conditions attached to these grants. First, the grantees had to pay annual quit rents of between £20 and £60 per township to the crown. The amount varied in rough proportion to the quality of the land. Within ten years, they were to settle their estates with one person per 200 acres, or about 100 persons per township. Finally, the settlers were to be Protestants from outside British North America, the sole exception being made for Yankees who had been in North America two years or more. The penalty for non-fulfilment of these conditions was to be escheat, or reversion to the crown. Two years later, in 1769, the island was granted colonial status separate from Nova Scotia, at the behest of the landed proprietors, who wanted to be within a small political jurisdiction which they could control. (3) The expenses of the government establishment were to be paid for by the quit rents.

These were the basic elements of the Prince Edward Island land question in the eighteenth and nineteenth centuries. In essence the colony had been saddled with a neo-feudal land system. For the average settler it meant that he could not own the land he worked. He had to lease it, usually at around £5 per hundred acres, plus two, four, or six shillings in quit rents, responsibility for which was thus transferred from the landlord to the tenant. Although this sort of arrangement was not uncommon in Europe at that time, the norm in the New World was freehold tenure. Consequently, from the very beginning, settlers were disinclined to go to Prince Edward Island. Many who did go to the island colony moved on, or their sons moved on. This reluctance on the part of potential immigrants, and lack of effort by most proprietors, meant that the condition of settling 100 people on each township within ten years was not fulfilled. In fact, throughout the entire colony there were perhaps 1,300 persons after the ten-year deadline had expired; (4) there should have been at least 6,700. Of those settlers, a large proportion were Roman Catholics of Scottish or French origin, and hence should not have been there. Indeed, no proprietor fulfilled all the conditions of his grant. Since the proprietors were unable or unwilling to settle the colony, they did not take the trouble to pay quit rents. (5) Eventually, the British government had to supply money for the salaries of the governor, the chief justice, and the rest of the civil establishment. Yet the lands of the proprietors were not escheated. (6)

The effects of the leasehold system were all-pervasive. Class tensions became acute, political struggles centered on issues like escheat, and the economic development of the colony was retarded. Even more than 30 years after the lottery, there were only 4,400 inhabitants. (7) Yet, eventually, people did begin to arrive in numbers. After the Napoleonic Wars economic distress was common in the United Kingdom, especially in the Celtic fringe of southern Ireland and the Highlands of Scotland. Tens, indeed hundreds, of thousands of impoverished Celts were faced with the choice of emigration or starvation. The poorest of these often ended up on the Atlantic coast of British North America because that region was the part of the New World closest to the United Kingdom and hence the fares were the cheapest. By 1861 the population of Prince Edward Island was 81,000. (8) The vast majority of these inhabitants lived off the land, a fact which underlined the importance of the land question in the life of the colony.

As the population grew, the tenants became increasingly vocal about their very real grievances. At least 60 to 70 per cent of the occupiers of land were tenants or squatters. (9) Furthermore, it appeared as though they would have to remain tenants or squatters indefinitely, since most landlords refused to sell clear titles to tenants on terms within their capacity to pay. Cash was very scarce in rural Prince Edward Island, with the result that in their early years on the land tenants might fall far in arrears in their payments. Crop failures could have the same result. Once evicted, tenants had no legal means of obtaining compensation for improvements, such as their very houses. Yet if they tried to pay off their arrears by working hard and taking large surpluses of crops to market, that too was dangerous. If a tenant looked too prosperous, a land agent might raise the rent or evict him in order to clear the way for a new occupant at a higher rent. Thus there was little incentive to produce a visible surplus, and consequently both the tenants and the economy as a whole suffered. It was a cycle of poverty, insecurity, and oppression. Islanders frequently referred to their colony as 'the Ireland of the New World', and this unhappy situation was unlikely to change as long as the land system endured.

Those who attempted to reform or abolish the leasehold system soon discovered that they had powerful and determined foes. The proprietors, who were often absentees based in Great Britain, were backed by a local élite composed of lawyers, land agents, politicians, and public officials. Together, the proprietors and the colonial oligarchy displayed a remarkable ability either to bend lieutenant-governors to their will, or to isolate and destroy them. Between 1769 and 1824 the one governor not to be recalled in disgrace accomplished this feat of survival only through allying himself with the most powerful local faction. His successor came to grief through association with a group known as the 'Loyal Electors', which has been described as the first political society in what is now Canada. The Loyal Electors briefly gained control of the assembly (which had been established in 1773), but the proprietors exerted their influence in London to have the governor dismissed and the society ostracized as allegedly being seditious. (10)

The Loyal Electors appear to have been composed mainly of United Empire Loyalists angry at being denied the clear land titles promised to them after the American Revolution. Although their ostensible aims were to counteract the influence of speculators and to gain clear titles for themselves, they too had been interested in accumulating land. Furthermore, their strength had been largely concentrated in the area around the capital, Charlottetown, and they had thriven in a period (1806-12) when the population of the island was still miniscule. Despite the allegations of seditious intent, there had been a faintly patrician air to the Loyal Electors, patronized as they were from Government House. (11) The next significant reform movement to arise, the Escheators, would be very different in composition, and would exist in a transformed social environment.

The Escheat movement flourished in the 1830s and 1840s, after the arrival of substantial numbers of Scottish and Irish immigrants. The Escheators took their name from their advocacy of a special court of escheat, which would investigate the titles of the proprietors (or 'land claimants') to discover whether they had met their obligations. Of course none had fulfilled the conditions of the original grants. Thus, according to the Escheators' plan, the lands would be forfeited and re-granted to the farmers occupying them. Some 65 per cent of islanders were Scottish or Irish (approximately two-thirds of these being Scots, who were overwhelmingly Highlanders), and this percentage more or less coincided with the proportion of tenants within the farm population. Back in the Old World, Highlanders and Irishmen had had considerable experience with landlordism. Such tenants were not inclined to accept the system passively. The attitude of the tenant has been aptly characterized in this excerpt from a recent poem:

> Ye'll get no rent for woods ye didn't cut,
> Stumps dug out with a horse I had to borrow,
> Land I plowed — — me and my old lady
> Who wasn't so old those days — — me in harness
> And her at the handles;
>
> A road I made with friends and relatives;
> And the wharf. When's there goin'ta be a wharf here?
> Don't bother with that. We'll manage without ye
> As well as we'll manage without payin' rent. (12)

Because the land agent was the most direct link of the tenant with the oppressive aspects of leasehold tenure, he was not welcome, and he was not made to feel welcome when he came calling. Means of underscoring this point ranged all the way from derision and intimidation to burning the agent's home and, at least on one occasion, murder.

The removal of civil disabilities from the large and impoverished Roman Catholic minority in 1830 combined with the low property qualification for the franchise to ensure that the strength of the Escheat movement was eventually reflected in the House of Assembly. The Escheators won a decisive victory at the polls in 1838, and they proceeded to elect as speaker of the assembly their leader, William Cooper. (13) He was a former land agent who had succeeded to that post in 1819 when his predecessor was killed by a tenant from whom he was attempting to collect rent. But by 1830 Cooper had changed sides and become a land reform politician; he entered the assembly after a tumultous by-election in the following year. (14) The Escheator-dominated assembly sent Cooper to London in 1839 to demand a final settlement of the land question. Yet although he had gone as a delegate of the assembly, the colonial secretary, Lord John Russell, whose sympathies were with the 'rights of property', refused to grant him an audience. (15) It was clear that the British government had no intention of permitting a court of escheat to be established. Having come to a dead end in the parliamentary process, the Escheat radicals focussed their attention on continuing the struggle in the countryside. They resisted collection of rents and distraint for rents, and intimidated land agents and law enforcement officers. Late in the winter of 1843 troops were called out to make a show of force in eastern Kings County, where the Escheat movement was strongest, and where disorders had recently taken place. (16) In a despatch, the governor, Sir Henry Vere Huntley, reported that news of the troops moving eastward had caused 'a large body of the people to abandon a march on Charlottetown. (17) That summer a leading radical assemblyman Duncan MacLean, was successfully prosecuted for libelling the government. (18)

While the radicals concentrated their energies on direct action in rural areas, a more moderate reform party took shape in the capital. Led by Edward Whelan, a brilliant young Irish journalist, and George Coles, a distiller who, although a well-to-do businessman, sided with the tenants for his own reasons, (19) the 'Reform' or 'Liberal' party argued that responsible government was a necessary prerequisite to solution of the land question. The Reformers, with the support of remnants of the old Escheat movement, took office in 1851, with Coles as the first premier under responsible government. In order to ameliorate and eventually liquidate the system of leasehold tenure, the Coles administration tried various expedients short of a general escheat. These were unsuccessful, and when the Reformers left office in 1859 the proportion of tenants and squatters among the occupiers of land was still between 60 and 70 per cent. (20)

The local Tory or 'family compact' party had regained office largely through dividing the tenantry along religious lines. (21) They attempted to deal with the land question through appointing a three-man commission. But when the commission reported in favour of the tenants, recommending that all tenants have the right to purchase the lands on which they lived, the proprietors successfully exerted pressure on the imperial authorities to disallow the award. The island government responded by sending a delegation to London. But Sir Samuel Cunard, the founder of the Cunard shipping empire, who owned one-sixth of the island's land mass, mobilized the proprietors to reject the proposals of the delegates. (22) These new setbacks left the tenants completely exasperated. Driven to desperation, they formed tenant leagues, organizations pledged to resist collection of rents. If a tenant were evicted, the leaguers were committed to prevent occupation of the victim's farm by anyone else; thus no rent could be collected. (23) There were public disturbances, and troops were called in from Halifax, Nova Scotia in 1865. Although most historians have minimized the significance of the Tenant League, or dismissed its activities as futile (given the repressive measures taken against it), (24) it is certainly arguable that its willingness to resort to illegality had positive results: in 1866, after the death of Cunard, his heirs decided to sell their 213,000 acres to the government for purchase by the occupants under legislation passed by the former Coles regime. This was perhaps the major turning-point in the struggle, and it may well have been prompted by the Tenant League's organized and calculated defiance of the law. Certainly, the decisions in the mid-1860s of other, smaller proprietors to offer sale of clear titles were popularly attributed to the climate created by the Tenant League agitation. (25) The leasehold system was only completely abolished after the entry of Prince Edward Island into the Canadian confederation in 1873. One of the terms of union was support by the Dominion government for a programme of compulsory purchases of estates. (26)

II

What were the roles played by Scottish and Irish immigrants in this story? The most obvious fact about Celtic immigrants to Prince Edward Island was their poverty. The historical geographer Andrew Hill Clark has written that

the great majority of Highland Scots and Southern Irish...advanced their circumstances very slowly over the years; they were yet in the 1850s (and many of them
still in the eighties) as close to the level of a European peasant tenantry as one would
be likely to find in the New World. Through the middle decades of the nineteenth
century, where the land was poorer, rougher, swampier, or less accessible, there
Gaelic, the Acadian patois, or a distinctly Caledonian or Hibernian inflection of
English was likely to be heard. (27)

This combined with the statistical fact of their numerical predominance (not to mention their Old World cultural inheritance) to ensure that the Scots and Irish played very large parts in all mass tenant movements. This was especially true of the Escheat movement, whose centre of strength was the most Scottish of the three counties, Kings. When a radical Escheat newspaper was established in 1836, it regularly included selections of Highland Gaelic poetry. (28) Although the actual leaders might often be non-Scots, such as Cooper and John LeLacheur, the rank and file were undoubtedly predominantly Scottish. Probably the most famous Escheat public meeting ever held was convened in December 1836 at Hay River in north-eastern Kings County, where a series of resolutions was adopted which provoked the majority in the assembly to commit the three Escheat members who had presided to the custody of the serjeant at arms for almost two full sessions. The official report of the meeting stated that when toasts were offered, 'An attempt was made to play 'God Save the King', but (we must tell the truth) our musicians are better accustomed to Highland Reels'. (29)

There were Scottish landlords as well as tenants, but ethnic kinship did not always override the antagonism inherent in the proprietor-leaseholder relationship. One of the best-known Scottish proprietary families was the McDonalds of Tracadie. In the 1770s John McDonald, known in Scotland as 'Glenaladale', settled some 210 fellow-Roman Catholic Highlanders in the colony. When they realised their situation, many left for Cape Breton Island and freehold tenure. (30) McDonald's third son, a priest also named John, encountered yet more serious difficulties. After completing his education in England and France, and doing missionary work in Glasgow, he returned in 1830 with 206 Scots and Irish as tenants for lands he had inherited. (31) For several years Father John acted as both priest and landlord in the area, as well as land agent for a brother, Roderick, until local discontent led to his transfer to another part of the island, away from his estates, where a Gaelic-speaking priest was needed. Unfortunately for him, he was sent to a district adjacent to Hay River. It soon became apparent that he and his parishioners disagreed over the land question.

When in March 1843 Governor Huntley sent troops to eastern Kings County to put down disturbances on the Cunard estate, Father John, who resided nearby, gave them accommodations. The rumour spread that he had concurred in, or even suggested the action of Huntley, with whom he was on friendly terms. Feelings became very tense in the parish, and after a visit in September his bishop, Bernard D. MacDonald, requested him to leave within a month. When he refused to do so, his parishioners took matters into their own hands. On 1 January 1844, led by the local Escheat assemblyman, John Macintosh (who had been censured, along with Cooper and LeLacheur, for his role at the Hay River meeting), they elected new elders and directed them to tell McDonald to leave. When he held the next Sunday mass, he refused to recognize the new elders, as these were usually chosen by the priest. Macintosh arose, demanded a hearing, and McDonald was only able to silence him by kneeling in prayer. The service then ended with the priest fleeing to the parochial house, and Macintosh angrily berating him. Contrary to the wishes of his bishop, McDonald took legal action against Macintosh and employed as his lawyers two Tory politicians. A jury acquitted the assemblyman, and the bishop ordered McDonald to leave the parish. Although much of the congregation was now boycotting his church, he would not vacate until the bishop suspended him late in 1844. Believing that the bishop and the neighbouring priests had conspired with the Escheators against him, McDonald, an island native, left the colony and spent almost all the remaining 30 years of his life in England. (32) This was an extreme case, but it indicated how deeply rooted was the resistance to leasehold tenure, when a congregation would combine against its priest on the issue, and when the local clergy, including the bishop, would feel compelled to side with the laity. Father John's elder brother Donald, another landlord (and also a legislative councillor and magistrate), had still more harrowing escapades, for at least one attempt was made to assassinate him. He himself went about, according to the governor in 1851, 'always carrying a loaded pistol in his pocket'. (33) Many buildings on his property were the target of incendiaries, and in 1865 barns belonging to his eldest son and heir, John Archibald McDonald, were destroyed by arson, almost certainly committed by tenant leaguers or their sympathizers. (34)

While Scots played very visible roles on both sides of the land question (but particularly as tenants), the part of the Irish is more difficult to trace because of their smaller numbers and more even distribution. Furthermore, aside from several politicians, few individual Irishmen reached positions of prominence in the colony. There were no Irish Roman Catholic landlords or bishops, almost no educational leaders, and even comparatively few priests in the period of the land question. However, from what is known of the voting patterns of the Irish, and from the literary evidence which survives concerning their activities at public meetings and political affrays and on other occasions, there can be no doubt that they were, as a body, strongly committed to the reform cause, and opposed to leasehold tenure. (35) The most notable Irish public figure to emerge, the journalist Edward Whelan, began his Prince Edward Island career in 1843 by emphasising not only the parallels between the island colony and Ireland, but also the common historical problems of Highlanders and Irishmen. As well as editorials on this theme, and the latest 'repeal' news, he published poetry and fiction with a Highland slant. For a generation, Whelan stressed the centrality of the land question, and came back repeatedly to his early argument that the Scots and Irish of Prince Edward Island were facing a common and historic foe: landlordism. (36)

It is tempting to assign a leading role to Irishmen in the Tenant League disturbances of the 1860s. The league itself was a secret society, and Irishmen undoubtedly were prominent in some of the most notable actions attributed to its members. (37) Furthermore, there had been an abortive 'Tenant League of Prince Edward Island' in 1850-51, apparently supported largely by Irishmen, which counselled withholding rent (although in narrowly defined circumstances), which explicitly drew upon Irish examples of how to proceed, and which planned to establish a link with the 'Irish Tenant League in Dublin'. (38) Yet there appears to have been no direct connection between it and the organization which emerged in the mid-1860s, aside from the fact that those areas which generated it tended also to support the later Tenant League, which, presumably, could thus profit from whatever lessons had been learned in 1850-51. (39)

The Tenant League of the 1860s appears to have been a more complex phenomenon than simply a carry-over from Irish agrarian radicalism. One of its most striking features was a distrust of politicians so strong that when an island-wide form of organization was adopted, M.P.s and political partisanship were specifically banned. (40) According to Whelan, a crucial new element in the tenant movement of the mid-1860s was the prominent involvement of relatively prosperous tenants of English extraction who, unlike the Celtic Escheat radicals of the 1830s and 1840s, could amply afford to pay their rent. (41) As Andrew Hill Clark has stated,

In general those of ultimate English origin (and these included descendants of people from more than half the counties of England, Loyalists, New Englanders, and disbanded soldiers) were situated where agriculture was most intensive and productive or in the best locations for ship-building or fishing. On the average they had more capital and more applicable agricultural skills. (42)

Islanders of English extraction were almost all Protestants, and tended to vote for the Tory party, which represented the interests of the overwhelmingly English and

Q

Protestant family compact. They had strongly supported the Tories at the election of 1859, when the latter had defeated the Reformers through an appeal to religious loyalties. At that time the Tories had also promised to use their close connections with the proprietors to bring about settlement of the land question; but the award of the commission they established had been disallowed. In these circumstances, they faced the distinct possibility of defeat at the next election. The Bible question of the late 1850s had ultimately been extinguished simply by giving the *status quo* a statutory basis, which amounted to an implicit admission that the Reformers had not been trying to eliminate permissive daily Bible reading in the schools, as the Tories and their allies among the evangelical clergy had alleged. (43) Given this, and the fact that the land question remained unresolved, the Tories were fortunate indeed that they were again able to discover —— or manufacture —— 'popish dangers' sufficiently credible that the Protestant constituencies could be persuaded to vote in a body for the government in 1863, thus maintaining them in power. (44)

From one point of view, the Protestant tenantry had once more been duped into supporting the family compact. Following the election of 1863 and its immediate aftermath (including an act to incorporate the colony's Grand Orange Lodge, which was disallowed by the Colonial Office), religious passions abated rapidly. The land question reasserted itself, and with the failure of the delegation to London in the winter of 1863-64, the Tory government proved incapable of finding a solution. It was only a few months later, in May of 1864, that the Tenant League was given its formal organization in circumstances reflecting distaste for partisan politics. (45) If Whelan's assertions about the English Protestant Tories — he even referred to them as Orangemen (46) — in the Tenant League rank and file are credited, then the apolitical bent of the society becomes more comprehensible. Given the bitter political divisions of the 1863 election, these Protestants could not accept working in an organization where George Coles, Whelan, and other Liberals would play prominent roles; (47) and given that the Tories had misled them twice in succession, with the commission and the delegation, both of which had proven fruitless, the English Protestants were willing to discard them as well. Politics had divided island tenants in the past; it would not be allowed to do so in the new organization.

III

Relations between Scots and Irish in Prince Edward Island were complicated by religious differences, since perhaps 70 per cent of the Scots were Calvinists of one variety or another. The bloodiest political affray in island history, the Belfast Riot of 1 March 1847, which resulted in at least three deaths, has usually been attributed to these religious differences. The occasion was a by-election in the Scottish Protestant district of Belfast, and several hundred men fought it out with cudgels. (48) While it is true that those on one side were Scottish Protestants and those on the other were Irish Roman Catholics, it is far from certain that the causes of the riot can be reduced to religion, or 'religion and nationality'. In the first place, at least in later years it was asserted by Whelan that the real issue behind the riot was 'a contest between landlord and tenant'; (49) and it is a fact that the leading Tory candidate, the English-born William Douse, was the land agent for the proprietor of the area, the Earl of Selkirk. Secondly, political partisanship was certainly a factor, with Scots supporting the Tories and Irish the Reformers. Finally, it is worth noting that intimidation at elections was not uncommon at that time in Prince Edward Island. Just 16 days before the riot, Whelan had in the assembly described the turmoil at the previous controverted election in Belfast as simply 'the usual effervescence of popular will, which always will, more or less, evince itself at elections', and no more of a disturbance than regularly occurred on market days in Charlottetown. Contested elections, he continued, always require 'some degree of intimidation'. (50) A few days previously he had stated, again in the assembly, that were Irishmen told to leave their sticks at home when they went to vote, they would soon also be required to leave behind 'their wit and drollery'. (51) If such attitudes towards violence at the polls were common, it is possible that the Belfast Riot was simply a routine electoral brawl which got out of control. The facts that most of the Irish appear to have been from outside the constituency and imported to add physical force to the appeal of the Reformers, and that violence on the scale of 1 March 1847 was never repeated, would seem to lend credence to this possibility. Nonetheless, when all this is said, the further facts remain that as yet no fully satisfactory explanation for the Belfast Riot has emerged, and that the combatants *were* Irish Roman Catholics and Scottish Protestants.

In addition to the very obvious differences between Irish Roman Catholic and Scottish Protestant, there is evidence of tension between Irish and Scot within the Roman Catholic church. Although the Irish outnumbered the Scottish Catholics by a considerable proportion, the Scots monopolized the episcopal seat from the time of the first appointment of Angus B. MacEachern in 1821 until the end of the century. They also tended to dominate the faculty of the diocesan college, St. Dunstan's. The first rector was a Father Angus MacDonald, and the names of most of the professors in the nineteenth century were Scottish. (52) These and other considerations aroused some resentment among the Irish, and as early as 1828 an Irish priest in Charlottetown wrote to the Bishop of Quebec that MacEachern 'is well known to possess prejudice against anyone from Ireland.' (53) If this was the case, then MacEachern was no different from many Scots of the day, both Protestant (54) and Roman Catholic. Furthermore, such tensions within the colonial Catholic church were certainly not unique to Prince Edward Island. One of Whelan's early mentors in Halifax had been a dynamic Irish priest, Father Richard B. O'Brien, very popular with the city's Irish population, who eventually returned to Ireland because of friction with the local Scottish bishop. (55) It would seem that the Scottish Roman Catholics of Nova Scotia and Prince Edward Island, who were themselves striving for acceptance and responsibility, were sometimes none too happy to find themselves in the same congregations as the ragged Irish.

Yet there was a more positive side to the interaction of Irish and Scots in colonial Prince Edward Island. There is ample evidence of common effort in such matters as building and moving Roman Catholic churches, raising money for Irish and Scottish relief in 1847, (56) and, of course, dealing with proprietors, land agents, and sheriffs. (57) Even between Protestant and Roman Catholic there does not seem to have been much outright hostility until the late 1850s, when it became profitable for one political party to exploit religious loyalties for its own purposes. Certainly there was nothing

Q*

to compare with the regular, almost ritualised violence between Irish Roman Catholics and English Protestants which disfigured Newfoundland history between the 1830s and the 1860s. The Belfast Riot should be seen as an isolated incident whose occurrence shocked both sides, (58) and lessened their disposition to resort to force. The everyday imperatives of coexistence in a small pioneer community seemed to outweigh inherited prejudices and suspicions at least to the extent of making physical violence seem counter productive. In the final analysis, pioneer islanders wanted to live together in peace, and not be confined to ethnic and religious enclaves from which they could wander only at personal peril. Harsh words were often exchanged over the years, but the hostility remained at a verbal level even in so impassioned an election as that of 1863.

One of the striking aspects to some of the bitter arguments over the years was the extent to which the spit and fire came from Old Country natives in a colony where, by 1861, the non-native-born numbered only 22.1 per cent. (59) There were two groups in particular who tended to be prisoners of their Old World pasts when perceiving fellow-islanders. The native-Scottish Presbyterian clergymen were prone to find a scheming Jesuit behind every sign of activity on the part of the local Roman Catholic church. In contrast, the priest of this period, although trained in Quebec or on the Continent, was usually an island native, and, as the product of a pioneer community where cooperation was essential, basically pragmatic in his relations with all his fellow-colonists. His Protestant counterpart was not a colonial, but a Britisher with the problems of Puseyism and the Great Disruption on his mind — a man who associated Roman Catholicism with the traditional enemies of Britain, and an increasingly react-ionary papacy. (60) On the Catholic side, Irish-born politicians insisted upon seeing local Orangemen as Old Country nightriders. Island Orangeism was a curious phenomenon given the lack of Protestant Ulstermen in the colony. It grew slowly until the end of the 1850s, when religious loyalties became entrenched as a central factor in local politic Whatever Orangemen were elsewhere, those in Prince Edward Island were non-violent, and in fact could best be characterized as simply farmers of Scottish and English extract ion belonging to a Protestant social group. Yet when incorporation of the local Grand Orange Lodge became an issue, Whelan and other Irish-born assemblymen responded with a ferocity which owed more to memories and parental stories of Ireland than to the realities of Prince Edward Island. (61)

Such are some of the aspects of Highland and Irish heritages in Prince Edward Island in the period dominated by the land question. Many features of Celtic life were transplanted in this relatively self-contained part of the New World, which was burdened with an archaic and oppressive carry-over from the Old. Some, like the common use of Highland Gaelic and the fierce religious loyalties, remained relatively unchanged. (62 Others, such as Orangeism and the 'tenant league' tradition of Ireland, were greatly transformed by the ethnic mixture and particular circumstances of the island colony. Only one generalization can be made with certainty: that if the history of Prince Edward Island is ever to be made fully intelligible, it must be seen in the context of the heritages of the peoples who immigrated there. They did not leave their cultural backgrounds on Old Country docksides. Even a movement like Escheat, whose name owed nothing to the recent pasts of Scotland and Ireland, was clearly a hybrid of the traditions of the two countries, amalgamating the intense loyalties of the Highlanders with the militancy and readiness to resort to force of the Irish.

NOTES

1. I am grateful to Mr Harry Baglole of Belfast, P.E.I., Mr H.T. Holman of the Public Archives of P.E.I. (P.A.P.E.I.), and Prof. Joseph Levitt of the University of Ottawa for their comments on this paper in the course of its preparation. I have also benefited from reading two unpublished papers written by Mr Baglole, entitled 'A Reassessment of the Role of Absentee Proprietors in Prince Edward Island History' (1970), a copy of which is in P.A.P.E.I., and 'The Origins of the Prince Edward Island Land Question: 1770-1805' (1971).

2. For the legislative and political history of the land question, see Frank MacKinnon, *The Government of Prince Edward Island* (Toronto, 1951), ch.5; and Francis W.P. Bolger, ed. *Canada's Smallest Province: A History of P.E.I.* (Charlottetown, 1973), chs. 2, 3, 4 (by Bolger), and 5 (by W.S. MacNutt). A greater sense of immediacy is conveyed by Harry Baglole and David Weale, *The Island and Confederation: The End of an Era* (Summerside, 1973), ch. 4; and Harry Baglole, comp. and ed. *The Land Question: A Study Kit of Primary Documents* (Charlottetown, 1975). The second and third titles have been reviewed at length by I.R. Robertson in 'Recent Island History,' *Acadiensis,* IV, 2 (1975), 111-18, and *Canadian Historical Review,* LVI (1975), 460-61.

3. See MacKinnon, *The Government of Prince Edward Island,* pp.6-7.

4. See D.C. Harvey, ed. *Journeys to the Island of St. John or Prince Edward Island 1775-1832* (Toronto, 1955), p.7; and Andrew Hill Clark, *Three Centuries and the Island: A Historical Geography of Settlement and Agriculture in Prince Edward Island, Canada* (Toronto, 1959), p.56.

5. By 1801 less than £6,500 had been collected, and £59,162/17 were owing; see Public Archives of Canada microfilm, Colonial Office (C.O.) 226/19, p.352. In fairness, there were other factors in the non-payment: e.g. the inadequacy of the collection system, and the likelihood that any quit rents collected would be put to the private purposes of the collector.

6. The only exceptions were lots 15 and 55, which were escheated by Governor C.D. Smith in 1818, and divided among the tenantry; see Bolger, ed. *Canada's Smallest Province,* p.88.

7. Clark, *Three Centuries and the Island,* pp.60-61.

8. P.E.I. House of Assembly, *Journal,* 1862, appendix A.

9. See Clark, *Three Centuries and the Island,* p.95, and Table III, on the same page. In Clark's words, " 'squatting' refers to the process by which settlers moved in and occupied land neglected or ignored by the nominal proprietors." (p.99).

10. See D.C. Harvey, 'The Loyal Electors', Royal Society of Canada, *Proceedings and Transactions,* 3rd ser., XXIV (1930), Section II, 101-10; and Bolger, ed. *Canada's Smallest Province,* pp.75-84.

11. Edward Palmer, the son of the Loyal Electors' leader J.B. Palmer, was absorbed into the local élite in the 1830s, and from around 1850 until the early 1860s was the leader of the Tory party of P.E.I.

12. Milton Acorn, 'The Figure in the Landscape Made the Landscape', in *The Island Means Minago: Poems from Prince Edward Island* (Toronto, 1975), p.47. For this volume of poems, many of them on the land question, Mr Acorn has received the Canadian Governor General's Award for poetry published in 1975. An interesting elaboration upon this tenant ideology will be found in the testimony by tenant farmer James Howatt before the land commission of 1860, in *Abstract of the Proceedings before the Land Commissioners Court, held during the summer of 1860 to inquire into the differences relative to the rights of landowners and tenants in Prince Edward Island,* reporters J.D. Gordon and David Laird (Charlottetown, 1862), pp.84-85. As succinctly summarized by Baglole, its import is that 'when land is purchased from the proprietors the price paid − even for productive farms − should be no higher than the value of land in a wilderness state. The proprietors must not be allowed to profit from the labour of the settlers'. (Baglole, comp. and ed. *The Land Question,* Section A, Document N, n.2).

13. See Harry Baglole, 'William Cooper', *Dictionary of Canadian Biography*, IX (forthcoming).

14. P.E.I. Assembly, *Journal*, 1832, app. A.

15. This rebuff was in striking contrast to the easy access to the Colonial Office enjoyed by proprietors and various Tory delegations over the years.

16. Until 1852 the governor had at his command a garrison consisting of about 100 men, whose main function was as a 'potential aid to the civil power'; J. Mackay Hitsman, 'Military Defenders of Prince Edward Island, 1775-1864', Canadian Historical Association, *Annual Report* (1964), 32. According to Baglole, 'For several years it was almost impossible to find a man brave enough to serve as sheriff or constable in Kings County'. (Baglole to author, 30 Jan. 1976).

17. C.O. 226/65, p.133, Huntley to Lord Stanley, 21 April 1843. In the same despatch, Huntley described the militia as unreliable. (p.135).

18. Huntley, who had directed the prosecution, also requested that sentence be withheld, in order not to make MacLean a martyr. See *ibid.*, pp.190-92, 198, Huntley to Stanley, 14, 24 July 1843; and I.R. Robertson, 'Sir Henry Vere Huntley', *Dictionary of Canadian Biography*, IX (forthcoming).

19. See I.R. Robertson, 'George Coles', *ibid.*, X (Toronto, 1972), 182-88.

20. See *ibid.*, 185-87. Even in 1861, following the sale of the large Selkirk estate, the proportion of freeholders was only 40.4 percent; calculation based on Clark, *Three Centuries and the Island*, p.95, Table III.

21. See I.R. Robertson, 'The Bible Question in Prince Edward Island from 1856 to 1860', *Acadiensis*, V, 2 (1976), 3-25.

22. See Phyllis Blakeley, 'Sir Samuel Cunard', *Dictionary of Canadian Biography*, IX (forthcoming).

23. The 'tenant's pledge' is printed in *Examiner* (Charlottetown), 30 May 1864; also see *ibid.*, 1 Feb. 1864.

24. See, e.g. Bolger, ed. *Canada's Smallest Province*, where the editor treats the Tenant League disturbances simply as a minor factor in the story of the island's entry into Confederation (pp.180-81); or Clark, *Three Centuries and the Island*, who ventures the opinion that the league 'may have done more harm than good to the cause of land reform', (p.93) while later in the same paragraph attributing further sales of proprietors' estates to the leaguers' agitation.

25. See, e.g., *Examiner*, 22 May, 19 June 1865, 21 Oct. 1867.

26. Although the resulting legislation was passed in 1875, it was another 20 years before the last estate was purchased; see MacKinnon, *The Government of Prince Edward Island*, pp.296-98.

27. Clark, *Three Centuries and the Island*, p.91. About one-tenth of the population was French Acadian.

28. See *Prince Edward Island Times* (Charlottetown), e.g. 26 March 1836 (vol.I, 1).

29. *Royal Gazette* (Charlottetown), 10 Jan. 1837. Of course there were exceptions to this militancy among the Scottish tenants. In 1831 proprietor David Stewart, upon visiting his estate for the first time, reported that a Highlander 'thanked God, threw his bonnet up in the air and thanked God again' as an expression of joy at meeting his landlord. P.A.P.E.I. Journal of David Stewart (as excerpted in *Guardian* [Charlottetown], 16 July to 24 Sept., 1949), entry for 28 June 1831.

30. See anonymous [John C. Macmillan], *The Arrival of the First Scottish Catholic Emigrants to Prince Edward Island and After, 1772-1922* (Summerside, 1922), pp.30-31; Rosemary Hutchinson, 'Emigration from South Uist to Cape Breton', in B.D. Tennyson, ed. *Essays in Cape Breton History* (Windsor, N.S., 1973),p.11; Allan F. MacDonald, 'Captain John MacDonald, "Glenaladale",' Canadian Catholic Historical Association, *Report*, 1964, pp.32-34; and Ada MacLeod, 'The Glenaladale Pioneers', *Dalhousie Review*, XI, 1 (1931), 319.

31. In later years one of those he took with him alleged publicly that he had deceived them as to the condition of the land to be leased, and stated that some of

the immigrants had left for the United States; see testimony of John Haggarty in *Abstract of the Proceedings before the Land Commissioners' Court...*, pp.117-18.

32. See I.R. Robertson, 'John McDonald', *Dictionery of Canadian Biography*, X, 460-62. His estate was left in the care of an agent, and distraint proceedings on his behalf were a factor in the Tenant League disturbances of 1865; see P.A.P.E.I. Accession 2514, James Curtis to John Morris, 14 March 1865.

33. C.O. 226/79, p.212, Sir Alexander Bannerman to Earl Gray, 14 Aug. 1851 (confidential), also see *ibid.*, p.214, proclamation dated 2 Aug. 1851; *Islander* (Charlottetown), 1, 22 Aug. 1851; *Examiner,* 10 Aug. 1850; *Royal Gazette,* 13 Aug. 1850. The following published account of Donald McDonald's misfortunes appears to be basically accurate: Isabella Lucy Bird, *The Englishwoman in America* (Toronto, 1966 ed.), pp.46-47. There is evidence which suggests that McDonald had amply earned unpopularity among his tenants: see P.A.P.E.I. Palmer Family Papers, testimony of Vincent Bell in *Public Documents on Various Subjects Connected with the Interests of Prince Edward Island Ordered by the House of Assembly to be Printed, April 23rd., 1841* (Charlottetown, 1841), pp.75-76; and Bannerman, *supra.*

34. See *Royal Gazette,* 23, 30 July 1850, 7 June 1865; *Examiner,* 24 July 1850, 12, 19 June, 20 Nov. 1865.

35. For a particularly vivid account of the reception given by a group of Irish squatters in the 1860s to a surveying party led by a proprietor, Robert Bruce Stewart (the son of David Stewart), see Moncrieff Williamson, *Robert Harris 1849-1919: An Unconventional Biography* (Toronto, 1970), app. 1, pp.202-07. As in the Macintosh-McDonald case, a jury proved sympathetic to the popular cause in a resulting trial for 'riot and assault'.

36. See *Palladium* (Charlottetown), 4, 7, 11, 14 Sept. 1843; *Examiner,* 30 May 1864, 21 Oct. 1867. When Whelan finally lost his hold on the Irish population of the colony in the mid-1860s, it was partially because of his break with the radicalism of the Tenant League; a detailed account of his deteriorating relationship with the tenant movement of later years is included in I.R. Robertson, 'Edward Whelan', *Dictionary of Canadian Biography*, IX (forthcoming).

37. See P.A.P.E.I. Accession 2514, Curtis to Morris, 14 March 1865; and affidavit of Bernard McKenna, dated 5 Aug. 1865. The tenants of Donald McDonald and his son John Archibald McDonald were mostly Irish.

38. See *Examiner,* 11 Dec. 1850, 13 May 1851.

39. Lots 35, 36, 37, 48 and part of 49 produced the island's first 'tenant league' and at least four of these were noted for support of the second. See *ibid.;* and Clark, *Three Centuries and the Island,* p.93.

40. See *Examiner,* 23, 19 June 1865. At this meeting (in May, 1864) the name 'Tenant Union of P.E.I.' was adopted, but the organization continued to be popularly referred to as the 'Tenant League'.

41. See *ibid.,* 21 Aug. 1865. Little is known about the leaders of the Tenant League, and this is not surprising, given the nature of the organization, for the emphasis was upon united mass action rather than individual leaders. One of the very few figures to emerge reasonably clearly was George F. Adams, whom the governor of the day described as 'a wild Chartist' from England. See C.O. 226/100, p.230, George Dundas to Arthur Blackwood, 6 June 1864 (private).

42. Clark, *Three Centuries and the Island,* p.91.

43. See Robertson, 'The Bible Question in Prince Edward Island from 1856 to 1860', *Acadiensis,* V, 2 (1976), 20-25.

44. See I.R. Robertson, 'Religion, Politics, and Education in Prince Edward Island from 1856 to 1877', McGill University M.A. thesis, (1968), chs. 5, 6.

45. One of the delegates, W.H. Pope, had warned that agrarian disturbances would result from failure of the delegation; see I.R. Robertson, 'William Henry Pope', *Dictionary of Canadian Biography*, X, 596.

46. See, e.g., *Examiner,* 1 Feb. 1864, 19 June, 7, 21 Aug., 4 Sept. 1865.

47. In fact, Whelan had played a role in the winter of 1860-61 in founding an abortive tenant movement, which was meant to become all-embracing; see *ibid.,* 23, 29 Oct., 31 Dec. 1860, 7, 14 Jan. 1861.

48. See P.E.I. Assembly, *Journal,* 1847, app. I; CO 226/83, p.166, memorial of Dr W.H. Hobkirk to the Duke of Newcastle, 10 March 1854; and H.T. Holman, 'William Douse', *Dictionary of Canadian Biography,* IX (forthcoming). Inquests were held for two Irishmen and one Scot. Three medical doctors appear to have been involved in attending the wounded, and one claimed to have treated between 30 and 40, some of whose injuries were 'very serious'.

49. P.E.I. Assembly, *Debates and Proceedings,* 1864, p.57.

50. Summary report of assembly debates in *Royal Gazette,* 2 March 1847; also see the remarks of Macintosh in the same debate.

51. Summary report of assembly debates in *ibid.,* 16 March 1847.

52. The publicly-supported college, Prince of Wales, was also dominated by Scottish professors, in this case Protestant. To a lesser extent, the same Scottish Protestant hegemony was apparent in the colony's Normal School, school visitor-ships, and grammar schools.

53. Archives of the Roman Catholic Diocese of Charlottetown, Bishop Angus B. MacEachern Papers, Father Thomas Fitzgerald to Bishop Bernard Claude Panet, 28 Aug. 1828. Access to this collection was granted by Father Faber MacDonald. For the official Roman Catholic (and Scottish) version of the differences between MacEachern and Fitzgerald, see John C. Macmillan, *Early History of the Catholic Church in Prince Edward Island* (Quebec, 1905), pp.227-28, 231-32, 264-65.

54. E.g. the proprietor David Stewart appears to have taken a particularly hard line with Irish tenants, even offering them inducements to vacate; see P.A.P.E.I. Journal of David Stewart, entry for 25 June 1831.

55. See Angus A. Johnston, *A History of the Catholic Church in Eastern Nova Scotia, vol. II; 1827-1880* (Antigonish, N.S., 1971), pp.166-67, 179-80, 215.

56. There was a joint fund, which was commenced shortly after the Belfast Riot; see *Royal Gazette,* 9 March, 6 July 1847.

57. It is worth emphasising the point that, however one accounts for the Belfast Riot, over the years the land question generated far more violence than did ethnic or religious disputes.

58. Shock and sorrow were the dominant sentiments expressed in the assembly debate of 13 March 1847 following Governor Huntley's message relating to the Belfast Riot; see summary report of assembly debates in *Islander,* 20 March 1847.

59. Clark, *Three Centuries and the Island,* p.121, Table V.

60. This attitude towards Catholicism was not confined to Presbyterians; one of the most contentious clergymen of these years was the Rev. David Fitzgerald, a displaced Church of Ireland priest.

61. See Robertson, 'Religion, Politics, and Education in Prince Edward Island from 1856 to 1877', pp.39, 88-93, 130, 138-43. In fairness, it should be noted that the bill's sponsor, W.H. Pope, introduced it in an extremely provocative manner, and that he did so on St. Patrick's Day.

62. For an example of a Scottish Protestant community in which the way of life, religious customs, and hierarchy of values changed very little over several generations see Andrew Macphail, *The Master's Wife* (Montreal, 1939; reprint forthcoming, with an introduction by I.R. Robertson); and I.R. Robertson, 'Sir Andrew Macphail as a Social Critic', University of Toronto Ph.D. thesis, (1974), ch.1.

Index